BEYOND WILD

BOOK FOUR OF THE "ALASKA OFF GRID SURVIVAL SERIES"

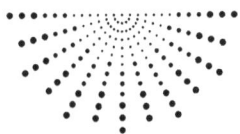

MILES MARTIN

ALASKADREAMS
PUBLISHING

Beyond Wild
By Miles Martin

Book Four of The Alaska Off Grid Survival Series
©2021 Miles Martin
Artwork, Photos, Original Poetry ©2021 by Miles Martin - All rights reserved

Published by:
Alaska Dreams Publishing
www.alaskadp.com

1st ADP Edition August 2021
PRINT PAPERBACK ISBN: 978-1-956303-04-9
PRINT HARDCOVER ISBN: 978-1-956303-05-6
This book was previously published by Miles of Alaska

Visit www.milesofalaska.com to find a bio of Miles, additional photos, stories, how-to videos, handmade artwork, and raw materials for sale.

I always had the wilderness life as a dream. In this picture I am 13, dressed and doing the same as when 63.

CONTENTS

NOTES FROM THE AUTHOR

The series I write is about survival. As my story progresses, survival is less about building fires, and more about survival for those who color outside the lines. Square pegs in a world of round holes. What do I do after twenty-five years of living alone in the wilderness? I'm trying to blend into a wonderful world that has other people in it.

This book covers the years 2000 to 2010, when I am forty-nine to fifty-nine years old. I am hopefully maturing and gaining more wisdom. I learn 'Survival' involves how to interact with others, make a living, being happy, and keeping independent and free, without feeling like a slave, or getting overwhelmed. I transition from having sled dogs as my only transportation, to depending on a snow machine, but still not driving. I run a successful internet web store, with slow dial up internet connection and a $100 program. Remote Alaska village life is explored and understood through my eyes.

There is action, when I am a murder suspect in a crime never solved. Headlines read, "Homesteader War." A forest fire destroys twelve of my trapline cabins and 200 miles of trails I cut, representing twenty-five years of work and supplies. A flood has me canoeing through my front door into the cabin. I recover, manage, survive, learn, move on, and prosper. There is a lot of 'meeting women through the mail and internet.'

I'm in GEO Magazine in Europe, Alaska Magazine five times, Gem Magazine, on TV and on my way to becoming an expert at what I do. The series of books follows my life and its changes. Partly a psychological/social study for an intellectual, and partly a high adventure along the lines of an Indiana Jones/ Crocodile Dundee character. Maybe this is a study of someone who fancies himself in these roles, and what that looks like, how that gets pulled off. Pretending you are a hero and good at stuff. Am I really? Or is it an act? Am I the Wizard of OZ, the man of magic, or Oz the humbug? Maybe I am not like Oz at all, but more like Don Quixote! It's not for me to say, I am simply recording the events.

Map of the Interior of Alaska

I describe the interior's map best in book one and two. I feel that's old news now. Summed up… It's a big place. Bigger than the human imagination.

#1 Fairbanks area, the hub of the interior. Grown since 1972 in book one, might be 100,000 now in population. Where I get supplies, sell my art, fly in and out of the state, and where all the government offices are that need visiting for permits, going to court, etc.

#2 Big Delta, where the houseboat was built (book one.)

#3 Nenana River and the village of Nenana, where I end up living.

#4 Yukon River, Galena, where I spend my first winter on a houseboat in book 2. Now boat that direction looking for fossils and fishing.

#5 Kobuk country, where I first dreamed of going in book two.

#6 Manley Hot Springs, stop here a lot, spent a winter here. Survey business requires coming in and out of here.

#7 Lake Minchumina, headwaters of the Kantishna River where I trap.

#8 Hansen Lake and Bearpaw, one of my homesteads and trapping areas.

#9 Lower Kantishna cabin, my main homestead and home base for trapline.

Note dotted line to Nenana, the airport is on this trapline trail.

#12 General area where mammoth ivory is found. Legally, fossils can only be taken from land that has mineral rights such as mine claim or native lands.

Some of these locations are more relevant in book one and two, but all of it is 'my stomping grounds' in my travels. The village of Toklat so bold on the Kantishna River has been abandoned since the gold rush days. This map is not all of Alaska, only the interior as it relates to my story, note the insert of the map on the state map.

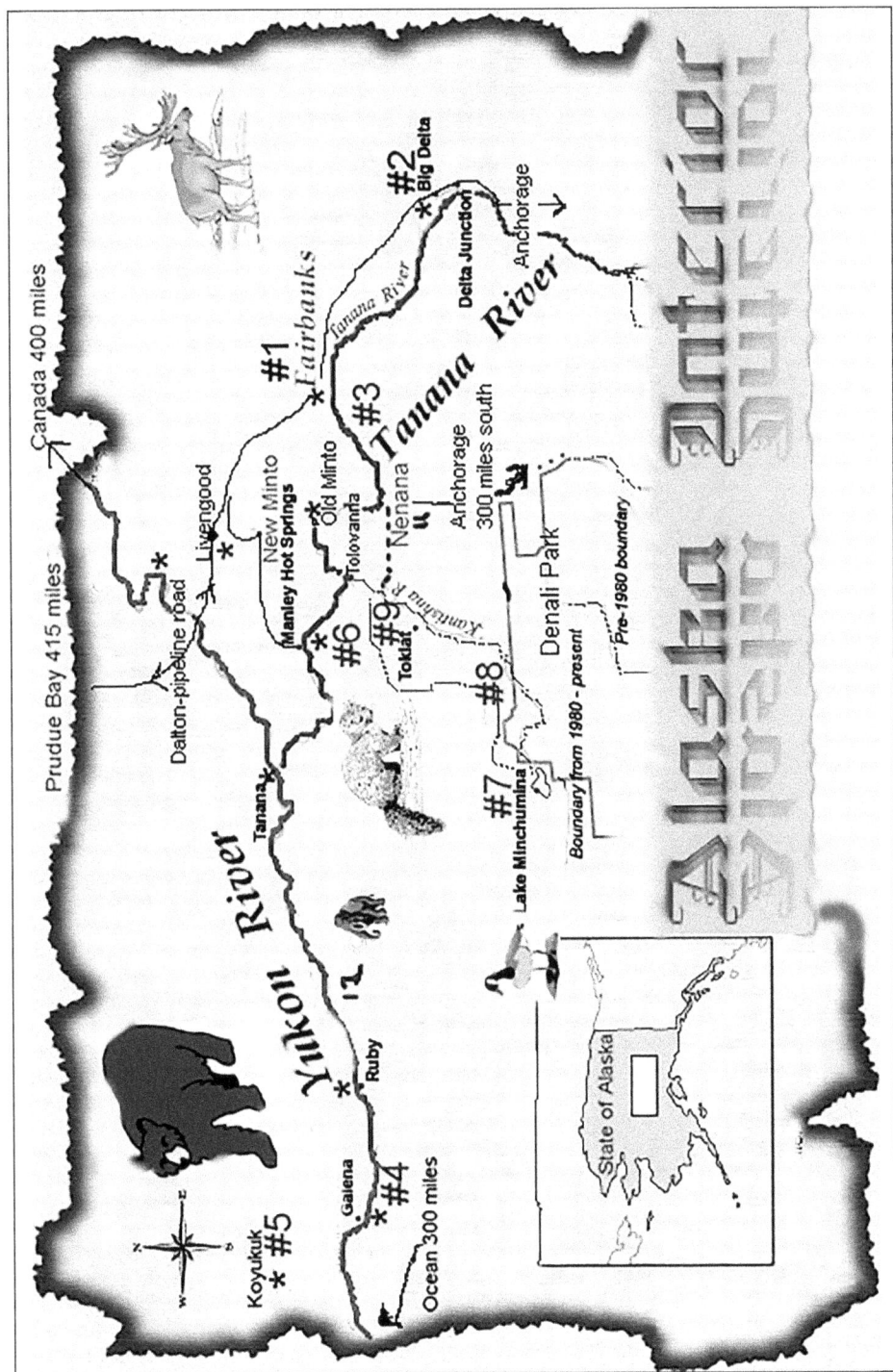

Alaska Interior

Prudue Bay 415 miles
Canada 400 miles

Dalton-pipeline road

Livengood
*

Manley Hot Springs
*
New Minto
Old Minto
**
Tolovanha

#1 *
Fairbanks

#3
Tanana River

Tanana River

#2
* Big Delta
Delta Junction
Anchorage →

Nenana
u.

Anchorage
300 miles south

Denali Park

Pre-1980 boundary

Boundary from 1980 - present

#6 *
#9 *
Tokat

Kantishna R.

#8 *

#7 *
Lake Minchumina

Tanana *

Yukon River

Ruby
* #4

Galena
Ocean 300 miles

Koyukuk
* #5

N
W   E
S

State of Alaska

PROLOGUE

MAJOR DETAILS AND SUMMARY OF MY OTHER BOOKS

"The life I once lived in the wilds, I now freeze in metal scenes." No. "The story behind the scenes is the wilderness life I've lived." I hesitate, as my mind tries to come up with something better, more summed up, more perfect, more catchy, a more exciting 'one liner' to spellbind my fans with. Like a quotable line from a movie!

"Smile when you call me that!" My unconscious replies: *You call that a knife? We* both smile. "Yeah, like that." So much, with so few words. It gets harder as I get older. The older I get, the less I know. I was smartest when I was about eighteen. Ignorance is bliss. "I do not just sell art. I sell a way of life and a way of thinking." This sounds better, and I recognize it from one of my brochures. It rolls off the tongue so easily from behind my table at a big show.

I read my Bio from my prepared brochure.

"The basics of my upbringing are that I was born in Hawaii in '51, but I do not recall much. We moved to San Francisco when I was three years old, then to Cleveland, Philadelphia, and Syracuse - maybe some other places... I forget. It doesn't matter. The main point is, I moved enough and gave up enough friends to learn not to make close friends. Also, there are many ways of doing things. I could never keep up with all the fads! Geez! I just got the cool bell-bottoms and black socks. We move, now I need the tight black pants and white socks, or I'm out of time! I learned early to just go with what I have and who I am. I had to! My parents would not keep buying new clothes to keep up with what is in at the new place. At fifteen, I got my first serious job on a ranch in Montana for the summer.

At sixteen, I went in the Navy during the Viet Nam era. I got out and wanted to live in the wilderness. I moved to Alaska at twenty-two years old. A wilderness life dream stayed with me since I was about five years old, of living like Daniel Boone."

I set the brochure aside. I have it memorized. My mind spins back in time.

Past Flash:[1]

I'm in my youth, I am considered talented at art. 'Gifted' is usually a term applied to me. I'm not sure how much attention I, or anyone else gives that. My peers tell me any guy who is an artist has to be gay. They try to beat me up. I'm not especially 'afraid,' as I am disoriented at being 'one of them' and not 'one of us.' I'm short, small for my age, and always new to the area. I win most fights. I am equally strong, maybe not stronger, but have incredibly fast reflexes. I run the fifty yard dash in well under six seconds, a school all time record. I'm smart, crafty, devious, innovative. I tend to win, even if it takes an equalizer of some kind.

The school system puts art in the same category as gym, recess, and study hall. " One of those classes you take as a break from real studies that are important." A class chosen by those wishing to avoid a real education; the lazy and incompetent.

I want to be an Indian. When we kids play cowboys and Indians, I am always the Indian. I take note that an artist among the Indians has an honorable role, like a shaman, almost the status of the chief! I wouldn't have to live among civilized white people... if I get accepted by an Indian tribe!

I just read 'Hanta Yo' translated 'Clear the Way.' I'm a bit young to read such an adult book. I see the story as a struggle between two ideas competing for leadership of the tribe. Which is better, the one who understands war and fighting? Or, the spiritual artistic one? Wait! I have some cool experiences as an artist. Good memories! All the girls that want to pose for the nude sculpture, remember?

Now I remember, glad my conscience reminds me of the good stuff. My **past flash ends**

I now believe, art is a form of communication. One needs something to say. Alaska may have done that for me—given me something to say. When I arrived in Alaska in 73, it was like a duck finding water. Christians have the term 'born again.' This is how I felt, on this day I was born. Like the Beatles line in a song, "I was only waiting for this moment to arrive."

These were pipeline years in Alaska, with big dollars to be earned. Not just pipeline work, there is simply a lot of money being passed around. I am able to earn enough money in a few months to outfit myself for a winter in the wilderness. Though my outdoor knowledge was mostly acquired by watching Walt Disney movies, I considered myself qualified to live in the wilds, and made arrangements with a pilot to be flown in. I did not consider much, how I would get back out. I walked the fifty miles through the wilderness to the nearest road eight months later.

I had learned a few things during those months alone, so assumed the next year would be easier.

This next winter my supplies are stolen, and I need to be rescued. I had tried to walk out at fifty below and didn't make it. This made good international headlines. I was able to practice my writing as a result- telling my story for Alaska Magazine and later the New York Times. I guess I was always a writer as well as an artist, but never thought about it. I spent more time writing notes to girls in class then studying, and wrote poetry (I wouldn't dare tell anyone) and kept a diary. When the family moved later in my life, I kept in touch with friends by mail. Maybe I lived that way—through the written word.

I used to write my girlfriends 300 to 700 page letters while in the Navy. I did not know that was unusual. I did poorly in English in school. No one told me 'writing' is 'English.'

In the wilds, I also wrote letters and expressed myself on paper. I felt as comfortable writing as speaking—maybe more so. Not that I understood the rules. Who follows speaking rules when talking? Who would understand us? *That would be weird!* We gesture while we talk. We use slang. We say "Da," we go 'welp,' and we pause, 'er-uh.' We use local dialect. Here up north we use native words. Locals I communicate with understand words like 'mukluk'; places like 'Minchumina'; terms like 'life in the bush'; objects of clothing like 'bunny boots'; or occupations like 'stringing steel'. I was not a good writer, I just wrote a lot. I assume my girlfriends understood what I wrote. That was the objective. What else mattered? Fine. So let this be a story about discovering ourselves, coming to terms with our failings and such. The Beatles did not do well in school. They were told they would never amount to anything, an embarrassment to family, playing that silly music in the garage. So who is embarrassed now, pray tell? *I listen a lot to my inner self.*

Art was made for myself, and as gifts to friends, at first. However, I went to the remote Yukon River village of Galena once, and had no money. My pistol was wearing out. I could not afford to buy a new one. Someone saw the diamond willow wood grips with the lynx bone cross inlaid. I shrugged and told the story. "The lynx hides in the willows, but I see it. The cross reminds us God is watching everything." The guy gives me more money for my wore out gun than a new one cost. The light bulb went on in my head.

I could not afford gemstones. It would be difficult to get them, or other ordinary art supplies when in the wilds. I also have little knowledge of such materials I can't get or afford. In time, I understood how to stop a tooth from cracking, how to get glue to stick to something greasy, how to get leather and steel to combine and stay together. This knowledge becomes my niche of knowledge not many people have. Being a mountain man is not an occupation, it is a way of life. Much like saying, I want to be a city slicker. A city slicker can pay the bills in many ways, as can a mountain man. As a child, my mind was set on being a "trapper!" Mountain man and trapper, were one and the same. Kit Carson, Jim Bowie, Liver Eating Johnson, The Mad Trapper, and all those guys had something to do with 'Furs' – spelled with a capital letter. Pronounced 'Fours,' and said with the thumbs in the pocket rocking back on your heels.

Being a writer, artist, trapper, and wilderness land surveyor become occupations. Yet the occupations are a direct result of the lifestyle. They all needed each other, so to speak. If I didn't understand the wilderness, my art and writing has little value, nor could I survey the wild lands, unless I knew my way around. I was hired as a saw man because I could make a camp, run a boat, was not scared of bears, did not complain about mosquitoes, and knew how to run a saw. Possibly these traits are more rare than folks with a degree in math and surveying. I am the highest paid saw man in the state. Surveying introduced me to the Athabascan villagers whose land I travel through, and from whom I got raw material for art and learned from. Teeth, claws, bones, antlers and hooves—by products of my trapping—become art materials. The stories I accumulated in my travels give me something to write about. I'm living the Jack London-Robert Service stories! This helped give provenance to the art, credibility to my words.

In 1978, I got my first dog team. This changed my life. Before this, I could not get to the villages in the winter. I could not seriously trap animals without traveling long distances. Over the next ten years, I cut about 200 miles of trail. I made okay money trapping. I, and most trappers, realistically earn fifty cents an hour for our time. By getting to the village to get mail in winter, I could sell both the furs and my art. Furs are worth more in winter than when sold in spring. I became less dependent on summer work to make all the money to support winter life. With the increased money, I can afford propane light, a few reference books for artwork, and an inventory of nice materials for my art. I can buy silver. Eventually I buy a torch to solder with.

In the 1990s, I still trap and grow a garden for my food, hunt and fish and feed my dogs from the land in a nomadic subsistence life. Life is ever changing. Several things went on that changed my life yet again. The houseboat I lived on is getting old. I owned more things, that no longer all fit on the houseboat. I am tied to the trails I cut, so no longer free to stop, live, and trap just any old place in a nomadic lifestyle. The native land claims went into effect. Native corporations selected the best lands. Nomadic subsistence 'hunter gatherer' turns into 'farmer.' I acquired homesteads that tied me down, following the steps one at a time to 'civilized' land owner.

The oil pipeline days of the '70s – 80s ended, and with that, good pipeline money. The population of the state increases. There are now more artists to compete with at the tourist shops/galleries and more hunters to compete for game. I can no longer go to town, do a show, and sell all the art I created all winter in a week. Having to hang around town for a month to sell my art changes my life. It is harder to grow the garden and keep up with bear damage and take care of the sled dogs. While in town, I cannot fish for the dogs.

Fur prices drop. It is harder to make any real money trapping. I get lonely and want to be around women and have a social life after twenty plus years alone in the woods. Laws change. I think Native issues get big. 'Subsistence' slowly becomes an 'Indian only' issue where it used to be a lifestyle issue, with no prejudice by race. The changes are slow. At first, society acknowledges prejudice is illegal. There are others besides Athabascan's who depend on the land.

At the same time, there is a recession in other states; lack of resources Alaska seems to still have an abundance of like timber, fish, gold, and oil. This is a big change. When acquired, Alaska was 'Seward's Folly,' less than 100 years, ago; within memory. Alaska, as a state, began with the fur industry and competition over fur seals, maybe whale oil. Now those items are going extinct even in Alaska. The shift in focus moves on, and with it, increased population, interest, and of course laws to protect those interests. People living off and depending on things like fish, blueberries and firewood to heat with, interfere with big business. There is a tendency with big money involved for greed and corruption to set in. Government cares what I do because it affects a bigger plan.

The biggest impact is when I am stopped from fishing for my sled dogs. I was arrested several times and 'won' in court. But won what? The right to keep doing what I had already been doing after hiring lawyers and spending time in town going to court? I won nothing. It cost me time and money I could not afford, and caused me to be viewed as an outlaw' a 'person of interest'. I was forced to buy a snow machine to haul dog food from town. This was also the beginning of the end of a lifestyle. I ended up using the dogs to haul gas for the snow machine—sort of a joke. However, the subsistence life, though seeming simple, is a fabric of threads tied together. Pulling a few threads out causes the whole rug to fray. The subsistence lifestyle is fragile. Workable if a person is adaptable, inventive, clever, resourceful. These necessary traits are greatly hampered by rigid rules imposed by civilization.

I'd had to re-cut my trails so a snow machine could go on them. Society put pressure in the direction of desiring me to be plugged in, buying gas, machine parts, being a consumer. It was easier to come to town to sell art and park the snow machine, then finding a place to tie up my sled dogs. It is easier to go get a load of firewood with the snow machine when you are in a hurry.

Survival is not in being bitter and fighting, but in understanding and adapting. Parallel to all this, animal rights groups are getting stronger. This as well happened slowly over a long time. At first it was only city folks. Bush folks laughed and thought how silly civilization is. None of us wilderness people could comprehend a time would arrive when animals had more rights than people. Various trapping-hunting issues come along. It becomes politically incorrect to trap, eat meat or hunt. All that as well, became more recreational, except when speaking of Indians.

Art becomes affected. More rules and laws came along having to do with what parts of what animals may be used in art. The parts I used to adding to my art, that I had easy access to, became first, inappropriate, then illegal.

It is difficult to just 'go back' to those good old days. In the old days my pirate flag was my permit to do everything I needed to. I was viewed as a harmless eccentric by most... at first... for a while. Maybe I only wanted to believe that. The time came when it was illegal to live without an ID card or a credit card. For twenty-five or more years I had neither—and needed neither. Cash once talked, now credit talks. Eventually cash became illegal for conducting some business. The bill that says 'good for all legal debts' is a lie. You can't rent a car, buy a plane ticket, get a hotel room, or pay to run the Iditarod dog race with cash, for example. The big question and issue became, am I going to go down with a sinking ship, an outlaw trying to stick with old ways that are not even legal anymore—or will I adapt, adjust, and accept the changes, be happier and survive? There was no specific time I was a mountain man... and then suddenly I was not. Or once a subsistence person... and then not. Partly "Define these terms." This next book is part of a transition, of constant change. As I gain wisdom, knowledge, skills, and new goals based on new experience.

Just what is survival anyway? As a youth watching outdoor shows like Daniel Boone, Rin Tin Tin, Zorro, Sea Hunt, Lassie, etc., I had a view based on having outdoor skills, a connection to the land. Reading my mountain man books about the heroes of the day, I dreamed survival was stuff like... how to build a fire, and such Boy Scout skills. In 'ending times', I saw coming as early as the '60s, I assumed those who could make it on their own in the wilds would be among the survivors. In my youth, society outfitted bomb shelters. We had atomic blast drills in school. There were many antiestablishment groups and deeds in the news—Black Panthers, Kent State protests, riots. Not all deeds and acts were violent. A great many people believed in tuning in, dropping out, dispensing free love, flowers, and peace symbols. There was Martin Luther King. There were communes, and co-ops formed. Also, thoughts of simply getting back to nature and getting closer to the land. There was the Whole Earth Catalog offering sources for survival supplies. I bought the Foxfire how-to book series explaining how to use these supplies. These things lead me to believe I was not alone.

This is still true today, but forty to fifty years ago seems different to me. The average physical health would allow such a lifestyle in the past. The Kennedy years I recall, had serious physical fitness required in school, with tests you had to pass to graduate. There was more reality about what life with nature was about, like the fact we might have to kill a living thing and eat it. We now face a more obese, chemically dependent society. Or maybe when I was young, ignorance was bliss? I do recall the 'over thirty' crowd when I was a youth, that thought the world was coming to an end when bell bottom pants were popular.

We'd all be back in the Stone Age soon after the nuclear wipe out of civilization. That was a widespread belief, with a few people doing something about it. That seemed sane to me at the time. Those who knew how, would have the best chance of survival. Now the term 'survivalist' seems to mean 'nut case'; to the police, 'person of interest'. 'Alternate lifestyle' now means homosexual. Or perhaps it always did. We could once buy survival food in local grocery stores in cans packed in nitrogen to last twenty years, so we could go underground while the surface of the planet was destroyed. Presumably, we could crawl out of the Earth and rebuild the planet from scratch. When young, I did not consider the surface would probably be radioactive for a million years. Still, it seemed like it would do no harm to know where food comes from... have some knowledge and skills related to providing my own shelter, medicine, necessities, and such. What harm is there in that? If that's nuts, I reasoned it is harmless enough, and hurts no one. *Why would you want to stop me?*

As I got older, I came to see 'survival' on many levels. There is a survival within civilization that has rules, much like the rules I learned in the wild. *No, the wilderness life is not about total freedom.* For example, if you jump off a cliff and think you are going to fly, you will hit the ground and go splat. You are not free to jump off that cliff and expect to live. It's called the law of gravity and this law does not discriminate. No matter where you are, survival is understanding your environment, knowing the laws, and being adaptable.

I start to work with fossil animal parts and gem stones in my art, instead of animal parts. I also become a large wholesale supplier of raw materials to others. A change from just local raw animal body parts of the past. I start traveling out of state doing shows. I move in the direction of computers, the internet, and the ability to work on my book and other writings with a computer. I get into editing my pictures —pictures of wildlife and scenery in the world I love, that I can share with others. I become more social and active in the community I live in. I am head of a Chamber of Commerce, serving on the library board and historical society.

This has rewards to offer, new to me, and an adventure. I can now afford gas and new equipment. Thus travel in the wilderness more than I ever used to. It is not a big deal now to take off on a 700 mile boat trip, and be back in four days. I can now go to the homestead in two hours instead of two days. I miss how it used to be, but surely there is no happiness in dwelling on what cannot be. Some of 'what used to be' still is. Partly there are just more secrets. I come home with 40,000 year old mammoth tusks, and just need to be more vague about how I got them.

I have a few friends who figured out how to live closer to the old ways than I now live. I am unsure if it would work for me as easily. Some guys sit around their cabin in the wilds all day and smoke pot they grow, are subsidized in some way, or have retirement or disability income, etc. In my mind they do nothing, have no life I'd be interested in. They survive because they bother no one. They bother no one because they want nothing. When society tells them to move over, they do. Their impact on the world, on others, is zero. They are not cause over their life. They have no adventures. This is perfectly fine for some who feel no need to amount to anything, or accomplish anything. The world needs sheep. Without sheep, where would fleece come from?

My body has changed and I do not feel as 'safe' out in the wilds. Thirty years of hauling firewood on my shoulders has had its toll. Or maybe we have a body we are given; some are designed to last 100 years and some simply are not. Much is heredity we have no control over. My eyes and ears are not great. I need high blood pressure medication, and getting diabetic. I require a balanced diet. My physical strength is gone. I'm forgetful. Much of this I might 'fight' if I had enough desire. In the old days, I never had to 'fight' my body! My body was my friend who did not let me down! When I lifted something heavy, my muscles simply grew and I roared, flexed those muscles, and my shirt would tear. It never 'hurt'. Plus the laws being different now affect my 'reason' for being out in the wilds. I enjoyed not knowing what day or even what month it was; enjoyed being free in terms of running my own life. If I can't do that anymore, much of the reward is simply gone! It is now a legal requirement to have electricity and a radio, because how else will I know of the latest animal harvest up to date changes? I accomplished most of my goals in the wilds, now it is time for a new game. My zest for life I was beginning to lose comes back as I face new challenges. It is time to go Beyond Wild.

Surveying homesteads on the Kantishna River 150 mile in the wilderness. Me far right.

CHAPTER ONE

YEAR 2000, BACK PROBLEMS

O n my hands and knees, I crawl away from the boat. It feels like it has been all day. Actually, it has been just two hours. My back is killing me. Beads of pain sweat drip from a white pasty face. Ten more feet and I rest again for five minutes. At least it is summer, weather is nice, so I try to feel grateful. I think I can make it home. Maybe half a mile to go yet. Perhaps another few hours, by dark. *Which is midnight this time of year in Alaska.* My conscience reminds me. Ha! The pain stops me from laughing, even from breathing. I'm not in a panic mode. I will make it.

Oh, oh. I hear a truck coming! "Yes! I hear it too!" With all my strength, I roll off the dirt road into the ditch so I will not be seen. As the truck comes around the bend, I recognize it as belonging to my best friend Josh. I hunker down so he will not see me. When we are hurting and weak there is no such thing as a friend. After Josh passes I know I have half an hour before he comes back again. He is headed down to the end of Tenth Street to feed his sled dogs. This is also where I keep my boat tied up on the Nenana River.

Getting back up to the road takes almost half an hour. I only get twenty ft. before I have to roll in the ditch again as Josh goes by on his way home. I know he has to keep his twenty-five racing dogs outside city limits, due to village rules. I now know the coast is clear, and there should be no one else coming by this way till tomorrow. I have all night to get home.

After two more hours I am at the spot I dread. I have to cross the highway without getting run over. I wish I could walk, at least this short bit. But hard as I try, I cannot get up on my feet. It is hard to believe the doctor is right, that walking will fix me right up. This pain medicine stuff he gave me is useless. Made from pineapple extract. All natural. Oh well. God gave us pain for a reason. So we know something is wrong. Masking the pain may not be a great idea. My body is telling me I should not be doing this, and to stop! Fine, but who else will check on my boat for me? *I can't just leave my boat tied up for a week without checking on it.*

I started out sort of walking. The doctor said to walk. I assumed I'd loosen up and feel better, not worse. Dang. A gap in the traffic gives me time to make my move across this two lane paved highway. A dust trail is left as I crawl. I must look a mess. There is no stopping to rest on the pavement. *No cars coming anyhow.* I'd get run over for sure laying in the middle of the road like this. But I have a high Jesus factor. Stuff like that does not happen to me. I'm blessed. Not everyone is as lucky as I am. I try hard not to let it make me stuck up.

Across the highway I get in the ditch so I will not be seen, and can rest up in peace. My legs start twitching in uncontrollable spasms. Maybe nerve damage to my spine? I should tell my chiropractor? *Naw. He'd just tell me to come in.* It's fifty miles to Fairbanks, the big city of 70,000. I have no transportation. Do not drive, never have. Anyhow, what's he going to do? What has he done so far? It's all about the money. I lie in the ditch and hope I do not pass out, wondering what to do. *At least workman's comp covers us!* Yes, this is true. Thanks for that. On my income, I'd have to kill myself. Just a fluke of luck I got hurt on the job! Not luck, that high Jesus factor again. First time in my whole life I was unable to show up for work. A horrible feeling. I lay here resting, thinking of how I got here.

SEYMOUR and I have been land surveying together for a great many years now. It seems like hundreds of jobs together. All over the Alaska wilderness doing home-steads, native claims, remote village work. He has his own plane now in 2000, and that makes our work more exciting. We fly in a small private plane, and land on floats on some remote river in the center of everything; the great outdoors. I moved out of the wilderness to live in this 1916 log cabin in Nenana. Sort of by choice. Sort of not. But, oh well. Life goes on like a train and we are either on board or left behind. There are things to look forward to in civilization, or so I tell myself. I gulp at the brave new world that has such things in it. Such things as I am being intro-duced to. The computer age. Totally different world than when I left civilization back in 1972 to be a hermit, mountain man, trapper. Anyhow, those nomadic subsis-tence days appear to be over, at least much harder to manage than in the past.

Past Flash

Seymour and I get another interesting job. A power line is going in between Healy and Fairbanks. The Intertie, to help bring electric power into Fairbanks from the new power plant by Denali, or just power from the bigger city of Anchorage. As saw man, I run point. The very cutting edge of civilization. I'm first on the ground, dropped in by helicopter into an LZ, like Vietnam, clearing the area, making it hospitable for a takeover. *It's exciting!* I get picked up at the end of the day, often five miles away. Dropped off, often alone with saw, gas, lunch and basic survey gear, armed for bears. I end up deciding where the power line will go. Or at least the small moves right or left of a swamp, or stand of trees. The first to see it. The one to cut the first tree down. That's me.

I am having problems from the start. My back hurts. I'm working in the rain with all my gear strapped to my belt, and those dang saw chaps they make us wear that do not fit, pull on my back. Being a short guy, nothing fits. Tripping on my chaps seems more unsafe running a chain saw then not wearing them. *But what do I know? I'm not being paid to think.* When not working for big companies I leave all the safety gear behind and feel more safe.

There is a new kid with us also running the saw. He can cut trees ahead of us faster than I can walk. I can hardly carry his lunch and gas up to him. I'm barely forty years old, but already I know I am not eighteen anymore. Seymour describes our work as, "like being in the Olympics," or any top athlete. In your prime at eighteen. At your peak at twenty-five, and on the way out by thirty. Wore out and a has been by forty.

So here I am, trying to keep up with some young punk kid. We take turns. It is my turn to cut for a while. I'm cutting a big dead tree, too tired and hurting to look up or pay a lot of attention. I have cut a gazillion of these. But this one has a dead branch way up at the top that breaks loose. When younger I would have heard it, or looked up more often to check what is happening to the tree. Sweat in my eyes. I can't see. Tired. The branch breaks loose and lands on my back, slamming me to the ground. I'm told I screamed, but do not recall.

I think I am okay. I get up and go back to work. Didn't hurt any more than the normal daily pains that come and go as part of the job. I do not get paid for complaining. No way out till the end of the day when the helicopter arrives anyhow.

If I cut my leg off I'd probably say, "Rats! Hey, can you cut trees for a spell, I think I need a break!" Take my belt off, wrap it around my leg stump, fashion a crutch and go back to work. "I can't work" is not one of the options. So I finish out the day. There is an assumption all I need is a good night's sleep and I'll be ready to go like always. As it has been for twenty-five years. In all those years, I have never been sick, nor seen a doctor.

But in the morning I cannot get out of bed. The first time in my life. There is no worse feeling than having to say I can't work. It's embarrassing. It's also the day, in my mind, you die. The beginning of the end. *If we cannot take care of ourselves, who will?* It also messes up the job for everyone else. I've always been the one you could count on, never let a boss down.

Workman's comp pays for me to go to a chiropractor with a back problem. An X-ray apparently shows nothing wrong. Hard to believe.

Past Flash ends

I lay here in the ditch, believing nothing is wrong. I've been seeing the chiropractor for two weeks now. He is an expert, so if nothing is wrong, then it must be true.[1]

Eventually I get home. Now I need rest. *I'll be better after I rest.* I cannot get up to fix any food, but assume in a day or two I can stand up and be able to get a meal fixed. Luckily I can crawl to the bathroom and back to bed. I still do not own a phone, never have in my life. No one to call, anyhow. *To say what?* The value of my life has already been summed up. It was not so long ago a nut case had me at gunpoint at the river right where I was looking after my boat. He was about to shoot me and dump me in the river. I believed him. No one especially cared. I got away only because an unexpected car came down the road and stopped. I suggested to the trooper I know that maybe we could set the guy up and I could be wired and…

"You can step in just before he pulls the trigger and arrest him, lock him up, get him some meds or psychiatric help or something." The trooper agreed, and thought it was a good idea, that might work. Later he told me, that there was no funding for a tape recorder. All the ones they have were in use, and none could be spared, but maybe in a few months. I did not have $50 to buy one. That's what my life is worth. Someone killed this Gene guy. Otherwise, it would have been me dead. I do not know who, but I am grateful. That's the kind of the world we live in.

If I can't get up to fix a meal and eat, then I will starve and will be found dead in my bed. That sums up civilization. Or, it is part of the subsistence life I understand, agree with, and accept, as a price we pay for a lifestyle we choose. In the beginning I asked what one did when we get sick. The old Indian smiled and said "We die." Possibility I'm going to die. I don't have anything to say to anyone. Maybe a nice Clint Eastwood type one-liner and a wink. *"Smile when you call me that"* or *"I'll be back!"*

I DO NOT DIE. In less than a week I can stand again. Workman's Comp calls to tell me they are not happy with the chiropractor results, and want me to go to a 'real doctor' at the hospital. Isn't a chiropractor a real doctor? Puzzling. But what do I know? I'm a savage from the wilderness. The real doctor tells me I have a herniated disk and would I like it operated on? If I do not, I can lie in bed and rest between five to seven years. My back might be sort of better again, about the equivalent of the operation. I know though, that after five years in bed, nothing will be the same again! That becomes a whole lifestyle. How could I ever get back in shape again?

The operation has risk. I could be in a wheel chair if the operation goes bonkers. I decide to go for it though, because I have Workman's Compensation. Three to five years from now they will not remember who I am if anything more is needed. Right now they offer this operation worth more than my house is worth. If the tree branch had fallen on me while out on my own cutting firewood I'd be dead. But then I might not have been pushing myself as I was. Hard to know.

The doctor does a routine checkup before surgery and tells me I have blood pressure off the scale—well over 200. They cannot operate till it comes down. I'm ordered to take some pills. The nurse tells me I would probably not live more than a few months with blood pressure so high. I thought the blood pressure was due to pain. But there is no proof of that, and this is not accepted as a reason. Meaning if I had not had the back injury I'd be dead within a few months of high blood pressure. I had not seen a doctor in... um... maybe never. Oh yea, once in '74, or so. So in a way, am I lucky I had an injury that got me to the hospital? See, once again, a high Jesus factor. *Am I ever lucky.*

As soon as I wake up from surgery I know my back is better. Even before I try to move.

"There is the possibility you could be in a wheel chair," The nurse said.

"I'll be fine." I say without hesitation. Just some recovery time. If I had my only home, the homesteads or the houseboat of the past, it would be hard to rest. There is firewood to cut and water to haul. No electric. The hot water in the tub in my new Nenana village home is almost a necessity for my back.

The new home in Nenana is... well... different for me. I have spent the past twenty years living in the Alaska wilderness, living out my life dream as a mountain man-hermit-homesteader-trapper. I was raised middle class, with my father being Dean of a college with lots of prestige in college towns across the country. I left so long ago, it is hard to recall life with electricity, running water, and bills to pay. As I step through the door of my new home, I marvel at having light by flipping a switch. I operate the switch up and down and focus on how it was built. *Amazing. Oh, brave new world that has such things in it.* At the sink, I turn the hot water tap and there is hot water! No need to fetch it from the creek, set it on the wood stove, and wait for it to get warm!

There is a wood stove, and I am glad for this. While being overwhelmed by the sheer class of it all, I am at the same time afraid. *Can I afford all this?* Nothing in life is free. I am used to providing everything my life requires by building it, or fetching it direct from the land. I have never paid rent, had a phone bill, an alarm clock, an ID, or a credit card. I do not get bills in the mail, I get checks in the mail. I am used to being smug about this, and feeling sorry for the rest of the world. Am I now on a path of destruction, getting plugged into the rat race? Is this the first move of my undoing? How will I ever afford the bills? What am I qualified for if I have to work? I've been taught nothing I do is worth anything. Seymour pays me as a saw man, but he does not have full time work for me, and 'saw man' is not a real job. I mostly enjoy it.

The cabin is an original village cabin in Nenana. The ceiling is hand cut whip-sawed wood, originally the hull of a paddle boat, turned upside down and used as a roof. The boards are twenty-two ft. long without a splice. The curve of the stern-wheeler hull is still visible when looking up inside the house. The ceiling is a low six ft. Maybe the bottom logs have rotted and the cabin has dropped, or maybe cabins long ago were built low, or people 100 years ago were shorter. This works out fine since I am short, and I have built such cabins myself on the trapline, so am used to this. *A Hobbit house.* Even though I bought it in 1996, I have not made use of it and moved in to it in 2000 because I preferred to live on my homestead on the Kantishna River.[2]

There was still some snow on the ground when I first moved in, but I had seen this cabin in summer with the flowers and bushes surrounded by tall trees. Like a sanctuary, with song birds and a greenhouse full of good smells and happy plants. There will be the smell of lilacs soon. This is the edge of town, on a dirt road with no designation, no road sign, no house number, and no mailbox. Two people going by in a day is normal. Nenana has a population of 300, but up to 800 come to Nenana to get mail from the outlying area. So Nenana is a hub for people like me, trappers, miners, homesteaders, Indians. Bush folks. *Thank God for that.* I might have a chance to blend in. *Maybe pass myself off at the bottom rung of 'civilized.'* This is on my mind as I soak in the bath. A luxury I have not had since I was a child. I think to myself here in the bathtub.

There is a developing issue related to 'animals' and how to deal with them. The loose dogs in town. I'm puzzled. I ponder what people in civilization do. There is a law on the book: "No loose dogs. All dogs must be under the owner's control."

This law is universally ignored, as if it does not exist. Puzzling. Though I am aware of all sorts of laws that are not real laws, just 'for the record' that everyone ignores as if they do not exist. *Don't we have way too many laws to remember anyway?* If the law is not workable, make it workable and realistic, or remove it from the books. There is something about how civilization works that I am missing. I have not been a member, so am not tuned in to how it works. Apparently, the laws can be randomly applied when desired. *Desired by whom?*

I have jello cooling in my entry way, and a loose dog breaks in and drinks it. I watch him strut off as if he owns the world. Dogs piss on my firewood. I have to put this wood in the stove. It is common to see village dogs running down the street with packs of frozen meat they robbed from someone. It is common for people to be bitten, chased, and run off the dogs' turf. I watched a child get knocked off a bike the other day. *Who runs things, who is in charge? The dogs?* In the wild, all this is not a problem, even a blessing! Some creature has the audacity to steal from me? How quaint! How naive, how cute, how droll. The creature, whatever it is, becomes my dinner. *Please, come try to take something from me, I am hungry, I am amused.* It's the trespasser who has a bad day, not me. The concept that I am the victim is absurd! In the wilds, I am king of all before me. In civilization I am to be a slave... to dogs? *What a big change.*

I assume there is some solution I am not grasping here, besides being a helpless victim. I believe the best solution is to go to the city council at one of the town meetings and address the issue. Get an official answer on record. Because those I ask tell me, "Shoot them loose dogs if they're a problem!" So what will the city council say when I ask why there is a leash law? Why is it ignored? Not ask in an accusatory manner, but with a puzzled attitude: "I don't get it, explain it to me." One thing that will not happen, is dogs having more rights than people, stealing my stuff, and there being nothing I can do about it. After much thought, I decide living in civilization can be much like the wild. The rules are similar. In both worlds, understanding your environment means getting involved. In the wild, I learn and study weather, animal behavior, plants, etc., because these things run my life. So if the city council runs my life in town, I want to find out who they are, how it works, and have some influence- effect.

Maybe the city will tell me there is a dog catcher to call. Or that dogs have name tags. Catch one and call the owner. Or catch one and collect a prize; there is a bounty on them, paid for by the owner. These are solutions I'd think would work. Loose dogs being a blessing to bounty hunters, a job for the unemployed.

I went to my first city council meeting last month while still living on the houseboat. Trying to be involved, care about what might be considered my community. Not just a place I pick up my mail, as it has been in the past. They meet once a month in the fire hall. There I was, to find out the meaning of life. Eager to learn. The entire meeting, two hours, was occupied with: "Who left the red underwear in the drier at the fire hall," and "Who has a right to use the washing machine among the volunteer firefighters?" One suspect on the city council says, "It was not my underwear, because I don't wear underwear!" Others had heads turned her direction as a most likely suspect.

Someone pinch me. This is a dream. Wake me up. This is Candid Camera, right? But no. This is our tax dollars at work. *Ha! I am sure glad I do not pay taxes, what a joke! But wait! I do pay taxes now.* Gosh, this is depressing. No wonder civilized people are so bummed out all the time. The bright side, *always look at the bright side*, this is survival. The bright side is, if this is the most exciting, important thing that has happened in the community in a whole month, then it's got to be an OK place to live, right? Considering what I hear in the news from around the planet. So I'm going to keep a straight face and not burst out laughing, and be entertained. We are going to get to the bottom of who left the red underwear in the dryer. *But if we find out? Then what?* Stay tuned to the continuing drama of the most exciting question of the month. Maybe we should get all the village women lined up and see who can fit into this underwear. "If it doesn't fit, you must not convict" *the famous glove from the Simpson Murder trial.*

So now on the agenda is loose dogs. Apparently word spreads. The agenda is posted at Coghill's store, library, senior center, and the gas station. Concerned citizens are coming up to me, explaining that yes, they too have been bothered by loose dogs, and something needs to be done! My answer is always the same: "Well, it is your community, why haven't you done anything about it?"

The answers seem vague and do not make sense. "No time. Do not want problems with others. No one cares anyhow, so why bother."

I'm learning more, since the subject will be on the city council meeting agenda. Apparently many citizens do shoot loose dogs when the dogs bother them. No one knows when, or who, for sure. Dogs disappear, there are gun shots. No one saw anything or knows anything. I have a variety of concerns with this. I am up to the task of shooting stray dogs that bother me! Not a problem! I am a hunter, own guns, know how to use them. But what about citizens who do not own guns, or children, or the elderly? Those loose dogs would be the most danger to the weak.

My next concern is safety and liability issues. A community of armed citizens blasting stray dogs on sight conjures up certain images in my mind. What happens if you miss and a stray bullet does what? Hits a person (me!), breaks a window, etc, etc. Who is liable? There might be wounded dogs running off. Also a loved well behaved nice dog that got loose one time that is not a problem dog, might get shot. There are arguments already. Who shot who's dog, and why! My plan is not to be a concerned citizen who wants a revolution, and change how things are done all by myself! I have a simple question, "What do you do? So that I may do the same, and get along. A solution that works." I suppose I have enough of an answer to mind my own business and just shoot dogs, know nothing, see nothing. Like everyone else.

It appears the loose dogs learn whose yard to stay out of. The dog shooters have safe yards. The rest of society here is living in chaos and terror. A serious accident waiting to happen, when dogs pack up and kill a child. Many are sure this is going to happen. Why is that any of my business, as long as I know how to take care of me? *What you do, or do not do, is your concern!*

I have memories from the past. Canada. Trying to help out, solve a community's issues at twenty years old. My thanks was to get deported, lose everything, a home and all I owned.[3] At any rate, the subject is already posted on the agenda with my name on it. *How do I get myself into these messes!* If a community cannot take care of itself, why is that my business!

So the day arrives. Maybe fifty citizens show up, gathered in folding chairs, chatting next to friends, dressed like simple folks for the most part in plaid shirts, suspenders, work boots. *No suits and ties in here. No briefcases.* It is my turn to address the city council. I express my concern in simple terms. "Most of you know me. I have been around the Interior for twenty years. I have spent most of that time in the wilderness, and have just moved into the village. I'm trying to adjust, adapt, fit in, and a big issue is the loose dogs I see in the community. Of personal concern is, these dogs in my yard are stealing things. My food, and my furs, turn up missing. Dogs are dumping in the yard, marking my firewood pile I have to burn, and in general being a nuisance. I want to know what it is I am supposed to do? What is recommended, and normal for the community? I have discovered after inquiring, that many other citizens have the same questions. Do you have an answer for us?"

The reply is short and simple, and comes from the mayor himself: "Shoot them!"

I reply: "I have no problem with this answer. I own guns, know a lot about them. I'm a good shot. It seems strange to me that it is every man for himself. There are children, the elderly, along with those who do not own guns, not in the position to shoot dogs. I have an image in my mind of unqualified people blasting away, chasing a dog down the street, with bullets flying everywhere. Or the possibility of a tourist being bit who is not as kind and understanding as locals are. If we say "Shoot that dog!" I can see lawsuits and bad publicity." I'm not sure how to explain further.

One comment comes from the public. "We used to have a dog catcher; Charley used to take care of it when dogs became a nuisance. He'd go around town and shoot them. But he does not do that anymore."

I am asked by the city council, "Miles, would you be interested in being the dog catcher?"

I assume the job is described as Charley once had it. Once in a while go around town, get paid to shoot the stray dogs. I do think shooting them is preferable to them living wild on the streets threatening people. I'm a bit in shock this is the official stand. *It's like the Wild West. I thought this was civilization.* I express interest, and ask the details. *Maybe they'll pay me!*

Many citizens give personal accounts. "I have a friend down B street and I am afraid to go visit because there is a loose dog that guards the street. I cannot go down that street," said by a soft spoken old lady who has a hard time walking, and is frail. Others have been bitten. Many will not go for walks because of loose dogs. Many citizens will not bike ride because they are chased. This has me feel the city's solution does not work.

The mayor addresses me: "Miles, new laws are in effect. You'd have to build a fenced in area to specifications, special diamond fencing, with a cement floor at your expense. You would have to catch and quarantine the dog. If anything happens to the dog during quarantine you are responsible."

I'm shocked! *My responsibility to a loose dog is greater than the responsibility of the owner? How odd! Is this for real? Is this a joke? Is this how people really live? By rules like this? Are you insane? I have to feed them, and take care of them, in an approved environment? Carry insurance and what not?*

I said, "No!" With an understanding laugh. Who else would want such a job? *No one!*

I am told in an aside, "The city is not happy either, but rules from far off are handed down to us to abide by. This is the legal position the city finds itself in. How they do it in the big city."

I sigh, and accept the words direct from the city council, right out of the mayor's mouth. I begin shooting dogs that give me a problem. Two to three a day sometimes. I'm a little upset because it disrupts my day. I have to drag them to the river and dump them, then wash out my cart. I'm inclined to bill the dog owner. *Yup I saw your dog all right. Shot it. If you buy another one, try taking care of it. I'll be nice and not charge you for the time it took to take care of your problem, but next time I might not be so nice. I'll charge you.* I am savvy enough to guess this would fly like a lead balloon. I think people have a right to know the truth. So people may have cause over their life. I'm not inclined to feed their fantasy, that little Cuddles was no bother to anyone, and maybe some nice person loved Cuddles and took him to a better home. *No. little Cuddles pushed the door open, came in my house and ate my dinner. I did not know who little Cuddles belonged to because there was no name tag. The local policy is not to try to find the owner, but to 'solve the problem with bullets'. I did not make the policy. I do not even like the policy. Any questions?* What's this living in denial stuff? An entire dysfunctional community! What is this talk of being a 'victim'? Me, the victim? I think not!

My outlook is not going over very well in the community. Or it is. Quite a few give me a thumbs up and 'Atta boy'. I discover however, in private, not publicly. There are those who push me into the lime light above the radar. So I may get shot down, not them. The fall guy. Someone says, "Hey there is this dog next door I do not like, giving me problems, can you take care of it for me?" *What am I? A hit man?* There is an assumption I hate dogs, love killing things.

"Yes, I love dogs. Had sled dogs for years. Cared more for them than people. I guess the answer is, I like dogs that mind. Just as I like people all right. But when a person robs me, or injures me, even threatens me, I do not like that." *Fascinating. That 300 people could all be nuts. Obviously it is not so, and it is me who has a problem.*

In the bathtub I sigh. I love life in the wilds. In the wilds I have no problems, only challenges, with difficult- but surmountable, solutions.

I almost forget. My father is coming to visit. All the way from Connecticut. I've never seen his home there. Have not seen him in years. Unsure why he wants to see me. Something about being there for me during my surgery recovery. But that's strange and does not make sense. But, oh well. Life changes. *What can we do together?* I prefer to be alone. I do not want anyone to see me till I am stronger. Especially family! Sigh.

The day arrives. I have no way to get to Fairbanks to pick him up. Dad rents a car in Fairbanks where he flies in, and drives the fifty miles to Nenana. He helps me through some of the hardest days. So yes, there are people who will step forward and help. It is just me, not trusting that, or depending on that. Help may or may not happen. Dad seems to enjoy meeting the people I know here. Josh especially wants to meet my father, the professor, the dean of a college. Josh, the Iditarod dog sled race winner, Athabascan Indian meets the professor. I grin. Dad and I go on a tour of the state in the rented car when I am able. He does not think much of my lifestyle. I'm sorry he felt the need to come here and help me. Honestly? I doubt I'd do the same for him. I suppose I love him. I suppose I have no clue what love is, and I simply 'feel something', do not know what to call it, and assume it must be love. Such is the way of dysfunctional families. On the bright side, he is lucky I do not hate him. Or I may be lucky he is willing to come here and take time from his life to help me.

"Miles, aren't the glaciers interesting?" We are in Valdez.

"I came here once with my buddy, Crafty, long ago on a selling trip, but we never stopped to see the glaciers. We went to the ski resort and I did a show there. Yes, it is good to take time to see the glaciers."

"Pretty amazing, all right! Glad we can share it together." It is nice seeing dad. But he'll be gone and out of touch soon. This is just a vacation. Or a short visit anyhow. About the time we start to bond he'll cut me off at the knees. His first question is the same as always, "Can you drive yet?" It's not about can or cannot. It is about a choice I made not to. He believes I am not capable, and I tend to live up to what's expected. Likewise I hear, "When are you coming home?" I ignore that age old question I have answered too many times and not been heard. I change the subject.

"Dad, I'm thinking of going to Germany to sell my art." I think this might interest my father, who also travels on business. He might think I'm coming up in the world. This has been on my mind. My German friend Helm has suggested it for two years now, and sounds serious about inviting me to his home in Frankfurt.

"I notice it is the German tourists who seem to like my art and lifestyle the most. So why not go to the source? Check it out for myself." I explain also, "Germany has new high tech computers that are capable of printing my book. Helm has a friend who owns such a company. Raak. I can meet with this friend. For short runs of books it sounds like this is the way of the future. Maybe $5 a book, sell 'em for $10 or so." Dad has a bunch of degrees. I do not know what in, as he does not talk about it, but think one PhD has to do with business.

"Without a marketer or distributor, Miles?" Dad knows at least a little about the book business. His wife, whom I do not know very well, has written and published a couple of books. She's a history professor. She had to write a book as part of getting her PhD. The books sold well and are popular. Dad goes on, "I thought of writing a book, but saw how much work it is and decided not to."

I can see how that can happen. I have been working on this book for how many years now? Enough years no one believes I am serious or will ever have it done.

"Computers make it easier, dad. I'm struggling to understand the computer. That is frustrating, but I took a basic class for free and learned how to turn on, access the internet and do email basics. It's all new. The beauty is, when you write, you can save it, later, move it and insert stuff, while the text moves ahead, you do not have to start all over like with a typewriter." Even though dad helped design one of the first computer programs—'Fortran,' computer language, he did not keep up with it. *Must have been a temporarily interesting project at the time.* When Windows came along and ran the program in the background, the end user no longer had to understand computer language. I chuckle and have to explain why. "I have to admit I spent a month's wages on my first computer, managed to ruin it in a week, and had to buy another one." Dad wonders why I'd admit to that with a smile. *Do most people try to cover their mistakes? Oh. Why?*

"I suppose, dad, I feel what I have accomplished is amazing. Something to be proud of. Of course it comes with a price, that's a given." I explain as best I can. Why not chuckle about the price? How can one learn without sacrifice and cost? Paying the price is what separates those who succeed from those who do not. Those who quit the first time they break something never have anything. Coming out of the wilds with no ID, no phone, no driver's license after having spent... what... twenty-five years alone in the pucker brush, living on a houseboat, not seeing anyone, and within a year, understanding computers. *Could you do that?* I wonder.

Dad put my art work up when I was a child in the halls at the university. Most assumed that he was'Miles', and complimented the work. We both have the same name. He dabbled in painting as a hobby, fancied himself very good at it. I think it upset him, having to say, "No, that's my twelve year old son's work." I was better at art when ten years old, than dad has been in his entire life. I am not wanting to rub that in. Dad has a formal education I will never have, that I admire. It's just not me.

Dad changes the subject. "I could teach you how to drive while I am here, Miles." He does not understand, physically driving a car would be easy. I run boats and snow machines that are harder to handle. It's psychological. Dad is more a part of the problem than the solution. No use going there.

"Thanks for the offer, dad, but as I have explained, I live a lifestyle that does not require driving. There is a post office and store within walking distance. I can get a ride with others once a month or so when I need supplies I cannot get locally." I do not explain I am seeing a potential to order supplies on the internet in the future. There are a few stores now offering items on the internet. Having a web site is becoming the rage, and in the local news. A few who created web sites got lots of business. It's all new, but seems to have potential. This new rage does seem to be among the young! Elders want nothing to do with computers. *As many elders wanted nothing to do with the new fangled telephones and airplanes when they first came out.*

This is the first time my father has seen for himself where and how I live. Seeing me work at the bench at my art, impresses him. "You're a real professional, Miles!" I make a custom knife for dad with his name on it. He goes camping sometimes and loves to sail, so might like a knife on the boat.

THERE IS a knock on the door. My Athabascan Indian friend Josh is here. "Hold on, Josh, while I throw some clothes on!"

My father came and went. Josh was impressed by him, the professor. There is often an irritation when Josh greets me, and wants to know what went wrong, what happened to me, that I did not turn out like my father. Did I turn out like my mother instead- ha ha? He often introduces me as 'the son of a college professor.'

"Mr. Maw-tin, how are you these days. Where did you get the truck?" There is a 1986 Ford crew cab in the muddy driveway.

"Hey, Josh. Well, I think I own it. I am not sure. Some gal left it here for safe keeping and left the state. Now she cannot return – some kind of legal problems, so is selling me her truck cheap, like $1,000. Runs good. Has the camper on the back so I can haul all my goods to the fair, covered, and safe."

"But you do not have a driver's license."

"'Ya,' well. I can have someone else drive my truck maybe. Or I can drive at night and just get there and park. I'm not sure. One step at a time, Josh. I only know I cannot go wrong getting a truck that blue books for $5,000, buying it for $1,000. Even if I turn around and sell it for $2,000. Making money this way beats working for a living!"

:)

"The man of opportunity!" Said with a smile, but a crafty smile, with hidden sarcasm in the voice. *My buddy, Josh. Always trying to bait me.* A lesson in forgiveness. For he too has his life story, and reasons for being who he is. *I'm curious about the personalities of people who are the best there is at what they do.* Josh is one such person. Short guy, like me. Wins the Iditarod, toughest race on Earth. No sponsors, no helpers, no money, owning only twenty sled dogs. Competitors often own 200, have a vet, handlers and sponsors, yet lose to Josh. *What makes him tick, what motivates him? How does he do it?* I ignore his sarcasm, and am extremely proud to know him. He may have not gotten over the fact I gave up sled dogs and have a snow machine now.

Josh will die on the runners of a dog sled. Without dogs, there is not much for us to talk about anymore. He is not seriously interested in anything else. On any other subject he is just being accommodating and polite. Is Josh happy? Successful? *If not, what good is being the best?* My mind wanders: *I heard of a study about people who are the best there is at what they do, gifted in their field. Many are very strange, and not especially happy, not the sort the average person would chose to be like. Gifted people focus so much time and energy on their chosen field they are often inept in every other area. Poe, Hemingway, Picasso, Benjamin Franklin, John Lennon, and many I can think of, were very troubled people. Many committed suicide, ended up insane, in prison, poor.*

I would not wish to be Josh. How many would wish to be me? Not Josh, who once said, "At least I recall my childhood, Miles. You do not, as bad as mine was, I remember!"

In my life I have had had many people who look up to me, and want me to be their guide, mentor, or guru. None got as far as step three, in a process requiring 100 steps to be in my shoes. Possibly no one can be me. *As no one can be Josh.*

I wake up with Josh's question: "Miles, you think you will ever get the houseboat back in the river?"

Josh has changed the subject. Willing to at least talk about boats, to be polite. He helped me pull the houseboat out of the water onto dry land when there was a flood. I park the river boat I use in the water at the bank under the houseboat.

"Kind of doubt it now, Josh. Unsure it would even float!" *Built when? Back in 73? Seems a lifetime ago.* Wood boats are not forever. It's been sunk four times and had a hard life. I trapped from it, and put a good 100,000 miles on it. All the dreams this boat stands for. Originally it was designed to be a paddle boat, run by steam. I worked with steam in the Navy, so understood it. I learned to run a steam engine. Steam never powered my boat. I got overwhelmed with the task of putting in a tunnel hull, and the power that runs that set up. I got the engine, the shaft, and the rudder. I even got the marine transmission to run the engine through. I do not have the knowledge or tools to put it all together. The transmission will not just bolt to the engine. The engine may be the wrong kind. I need a marine engine with strong thrust bearings. I did not know this when I got the four cylinder Saab off my friend Will. No money to pay for help. Anyhow, my life seems not to be going in the direction of life on the houseboat in the remote wilds. Been there, done that already.

"Josh, the new Honda four stroke on the river boat seems to be the way to go. You going to try the four stroke engines?"

"I'll wait till you try it out more, work all the bugs out. Give me a report!" We both laugh. He does not fully trust white man's products. For good reason. We talk about the old ways a lot. Josh used to be captain of a big steam boat, the Nenana, on display in Fairbanks. I have seen a picture of Josh at seventeen years old, behind the wheel of this 120 ft paddle boat that draws only two ft of water. Josh also made money cutting cord wood by hand with a whip saw and selling it to steam boats. Look how much has changed within his memory.

"How much gas did you burn last trip coming up from Minto, Miles?"

"Well let's see. I figure three gallons an hour, maybe twenty miles an hour average. Maybe five gallons, Josh."

"Sounds good all right. I burn at least ten gallons, and in the houseboat, you used to burn as much twenty gallons between here and Minto!"

Yes I recall. Not being able to afford the gas anymore is one major factor in a lifestyle change. The houseboat averaged a gallon a mile. "Gas used to be 80 cents a gallon too, remember? Now geez, up over $1. Who knows where it will stop? Might get over $2 a gallon! Then what! We are going to be dead in the water." It's a good reason to think about four stroke outboards that burn half the gas as two stroke.

"Your back feeling better? You aren't down for the count, are you Mr. Martin? Hate to plan a funeral." He's trying to depress me, but it is not going to work.

"I feel pretty good, getting stronger by the day. I should be up to setting up for the fair in August." Fair time is a big deal to me these days. I can make half a year's wages in two weeks.

There is concern if I will ever survey again, if my back will hold up. Or another issue to face. I could force myself to survey since I need the money, and work till I end up in a wheel chair. I could choose, like Josh, to never change, and end up how? A physical life is good for how many years on a body? Then what? What is the smart thing to do?

Friends, customers, fans, want me to feel guilty for changing. As if I let them down in some way. The football hero who didn't make the touchdown and gets booed by the very people who an hour ago wanted to buy him a beer.

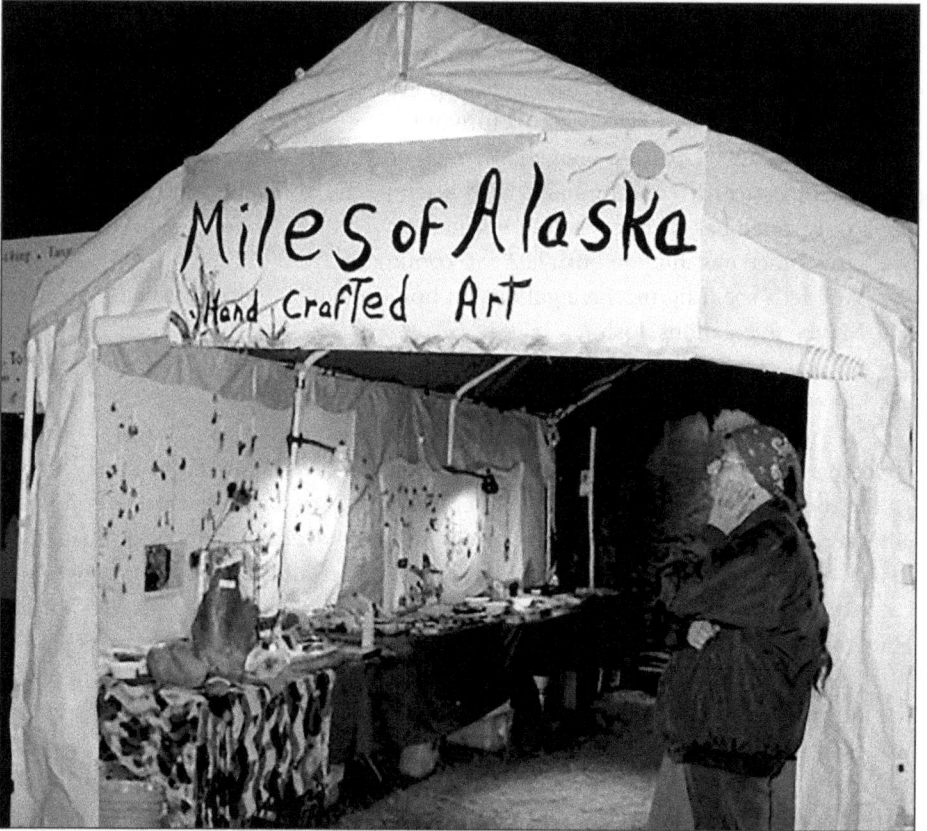

My booth and handcrafted art set up at the Tanana Fair each year.

CHAPTER TWO

MAMMOTH TUSK HUNTING, QUOTED IN FAMOUS BOOK, MAIL ORDER RUSSIAN GIRL

A letter arrives with a copy of a book. (!) I am excited as I recall an interview with this famous scientist who is the world expert on ravens. A note in his book tells me to turn to page ninety in 'Ravens in Winter' by Bernd Heinrich. He thanks me for the duck feather and hand painted envelope: "Nice Raven scene you water colored!" I eagerly turn to see my name and contribution in print, being read all over the world.

Bernd had written me, and asked if I knew any raven stories, if I knew of any reason to believe ravens work together, to help each other or show intelligence. I told him some raven stories as I knew them. I arrive at the spot.

"It is common to confuse personal interpretation with observations. Because there is so much engrained folklore."

Hmm, yes, well, whatever. The first words are about someone else he interviewed. I read on:

"A woman from New Orleans who read my article on ravens in Audubon Magazine, which I had written when I had just got started to find out how ravens share, wrote me: 'I did not have as much trouble as you did showing that ravens share. I see them at the feeder-they even feed one another.' There are no ravens in New Orleans, nor anywhere else in Louisiana. Perhaps what she actually saw were several large dark birds (Crows? Grackles?), one of which fed another one or two (probably their grown offspring traveling with them). But a trapper in the north woods might be more unbiased.

I had read an article about a trapper/writer near Nenana, Alaska, and knowing he would be familiar with ravens in the North, I wrote and asked him if he had seen crowds of ravens at carcasses. I also told him the reason for my interest. He had a lot of raven stories to tell. First, he said, "Everyone" he knew, knows that ravens share their food. He was surprised at the ignorance of us armchair scientists so far away, who didn't believe what people like himself who had lived in the woods all their lives knew.

For example, the ravens knew the destructive power of his rifle, and they kept just out of its range. Nevertheless, they were "clever enough" to raid the fish he kept on racks for his dogs. They did this by posting a "twenty-four-hour guard at his cabin." (How did he distinguish this, I wondered, from birds waiting for an opportunity to feed?) As soon as he got up, a raven was there to see him and "spread the word" (read: Flew away, and/or called.)

He claimed that one raven "followed" him all day. (Read: He occasionally saw a raven.) It then "reported back" to the others so they could all leave just before he got back from his day on the trapline. (Read" He saw several leave together, and there were none when he got back to his cabin door.) Many of the birds "raided" (fed from?) his fish rack, and his idea of them "getting out the word" to ravens for miles around is that the one who discovers the food calls, and the summons is heard by all the birds in neighboring territories, who then also call, in an ever enlarging ring of information sharing.(An interesting thought). It was no mystery to him why the birds would do this: "gossiping."

"It seems obvious," he said, "that the birds get excited, and they simply can't hold on to the excitement that lets the others know" (Very weak, incontinent birds, these). And why should they evolve such transparent excitement? That too was "obvious": "Because it is best for the species." This stock answer explains nothing, any more than saying "God" created the world when you really have no idea.

It was disturbing to me to see someone so fancily blur the distinction between observations and interpretations and then even go so far as to make numerous deductions that he believed to be self evident without the slightest shred of evidence for even one."

I sigh and put the book down.

I make a distinction between telling a story and offering proof. I agree with myself. Proof is dry and not fun, stories are entertaining. I told it like a story, as requested. I was not asked if I had any proof, nor was I told the request was a scientific one. The word 'story' and 'science' do not belong in the same sentence.

It is true I suppose. It is hard in the wilds to offer 'proof' of much. All there is, becomes an opinion. What experiments can I run, with what equipment? I had read what Bernd had written earlier someplace – where he spoke of moving into a remote cabin in winter to study ravens. They did not know he was there in the cabin, and so he studied them in their natural state. I wondered what proof he had that he was undetected. How did he know for sure he was not a factor, had zero effect on what he was studying. I felt at the time it is almost impossible in winter to go to a cabin and not have ravens know you are there.

We leave footprints in the snow, sounds, smoke coming from the chimney, etc. Much of what I have seen with ravens I think has to do with the fact that I became part of the environment, accepted as part of the wildlife. I read how long it took Jane, that famous naturalist, to be around, and accepted by gorillas before she saw them in a natural state. Years. A lifetime. I also read a scientific study on how vultures signal to each other, and all come in on a new carcass out of nowhere. I did not think it a huge stretch to think ravens are as capable of such communication as vultures. I did not think my beliefs are so farfetched. But yes. I suppose I should just shut up. Keep what I believe to myself.

I understand better. Yes, the Eskimo who told me of the white scientists from the city who came to his village to study, and tell his people all about wolves. Scientists who could not identify a wolf track filled in with snow, or had no clue how old the animal or track was, or if it was a male or female. Educated idiots he called them. Most Eskimo children know such things. There were the biologists who came up the Kantishna River to study salmon. Lost, did not know what river they were on. Looking for salmon at the wrong time of year! Telling me this is a disaster, there are no salmon! They did not ask when salmon were here. They did not ask the locals. We would have said: "No salmon now? Not surprising. In a month we will all catch them by the hundreds and almost be able to walk across the river on the backs of salmon, but no, not now."

There was my friend in Tanana who took the scientists to an island where there were ancient artifacts. My friend found a jade ax head at the digging site on the beach by the boat, and showed it to one of the scientists. It was not supposed to be there. There was no known trading between jade country, and this far in the interior of Alaska. The scientist took the jade ax head, and tossed it in the river saying, "This does not exist." The assumption being it did not fit in with the scheme of things, did not support the hypothesis formed, did not fit within the scope of the grant money funding the expedition. Or a fact not accepted because it was not a scientist who found it. Other such events come to mind... But oh well no time to dwell on it.

People in the wilds who hunt for a living, who work with animals as a way of life, who depend on them, have different thoughts than scientists. I feel bad that I might have offended him. *I could have been more polite with my view.*

A voice,

"Honey what are you doing up so early, it is four in the morning"

I smile back as she stands over me in her bathrobe.

😀 :)

"Did I disturb you? Sorry." I have always been an early riser. 6:00 am would be late for me. Unsure if I have ever in my life slept in till eight. "I was planning to come back to bed when I heard you stirring, so I could be there as you woke up."

"Very kind of you, sir." She chuckles. "I do not know how you can get up so early, good grief, Miles. I need my cup of coffee in the morning before I can even function!"

Yes. I understand. This describes most people. I do not even drink coffee. As far as I'm concerned, by watching people, it's a drug. I do not want any chemical controlling me. But rarely say anything to others about what they do with their life. I have enough trouble keeping track of my own. Brooke is looking around absently sniffing the air.

"Miles, what's that horrible smell?!"

"Horrible smell?" I give the standard male, blank look, with the words "Huh?" That look that the male of all species has used for the past million years successfully. She looks around and sees a pot on the stove, and concludes the smell comes from the pot.

"What are you cooking?"

"Well, not really cooking anything. I'm boiling a skull to clean it. Part of my occupation."

"In one of my cooking pots?!" She says in shock.

"No. I have my own special pot I cook in." In truth, if no one else were around, it would not bother me to cook a skull in the same pot I eat out of. *It's all meat, what's the big deal?* I'm getting civilized enough to understand Tarzan did not even have a pot, and few want the details or direct experience of just what he ate and how. I'm at least smart enough to know I can't cook a carcass in a woman's pot. It's just a woman thing, I guess. Women are fascinating. But what 'men' are to women, who knows? Children at best. Yup.

"You are such a child, Miles!" But at least she is smiling and saying that fondly. For now.

☠

The first week of romantic bliss. I explain to her what I am reading about the Raven guy. She is not interested.

"Come back to bed, Miles, it's too early to get up." Yes it is common for me to be up at four AM. When my partner wakes up, come back to bed. Many aspects of my life do not fit so well with the ways of the civilized. I explain about the skull before we fall asleep.

"The smell of money! I know people in every village in the interior of Alaska, for

1,000 miles in any direction. I lived on the houseboat all over. I worked years ago as a forest fire fighter and met the village fire crews. I am a land surveyor who has surveyed 300 remote homesteads and had many remote village jobs. Over a period of twenty years, word has got around that I'm someone interested in teeth, claws, bones, skulls and related items. From far and wide, remote people bring me 'stuff,' road kills, byproducts of the fur industry there is little market for, parts of animals killed for food or self defense. I think of it as being the garbage man. Dealing with man's garbage in a sacred way."

"But it stinks, Miles!"

"Oh. I suppose. If you had a child, would baby poop bother you so much you would not take care of your baby? When you love something, you do not think so much in terms of it stinking." I'm trying to explain a viewpoint in ways she might understand. To many of my customers, teeth, claws and bones are valued sacred items that have deep meaning. To many I am as a shaman. A wizard, man of magic, my name spoken in awe. Am I a con artist and just play into that, or do I actually believe it? Even I do not know for sure. I thrive on the attention and hopefully respect. Few know the details of where that wolf fang comes from. I'm the man who works in the background taking care of your dirty work. No, I do not suppose I have a normal occupation. Not everyone smiles tolerantly. Not everyone is kind. Not everyone thinks I'm a harmless eccentric kook. Many view me as 'dangerous.' For now, I can fall asleep in the arms of someone who will put up with me, for a week or so. Such women come and go. I never knowingly get involved in a week long fling. I am always hopeful this one will... oh... be filled with forgiveness and understanding. Dare I even think, *shared goals, common interests, Love?*

"Why don't you do this cooking outside, Miles?"

"How would you like to be asked to cook outside?"

"But cooking meals does not stink ,Miles."

"Ok. Well how would you like to change baby diapers outside?"

"That's different. You need running water, good light."

"And my job does not require that as well?" If she and I last, I might build an outdoor cooker, maybe a shed to cook in. What is so cool about this new property in town is, I have nine buildings on it! None have any value except the new shop built in the late '80s, with cement floor and steel beams, about forty x forty and two stories. The home has zero value, just rotten logs and warped floor, with bad wiring and no plumbing (its own electric, with a well-not hooked up to city water yet). The other buildings are sheds with roofs that do not leak, is all that can be said. Ok for storage or a carcass cooking shed.

It's just one project, in a long list of things I ought to do when I ever get time. I already put in fifteen hour days. It's one reason I learned to get up at four a.m. so I can get things done. Reviewing how I feel, and why this has to be an issue. I sigh. I have been cleaning skulls and such in the house since I was twenty years old. It is a way of life filled with good memories. The smell of money. To be told to do this outside is to treat it as something unworthy, to not be welcome in my home, kicked out. Psychologically, that part of our mind is not rational. Sometimes we can get past it with a stronger rational part of the brain. If we have a strong enough reason. If I felt accepted and loved, I might not feel like I am being kicked out of the house.

In a week, this is not love. It is, maybe checking each other out to see what we each stand for, who we are beneath the public mask. I lay awake thinking as well, I consider this my home, not our home. A week is not long enough for much to be 'ours.' In many relationships, the couple got together young and acquired the goods of the world together. Each making some sacrifice and contribution. Put another way, if it was me coming to her home, I would consider it her home, her stuff, and I am a guest till I have contributed. Or politely saying, no I cannot accept her rules concerning her things. But anyhow… I nod off to sleep.

WITHIN TWO WEEKS this Brooke gal is gone. Josh asks me about her.

"The man with the golden pen! Hello Mr. Maw-tin." I nod hello. "So you seem to attract lots of women but cannot keep them. You must have one heck of a line for them." I only nod. I am used to Josh and his way with words. "So what happened this time?" I may as well tell him about it. If he understands or believes it, agrees or not, is up to him.

"Brooke wrote me she was independently wealthy and I would not have to take care of her. She made a lot of money running a greenhouse." I explain how I am impressed, because I know a little about greenhouse work, and if anyone can get wealthy at it, they are a hard worker, smart, with a good business sense. All qualities I admire. She has a son she leaves behind with her mother so she can come check me out. Just got divorced. Another viewpoint shows up when I get the details. Her independently wealthy fortune is a flat $50,000 as a divorce settlement when the house sold. She wants to take her son to Disney World, buy a jeep, load everything she owns in a trailer and bring it to Alaska to move into a new home we acquire together. Oh, and not have to work for at least a year. She needs a break.

Josh comments, " All that would be hard to do on $50,000, Miles!"

"Exactly!" I explain to Josh: This is money her husband earned. She had a greenhouse sort of, that he subsidized as her pet hobby. It looks to me like the greenhouse did not break even, but cost money to operate. So her grand future greenhouse plans she speaks of will not make any money, but cost. She got a divorce because her husband was boring. It is difficult to sympathize and respect that as a good motive for divorce. I may well side with the husband. In every other way a good man – hard worker, with his only fault, being boring. She wanted some spice in her life, a bored housewife, and got it. But she does not have enough money to get through all her dreams. The money will be gone before she gets as far as the jeep, trailer and moving all her stuff to Alaska. She in fact wrote me from Virginia, that wow, moving to Alaska was going to cost a small fortune! I get the impression she is from a poor Virginia mine area where fifty grand is a fortune, but maybe never had to manage money before.

I tell Josh, "We never had a fight or got mad at each other. She does not have the money to do all she wants. I could maybe come up with the money if I was motivated. I do not want to contribute to her year off vacation. I do not think she deserves a year vacation at my expense, or anyone else's. It is time for her to learn how to work."

"No matter what her curves are, Miles? You know it's not free!" Which reminds me, she had told me she wanted to make money growing basil, and had me plant my entire greenhouse full of basil. I planted 500 plants in anticipation of a joint venture. The greenhouse is one of the nine structures I got with the property, a rundown twenty x twenty greenhouse with raised beds. I'm building it up to work again. I had to change the used up soil, and do some structural repairs. Hard to get much done while recovering from a back injury. The fiberglass covering is twenty-two years old, and barely lets light in, but enough to get me started. *What am I going to do with 500 basil plants?*

"No market for that fresh here in a remote area, but think dried does not weigh much and can be shipped all over the world if we got a business going." I had visions of 'My Lady' set up with me selling herbs and spices to the yuppie-hippie crowd, while I sell teeth and claws to the same spiritually lost groupies. The vision is so strong it is a physical pain and longing.

Josh laughs, "Yeah, women are good at supervising, huh?" I know it is not always true, but it's a guy joke one needs to just let go and give a 'you got that right' nod to, so we can be friends with common thoughts. "Miles, you need a ride to the fair this year?"

"No, Josh, but thanks for offering. I got the truck. I think I have someone to drive it in for me." I feel behind a rock and hard place dealing with civilization stuff, yet not being plugged in. I need to drive what, three days out of the entire year? To do that I need to? Get a year's worth of insurance? Do the whole license bit? No wonder town folks are so often broke! They are paying too much to the mafia for protection. Do I want to be there broke with them? Should I try to just drive in, be careful not to get busted? It's only one day a year, and one day getting back! That seems not to be possible to pay for, and be legal about. *I need more money in this new lifestyle, that is for sure!* I am reluctant to depend on someone else to drive me. I have heard in the past, so expect to hear now, "Oh, it's today? I forgot!" Or something similar.

Josh asks me about a boat trip looking for mammoth ivory. I mumble something vague. Josh is a nice guy, good friend, but being Native, he does not understand white man ways all the time, and has got me in trouble before. I got out of his problems in the past… but, well, it is sometimes just easier to not have to explain myself to people trying to create problems. Well meaning Josh will retell any story, and pass on any information with his own interpretation, to anyone who will listen.

"Miles knows how to fool the authorities, good for him!" That is not useful information to share. Kind of like, why call the IRS if some tax issue comes up? Best if they do not know who you are and do not have your phone number. Getting on the radar and becoming 'a person of interest' is not desirable.

This is in fact the time of year that is good for fossil hunting. Summer heat has melted the ice cliff. *At the legal mines, don't forget to add that!* Water level is good. I never tell anyone where I go, when I go. I am simply 'gone' as is often the case, to one of the homesteads, out surveying, and or, hunting- fishing. I get asked about the past by a friend, and write back an interesting story…

From my diary
Aug , 2000
The Mammoth Flower

I have told you many times about the mammoth tusks and bones I find. Now you want to know about this trip and the Mammoth flower, the flower that doesn't exist? It is a long story and I guess I can start with the weather!

There has been heat and also rain. The rain helps the permafrost melt and gets the river water raging, which can rearrange any tusks in the creek bottoms. The heat helps melt the mud banks so they slough off exposing hidden tusks. The tusks are the whole reason I go there, and can pay for the trip. I have six days free. Two days to get there, two days to hunt and two days to come back. I'll have to travel long hours for it is a remote area. I've been fossil hunting off and on for almost thirty years, and have seen and done a lot of things at the mammoth graveyards. Certainly my mind fills with memories of tusks found and sold; interesting events like the grizzly in camp…

"But, Miles—I want to hear about the flowers—not all the other stuff!"

"Yes, well you shall see—it is all tied together- all part of the story." Among the memories is the finding of a flower I'd never seen before. I thought I knew my flowers being an artist, and studying all types of flowers. I was taken back one season by a whole field of flowers I couldn't identify. Not just 'could not identify,' but these flowers didn't even come close to anything I knew of. The stem is seven ft. tall. But my mind is not on this, as I take off on the trip. My mind is on ivory. As good luck would have it—the weather clears up. As better luck would have it, the water drops the very day I leave. This is good news because much of the creek debris where I am headed gets left on the banks as the water drops. The sooner I get to it the better, before animals or other hunters get there. I have a new boat to try out this season, so am excited about how it performs, but am unsure how much gas it will burn, or what the payload will be. I am headed far off where I will not be able to get gas. The last stopping place of civilization charges over three dollars a gallon. I have a spare engine and lots of food, as well as all the tools needed to dig up tusks. I also have clamps -- so tusks do not break as they thaw. They are often still frozen - having just fallen from the permafrost after 40,000 years.

Just one of those places tourists never find, off the beaten path, 'in the middle of nowhere.' (But I call 'the center of everything'.)

"Yes, yes, Miles we all know how you feel about your wilderness life and have heard it a million times- tell me about the undiscovered flowers!"

The fall colors are out, red and yellow reflected on the calm waters. Does life get any better than this? Certainly I can feel sorry for the rest of the world... but hopefully everyone else feels the same about what they are doing with their life. All of 'this' though, has to do with the background; the big picture behind a simple flower.

I arrive at my hunting grounds after the usual two days of travel. It is like another planet here. There is the constant sound of mud dripping; the smell of 'old things', that only mammoth hunters know the smell of and there are only a handful of us 'professionals' who can tell the stories. It is late and I am tired, but cannot resist a quick check of the area for tusks. I have listened to the hum of the outboard engine for fifteen hours today. I have seen no other boat, crossed no bridge, nor seen any road. I have in effect, passed through the Star Gate.

It is time to go back and re-explore ground already covered. I wonder vaguely where that field of odd flowers is—that I see now and then.

Are there good years and bad years or certain times of the season to see them? Do I keep missing the exact spot? This is not on my mind as I 'discover' a cut I had missed and realize, some years I can't find it, and other years the opening is accessible. This is a narrow cut that gets plugged with mud. There is a 'secret' way around I often forget, or am too busy to ever deal with. Once past the hidden entrance, this cut opens up again and goes in a long way – leading up to the top of the bluff. I have never found any ivory up this way—or no, there was that tip I found here once hinting of bigger things possible. And didn't I dig up that seventy-five pound leg bone here?

Up this secret cut, I discover the field of hidden flowers I had thought I'd lost—or thought grew but once in a blue moon. They are not in bloom this time of year, but are in seed. Sure enough, the stems are seven ft. tall. Not as big around as my arm as I once remembered, but larger around then my thumb. The leaves look like dandelion leaves. And the flowers are yellow – small and fuzzy- sort of nondescript. I'd managed to bring seeds home one year and actually got them to grow! I discovered they need a different environment than I provided though. They did not get very tall. The next year they came back in the five gallon bucket I had them in, but were not healthy and didn't come back a 3rd year. I think they must be perennials. Who knows how long it takes for them to get a root system to produce such huge plants? I speculated they start from seeds that have been frozen in the ice since the mammoth days and thaw out and grow here. They only grow where there is mammoth dung, and decay from that era. I have seen the flowers elsewhere, but always where there is ivory. Enough to know if I spot this plant I am in mammoth country.

I told 'plant people'. Some say "Very interesting" and leave it at that, or do not believe me. No one was especially interested in the plant I managed to grow for all to see in the bucket. It was a smaller version and no one knew what it was, but no one was especially concerned.

"Something in the Senicio family?" Surely it is just a flower and nothing to fuss over. I took pictures once, not of the tall field, for this area is so hard to get to I never have the camera with me. I am so wore out and covered in mud I am lucky to just get myself here! Everything I bring with me is covered in mud and banged around. A camera would get ruined. I don't feel overly motivated to 'prove' what I see. Scientists treat me like the enemy- call me a grave robber, criminal. Heck I'd brought the real seeds and grew them- and who was interested? The area is five acres big, not huge, but rather odd when flowers are growing over my head. What else have I found that is interesting?

Hmm—Yes, I once brought an unusual bird bone to the university and no one wanted to see it. Actually I felt rather insulted. It had taken me considerable effort, personal money, and time to get this here—so this too has a lot to do with the 'story' of the mammoth flower. I knew it to be a wing bone off a bird that would be the size of a dodo or moa—but in Alaska? Perhaps a vulture? (I speculated). But no one wanted to look at it. I am after all, not a university educated type—and I get the impression the common person's word means very little. Or? Maybe every day people stop in saying they discovered something interesting - "Come look!" And that gets old, and scientists are busy. I had proof in my hand. No one would even look up from the desk. Why?

I thought science was about the art of curiosity and investigation, so I'm confused, treated like an idiot as if, "Oh that's probably a chicken bone some stray dog dropped." This is not just one person, or one time. I think, surely in general this shouldn't happen! Yet, I recall there was the cave bear tooth I brought in and was told this bear never existed in Alaska. Someone must have dropped it in the wilderness. Perhaps (but not likely), but why make such an assumption? Why not ask questions? But no, just "impossible." There is the view of the raven expert in his book. Do I have an attitude problem? If so, which came first, my attitude, or a reason I acquired it? Is this part of an authority issue I have?

"Oh, Miles! You always exaggerate and are so negative it is hard to listen to you sometimes, you get so carried away!" Humph!

"Yes, well, it is all part of the mammoth flower story—beyond the Romance." Yes, I imagine one day the flower will be 'discovered' and there will be a fence around this pristine wilderness spot. Tour bus with guide, and signs like 'Danger, Ice!' will be in the pictures taken. Little old ladies will spray the nasty bugs and peer through the glass window, and it will of course be highly illegal to step off the bus without permission. "Back to the subject, Miles?" My mind wanders and I ramble on...

A fellow mammoth hunter found a copper arrowhead imbedded in a mammoth bone. I find it regrettable that such knowledge can't be shared with the world... that the last place he'd ever go was the university. He told me I was a fool to even talk to 'those' people. Another friend found a prehistoric human skull in the river bank and with some 'Eskimo' looking artifacts in the Interior, where they shouldn't have been. He told the university. A representative came and the area was closed and made illegal to enter (I saw the 'no trespassing' sign when I went to see where he was talking about) yet the university did nothing; the artifacts wash into the river every year and are lost.

I stand in the mammoth flower field—perhaps the only human being to ever stand here. All 'this' I'm thinking of, is also part of the mammoth flower story... the whole issue of 'people like myself' mammoth hunters – making art and dealing in the economics of fossils; interesting objects; bits of valuable knowledge; trying to pay bills by living in the wilderness doing what I love. Does life get any better than getting paid to do what you love?

"Well, Miles – you probably went in there with a bad attitude to begin with; dressed in rags, claiming all sorts of crazy things! No wonder they don't listen!"

I think about that conversation, and the fact the University of Alaska once had more mammoth tusks than it knew what to do with, so dug a pit with a bulldozer and buried them as a way to store them. There must have been hundreds and many tons. Now the university can't remember where that pit is. That is how much they care about 'precious artifacts'. Whoever donated the tusks were fools. Probably worth on the market a cool million dollars. What a waste—when I see it as people like myself offering such things to the public as art, displays for all to see, know about, get excited about. In my humble opinion, this is what generates 'interest' in old things in general and ultimately results in an interest in preservation and university funding. If few people know about it, can touch it or tell about it or see it as art, then there is little interest. It seems to me there is room for both—the knowledge and a few items on display—and some of these items—most- reaching the private sector as art and jewelry to be seen, admired, worn, talked about. All this, too, has to do with the mammoth flower story. The lack of trust between different lifestyles and ways of life creating misunderstanding and no sharing of knowledge—it's the story we tell with stars in our eyes around many camp fires swatting bugs. What is life without a dream? My mind is wandering. I change the subject. I'm explaining in general how it is with the people who find things and the people who document the find and record it as a 'discovery'.

It doesn't even matter really—if I'm full of dung, if the flower is undiscovered or not. Not really. What matters is it could be. And if this flower is really unknown and if I am really the only one who has ever been here and if I can prove it or not or if I can find a tusk and sell it, isn't really what it is all about. It's about memories (and not so much the gold as the looking for it...)

The memory of bending a seven foot stem so I can blow on the flower. I scatter the seeds to the wind... the way the fuzz feels on my nose; waving the seeds away and wishing them luck wherever they go with a happy smile on my face.

I remember now how to find this hidden cut with the secret hard to find entrance hundreds of miles in the wilderness. A place where flowers grow that man has not yet named—isn't ready to know about, but mammoth hunters call 'The Mammoth Flower.' Believe it or not; but go; leave me in peace—**I'm done with my story for today.**

Much of my social life is beginning to be on the computer. In the old days I had ads in Mother Earth looking for a soul mate, a life partner that I never found[1]. Now the computer age is expanding my horizon, offering a chance to meet people, mostly women, from all over the world! In some ways the computer is helpful and working out well. Because... well... *because I was raised somewhat open mind, compared to most.*

My father is always working with students and teachers from all over the world. That world came to the house and was treated equally. Sometimes visitors would cook for us, or we would visit them. I got to try foods from all over the world, discuss cultures, and explore life choices. I was exposed to spiritual beliefs from many cultures, as well as many occupational ideas.

I was always curious how people around the world solve life's basic problems. How to keep warm, eat, get money. How to find and live with a mate and such things. With my Alaska dream and love of the frigid country, my thoughts some-times go to Siberia, because Russia once owned Alaska. The climate and terrain would be the same. Only Siberia might be even more remote and wild. It is difficult to believe big government gets to remote places in Siberia to bother subsistence people. Is it possible they then are more free in the way I wish to live? Would it be like Alaska 200 years ago? I am curious and full of questions. This is an email from a girl in Russia that just arrived...

"**Hello Miles!** I am 27 years old. Mine birthday of July 30, 1975. I have growth of 172 centimeters and weights of 54 kg. My profession is an the designer of a landscape.

Now I work in the commercial firm as a the designer of a landscape. I want to inform, that I do not smoke, and I do not drink strong spirits drinks of spirit. But sometimes I love to drink in the good company not a lot of grape vine, though it happens very seldom. I want to you to speak, which I love various music, but basically classical.

I to not have children! I was never married! What you to love to do(make) in free from work time? What you to love from the foodstuffs? About my hobbies... In my free time, I study English (I want to hope for success), and go to the sports club, in the evenings. I like music. I like dancing, but not often, because I don't have a lot time for them. At the same time, I like cooking, bat not every day. Some time, I like sewing, when I have any mood, and I like own clothes. It's my favorite hobby.

I very love the see, but I don't have an opportunity to see it often (in our area, there are many nice forests, rivers and likes, but not the see). The sin, the beach, and the see with lovely man... It's only my dreams. (I think, that I too romantic today,) and I believe in love. Well, I'm a very friendly person, I love meeting the people that come my way and making new friends. What am I looking for? I'd like to meet a man, who can become good husband. I want to live a happy family life. Where? It's not important. I'd like to be together with dear man. I believe that relationships between people must be bused on trust and respect. I value in the persons: the honesty and the seines of humor. If you would like to talk, please write back to me. I've promised to you, I'll answer all you questions frankly and honesty. I hate any lie. Some attention, kindness, and care will make me happier. As for my location. I live in Cheboksary. It is a small town by comparison with Moscow. Cheboksary is the capital of Chuvashia Rep. It is about 950 km on east. **Tatiana (Tanya).**

P.S. Send the photos, please".

I send a reply, letting her know I am probably too old for her, but have an interest in remote Russia and would like to correspond. I smile. She seems human. She seems like a woman, with concerns anyone might relate to. This is not the Russia I was taught about. I am all the more convinced I need to make up my own mind about people, situations, lifestyles.

Before sealing the envelope, I put in one of my usual iridescent duck feathers saved from a meal. The envelope has been hand painted with spring flowers. She is very beautiful, dressed in Russian fur. The scenery looks similar to what I know, with the same trees and ducks on the water behind her.

My diaries are now written on the computer for the first time

June 16, 2000—Boneyard trip

"Should I go to the Boneyard and look for mammoth tusks on the Kantishna River, Jennie? You know I may not have the time this summer I'm used to. I'll be surveying, there is the greenhouse to tend, the Nenana Cultural Center to buy art for, and other obligations. This might be a good time. I feel right about it. All these days of heat, with the chance to go early in the season before any other mammoth hunters arrive there."

"I think you should go, Miles, you've been working hard lately and need a break. Do you think your back will hold up?"

"Ya, ya, ya, not to worry!" Packing should have been routine, but it doesn't seem to be. I had been away from the river long enough that I now have to think about it and make a list. There is a tent, a sleeping bag for camping out, enough gas to get to at least Toklat. And how far is that again? 200 miles—somewhere in that neighborhood. How long will that take and what do I burn an hour? Food and tools for the engine need to be got together. There will be hose clamps to bind up any tusks I find; plastic bags to cover ivory and keep it wet so it doesn't crack. I want to bring a rifle and way to hunt meat to eat, and the fishing pole, bug repellant… and so the list goes on. I make a pile. I will leave the same day I decide the time is right.

I leave my diary and write direct from memory.

The computer diary is new to me. Helpful, organized, readable, and compact! "The wonderful world of cut and paste too!" Yeah, so we use it more often than we did penciled notes. I notice, we read what we entered, and it helps a lot to jog the memory. We read, and 'Oh yeah, now I remember!' A memory link opens and it is like we are right there! You notice that? "Yes, it's like present time huh?"

I TELL no one exactly when I'm going. All day is spent getting ready. It is 5:00 pm in the afternoon before I am packed.

Should we wait till early morning? No, I will get some hours in on the river and camp someplace along the way. If all goes well I could be at the mammoth grave-yard by sometime tomorrow. I leave with eighty-five gallons of gas, expect to be gone only a few days, because I'm due back in Nenana to survey in Fairbanks by the weekend. The weather has been record hot. This is one reason it will be good to be on the river. The heat should have the frozen cliffs sloughing off, exposing tusks. The winter had more snow than usual, so there should have been a good run off in the spring. These situations will contribute to good conditions for hunting. There is no weather report or anyone to contact in the area I am headed. I have received permission from the miner who owns the land, who is rarely there.

The boat gets on step well enough. This determines the length of time the trip will take, which is always critical. In two hours I'm at a good fishing creek, stop to test the waters and maybe catch dinner. The creek takes a while to navigate. The clear water looks inviting if I were a fish. Nothing is caught in a dozen casts, so I decide to press on.

The village of Old Minto is the next reference point and time check. Lots of driftwood in the high water has me running the boat defensively, which slows me up some. Minto takes longer than it should. Gas consumption is good, maybe one and a half gallons an hour. I am constantly looking at gauges, figuring speed-gas-wind, balance. I think of my civilized friends who think this is odd!

"We don't do that when we travel, geez, Miles!"

I review such conversations as I travel. "My survival depends on looking out for myself." I realize in civilization, there is little need to keep track! An alarm tells a driver they are low on gas, pull into a nearby gas station of your choice. Break down, call 911. The insurance company, the lawyer, the tow company is there to serve. It's all covered on your AARP policy. Someone will look out for you. Who keeps track of how drafting behind a semi-truck or the wind speed effects gas milage, with concerns, if you can make it or not! Ha! "Yeah, and here we are watching tenths of a gallon with interest." Remember that time on a 300 miles trip, we were a cup short on gas and had to borrow half a cup from Al John! I only smile, looking at my gauges.

Next reference is Tolovana Roadhouse, twenty-five miles from the Kantishna, my old stomping grounds. I compare fuel, time, load, wind, with other trips. I'm going over 800 miles. I do not want to come home with more than ten gallons left.

The sun never sets this time of year, so I can run as long into the night as I want. Tolovana Roadhouse comes and goes, Dim's fish camp is a few miles. I'd rather camp near the mouth of the Kantishna, so now I think about a place to stop. Rock Creek seems nice. I can fish here. Maybe I will just sleep in the boat. The mosquitoes are not so bad out in the open. If I park in the middle of the creek, maybe the bugs will be fewer. I tie the boat to an old dead tree in the middle of the creek. The fish pole goes in, and I have a pike grab the lure as soon as it hits the water. Pike are easy to identify, as they are the sharks of the fresh water creeks here. They grab and run with anything that moves. The line screams off the reel. It has to be a pike. The line snaps. I have plain fishing line on the new fish pole. Rats.

I take time to throw away the light line, and put Alaska fish line on instead, my standard fifty pound test. A leader is added, a silver spinner, and I'm ready to fish. The same pike follows the lure. I see through the clear water he is still trying to swallow the first lure stuck in the side of his mouth. But he will not grab the second. It is hard to read a pike's expression—or believe a pike is capable of thought. But it sure looks like the pike is thinking, "This tasty morsel is hard to swallow and maybe I'm not as hungry as I thought."

I am able to get the pike with a spear by luring him near the boat with the spinner. Then I got another smallish pike two feet long on the next cast. Two fish are enough. I decide to get the stove out, get ready to sleep here. Upon investigation I see I didn't pack the bag that has the tent in it as well as the mosquito coils and some other camp items. "Darn!" Going back is not an option. There is a tarp to sleep under, and bug repellant to put on my skin. A pile of my extra clothes will do for a mattress. A small alcohol stove cooks dinner in a mess kit pot. Pepper, rice, dry onions are added to the fish stew cooked right in the boat. The mosquitoes manage to find me as the evening cools off. Rain clouds roll in. A double rainbow shows. I get the digital camera out and get a good picture. The pike are photographed.

Yawning, I decide to get some sleep after my fill of fresh pike. No I'm not especially fond of fish, but if it is fresh like this, it tastes good enough. The mosquitoes this year prove to be out in record numbers. The bug repellant is good for an hour, then has to be put on again. I get an hour's rest, then decide this isn't going to work. Dim's fish camp is five miles further. No one will be there, but I can stop and get in out of the bugs.

About midnight I arrive at Dim's, too tired to do much but stumble up the bank and go in the open cabin. I fall asleep away from the bugs. Bears have moved into the cabin. This looks like porcupine dung pellets all over the bed I'm sleeping on. Oh well. About 6:00 am I'm up and ready to press on. The sun is out stronger. It never really got dark.

Dim's place is up against a steep purple bluff. As a rock guy, I think this could be rhodonite, maybe a low grade. Very bright with the sun on it. Dim Burke will have a lot of work to do here. I'll have to let him know about the bear damage so he can bring repairs with him. The torn door allows other animals to come in! This is Dim's fish-camp. He has his main home in Nenana.

The river runs with drift wood, but there is no wind. I know Moonshine's main camp is another six miles. I think he and his wife Wren might be home. Before 7:00 am I arrive, and hear his sled dogs barking. I think he will likely wake up from the dog ruckus and maybe he is an early riser, so decide to at least stop and look in to see. It would be nice to get caught up on the latest news from the river. Wren comes out of the cabin and says they stayed up late and are sleeping. I wish her well and tell her I may stop on the trip back through in a few days.

Manley Hot Springs is next. Forget the mileage, maybe fifty miles. There is no planned stop. The boat landing is on the river, but the village will be six more miles up the springs slough. If I was not pressed for time, I might stop in and visit friends, get a meal at the lodge. I often do this on trips downriver. My survey boss Seymour lives here.

There is a single boat tied up at the landing, a few trucks parked there, and that is all I see. At a steady twenty-five miles an hour, I keep going, eating up the miles dodging drift logs. Next stop will be Squaw Crossing, the mouth of the Tanana. This can be a tricky crossing with a lot of shallow places. It is a good place to get through and be glad about. The crossing is another few hours of running time ahead of me. The heat of the sun bears down. I am glad to be on the river in the breeze created by the movement forward, catching the cool damp river air in my face.

A barge is on the river, but I am not sure which one. I wonder if the captain will recognize my boat. I wave as I go by, but see no one aboard. The push boat has two heavily loaded barges ahead if it. All supplies are for downriver villages that have no road access.

"Fish Creek, almost forgot, better stop and see if there are any fish!" I almost miss the turn, but swing in for a few moments to drop a line overboard. The first cast has a pike. After five casts and five fish I remember I can't eat this many! Since there will be a gas stop in Tanana, I will give the fish away there. At Squaw Crossing, a sand-hill crane flies up in front of me. With quick reflex I grab the shotgun and down the male bird. This will keep longer than the fish, and will feed me for the trip. I haven't had bird in a long time, so look forward to a taste of the old life I lived.

Squaw Crossing is rarely simple. However the past few years, there has been a channel going far to the right behind an island. It is narrow and long, but if it is open, no wonders where to go. This avoids figuring out the flat section several miles across with no reference points. The low morning sun is glaring off the flats. I have to slow up. All the drift at least shows me where the channel is through the flats. However this right way through against the far bank is open this trip. There is permafrost that never melts, but creates ice ledges hanging out over the water. Here and there I have to duck under a ledge and go through a dark tunnel. Black sold ice drips from above.

TANANA VILLAGE IS AHEAD of me and I pull in. There are two roads of mud, with a handful of trucks in the village. There are more boats tied up at the river than there are cars. Everyone just pretty much picks out a spot they'd like to tie up a boat and it becomes their spot.

It takes me a while to give the pike away. I end up walking a mile to the Elder cabins. The seniors look forward to eating fish. I fill up on gas, realizing I'm paying $2.50 a gallon, "Ouch!" It might have been smart to haul enough gas for a round trip! I wasn't sure where the other gas tanks are and was wanting to get going and not wait another day, so here I am buying gas in Tanana. The time is about noon, so I figure another few hours I can be hunting for mammoth ivory on Clear Creek. I do not mind supporting the village of Nenana with high gas prices. They need the money and have little sources of income. I grumbled but once I see the situation I understand.

THIS MIGHT BE the Cosna River, I think to myself as I go by. There would be fish here too, but I'm about fished out for the day. This stretch of the river is not as familiar to me as the Tanana River to Manley Hot Springs. The boneyard will be recognized when I get there I'm sure. It is hard to keep my eyes open. Didn't sleep well last night.

Maybe I will stop and camp at Reinhardt's. I do not stay here often. *One time with Crazy Lawsen.* Clouds start to magically appear, there is lightning and thunder. Another rainbow is worth taking a picture of. One bright flash of lightning has me wondering if I should get off the river! Smoke starts to form where it looked like the lightning struck. The digital camera records the first smoke of a major forest fire. At Reinhardt's, I stop and unload my camping gear, major gas load, and get the cabin set up for later. I will come back here to spend my nights. In an hour I'm ready to press on to the boneyard[2].

The smell of the oil filled cliffs is a reminder of trips in the past. The peregrine falcon is at her nest. I am glad to see her again. She lives off the swallows nesting in the cliffs. My eyes are watching for tusks in the cliff. I know the likely places to look. The heat and snow runoff has got the cliff active as I suspected it would. Sections the size of houses have fallen off within the past hour. If such a section falls when I am beneath, I will die. Some smaller pieces fall off and land in the water next to me, but I pay it no mind. Since I am so tired, the plan is to scope it out today, see what I'm up against, where the cliffs are falling fastest, see what the creeks are doing, and see if there are any obvious tusks showing. Maybe there will be time to poke around and give a preliminary inspection to favorite spots.

A few logs look like tusks, but I cannot be sure till I circle around and get up close, hit them with a pole and see how they sound. A special probe has a steel point that has a unique sound when it hits ivory compared to wood. The other end of the probe has a small shovel so I can do some quick investigative digging.

A few times, I tie the boat up, get out, and inspect an area closer. The plan is to do a better job tomorrow. Nothing exciting. One old bone is tossed in the boat. It looks like a bison from 40,000 years ago. One object way up the cliff could be a tusk. Staring into the sun, it is a long climb to check it out and I'm tired. *May as well check it out though.* As I get closer it looks more and more like a tusk. 200 feet up above the boat I get to it and see it is! There is a toe hold stick next to it. From this position I have to get out my ax and chip away at the frozen mud. There is too much of the tusk still frozen in the ice, so decide to get down. Come back up in the morning with better digging tools. No one will come by between now and then. A little time is spent checking out the rest of the area in case there is something else obvious I can pick right up. One year I found a tusk right at the waterline on the Nowitna River, near here, ready to roll into the boat, and it had been a time like this, the first day I arrived, tired, waiting to make camp, but too eager to look around first.

A bald eagle sitting on a tree stump watches me intently and lets me pass by within fifty feet. I am too occupied looking for ivory to pay the eagle any mind. Geese and ducks are all over the place, flying up constantly, so there is the sound of honking and wings flapping that never really stops. This is normal background noise, and I pay it no mind. I am intent, looking for ivory. Suddenly a rumble. Mud letting go as the sound of a glacier calving. Instantly I spin the steering wheel away from the cliff without even looking. This time the section letting go is truck size and 100 feet away, only a slight danger. A new section is exposed to investigate, so I turn the boat around to see what is new. A thin shell layer is spotted, which was the bottom of a prehistoric pond in the days of saber tooth tigers. Sometimes interesting things sink to the bottom of ponds, so I watch the shell layer. A falcon swoops and hits a swallow. There is a brief flurry of feathers.

This only vaguely registers, intent on images in the mud, telltale signs of the struggles of a mammoth in trouble. Prehistoric log jams are a good place to study up close. Many mammoths died in flash floods and got swept down river. Or so I believe. Scientists I read of and talk to, deny my theory. Possibly the mammoth died earlier and the bones later got washed, but I do not think so. I have learned to keep an eye out on the upstream side of the jam. Dead mammoths in the river float up and the heavy tusks flip them over. The tusks drag on the bottom as the dead mammoth floats downriver. Tusks snag on the bottom in roots like at log jams. I look under the log jams. A leg bone? I turn the boat around slow to go back and look again. Bones will be at least twenty feet above the tusks. I learned this from Crazy when we were together here once. I focus below the bone, in that layer of blue clay. Nothing. I move on.

I try to put my mind in neutral, pick up the vibrations from the past, like being in a trance, going back in time. *If I were a mammoth, where would I be.* What would I be doing? Why would I be here? Where would I step? Sometimes I have paused at a spot that shows nothing, gone up to this nothing spot, and slowly stuck a prod in the mud and hit a mammoth tusk. The art of mammoth hunting is subtle and requires delicacy, being in tune with nature, and the past. Some say mammoth hunters are a little crazy. I only know of a handful of serious hunters who are successful. Many things I do in life I simply 'do' trying not to elaborate on how or why. Being too far out of tune with civilization is not safe.

Crazy Lawsen told me the ravens speak to him, "Tell me where the tusks are." I think he's nuts.

The bottom line being, "Do you find tusks?" I sigh, nothing obvious showing. *Speak to me.* The cliff doesn't answer. I expect no answer. My mind wanders. I might be a detective looking for clues, asking the clues to show themselves, to speak of the culprit, tell of his life and habits; clues that may be found. What brand of cigarette might he have smoked? Was he left or right handed? Why was he here? The clues are sorted and a story is told. *Was this a mammoth breeding area where the young and foolish perish in great numbers? Does a predator bone found nearby indicate a good place to hunt… or scavenge? If there was a rock outcrop, would a predator sit there in ambush? As the only high ground in an endless swamp.* The smell of prehistoric rot we call 'bone-yard smell' is in the air. Black oily dirt in different concentrations tells me how much animal matter is here. This oil can identify the correct aged layer.

The remains of decayed stuff from ages ago is visible. One tree limb way up high catches my eye. I turn the boat around for another look. It could be a tusk, but too far up the cliff to tell. The boat is pulled in and tied to a fallen tree stuck in the quicksand mud. My tonker stick is in hand as I climb the mud. The stick helps me get a purchase on the cliff which is not straight up, but steep enough that if I slipped I'd roll all the way down to the water. Survival would be unlikely. The water is freezing—literally. Chunks of river ice are still on the bank here and there. This shows how fast winter changes to summer, with hardly any spring. The swirling silt-filled water is ninety feet deep here, with such undertows, entire trees get sucked under and never come up. This isn't—can't be— on my mind as I work my way up the cliff. As I get closer I am more certain it is a tusk. I'm 200 feet above the boat now and here is the tusk (!). I am very excited, as it looks like it is in perfect shape. I guess about two feet of it is still held in the ice. I cannot free it with the digging end of my tonker stick. I am able to clear away only six inches of mud before hitting ice. Blue clay surrounds the tusk, which gives the ivory a blue color, very desirable on the selling market. The tusk looks to be about seven feet long and 100 pounds. A small rivulet of muddy water flows a foot away from the tusk and cuts a crack in the cliff. At some time it will cause this section to let loose. I divert the rivulet to the edge of the tusk by digging a trench.

Overnight the water running over the ice will help melt it and make tomorrow's work a little easier. I will have to come back in the morning to get it… back up here with the ax to chip at the ice. I am too tired tonight to climb back up the cliff after returning to the boat. Once again there is a good find within a few hours of arriving. The rest of the area is investigated for anything obvious. A few places are noted as worth coming back to later. A bison bone, the toe bone of a mammoth and an unidentified leg bone are found at the water's edge and put in a plastic bag. Such items have only a small limited market and are sold by the pound, barely worth hauling out. Seems a shame, something so old and interesting, having so little value in the public's eye. *Oh well*—and my sleepy thoughts drift to the tusk as I boat back to the fish camp for the night. I have seen no one on the river and do not expect to, so my two finds will be safe till tomorrow. There is an old cot in one room in the ancient cabin. An empty table and tree stumps for chairs occupy the other room. I set up my camp stove, get river water, and cook up the sandhill crane I shot, along with noodles. The lightning fire has grown. A big plume of smoke bellows up behind the cabin. It would be possible for the fire to reach the cabin during the night. I wonder if I would wake up if the fire came. I am tired. I idly ask myself if it is safe to sleep here the night. The alternative is to sleep in the open boat in the bugs and rain, or travel a very long way to the next fish camp. I take a chance on getting burned up. Hopefully my high Jesus factor will kick in. The ability to be lucky and to have good survival instincts.

I fall asleep smelling the burning forest, but it is too far away yet to hear crackling fire or the rushing of panicked animals in front of the wall of heat. Early in the morning I hear a barge coming. I get up to look out the front door. The weather has cleared; the fire has subsided some, and I feel rested enough to put in a good day at the boneyard. I skip breakfast, pack the left over crane and noodles to have as lunch later and am back up the cliff with the ax by 6:00 am. It is nice to be working before the heat of the day sets in. The rivulet I had diverted has cut the ice only a little, and piled up a lot of mud on the tusk, so maybe hadn't been a good idea after all. There is a small pobble, a local term that refers to 'not a pebble and not stubble', but an annoying little knurly branch one might trip over on the trail or need to grab while climbing, knowing it will not be of much help. So there is this little pobble thing to get one foot on to brace myself as I swing the ax. It is very awkward clinging to the face of the cliff while swinging the ax. Every few minutes I have to switch hands and shift my other foot to the pobble stick I stand on. When the tusk lets go I do not want to go down the cliff with it. I have a brief image of being found by a passing boater, impaled by a mammoth tusk, spread eagle in the bottom of my boat. With the mammoth getting the last laugh.

It takes about half an hour, but it feels like several hours to get the tusk loose. Finally it is free and I let it slide past me down the muddy rivulet trough. I think it will not make it all the way to the river. There is a ledge at the bottom it will rest on. I have to guide it down most of the way. I do not have to carry the weight of it, or take a chance slipping on the cliff. A picture is taken before the tusk goes in the boat. A perfect tusk from base to tip, without a crack in it. Retail, it will be worth in the neighborhood of $10,000. I need to take care of the tusk, or it will crack and have much less value. I put hose clamps on it right away, and keep it out of the sun. After being frozen for 40,000 years, it will rebel against the temperature change and being dried out. As it thaws and dries it will want to swell, twist and crack. The clamps stop it from expanding. The drying aging process will take perhaps months. It will be kept covered in plastic in a cool dark place to dry slowly. I will not be able to sell it for many months, unless I am willing to settle for half the price. I learned my lesson on the last perfect tusk. I sold it wet, for $2,000, and was happy to get that. The wholesale buyer, my buddy Tusk, sold it for $10,000. This middle person took it to the Tucson gem show and got $26,000 for it. I confirmed this by talking to the buyer in Tucson a year later. Most mammoth tusks are a by-product of the gold mining industry. The tusks are secondary to finding gold.

A bulldozer clears topsoil over gold bearing bedrock, and sometimes digs up tusks, usually damages them. If not, the miner sets the tusk aside, and keeps looking for gold. The tusk sits in the sun and cracks. The miner deals with the tusk at the end of the gold season, when he has idle time. By this time the tusk is in pieces. The miner is reluctant to deal with the ivory seriously for another reason. If word gets out the mine produces mammoth remains, the mine can get shut down as an archeological site. The miner is usually unwilling to risk having his mine shut down, so tusks are sold in hush-hush deals under the table, and the miner has little interest in taking good care of them.

Many large mine operations turn up vast quantities of tusks. Many dozer operators and workers are told when tusks are found, to bury them, leave them be, and not say anything. Consequently few good tusks reach the public's view. My mind goes over these facts as I think out a plan for the inspection of the rest of the area for more tusks. I now have two tusks.

I do a lot of climbing, and a lot of turning the boat around to look again at an object. But the tonker stick tells me it is wood. Many likely spots turn up nothing. I stop to eat cold crane and noodles, washing it down with silty river water. The day is getting very hot. I enjoy being next to the frozen cliff and getting the cool breeze off the ice. Mosquitoes are out in dense swarms. To fall asleep here would mean being sucked dry in a few hours by these blood suckers. I keep putting chemical poison on against them, but the poison makes me groggy.

My bad back acts up after going up and down the cliff. I could wish I was younger. Some places I decide not to walk up, even though they look interesting. I'm just too tired. I pull into a place I can tie the boat, and look for a log to rope it to, and just to the right of the log I select, is a tusk. Only a foot of it sticks out of the water, but I know right away this is a tusk because the Yukon River has washed it clean, so it has that distinct ivory look. I am unsure of its length, but the tusk is very large in diameter. If I pull on it, maybe it will slip into the river and be lost to me. It could be too heavy for me to lift. I decide to tie a rope to it before disturbing it. The rope is solidly tied to the boat and I pull to get a feel for how big and how stuck it is. The tusk moves easily. It turns out to be just a two foot section of a tusk that was once ten feet long. But even this two foot section weighs about thirty pounds. I'm sorry the tusk is not whole, but glad to find what is here. *Maybe the rest of it, or pieces are in the mud around it?* The tonker stick pokes here and there. Several pound size chunks of tusk are found in the mud nearby. The remaining 100 pounds of tusk must have sunk in the river, or still be up in the cliff above, frozen out of sight. The matching tusk likewise may have already gone in the river, or be buried deep in the frozen cliff someplace. Grizzly bear tracks go up the side of the cliff. Bears sometimes dig up tusks and bones to chew on. Sometimes the bones still have meat on them.

The rest of the day is spent checking out likely areas spotted last night. The constant climb up the mud cliffs and back down is making me tired however. In the rivulet of a mud stream coming off the cliff I find a bison horn in good shape. This is a nice find I can use in my artwork. Since I am tired, and have already found enough ivory to make the trip worthwhile, I think about calling it a day and head back to the camp, to pack, and get a start back towards home. If I can leave camp by 4:00 pm, I will get to the nearest village in time to catch the store open and get gas for the return trip home. The forest fire has picked up again, but does not seem to be headed toward the river and cabin. A boat has pulled into the camp. I spot it way ahead of me. I hope there is not a problem. The new owners may not like strangers staying there. A sign on the wall written on an old box asks visitors to keep it clean. I am also not sure how these people will feel about using the camp to go look for ivory. Among the Natives it is taboo to mess with the boneyard. I'm not certain why. Something to do with the ancestors? A fear it will bring bad luck of some kind?

When I get to the camp I see the visiting boat is fancy and not from around here. I am greeted by a woman who asks if I am Miles. She says she knows me, and is the sister of someone whose name I recognize.

"Cynthia? You are her sister? Well yes, I had hoped to see her in Tanana at the store she owns. She sometimes buys my artwork and I have some things to show her!"

"Cynthia is in Fairbanks for another week. She gave me a pair of your earrings that I just love! I get comments on them all the time! Do you have any of your work with you?" As she speaks, two guys come down the path from the cabin:

"We thought someone might be around, we saw the fresh goose on the table!" I didn't mention it is a crane. "Did you see all the old stuff around here?"

I had in fact taken some pictures of an old boat with trees growing all around it, and an old wood cook stove with fancy chrome lacework. I saw an old forge for blacksmithing and a brass bed frame, along with other things. Newspapers covered the wall to keep the draft between the logs out. I saw one with the date 1932 on it. I am introduced by the lady, and it turns out one guy owns a local airline, has several planes, and appears to be well off it looks like, with this fancy boat. They all want to look at my artwork. I dig around in the trashcan I use to keep supplies dry, and find the box with my art in it. So here I am out 'in the middle of nowhere,' doing a private art show, and several items are picked out. I make a few hundred dollars. Life can't get much better. Gas for the trip is covered by the art sale and I still have the tusks.

"Oh, do you want to see some tusks I just found at the boneyard?" They are all excited to see this ivory and hear the story of how it is found, how old it is, and what it must have been like back in those days around here. They all want pictures of themselves by the tusks.

They are off and on their way to Ruby where I get gas. My watch has stopped working so I no longer know what time it is, but figure it must be getting close to 5:00 pm; I hurriedly pack my gear and take off upstream towards home. I hope to get through Squaw Crossing, and camp in good water up the Tanana. I know from experience, that if a wind comes along, even a breeze, the water gets very rough in the crossing where there is a large stretch of open water.

Did I pass Tanana and go on the wrong side of an island? I had done this once before —missed Tanana and the mouth of the Tanana River and had gone almost to the rapids before realizing it! I answer myself, "You are supposed to pay attention, let me know!"

The wind is up and it looks like rain. With all this drift in the water, it is not a good time to be out in waves that hide logs. I have to get the boat off step and go slow. It is not a good time to be lost. I decide to turn around, certain that I missed Tanana. I go on the other side of an island and am sure Tanana is only a few miles behind me. *But no-- this does not look familiar to me and there is no Tanana. Is it upstream, or downstream from me?* A fish-camp is recognized. I think this is downstream of Tanana, so I have to turn around again and go into the wind, waves and drift. It is not a good time to be out on the river. In this kind of weather boats get swamped. I recall the story of another mammoth hunter who found eight tusks one year. He had them in a boat, got in a wind and had trouble. He tied the boat up to make camp. The waves swamped the tied boat and sank it. He lost all the tusks and his boat and had to be rescued. Now it will be difficult to get to Ruby in time to get gas, but I manage to without serious trouble and I am of course fifteen minutes too late to catch the store open, and it is pouring rain. The entrance to the store is the entry way for the post office, and has public benches and bulletin board. I hang out there till the rain stops. I had hoped to stop for a hot meal while I was getting gas, so hadn't eaten anything since lunch and skipped breakfast, so am pretty hungry. It would take a while to cook anything up, and I'm not very motivated in the rain. A Native in an old truck tells me there is a guy who sells gas after hours, but I do not understand his directions. I walk over that way, but see no sign or anyone to ask. I know Paul Starr who lives here, and I think I remember where his house is. I know his father Al better, from the Kantishna River near Minchumina. I have to go around the block a few times to zero in on his log cabin, and there is Paul out front. I'm trying not to see a lot of people in Ruby, or hang around long since it is impolite to get ivory at the boneyard. *Telling potential customers ivory comes from a mine and some bulldozer dug it up, well, what kind of story is that? It makes a better story to say it comes from the boneyard!*

Paul greets me, "Hi Miles, where you been, where did you go?" I pretty much had to answer, but am sorry to be asked, and have my business inquired about. He reminds me about that time I stopped by his trapline cabin and my sled dog got loose and ate all the beaver carcasses and got sick! He laughs. Adding, "Well, we sure liked that honey you gave us, thanks again!"

"Paul, can I get gas someplace, heard some guy sells it but couldn't find the place".

Paul gets on the phone and tells me I'll be met at my boat to get gas, $2.50 a gallon. Ouch. but who cares? I just sold some art and have all this ivory with me. What's a few extra dollars in gas?

The rain has stopped, wind is calm again. I get the gas and take off even though it is after 8:00 pm. I can't afford to hang around Ruby with people knowing or suspecting I have ivory in my boat. Some local vandal could jump me. I'm the wrong color. Whites have few rights around here. I'm a lot happier to be back on the river again.

The engine smacks another log hard. My heart stops a moment as it does every time. Wondering if this will be the time the gear case cracks and I lose oil and burn up the gears. I'd be in a pretty pickle then! Tired, really tired. And still hungry. But I better press on. There is a cabin way up by Manley if I can make it. This would be another good place to get out of the weather. Certainly I will not forget to pack the tent again! I'm falling asleep at the wheel about midnight when I pull up to the camp. Hungry enough to think about eating the dry noodles before cooking them. But I get the stove going, water on, rest of the crane cooked and I have a goose in the boat now, but will take it home with me to eat there I think. As the meal cooks I go to the boat again, and get the rest of the gear I need to spend a night. I have bug poison, rain gear, gun, dishes, soap and pail of water.

This camp is way up a hill with a good view, but not fun for packing things back and forth. There is no bed in this camp, so I spread out on the floor and go to sleep after eating a big meal. The rain and wind start up again. I am glad to be indoors. I drift off to sleep to the sound of rain pitter patter on a tin roof, and mosquitoes buzzing around my poison covered face.

This cabin also has no door, so I keep the gun handy in case a bear wanders in. Morning comes with gray light and heavy clouds; it is still raining and the boat is full of water from all night rain. If I get the boat up on step I can pull the plugs and let the water drain out. But a lot of things got wet. Mostly the ivory, but think this will not hurt it too much. Better than the heat maybe. I dress in long underwear, many layers of clothes, gloves, rain-gear and wool hat. I smile at the contrast of only a day ago, when I was sweating in a tee shirt! I have to stand up in the boat to see as the windshield is too wet to see through. The windshield wiper I thought I kept on the dash that I could use by hand to clear off the glass seems to be gone.

My back hurts, rain in my eyes, can't see, dodging drift. It's not exactly a vacation right now, but I'm used to this. Not all days of travel will be nice. The Manley landing is passed, Moonshine's fish camp, the mouth of the Kantishna. Just eating up the miles in the rain, wind and drift.

Hours go by with the engine purring. No one else is on the river. About noon I pull into the landing on the Nenana River. The three wheeler I left there to get from the landing to home has a flat tire. The spray can of 'fix a flat' is in the basket so I juice up the tire. I have to make a trip to the gas station for air. A few essentials are grabbed out of the boat. I head home and then go get air.

Once home I feel beat, so decide to take a nap for a while. Everything in the boat can wait. Later in the afternoon I get the tusks up to the house. It is time to wash them off, put a special coating on, and set all fossils in plastic to dry slowly. They will rest in a cool place for at least a month before I even know for sure what I have. Hopefully the nicest one will hold together well as it should with bands on it. The colors look good, with a lot of blues, blacks, and tan mineralized into the ivory over all those years.

THIS WAS the only trip I have time for this year for fossil hunting. I try to go at least once a year. It is time now to get some more sleep…

Email Jennie first.

"Hey Honey- guess what!"

So if this were a real story based on facts and real events it would be illegal right? My conscience is always worrying and trying to look out for me, as I can't look out for myself. I reply to Jennie after telling my tall tale,

"Yea, but luckily this is all a fish story, not based on fact right? Kinda like writing about unicorns and stuff, right?" *I'm with you! I'll be your witness if we go to court!* Geez so much these days is about being careful and 'If I go to court.'

CHAPTER THREE

CHAMBER OF COMMERCE, TANANA STATE FAIR, FISH & GAME, WOLF CLAWS

Another issue comes up that involves the community. There was a 'River Daze' meeting last night and I went to it. This village event celebrates the arrival of summer. There are vendors selling wares, contests, events and such to raise money for the city, and to just have a good time. Nenana puts on a raft race that this whole celebration revolves around. Rafting the seventy miles from Fairbanks to Nenana takes a full day. Participants have a great time! The new rules of 'safety' and insurance and all the updated regulations are putting a damper on the race. Someone on a homemade raft was drunk one year. This raised a liability issue. We may need insurance we can not afford.

I suggested a boating event, not a 'race,' but like a treasure map, with 'clues' that lead you down the river toward the prize. It could be a crossword puzzle based on Alaska trivia, or river trivia, mixed in with trivia from a sponsor, like from a boat shop in town. This way people wouldn't be racing in a hurry and getting in trouble. They would have to solve a puzzle as they go along. Anyhow, I know the boat shops in town, and I'm going to talk to them about being sponsors and setting it up, as a way to sell boats to us village people (we all have boats.) A big issue with any event is the money. Someone to pay for it all would help a lot.

In a way I'm reluctant to 'get involved.' Too often it's expected for us to 'volunteer,' and everyone else goes along for the free ride, living off your energy. And, if anything goes wrong? *Guess whose fault it is!* There is little reward in it. A lot of work. No money. It's easier to just mind my own business, help in some ways, but no more, no less than anyone else.

I don't like the idea of being the one others rally behind, and depend on. I believe in people helping themselves, and not getting on someone else's band wagon. But. (Sigh). I find myself going to 'meetings' every other day or so now. And? And 'caring' (even worse). Ya... well. Memories... from long ago. I got set up by a small town, lost everything I owned, because I 'got involved' in local politics, I suppose. The 'opposition' cleaned my clock. Lost my home and everything I owned over it. Its old news many times repeated. I'm pretty bitter still, and slow to get into other people's business. I was only twenty years old, a while back. Sigh. All the 'pressures' of being in civilization, now that I am back. There were a lot of good things about being alone. Hmmm.

I'm chatting with someone in the community. "Well... anyway. Oh yes, you, everyone, will say how good it is to help others, and get involved. But I notice it's said from the bleachers, egging me on."I try to chuckle good naturedly. Make it a joke, shrug it off. I'm still 'alone.' It is still hard to get people to just show up at a meeting, much less do anything.

"Miles, there is talk of getting the Chamber of Commerce going again. The Lions Club is disbanding." The Lions used to get involved with various community issues, including chamber related topics. "It's so disheartening to see the bigger businesses ripping the town off, getting away without paying city tax, or their water/sewer bills, because they sit on the city council. They 'rah rah' to get others to work, while they skim the money, and the city is broke again. Some business in town has a monopoly and takes advantage. Such things drag me down into depression. You talk about it too sometimes." Do I understand?

"People!" I say with disgust. *But some people are ok, yes.* I meet some truly great people sometimes, so maybe it all balances out. I think I'm just too sensitive about everything! I let things get to me too much. My survival may depend on being able to just step back and regroup, get involved in my art, or the woods, like a 'Zen' thing, like 'meditation.' Let the quiet and peace wash over me in waves. Now, no Lions Club, talk of needing a Chamber of Commerce instead. I like the idea of discussing money and profit. Stop talking about how great volunteer work is. Let's pay people. "Well, better go, I have to try my email connection again to try to get it to work, and get productive in the shop. So far though, I can't get through to get assigned a phone number to call to check my email." It's some free deal, and suspect like everything else, it isn't really 'free' but has 'problems' like it's too busy to ever realistically use. Hmm...

😊 :)

Time to pack up and get ready for the big Tanana State Fair. It is August of 2000 and I have done this fair off and on now since 1973. The fair and income with its connections has become more important each year. I run into my buddy, Will, and fill him in on what is going on.

"I know how you like the good old days, Will. It sure was easier during the oil pipeline in the '70s and '80s to make easy money, huh!?"

"You got that right, Miles! Making a living is so much more complicated these days. We are headed for ending times." Will has been a friend for a lot of years so I am familiar with his ways. Such a big guy compared to me, with arms the size of my body. His slow country Iowa farm drawl is familiar. "So, Miles, have you got your own space at the fair this summer and have a tent for it and the tables and everything?"

"After all those years of living on the houseboat and remote homesteads I have a place in Nenana now with lots of storage room. One advantage is the ability to reserve a shed for nothing but the fair booth and displays!"

"I remember when it did not take a booth and entire shed to hold the materials needed to do the fair."

I too recall the days when I showed up at the fair with a shoe box filled with new art, and that's it. I walked around and made some good money. But define 'good money.' In some ways I despair. "Will, The Natives and remote homesteaders used to show up with a tree stump to sit on, and a blanket to lay out wares. They would sell Native crafts, furs, fish strips, etc., and there was a real flavor of Alaska that those who attended wanted, appreciated, and paid to come see." Will and I talk about those times, when the concert used to be free in a big open field around a bonfire. But the police could not properly watch and manage the crowd nor easily look for drugs. The fire was a hazard. Booths were needed that met standards, were up to fire code, and such. Permits and a business license became needed by vendors so the city could make money. Oddly, in the early days there were no complaints about the fairs not making any money. The fair did fine! "Perhaps the fair's costs increase with insurance and property rent going up?"

Will just point out, " Lots of complaints all around now."

Fair attendees do not like high parking costs, increased entrance fees, the lack of the old family pass and the lack of interesting vendors and concert issues. The music after 9:00 pm is slow dance music, so the crowds do not get riled up and worked into a frenzy like in the old days. Not everyone prefers slow dancing, and will pay for it. Well, I do not want to dwell on the negative. Talk of money got me thinking of saving money and how burning wood for heat is rewarding.

"I cut log jam wood piled up on this one sandbar, Will. Every year the same sandbar collects a winters worth of wood for me."

"I tried cutting river wood but it's too full of silt and hard on the saw so I quit!"

"I know that's a drawback. I put up with it. I make my own chain loops for the saw so it cost me $5 for a chain. I go through two chains a season, so not so bad. Every two years or so I need a chain bar. I'd just rather not cut live trees when I can deal with trees already dead, already down, already done with their useful purpose, so to speak. It helps the environment to not go kill trees." A lot of people girdle trees to kill them. Let them stand and die and dry out for a year or two before cutting.

"I never took you for a greenie, Miles!"

"Not about being a greenie bunny kisser, Will, just being practical, maybe. Hey, I don't have to cut the tree down or limb it, so it saves a lot of time, already stacked up even. All I have to do is section it and roll it into the sled!" I make light talk of caring about the environment and being considered a conservationist. We get back to the subject of the upcoming fair. "I always have a good time and do well, so… 'whatever.'" *Who knows why it is as it is. Out of my control. I deal with what I can deal with.* "You were asking about John the knife guy? Yeah, I got a story about him." I tell Will about John, the Knife guy, who has been setting up at the fair forever! Talking to Will spins me into…

Past Flash

I get this knife from John a pile of years ago. I forget, maybe we traded. A really beautiful knife, custom made, that he did a good job on. John told me it comes with lifetime free sharpening! Anytime I saw him set up someplace I could hand him my knife and he'd sharpen it, for free! Very generous and kind of him, but I know how to sharpen my own knife, so forgot his promise.

I'm at the fair with my trusty blade at my side, as usual. Yeah, usual blade of grass bouncing out of my mouth, bearskin hat flopping. I hear a, "Hey Miles!" from across the way and spin around. It's John hailing me. I saunter over, big grin, shifting my blade of grass. With hand out to shake mine over his booth table set up for sharpening knifes, "Let me see your knife, I'll sharpen it for you!" Sure why not. I hand it over and begin telling him the latest news. Before he begins, he does the usual ritual of anyone about to sharpen a knife. He runs a thumb nail over the edge to see where the dull spots are, but pauses and frowns with concern. I'm puzzled what the concern might be. "Miles!" long significant pause. "There is a nick in the blade!" I make a show of my hands and lean forward with a, 'and your point is?' look. It is a working knife of course, so there might be a nick. So what? "How did it get here?" He is holding the knife like it is his baby. I do not have a clue how the nick got there. So he asks "Well, what was the last thing you were doing with it?"

I have to stop and think hard… go back in time. I brighten up when I recall. I happily say, "Cutting the heads off of nails!"

He has a horrified look at how his custom blade is being treated, but pauses and has a 'working his brain' look asking: "Well, did it work?"

"Sure. Oh yeah. I had a little trouble, had to beat the back of the blade with a hammer."

All over again "My poor baby!"

My Past flash ends

Will and I chuckle because we both know what kind of use a knife goes through in our hands. I sigh and tell Will what happened, just last year. "Yeah, Will, the fair decided knives will be illegal on the fairgrounds. John is told he cannot sharpen them, or sell his custom knives anymore. John is on the fair board, representing the vendors at the time he was told. He jumps up at the meeting in anger to protest, and falls over dead from a heart attack. Been doing the fair for like, twenty-five years. Donated his time, been on the board, a well liked respected guy among the vendors. So now, there's this new rule, Will. We can sell custom knives, but we have to personally escort the customer off the fairgrounds and hand the knife to them off the grounds. Who in their right mind will shut down a booth to spend half an hour walking a customer off the grounds? Lose $100 in business to make $25 profit!?" But it puts the liability on the vendor—so if there is an incident or problem on the grounds involving a vendor's knife, it can be said he knew the rules and was told and—well, we see where that goes.

Will understands. "Yup, the difference between what is in writing and how it really works. In the end any of us can be arrested at any time for who knows what, it is just a matter of who they want and why."

"They, Will? Just who is they?" We both laugh. Them and us. It is supposed to be 'us,' period. Of the people, by the people and for the people. Standing up for each other. But again, no use going there. Now a fair without John. The thought is lost when I see Dan and Vision running the Patty Wagon. Will wanders off with a vague word about meeting his brother to fix a car. "So, Dan, did you assign me #1 in the book?"

"You bet, Miles. Good to see you. I guess you do not collect grease for the sled dogs anymore?" For years and years Dan set aside his used cooking grease so I had thirty gallons of free grease for the sled dogs in winter while trapping with them. It's a bad subject.

"No, Dan, got rid of the sled dogs. Plugged in now, the man of steel, got a machine to do the job now!" Dan chuckles. He works with the Iron Dog snow machine race that follows the Iditarod trail after the race dogs go through. I think Norman Vaughn is now part of that. My friend Norman is now too old to run the dogs in the Iditarod, being in his 90s now. While we talk, I am thinking that when I need something to eat I can walk up and say: "Put it on my tab—that's number one" loud enough for everyone around to hear.

"Ooh, Aww, and how does he rate?" And we begin to tell the story of Alice's restaurant in two part harmony. How you can 'git anything ya want' at (?) Where?...*Miles booth just down yonder—Miles of Alaska—stop in. Cause I'm the man that's why.* Waiting for the customer at the Patti wagon to say:

"And what do you make," so I can give my next line in this skit... it's all rehearsed. "How do you do that fine work ?" comes next. *How do you do that? I back up and look at my reflection. How do I do that? I tilt my felt hat with the owl feather in it, shift my blade of grass to the left, and with the right amount of pause and correct grin say* "Talent!" to the mirror.

"Miles!? I loved your book and need another copy! Put me on the list for book two!" Both Dan and his wife Vision have read it and I am glad they think it is well written. I have been selling the book well at the fair. I figured, those who buy my art want a story about the artist who did the art, right? Here's the book- the whole story! After all, my story is what separates the art piece from 'made in china', right?

I say it to myself again: *"Talent,"* and a third time: *"Talent!"* Looking like I own the world, I walk the grounds. *It's show time!* (From the movie All That Jazz.) Drumming up business. Checking out the crowd flow, looking to buy, looking to trade, looking to sell. The wheeler dealer man of magic, shaman, guru, running a dog and pony medicine show. Most important, *And proud of it.*

It's hard work, if one cares to call it work. I care to call it 'getting paid for having fun.' Up at 5:00 am, working till I drop, about 10:00 pm. The fairgrounds are on the edge of Fairbanks. Flat country. The Chena River is not far off, so the sandhill cranes come in off the river to land in the fairgrounds field. I assume this field is deserted when there is no fair going on, and the cranes own it. Every fair time, in the early morning, year after year, one memory is the sound of the cranes. Looking out my fair tent where I slept, I see cranes fly thorough the morning fog and early pink sun. I stare at the sun as part of my morning ritual, to see if I can spot God, or the chariot He uses to haul the sun. I think I see the string of horses running out front, but it might have just been a cloud formation. Their manes look bigger and longer than their bodies. Staring, I think about relationships. First with God, then women – of course. We all know guys have a one track mind. But, weird, instead of women, I think about my first sled dog.

Past Flash

Kenai tangles with a porcupine, and gets a mouthful of quills. He lets me pull the quills out, but for some reason hates seeing those pliers. He lets me use them, so long as he can't see them. *Much like people at the doctors who do not like to look at the needle.* I have to come up from underneath, while Kenai stares wild eyed, but sits still. I'd work a quill through his tongue. In one side and out the other, by the dozen. One quill has to be worked behind his eye and around and out the other side. Not a job for the squeamish. He will die if I do not do this. Out in the wilds, no vet, no drugs for my buddy. There are other quills that went in behind the eye that I can not reach. Almost a year later, one quill must have gone in the brain and Kenai goes crazy. As a sled dog he gets slow, forgets his commands, picks fights, becomes undependable. The other dogs are getting a bad attitude from him, wanting to know why he gets special favors when he isn't doing his share. I have to shoot him. Lessons, always lessons. It never ends.

Past Flash ends

But anyway. Strange, to think of that time so many years ago pulling the quills out as he sat there, trusting me. We were bonded, a team, risked our lives for each other. I thought those memories got burned out of my brain from the shock wave of the bullet blast that killed him. Survival can't be filled with nightmares, or regrets, or even nostalgia we can't bring back. Like the Native believes, when someone dies, you can never speak their name again. Concerned, maybe my mind is getting filled and over stuffed with events I want to forget?

My conscience has a plan. *I can scan disk and defrag for you. Kind of like what you showed me works with computers. Re-file stuff, make sure it is all in the same format and operating system, so you have good fresh RAM. Stuff you do not use much will get put far away and hard to access, but in return, stuff you need will be there faster and more clear!*

I pause and wonder. Sort of like a Zen thing? All I have to do is sit here and hum —and you make all the data compatible? *See how important it is to be friends with your unconscious!* We both grin. I have never been to a barber, but think it might be like that. Just sit there and RRRRRRRRR. When we are done I am a new man with a new look.

Insert new green twig in mouth, set mountain man hat on appropriately crooked. Make certain socks do not match. And greet the day. *It's show time!* I look at the strange yellow orb in the sky. I begin reloading a new day. "Sun!" I say, seeing it for the first time.

"Hey Miles, good to see ya!" An Athabascan Native comes up to me with warm smile and outstretched hand to shake. I sadly do not recall who he is. I smile fondly in return, and put my hand out, assuming that as we talk, new data will get filed, and there will be some connection to an old lost file.

"You been back to Galena lately?" *So we know this guy is from Galena. Must be the houseboat days when I lived there on Jack Slough.* My unconscious goes *Friend!* and puts this new data in the friend file.

It's been over twenty years ago when I was in Galena, and I still run into people who remember me regularly. I ask about Edgar. He was the one who got me interested in the Kantishna River, all his talk of the old days, running the barge up there. It was because of him I found this river, which changed my whole life. This fellow tells me Edgar is in his 90s now and still asks about me, wonders if I made it or not, if I'm still alive, still in the country.

"Well, when you see Edgar, let him know that I settled in on the Kantishna and did well there." It means a lot to me that such a well-respected man remembers me in a positive way. "He used to think I was one of his grandchildren!" This was always funny to me.

He'd get closer and stare in my face, after a pause saying, "You're not one of my grandkids!" Indignantly spoken, as if I should be related to him. This Galena resident tells me I do look like his grandchildren, something I never knew. Gosh, twenty years ago. It's hard to imagine him still being around, almost like he's a forever person.

"I think I'll get him one of your custom knives. Let me see that fish knife there, Miles." It's a nice custom knife with local birch handle. I acid etched a salmon on the blade.

"Its local wood, with my freehand etch. I am not set up yet in the shop to do the custom steel work, so order the blank blades from someone else. Good Sheffield steel. I cut fish, so know what shape blade would be good for that. Nice to see it go to someone who will put it to good use!"

"Let me see the beaver skinner." It is someone else who heard me talking about my knives. Two knives are sold at $400 each.

"Keep them wrapped up guys, there's concern about knives at the fair, so make sure you stay safe." I tell them how technically, I am supposed to escort them off the grounds.

"We do not need baby sitters." Said with disgust.

I'm sorry I even mention it, but do not want problems if they take a knife out to show a wife or friend and get asked where they got it. Saying anything about, 'In case you might stab someone with it.' This direction of talk would be like suggesting someone might go nutso selling them a hammer, so please don't smash anyone's head in with it because 'I might get in trouble for selling you the hammer'. Crafty already got escorted off the grounds in handcuffs last year. He was not selling switch blades to kids. It was plastic switch combs kids flashed around like knives. But one must have been real, as it all started when a father got mad his son had a knife.

"Hey Crafty! Was just thinking about you!" Crafty is stopping by, right when I am thinking about him. He still reminds me of Grizzly Adams off the TV show.

"What it is, bro?"

I move the hand jive wiggle. "How's it hanging ma man!" I give my imitation druggie head bob. Crafty is used to that, and does not respond to my act.

"So what were you thinking, Miles, how much more money I am making than you?"

"Something like that!" We both laugh. He still makes ten times what I make, but works hard. Money is his God. This is all he does, sells crafts. He has to have employees, which is a whole new level of business with Workman's Comp, insurance etc. He knows ways out of that. Subcontract. He's looking for Wess.

"Wess the mess? Haven't seen him since this morning, Crafty. Showed up in his '60s tie dye shirt and hippie hair, asking if he could set up out behind my tent, borrow a cord and my power, and sit out back carving. He had his bongos with him." Wess is a gifted artist, but seems to distract business. Who can do business with him playing bongos and yelling at people about world peace. I'd look like a head shop. Crafty understands; he has hired Wess before; we both help out when he is down and out.

"Miles, I lent him a hammer and nails. Maybe he plans to build a lean to and try to sell somewhere on the fringes." I cannot say much about that, it is how I used to sell not so long ago.

"I got customers to deal with, gotta go Crafty, I'll send The Mess your way if I see him. Sell a lot, make a lot of money."

"You too, Miles, booth looks good this year." I used Crafty's ideas. Old card tables are set up with used doors laid between. A nice cloth cover is laid over them so no one ever knows what is under that cover. I at least have matching cloths all around. I make my own display stands of moose antler, drift wood, and materials the art is made from. As usual, I have the tent divided. The raw stuff in the very back, the kids stuff in the very front, the women's and the men's divided, and a small area for the under $10 crowd. I can usually direct a customer to one of those areas.

"Got any rough jade,Miles?"

I am talking to someone else. I just point to the very back and say, "On the left with the other stones," and keep on talking. I get jade from Crafty, wholesale in trade for my art and knives. I'm learning though. My buddy Crafty was calling his '10% off retail,' his 'wholesale trade price,' trading to me at my half off keystone price. He tries hard to trade his retail to others wholesale.

"Huh?" Someone asks me.

I snort: "It's like a shell game, and you better figure it out fast!" And then explain: "So let's say he has mammoth ivory you want, and his retail is $50 a pound. Wholesale if you buy a lot, is half that, called keystone, at $25 a pound. Let's say he wants your jade. You want $10 a pound retail, and sell wholesale in volume at keystone $5 a pound."

"Yeah, ok, so how does it work then?"

I go on, "Ok, so Crafty tells you he will give you a deal at 10% off if you trade. But he means 10% off retail, so $40 a pound. Not 10% off wholesale at $20 a pound. Big difference. Then he wants you to trade yours at wholesale, so $5 a pound for your jade. The bottom line is, his pile gets bigger faster than your pile."

I hear from up front: "Hey, Miles, what's with the two cans here?" .

"Oh yes. Well, read it. One coffee can says, 'Put your money in here,' and the other can says 'change is in here, have a nice day.' if I'm gone or busy you use the cans."

"Does it work? Dang, Miles, you are trusting!"

"No, I'm not trusting. Everything in here is radioactive. When you buy it, I deactivate it. If you steal it, then over time your teeth get loose, your hair falls out, and you go blind."

Long pause before a reply. "Is that legal Miles?"

"Try to prove it. Most people haven't got the money to test for radiation" I like this rumor to get passed around.

"Hey, Miles!" I hear Crafty holler. "Need any mammoth teeth? I got a deal on them, today only." I come over to take a look, and wonder what it is he wants in trade. "I heard you found some ivory this season." He adds "Legal stuff of course, from a patented homestead on state land."

I follow with, "Of course!" Just in case one of us is wired, working for the Feds. "What you want a pound, for fair C grade ivory, Miles?"

"What are the teeth worth, Crafty?"

"You first."

"Ok. Wholesale to wholesale?" He frowns but says nothing as I continue, "C grade for the fair? Retail $1 a piece for quarter sizes, That's about $15 a pound, but your wholesale, let me see, comes out to about 30 cents each, so call it $8 a pound. But if I give you such a hot deal, I need some slack on the teeth!"

"$100 each"

"Crafty! Crafty! My buddy Crafty, how can you do me this way?"

"Ok, $80 each. I need to get rid of them. North sea stuff." I can tell by looking. Not as good as Alaskan. But $80 each is good. I think I can get $200 each on the internet. Crafty still refuses to take the internet seriously. He thinks I might get $120 each or so, from the only market he knows—local. If he was not Crafty, I'd be open with him and tell him what I expect to get. Crafty set the rules of the game. You snooze ya lose. So Crafty gets twenty pounds of junk ivory I have no real market for —but he does in his Fairbanks shop with a market for low end tourist sales. My ivory market is higher end knife makers around the world, none of whom want garbage. " $300 in trade, so three teeth."

"Four teeth—three at $80 is not $300. "

"But four is $320. Give me another pound of your ivory."

"Crafty, how about three teeth and more jade at $3 a pound, an incredibly low price." I happen to know he has more jade than he knows what to do with, and wants to unload it. Yup. I go back to my booth with my goods. Jade at $3 a pound. *Beats working for a living. Walking around listening and observing early in the morning pays off.* "Yes, learned this from the top sellers in the world, in Tucson at the fossil show." I move the jade for $10 a pound by the piece. I talk a lot like Crafty when dealing with another customer.

"You need three pounds? I can go $5 a pound. Not enough money? What you got to trade?" I have a list of stuff I might be interested in. "Dall sheep horns in the garage? Pretty old and oily, no good for display now, huh. I'd have to cut them up then. I can go five pounds of jade." The guy will bring the sheep horns tomorrow when he brings the kids to the fair. So $25 worth of jade. But not really. I traded for the jade at $3, so the horns cost me $15. But no, I traded mammoth ivory for the jade.

☺ :)

And the sheep horn? It's off wild sheep, in good shape worth $150 a side. This has to get cut up, but still, one set of pistol grip roughs from part of the horn sells for $75. It's all about connections. Those that have. Those that want. Those who connect the dots. The internet will be perfect for keeping track and wheeling and dealing worldwide. I just have to figure out how to use the computer. Right now, no digital camera, no picture program, no knowledge. I can barely turn the computer on and figure out how to get email. Few others understand either. It's all new stuff that is just catching on. Crafty thinks computers will fade away as a useless gadget, so has zero interest. Maybe someday I will leave him in the dust.

Crafty is limited to who he can physically sell to. On the internet I can have, in theory, a store in Nenana, Alaska with the equivalent of a hot New York downtown address. No one else I talk to visualizes it like that, so I stop talking about it.

Deeds will do their own talking. Or. It's like chess. My competitors move a pawn, jump to the side, then move with the horse. We all study the game table. My present moves appear to imitate the moves my competitors make. They think I'm playing chess. I smile and nod as if I am. If I lose, I act like that is ok. Competitors keep a poker face believing I am a fool, sucker and mark. 'Miles has a good attitude, just a little slow!' If I win? 'How'd that happen? Checkmate? Does that mean I win?' I'm not playing chess. While others bring money to the game acquired in the game, I have a secret source of income I can bring to play with.

"Another few days left of the fair, Joe, does it look like you'll make some money?" I'm making my rounds, chatting with vendors early in the morning. I rarely meet anyone who gets up at 5:00 am as I do. Usually just the security guards on their bikes. But by 8:00 am, the grounds begin to stir. Dan at the Patty Wagon is up cutting French fries, the fryer is on, and coffee made for those that cannot wake up without it. Dan is short like I am, long white hair, round happy face, looking much like a Hobbit. Joe, the vender, is slow to reply, being one of those who needs coffee first. It is often part of one's culture to not disturb anyone who just woke up. So I made the initial invite to talk, but understand Joe is still asleep. Sam, the vendor comes up to the Patty Wagon and seems more alert and awake. I repeat the same question to him. Tall, skinny elderly guy who is spry – full of energy and ideas.

"Looking good, Miles. People always have to eat. I have a new sauce for my burrito this year the customers seem to like. I am ahead of last year, so far, anyhow. You always look busy when I go by, Miles."

A miner I think I know, comes up saying he is looking for me. "Miles," he pauses and looks around, then steers me to a table so we can talk in private. "There have been a lot of bear problems this year around Manley." I had read about some incident in the paper—a grizzly chased a guy on a bulldozer with no fear of the dozer. "Anyhow, Miles, the grizzly that chased the dozer got into the cook shed and later tried to get in the bunkhouse. One of the workers shot it coming through the window." He explains how such things happen now and then. Self defense is legal, but you have to make a report. He has no connection to the outside world to make a report within the legal five days after the event. Now, the skull must be turned in to Fish and Game in Fairbanks—for him, six hours away. "Long ago I made a report, and had to prove it was self defense. I came into town to explain myself. Cost me two days down time at the mine. Thousands of dollars loss. Never again." I nod that I understand. "So anyhow, Miles, usually we just bulldoze the bear into the pit with the rest of the overburden. Or shove him in the river. No more problem. But I thought of you, and cut the claws off." He takes a paper sack from his pocket and shows me huge five inch claws and just gives them to me! "I know they are not legal to sell, but heck, I sure hate to see waste. Hate to dump the bear into a pit like that, but that was what I was ordered to do by the boss, geez. I know you. You have a good reputation in the villages. I think it's legal to give them to you, but who knows."

Yes. 'Who knows.' Probably legal only if you reported the self defense and proved it, and then the bear would get confiscated, or you'd be told to bring it in to town. I know how hard it is, and how costly to get to town. I know how short the mining season is here in Alaska, how every day counts. I also know it was not up to him, but his boss, and even if legal, his boss might fire him for not burying the bear as ordered.

"I think we uphold the intent of the law. There are also laws about wanton waste; no one killed this bear for profit. No one is promoting the killing of bears. Anyhow thanks a lot. I really appreciate it. I may make a necklace for myself. I also know some subsistence Natives who need such claws for ceremonial, spiritual needs. I may make something as a gift for you." I have to hide them under the table, and maybe study up on the laws more later. I'm never sure if I have the latest version, and there is no one I trust who would give an honest answer if I asked.

A village magistrate, close to being a judge, told me, "You are responsible for knowing the law. The legal system is not responsible for making the law available to you. Not only that, those in the legal system are allowed to lie. The best way for us to spread the word, is to arrest someone." There was more spoken in the long, enlightening conversation. Such as, few cases go to court. Yet it is 'going to court' that sets a precedence for creating interpretations and changed laws. In some cases it appears the court, the legal system and those backing the legal system, have reasons to not want laws changed. It appears, they make sure cases do not go to court unless they want to move in a direction the legal system run by politicians wishes. There are no updated, workable laws on some subjects. One of those touchy subjects is subsistence, related to animal protection. I've reviewed this subject many times with lawyers, politicians, guides, Natives, judges and conservation groups enough that I think I have an accurate grasp of the situation.

"Miles, I was cleaning out my garage, and see I have some ancient walrus bones and mammoth ivory." The guy needs fair money for the family, and knows I buy stuff like this. All old fossil material, not endangering any species or anything, so I do a part trade, part cash deal. Some material I high grade and keep for myself to turn into art, and some I sell as is to those who come looking for such interesting materials.

"Miles, what you got new this year?" This guy looks familiar but do not know the name.

"I just got this fossil bone and ivory in an hour ago. You are the first to look at it." He is an artist, but knows others, so gets some extra material he can high-grade and sell to his friends. Maybe pay for the material he needs by passing it on. I'm selling more raw materials this season than my finished art, but at least something is selling. I keep saying, "Survival is about being adaptable." A Native artist friend comes by to chat. He has a new Russian wife he met on the internet. I give him one of the grizzly bear claws, since he is Native and can sell it once he turns it into art work.

"Thanks, Miles! Too bad you aren't Native, you could sell it yourself! This trading going on is how the old way was, so my father tells me." I understand from oral history, people were not as greedy, and shared more. I did not expect anything in return. People give me things, I give things, it all works out. Building friendships, trust and good will is worth something. Now and then some money passes between us, but mostly more stuff! Ha! Yes, legally it is a gray area. There is a reality here as well. Laws are so complicated, few understand them. Natives can do this, low income can do that, some is ok in the state, some is ok in the country. Some can be turned into art and sold. Boxes of goods get traded. Those receiving may not even know what is in the box, or what the item is when they see it. Even big dealers at shows get mixed up or do not care!

A dealer in Tucson had mastodon ivory inn his bin of mammoth ivory. I came across a piece of white walrus ivory. The dealer only shrugged his shoulders and did not care, saying it was all ivory and so what and who care? The difference between white walrus ivory and mammoth ivory is ten years in prison. I wake up from my private thoughts and smile.

I love the thrill of moving big wads of cash in and out. There is a visual impression burned in the brain of stacks of bills divided into denominations that completely cover a table. At least several thousand dollars. Much gets reinvested here at the fair, but still, I'm a feely-touchy person, and recognized this! Way back when I began trapping, I got paid at the end of the season with one big lump of cash. There's just nothing exciting about a check in the bank. Anyhow, I hate banks, always have. 'Cash!' I am in control of that!

😀 :)

The king's henchmen can ride through the streets prodding merchants in a shake down. They go right by me as I am dressed in rags and mumbling nonsense, but with pockets full of cash they never see. It's a way to survive. *I smile at me.* Reminds me of the Robin Hood days, Sherwood Forest. A band of merry men in the forest poaching the King's deer. It's no longer God's deer. The King never sees his deer, nor wants them, nor knows how many there are, but those who get caught eating them are publicly lynched.

I ask, "So what constitutes ownership?"

I yawn at the end of another seventeen hour play-day. I cannot fall asleep till the rides shut down at midnight, but there is quiet in the craft area after 10:00 pm. The big craft tent closes at 10:00. I used to set up in that tent, where a table and spot is rented by the day for $50. Now I am across from that tent in my own ten x twenty spot. In my sleeping bag on the ground in my tent, I nod off to sleep.

Sandhill cranes flying overhead awake me at 5:00 am. A raven tries to imitate the sound of the cranes. From inside the tent I imitate the raven. There is a significant silent pause. I only smile and wait. There is one tiny 'pop' sound the raven makes by swelling his throat and letting the air out fast. I wait the same amount of time, and imitate this pop, by using my finger on the side of my cheek. Then do it again, with a tone lower, and a tone higher, done as a question. The raven mumbles. Then begins to yell. Had I said the wrong thing? Said at the wrong time, or out of sequence? All I am pretty sure of is, the raven is very upset and it has something to do with me. Other than that, I would not venture to guess. Now and then a raven will try to imitate me. I imitate him, and then it is like we test each other, an octave lower, an octave higher, or two times instead of one time. We see if the other figures it out, and can or will, try to imitate. Oh, goodness no, I am not trying to prove anything. I am only greeting the day. I would not want to hang out with people who prattle on about talking to, living with, and understanding ravens! What a bunch of weirdoes! Too polite to tell them my private thoughts. I'd rather just not bring up the subject publicly.

I've been imitating birds all my life. I got started when someone read me various Indian stories. Back in the days when books were written about Indians taking scalps, sneaking up on wagon trains, farmers, homesteaders. Indian fighters were heroes. The Indians would talk to each other in bird songs and animal noises, while the unsuspecting farmer cleared the land on the edge of the forest without a clue what was going on, or about to happen. I decided such a skill might be very handy some day. Mostly I imitated song birds. As I grew up, I enjoyed the bird calls for no other reason than they sound nice. I now suspect, even when young it was not just about how I might sneak up on someone by making them think the sounds they heard were just a bird scratching in the forest. But, anyhow, time to get the day going. I stare at the rising sun as I scan disk and defrag my brain. I'm usually working within ten minutes of waking up. A yellow orb I never saw before in my life. A new fresh hard-drive full of ram. I smile. "Sun!"

With towel and toothbrush in hand I head across the grassy field for the rest room and public shower. Another day begins. *It's show time!*

"Wow, Miles this is beautiful. I have never seen anything even close this. How do you do this? It is a new line of work for you, it looks like!" This person must know me, but as usual I do not let on. I have no clue whom they are.

"Thanks for the compliment. Yes I moved to the village, have electricity for the first time, and so acquiring equipment knowledge, and my art takes a new direction as a result."

"But how do you do this, Miles?"

I give my usual grin, and reply "Talent!"

"No, but really I'd like to know, I'm curious."

I give a deep inward sigh. *Been here, done this, so many times and it is so disappointing, but oh well here we go…* "Well the metal cap you see is lost wax cast."

"Lost wax? What's that?" This is like asking a builder of a sky scraper how he did it, and as he begins to explain a hammer and nails, gets asked what a hammer is. How will we ever reach the end of the story? In how many years? But. Ok.

"Lost wax is a process of duplicating a carving done with wax, in metal. Wax is easy to carve compared to metal. Wax melts and disappears. So when the wax is carved, it is put in a can and covered in a wet plaster. The plaster hardens and is then heated. The wax melts, leaving a hollow place in the plaster, an exact negative of the wax. There is a passageway made leading to the hollow."

"It sounds complicated! How did you learn this, what school did you go to? Or who did you work under?"

I go on to explain. "No school, no teacher. No book really. Maybe a lot of books. I forget the names." It does not matter. I think I understand the process, and begin trying. If I get stumped along the way, I open one book and look for that stage, and if it is not described well, or there is no picture, I pick up another book. I only study the part I do not understand. I only read enough to get to the next step. I do it about... oh... a hundred times, and begin to get the hang of it. I never stop learning or adapting.

"Where do you get your metals?" There is an assumption I have a source, an art catalogue. But I get scrap metal from anyplace. Copper from wire and pipes, bronze from old boat propellers.

"But how do you know the melting temperature?"

I do not know the melting temperature. It does not matter a lot. I just heat it with a torch till it melts. Since I do not reply, the talker is more frustrated and even further disillusioned, saying, "I'd think knowing the temperature would be critical!"

"Well, then, when you do it, I suggest you work with known's; that's a good thing, you are already thinking and have an opinion. But you asked me how I do it."

"But Miles, you have no way! Every time you do it, it is an experiment; that is not scientific!"

"Exactly! Now you got it! It is not scientific, it is artistic." Right back where we started: "Talent!" Kind of like jazz or rock and roll, not knowing how to read or write music, but being a musician. Or like a cook who never reads directions and can't measure. A splash of this, a dash of that. Every time the song is played it is different. Every time a meal is cooked, it's a different meal. Something no one can duplicate. One time. One of a kind. Never to be repeated. The spice of life.

Forty years after Jimmy Hendrix dies, I only have to hear the first three notes to smile and know that's Hendrix playing. No one can imitate Janis Joplin. Again, forty years later we only have to hear the word 'Janis' and by word association the next word is 'Joplin!' The one and only. I do not know the names of any chefs, but assume there are those who cook, that if one tried their meal, the name of the creator would be forthcoming. No one cooks like so and so. Among artists, no one paints like Andrew Wyeth. Or Audubon. No one can imitate Hemingway, Jack London, Robert Service, or Poe's writing. Like that. *How do any of them do it? They simply 'are.' I think, therefore I am. Is there a recipe? A set of schematic's, a formula?*

I think all successful people have certain things in common. They all have passion and are driven. They tend not to give up. They tend not to listen to what anyone else has to say, or take advice, or pay attention to critics. Few have close friends, even though they are known by many, they are loners and isolated.

I cannot get past the beginning when discussing my trade with anyone. Perhaps if I hung out with professionals, like-minded folks in the same business? Mostly I'm snorted at, and told I'm not doing it right. I am not trying to be stuck up when giving a one word reply. Just trying to get out of the awkward question gracefully, by being funny. Or even stuck up. Because, you do not really want to know how I do this. If you did, it would take twenty years of listening. *Will you still be around in twenty years listening?* No one knows how I get the castings to look like this. It can't be done. I explain it to a jewelry friend who runs a shop here in Fairbanks .

He asks: "How do you get the two metals in one casting to come out like that?"

I'd only learned how to cast six months ago. I told him how I melt two metals in the crucible at the same time.

"But the metals will mix"

I tell him no, "Not if you do not use flux, do not disturb it, and have the metal with the highest melting point on the bottom, way hotter than suggested. I melt the copper first."

"No one casts copper Miles."

"Exactly. Now you got it." Yes, you begin right off doing something no one else does. Right from the get-go. Right off the starting line. I zero in on, "Who ever heard of that!" Suddenly I'm interested.

So I go on, "So I melt the copper first."

"But it has such a high melting point and the plaster can't take it Miles, how do you get around that?"

Well, luckily, no one ever told me that. That is not what I discovered. So I melt the copper. The spring arm is wound up ready to let go. I have another crucible with melted brass. I gently pour the melted brass on the surface of the copper. Maybe the hot copper mingles with the brass to some extent, but at the bottom is pure molten copper, and at the top is pure molten brass. Both at different temperatures as I let her rip.

"Kind of like I hear fresh water and salt water do not mix for a long time, and rivers make currents of fresh water out in the ocean." The metals enter the mold spinning and twirling and make a marble cake effect. I'm now trying to study that half a second time period, and figure out how to control the slip stream. If I could design the crucible different, maybe have it split, I could more easily separate the two metals in compartments that spin through the same hole. So far I am stumped. But heck. I have only been casting six months. I'm already so far out in left field that I am out of the game. Basically creating my own game.

Anyhow, trying to explain what lost wax is. I never got to the part about creating the rubber mold to cast the wax once an original is created. This is one of the real secrets. The ability to cast 100 waxes from the same mold and altering each casting. I use all different metals and it is all an experiment. The castings do not in fact look the same, because I figure out some ways to make molds that cost less and are faster than the average bear. *Yogi! Remember Yogi Bear?* I answer my conscience. "Hey, hey, hey, better than the average bear" *Ya, our buddy Yogi the cartoon bear.* When we were kids, Yogi outsmarted the park ranger all the time, getting the picnic baskets from the tourists. *Free lunch.*

The next phase of, "How do I do this," is the tumbler we bought and experimented with. *Luckily we did not read the directions, huh?* We did not know what grit to buy for each stage, nor very much about the liquid used as lubricant when polishing. Rio Grande, where we buy stuff, asked us to come to the big Tucson show and demonstrate how to tumble polish amber. Apparently no one knows how, and we figured it out. All we had to do was think about it with an open, blank mind. It involves weights, speeds and liquids, no one ever heard of using. Luckily we were too ignorant to know any better.

Ya, often the ideas back fire. *Ya, that's why so few listen to us, huh?* "Yes, I think that has a lot to do with it." I calculate in casting for example, that at least a third of all my work goes bonkers and needs to be re-melted. As much as a third of all my art goes tits up. But? It only takes one casting in thirty to be awesome. This makes up for the third loss. One casting can pay for the entire batch, if that one is unusual, interesting, sought after. One problem with experiments is that they tend to fail a lot. *Edison tossed out 9,999 light bulbs that never lit up.* My famous quote! I reply to myself with a smile, "Till one did, and paid for all the rest." Most people who ask how I do something, focus on some mistake, stop there, and dwell on it. Come to the conclusion I am a lucky idiot, and stop taking in any new information. Edison's wife died young and neglected, from mortification at her idiot husband. *Does anyone remember who she is?*

The first computer we got lasted a week. The first snow machine, the first camera, the first of a lot of things, got sacrificed. Sometimes even the second one. About then, no one wants to talk to you, and you are the laughing stock of your community. Full of do-do, the humbug Wizard of Oz.

Ok, I suppose it gets rid of the competition. No one wants to walk in our shoes, that's for sure! Or more like, it requires the ability to live an isolated life. Motivated totally from within. If you have to ask someone how to do something, you are already a follower. One of the sheep. How would I kindly say that to anyone? "Talent!" Big grin.

The customer looks at me dubiously. So I add "Do not pay attention to that man behind the curtain! I am OZ!"

"Ya', well Mr. OZ, the man of magic, guess I'll take that belt buckle. I know I will never see another like it anyplace."

Good choice! Will that be paper or plastic? Next! But say instead… "Good choice. Yes I like that one too. If you ever have any problems with it let me know, here is my card, lifetime warranty on it. Have a good day, maybe see you here next year?" *Yes ok, you are right, probably better to be polite.*

I feel driven by conflicting forces. On the one hand, I care and want to share—to promote a lifestyle, a way of thinking, to be kind, to teach. I also need to make a living. I also am sad, hurt, discouraged. I want respect, but understand it needs to be earned. At the same time afraid of any respect and positive attention. The jester outlives many kings. Thus, being seen as an intelligent and powerful person of influence can be a dangerous thing. Better to temper that with 'but eccentric.' *And so harmless.* When the king's horsemen ride in, scattering everyone, waving swords, demanding more taxes, demanding to see papers, permits, pay dues, file this, file that, inspect this, inspect that, I wish to be a clown with a silly grin in rags. That the henchman may scowl with raised sword, but be distracted by that well dressed flush looking guy over there who can put money in the henchman's pocket. Maybe he will just pass me by, usually does. Survival. It has worked in the past. *We tend to repeat what works.*

I never really wanted to be part of society like I am now, so now what? Stuck in such an unsafe, scary environment. Now what? Hovering on the fringes. Incognito. Like the guys in the Star Wars movie, just before they snaffle a space ship. *Yeah, even Jesus went around barefoot in rags disguised as a beggar. When he was discovered, how did the Romans treat him?* No. The truth does not set us free. Even the best get nailed to the cross.

This very subject comes up in the evening, chatting with people who know me, who I do not know. "Yes Miles, that sucks, John the knife guy, all the new rules and the direction of everything." Pause.

Another vendor speaks. All heads turn to the new speaker... "Yes we need a revolution or something, like it's time to toss the tea in the harbor again."

I have not replied. Just talking like this could get someone locked up. I wonder if we have freedom of speech. I think that anyone who badmouths those who defend and take care of you or – even those who simply have power over you, is not bright. If such a person gets slapped around, I am not surprised. Sad, but, oh well. *When a sled dog wants to bite me and spreads unease thorough the team, I shoot him. We cannot bite the hand that feeds us and expect no price to pay.*

I respond: "So ok, let's say there was a revolution. Who would you like to take over and be in charge?" No one has an answer. No one has thought it through to its conclusion. Anyone can complain. "So tell me what the solution is. Because I do not know any group I want running things. Nor do I think there is another country that is any better." I conclude all governments everywhere are the same, pretty much. It's all about control and power. If there were a revolution and we were weak, how would any of us enjoy Chinese or Russian rulers?

Looking at the average citizen, my honest opinion is, most people cannot run their own life without being told how. Most will not behave, or be moral or ethical, without someone bigger than them with a stick. The sheep bleat, but they do not bleat to be free. They bleat because the shepherd is not there instructing them what to do. It is raining, and they are afraid. Not bleating at the joy of being wet. *And, where would the world be without sheep?* I answer myself, "In truth, all is as it should be. Sheep are necessary, fulfill a useful function." Without sheep, where would fleece come from?

So no. I am not interested in a revolution. At least not the sort these guys talk of. Maybe just get back to what our country was founded on. Or was it always romanticized? Neither women, blacks, nor Indians could vote in the beginning. Ours was advertised as a form of government that called itself a democracy believing in equality. We were never a democracy, nor has there ever been equality. No matter what era we go back to, there was stuff going on behind the scenes few of us would be proud to know about. Our entire country is based on genocide. So where does that leave us? Our land was already inhabited when we arrived, and we made an effort to wipe the indigenous race out. Our politicians have always spoken of democracy, and the need to uphold and fight for it. Yet our country is not democratic, and never was intended to be. It is a republic, with representatives. The conversation winds down. Every era said about the past, "but aren't we lucky all that is over!" Only, it never ended.

"Well, guys, nice talking to you, but it's been a long day for me and I need to rest. Got a big day coming up tomorrow."

The night security guy walks by on his rounds as I get ready for bed. "Hi Miles. Have a good day today? Looked like your booth was busy whenever I came by. I still have my eye on the wolf claw with the opal on top. If it is still there at the end, maybe I'll get it."

"Yes, had a good day. I'll set that necklace aside and we can work something out. I can give you a wholesale price or something." My prices are not set in stone, often not even marked. I can get my work into hands I choose to, those I think deserve something, or earned it, in my opinion. So no, we are not equal. Maybe we are created equal off the starting block. But deeds, what it is we do with our lives, can determine what happens to us. With this in mind, I simply want to be among the protected. I like to think I contribute and do my part.

I am able to check my emails at the fair office. I think my Russian friend Tatiana is moving on with her plans and life. This is fine. She's a bit young to see as a life partner. *Or more I am a bit old, ha!* She had spoken about her family, her mother who is sick and no way to help her, and hinted she wishes to be able to help her mother if she leaves. There had been talk with friends to be careful on the internet with young pretty Russians wanting to become US citizens with Americans who had money (marry, then dump them). I do not have money! Ha!

I was glad to have met her. She has sent pictures I think are amazing. Ducks on ponds that look exactly like where I live! Same ducks, same plants growing. There had been a picture of her with her friends, her with her coworkers, doing church scenery on a wall, expressions on the girls easy to recognize. The jokester, the serious, the covered in paint, the dainty one. Human. Normal. Like if I were there, we would laugh about the same things, and feel the same about our art and purpose. I see the picture of her at home with her mother and the cat. The furniture, the way the cat sits on the lap, the way everyone dresses, is all very human. I can smile and guess what each is thinking, even the cat! Ha! *I could be comfortable here,* I think.

I can see how the internet will open the world in new ways. Governments will not be able to easily stop people of the world from meeting. Discovering each other. Finding out people in other countries are not monsters just because they are different, or our government says so. I smile at this woman fondly, and wave a happy good bye through cyberspace as she disappears from my life, along with hundreds of others I have met by mail and internet over the years.

WHILE I AM in Fairbanks I head over to a couple of shops where I have art on consignment. At the Yukon Quest store, Phil is working today. He is my connection there. "Miles, glad you came in. Fish and Game showed up here and had me pull the bear claws you had here for sale" I'm shocked. He gets the claws out. I see them; they are not bear claws, but wolf claws, perfectly legal to sell. But Phil is all agitated, telling me he does not need any problems in his shop with illegal stuff! Considering not carrying any of my stuff at all. "Who needs the government breathing down your neck!"

I explain I am puzzled. "These wolf claws should be no problem. I wonder if the agent does not know wolf from bear, or is yanking my chain harassing me or what. Trying to put me out of business?"

"The agents name is Bob Hunter."

I write it down. I call. He is not in, but I explain what happened, and talk like I assume it is an honest mistake. I'm polite, asking if someone could please straighten it out at the shop so the claws can get put back out, and I can continue good relations at the shop and conduct my legal business.

"Sure, sure, sorry, we'll get right on it!" But nothing ever comes of it. The store will not carry my stuff. Whatever I have to say is irrelevant compared to what the law officers say. As far as the store is concerned, I pulled a fast one on them, tried to sneak in bear claws illegally, calling them wolf. Will they then spread the word around town? Is Fish and Game just too busy and 'forgot,' or is this harassment? What would it take to find out? I'm going to go to the government and make accusations? Me and who else? Been there and done that.

Sell other things? Like what? It took a lot of years to be the tooth and claw guy. I have the connections, the knowledge, the customer base. It's what sells. Anyone can sell 'rocks,' but who has connections for stuff like wild sheep horns, wolf claws and such? Anyhow. Whatever. A thorn in my side. Bothersome, but not devastating.

"Miles, why are you always out there waving a red flag at the bull, pushing the legal line, testing where the fence is?"

"Um… because someone has to do it?" Hmm "Um, because it's a personality type?" I have no adequate answer. Many walk away shaking their heads. Maybe I am too used to being wild and free. All those years alone in the pucker brush with no boss, no tyrant, no rules but my own, and I got spoiled? Maybe remembering how I was raised in another time, and not keeping up with the changes? Raised in a time when personal freedom mattered most. When a guy's home was his castle, and unless you were bothering someone else seriously, you got left alone. When we had a Bill of Rights and a Constitution? Days I will not let go of? *Give me freedom or give me death!* Days like that? Or, if you believe in something, you need to stand up for it. Who knows?

I forget the bad stuff. *Ignore the bleating sheep!* "Yeah!" I imitate a sheep, "Master, master over here! One of the sheep is looking over the fence, quick come stop him, I'm worried and afraid!" Me and I wave our hands in a concerned homosexual way laughing. New customers compliment me, look up to me for my lifestyle. I get brave again, and want to stand up for my rights and all that.

I have an appointment to meet Seymour, my survey boss, at Crafty's shop. I'm here passing the time thinking. Seymour lives in Manley Hot Spring about a five hour drive away, but like me, this is where he comes and gets his supplies. I pass by the Hot Springs with my boat all the time. We have another wilderness survey job ahead of us. I have not heard the details yet. We feel like we do specialty work. Remote, hard to get to places. I'm not sure yet if this job requires my boat or his float plane. Seymour shows up, and once again I think how he looks like John Lennon. Same glasses, same hair style, same purposeful stride, with the long legs.

"So what's up Seymour, good to see you!" I feel like we are two hit men working for the mob, about to discuss our contract. We step out the door and pause, both look to the right, look to the left. In the truck, getting ready to hear the details of the hit.

"Your back OK, Miles?"

Yeah, the last job we got a helicopter ride to the LZ, like James Bond, by a Vietnam War pilot, who liked to fly full speed just over the tree tops. He thought we'd be scared. We only smiled. He tried to be careful, but seeing us smile, he did his usual stuff. At one with his machine, dodging treetops, then straight down over the cliff. Safer than getting shot at, but not what the public would be used to.

"Not as good as I used to be, but you said this job was not a lot of saw work, just some remote village locations?"

"Ya.' We've done it before. Gravel volume survey in Tanana." I get to climb over a gravel pile in a grid while he shoots the locations with a laser that gets recorded in a computer program. Piece of cake. For $28 an hour. About five times minimum wage. "We need to stop at the Surveyor Exchange for materials." It's common just before a job to go here to get corner posts, trail ribbon, and odds and ends.

SEYMOUR IS CHATTING UP FRONT. I am looking around elsewhere. My ears perk up when I overhear two other surveyors buying stuff too. One is saying: "Darnedest thing happened. On a job at Fort Yukon. We were short handed and wanted some local hire in this remote Native village."

Other guy replies: "Yeah! Local hire in the villages is part of most contracts these days. Hard to find local reliable skilled labor, huh?"

"Exactly! This kid comes up to us. Of all things he has a plumb bob. Now why would some Indian village teen have a dang surveyor plumb bob?" My minds wanders to old memories from years ago, golden oldies, knock out nifties of the past...

Past Flash

Seymour and I are surveying a road in Fort Yukon. We fly into the remote bush village in Seymour's plane. Elite team sent in to do the impossible...as usual. A village of log cabins, dirt roads with no connection to the outsides world; not much civilization going on. No place to stay, no place to eat. No white people but us.

I'm in the middle of the main road concentrating on holding the plumb bob over a spike. Seymour is measuring a distance to me with a laser (EDM we call it). A village Native kid, about eight years old strolls up to me, looking like he owns the street. I'm annoyed. He's in the way. Bothering me. Asking stupid questions. I almost tell him to get lost. The WC Fields routine. I guessed this was not going to work. It might even make problems. He's Native, I'm white, this is a Native village. He's probably related to everyone here, including the guy who hired us to survey. The kid is belligerent, looking for trouble. If Fort Yukon had a street gang, he'd be in it.

"Hey kid. Aren't you supposed to be in school or something?" *As in hint, hint, don't you belong someplace else?*

He drawls, "Naw. Not going today. Don't feel like it. Waste of time."

Uh-huh. No use telling this kid much. He's made up his mind. Adults are stupid. Parents probably drunks, no food in the house, and he's street wise. Seems smart, bored, and sees no future here, and nothing he can do about it. I feel for him, but not enough to care to do anything. It's a cruel world, and some will make it, and some not. He's nobody to me. Just in the way, bothering me. He's the walking dead, so I ignore him.

"So what-cha you doing here? Why are you standing here in the road staring at that string?" His tone is that of someone sizing me up, to see if I can be rolled.

I try to explain what 'surveying' is. In the village it is common to get the comment and question, 'Is it still there? Ha, ha!' Getting paid to locate a road everyone knows is there, is a cool scam, all right. I explain there is a guy down the road he can't see, looking through a telescope thing that has a laser. This guy you can't see is shooting a beam of light you cannot see, called 'infra red,' into this little mirror on the string. The light bounces back to Seymour. The instrument measures how long that light takes to get back and knows from this, how far away I am. As in, down to the width of this string.

The look on the kid's face tells it all. Even to me as I explain it, this sounds like the most ridiculous line of lame crap anyone could tell. Who can really understand it? Who even knows what light is? Traveling at 186,000 miles a second, and some instrument is really going to time it over a quarter mile and know to the nearest thousandth of an inch where the reflector is? *Top scientists cannot tell us what light is!* Ha! If it's all Greek to me, imagine how it looks through the eyes of this village kid? Even experts can't tell you if light is a wave or a particle. His expression tells it all. I can't make up a better story than that? It's right out of science fiction. I smile. I decide I'm going to have fun and mess with this kid. Or more like give this kid one chance to get it. Like in a country song I heard. Guy's woman is leaving him. He wants to know why, and she says, 'You got five minutes, to figure it out!'

I'm only going to say it once. I'm not the kid's parents, this is not my community. I'm on the payroll, I'm going to be gone in ten minutes, forever. So I sigh and explain it to the kid. Quick and dirty. "Ok kid, can you keep a secret? I just came through a wormhole. I'm from the future. We are on a mission. We are here to retrieve something that got left behind on a previous visit from our planet."

Kid goes: "Yeah, right! You think I'm stupid?"

About the exact attitude as when I tried to explain what a laser is. It's all Star Trek stuff off the TV, science fiction. I shrug my shoulders like I could care less if he believes me or not.

He says, "Hey, that's cool, what you did with that string!" I had just flipped the plumb bob up and into its sheath after Seymour told me he got the shot over the radio. No big deal. Seymour will be setting his back sight now, so I have some time before he moves up with the equipment. I figure I'll have fun with the kid. What the heck. I'm bored too.

"The string? It's a plumb bob, kid. The most important part of my job. Let me teach ya.' It's important. First ya' got to learn to stand right. Like a cowboy about to draw a gun, like this" And I show him. "You got to take out the plumb bob without looking, like this." I do it slow without looking. "Then you spin it over your finger like so, and let it drop, but stop it just before it hits the ground without looking. Like this" I stop it and the brass pointy weight hangs suspended without moving. He's impressed. "Here kid you try it" He thinks it is cool to let him try. "You need lots of practice, but that's the basic move. You got to speed it up eventually, like this!"

In one fluid motion I spin it back in the sheath like a gun after a shoot out. I stand like a gunslinger waiting for the draw. Fingers twitching. With that special bored look, that look you might practice in a mirror to get it just right. I make sure the kid sees this is all important, how you stand, how you move. It's all about moves. The blade of grass in my mouth shifts just so. Like John Wayne. Talk slow. Shove your hat back to be ready. Build up the tension. Till just about when everyone looking is about to bust. Without a flinch, faster than the eye can see, there is a 'swish,' and the plumb bob is out, dropped, and over the nail in the road without spinning.

The kid just goes, "Wow!" and his eyes bug out.

Just like a movie star. I tell him again it's called a plumb bob. It's a cool toy and I can see he wishes he had one.

"It's more than a toy, kid." I tell him. "So what we came here for is about three feet under this road, right here under this nail."

The kid tells me: "I was born here, right across the street." He turns and points to a rundown hundred year old log shed with the door off its hinges. "My grandfather was here before that, and there is nothing under this road. No way anyone put anything under this road."

I know it is here because it was put here in 1916. The metal detector found it. I'm called the chain-man. I'm the first man on the ground running point. Sniffing out surveyor spoor sometimes a hundred years old. Doing the impossible. Reading notes, looking for marks on ancient trees. The one who greets the bears. The one who arrives before there is a path. Where I go, everyone else follows. The line forms behind me. The most important job to all civilization. A God among mortals. But what will the kid know about such things?

"It's here. It has symbols on it, about this big." I show him with my hands. "Made of shiny metal from my planet. There will be an 'x' and some numbers in each corner. We need to read the numbers. We cannot leave without the numbers. It's the coordinates for the Star Gate that gets us back to our time." I tell him very matter-of-factly. I'm not trying to impress him, or con him. He does not believe me, so I grab the shovel and hand it to him. "Go ahead, dig, and see for yourself." He half-ass digs, knowing there will be nothing there, but he's bored, and for some reason I want a hole here, and he goes along with the con to get him to dig for me.

Tink. He hits metal. I just yawn. He digs like crazy and I casually look in the hole with elaborate nonchalance.

"Uh-huh, yup." The kid's mouth is hanging open. He is ready to believe. *Seek and ye shall find.* He is ready now to go through the Star Gate. I am Obi Wan Kenobi. He is the grasshopper.

"Tell your parents you want a plumb bob. Practice the moves like I showed you. Tell me what is it you are going to ask for?"

He says "Plumb bob" in the same tone of voice as if he was going to ask for Darth Vader's evil sword of light.

I tell it straight. "Practice with it every day. Count how many times you can do it right. When you get to 10,000, call me. Here's my phone number where I get messages when I'm on earth. Maybe I can get you a job with us. I'm not sure you can decompress going through the Gate, sometimes it makes your nose bleed, but we'll worry about that later. Oh, and keep it a secret, between us, don't blow my cover. We have to retrieve this message and leave without any problems." He nods his head dumbly.

Pretty much the last I ever saw of the kid. Seymour shows up and it's time to work, no room for a kid hanging around. I forgot about him, just another kid in another village. One seed of many. **Past flash ends**

Now, years later, here I am at the Survey Exchange in Fairbanks with Seymour. Another surveyor is here getting bearing tree tags like us. I overhear,

"Never saw the likes of it. We were looking for local hire, like a saw man, and this teen Indian from the village comes up to us, and of all things he has a plumb bob! Go figure! Darnedest thing. He stands like some kind of gun fighter, and without looking, draws that thing so smooth, and it stops just before it hits the ground and never moves. I never saw anyone that good. Like a movie star or something. Where would he ever learn a thing like that? Truly gifted. We hired him right there on the spot. Hell of a kid. Thinking of sending him off for some classes and hiring him permanent. Kid like that hasn't got much of a chance in a village. Be a whole new world for him here, almost another planet, in another time."

I never said anything. Kid probably forgot my name, lost my number. Just a fluke I ever heard anything. *Huh.* Yeah, "Huh." Makes me wonder about other conversations, and what effect it has I never hear about. These thoughts are interrupted by 'life' present time, the real world, of making a living, and getting the bills paid. Not always much time for reflection.

Seymour is speaking, "We need some bearing tree tags for a small side job. Should be no cutting. Total job about three days." I nod, as the boss tells me, "You can boat to Manley and meet me there. You will pick up some of the heavy stuff we need. I will fly to Tanana and meet you there with the plane. We may need the boat to get around to the back side of the village where the gravel pile is."

I understand from past jobs there is a discrepancy we need to work out between two parties. Villages often sell gravel. Sometimes a private person sells to the village, or the village sells to a company putting a road in. Each truck load of gravel is worth a lot of money. Someone is buying it by the truck load. A disagreement comes up as to just how many truck loads did you say you delivered? That is where we come in. We can tell you to the nearest truck load how much got delivered. Thousands of dollars are at stake here.

Looks like I get boat rental as well as salary. Getting paid for having fun, or doing what I like to do, is how I have tried to arrange my life. How much better can life get than to be paid for running a river boat past your favorite fishing spot? *Hey, hey, hey, smarter than the average bear!* Seymour gives me a ride all the way to Nenana, fifty miles, since I do not drive. He's a good guy to work for. Nice of him not to comment about how much out of the way, and how much time this is, driving me home. That's an extra two -three hours of his time. My boat is tied up at tenth Street on the Nenana River, right at the mouth where it goes into the Tanana River.

The trip to Manley is about 100 miles, then another eighty miles to Tanana. I may stop on the way back to go up the Kantishna and check on the homestead. I could also keep going past Tanana and make a trip looking for mammoth tusks. There is a miner whose claim I can look for ivory on. I haven't decided yet. Much depends on what the weather does, how the job goes, how my back holds up. I have to remain adaptable. I load eighty gallons of gas in the boat. I can use the truck with fifty-five gallon drums in the back, and siphon direct into fifteen gallon containers in the boat[1] There is a permanent thirty gallon fuel tank I run off of. Usually the fuel tank is a day's worth of running. I'll burn about three gallons an hour. But as much as five gallons an hour. A boat does not slide on the water as easily as a car tire rolls on a road, so there is a bigger difference in fuel economy, depending how the boat slides. A dented bottom or weeds on the bottom can affect mileage by a gallon an hour. How I load the boat, how I trim, what pitch propeller I have, and if the propeller has a chip or bent blade effects my fuel consumption a lot.

Moving the full fifteen gallon containers is slow and hard with my still healing back. I sigh. I could at one time in my life lift a fifty- five gallon drum of gas. 380 pounds. Now I struggle with 100 pounds. That's discouraging. Guess I'm lucky to have a back at all. Some back operations result in, well, less than satisfactory results. It takes me a whole day to get ready to go, when it used to take me an hour.

I have some outdated emails to review, sort, file and figure out what to do with. Trying to remember what ever happened to this Wilderness Rose? Do I owe her a reply, or was it she who stopped writing me? I review the contact.

Original Message Follows—

Subject: hi
18:31:56 -0700
Sounds like we have some things in common if you want to email me.
This is a copy of my profile:
I'm a lady who loves the country life. I live in a cabin out in the country. I love the

fresh air and the sound of a creek running through. I work at a second hand store and volunteer at my church's clothing/food bank/thrift shop. I like to sit out on my front porch and listen to the sounds of the night. I like thrifting. I have a great personality and am a very friendly mother of three teens. I'm also 4'11" HWP have long light brown hair and hazel eyes.

AGE: 49

My reply :

Hello Wilderness Flower. Yup maybe things in common? Cept I do not know what 'HWP' stands for (House Wife with Pimples?). I have been working summers and able to be more free in winter for the past few years. I'm a wilderness land surveyor with a friend. I'm just the chain-man but we travel to remote villages all summer and it pays well. I like garage sales, thrift stores, and making my own things, hardly ever get things new-like clothes. I have a web site if you would like to visit; has pictures, a bio, my art and links to my village home page which I created. Hope to hear from you.

Email ends

There are some other emails from other women. *Hmmm. Oh well. Time to head out on the river.* "Yeah, time to go." Letters get saved in a folder. I realize the 'stuff' I now have in the computer would fill a house full of file cabinets. Ha! It all fits in this little computer box. How? Amazing!

Mammoth tusk in frozen cliff.

CHAPTER FOUR

WILDERNESS RIVER TRIP SURVEY JOB, BUNNY HUGGER WOMAN, MOOSE HUNT

I'm lucky the weather is fine. Blue sky without a cloud. In some places the reflection on the river is as clear as its image above the shoreline. Which is the reflection? There is a stop at the mouth of the Kantishna to see if there are any pike in the clear water at Rock Creek. If there are, I usually know within a cast or two if it is worth spending more time. This is the place I stash gas for the return trip. It is worth leaving a fifteen gallon tank. That's 100 pounds I do not have to haul with me. Gas is siphoned into my running tank as I cast for fish. Three nice pike are caught in the time it takes to siphon gas and eat a snack. The fish are cleaned in the creek. There are fresh otter tracks in the mud, so assume the guts I leave will be found and eaten.

Coming up on the Tolovana Roadhouse, I look towards the wide crossing. The Road House is empty now. Until the late 1960s, it was used as an overnight stopping place for the mail carriers running sled dogs in winter. A friend bought it and got a grant to fix it up as a historical site. He takes people out on dog mushing trips from Nenana in winter, but so far has not been spending summers here. It is a marker for me, a place to know I can stop in if I am having problems.

As I begin the crossing, I see someone like me about to enter the shallow part of the crossing. It looks to me like they are reading the water wrong and will not make it through where they choose to go. It is not a huge big deal to touch bottom as the river is silt, not rocks. Sucking mud up into the cooling system through the water pump is not great, and running aground and getting stuck is no fun, but better than hitting rocks like in some rivers! Going slow means less danger to the boat and engine, but the boat sinks more in the water going slow. So speed = traveling higher on the water. A trade off with slow = more safe.

"Blam rrrrrrrrrrr- sputter, sputter...silence" The sound of someone who did not make it through. I slow and get within hollering distance. Someone I sort of know from downriver but can't put a name to the face. This guy is alone with a load about like mine drawing about as much water. He gets free by pushing off the shallows with a paddle. He is about to give up, figuring he cannot get through. I think there is a way, so I motor around in a big loop and wave to this guy to follow me. Not much risk to him, as if we cannot get through, it is me who will hit first and he can just watch and not get stuck.

I circle back around to make sure my unconscious has left my body and is out there in front of the boat giving me a depth reading. The driver of the boat behind me is yelling,

"There's no water, we can't get through here. I think we have to turn around!"

I pay no attention as, in a trance I tune in on my unconscious messages, *nine inches, nine inches, coming up on a ten-er, we got eleven, closing on eleven, with a lock, a mark," I memorize the spot. And back to nine...* Still on step I complete the circle around as my unconscious talks nonstop with information about speed, engine rpm, water depth, bottom condition... *See it?* The shimmer on the water. The eye of the needle, I see it, but don't bother to respond. I'm taking a dangerous side slip in the nineteen foot Carolina Skiff; fifty horse Merc screaming in my ear, trying to keep an eye on the water pattern. The channel is as wide as my boat that wanders through a crossing, stagnant as a lake. I count the engine rpms, which helps me know water depth. As the prop struggles to pull water, the resistance of the water crossing the bottom, drags the engine. It's the same with airplanes I'm told; as they approach land, it's called 'ground effect.' The change is only a few rpm per thousand, but I feel it through my hands on the wheel. "4950--4951..."

The boat behind turns with me, thinking I've given up and we are turning back. I pay no attention, as I complete the circle to tackle Caribou Crossing. I watch the surface of the water, watching—waiting for a sign, keeping an eye on my wake, catching the change in wake pattern that tells me the shape of the bottom. I wait for the word from my unconscious, as rpm increases with throttle 'peddle to the metal' guzzling nine gallons of fuel an hour. I have a heavy load that is hard to get on step, and as I circled, the boat has lost plane. Now that I have a straight shot, the nose of the skiff slowly comes down. Rpm's increase as we climb up the water and flatten out. We are committed now to the crossing. If I miss the slot in the bottom of the river, it will likely cost me my engine lower unit, over $1,500. Probably not cost my life, but I could get stuck high and dry to where it takes a day to get off. I still don't see the slot, but I'm confident I will.

Trim! I repeat "Trim!" To the man at the helm. I trim, and the sound of the water on the hull changes along with the rpm and speed. My unconscious reads off the depth to the nearest fraction of an inch below the prop. We aren't in the shallows yet. I have to be hydroplaning before we hit the crossing. *Six inches, six inches, five and a half-six inches.* I feel the rpm through my fingertips, *We have hydro plane.* I calmly say out loud, "Of course" Followed immediately by *Crossing.* We had a whole inch to spare, not even a close call. If we hit the crossing below warp speed, we could kiss it all good bye. Only at warp can we run this shallow. If we reach hydroplane and miss the eye of the needle, we are moving fast enough to send the boat 100 feet up on a sandbar. There is only one way to make it, and that's to go for it at warp speed.

There is a pause as my unconscious holds my breath. At hydroplane there is no longer the sound of the hull on the water. I can steer by leaning my body. The wind holds me back in my seat, waters my eyes, and sucks my breath away, as the inches of water below drop away, knowing the water will be there, enough, just enough…*one inch under an inch; half inch.* The ground effect flattens the boat, as rpms redline, flatter and flatter, till only the prop touches the water. Like sonar—*contact coming up.* We touch the bottom, bump the bottom, but I know there's enough water to make it. It would be easy to panic, back off, and 'lose it,' bite the big one. It takes a certain insanity to do this.

I hand watercolor all my envelopes to everyone, even my bills.

The people who make these boats and motors say it's impossible to run a prop that's over 11 inches in diameter in water less than six inches deep. I'm glad I'd already done it before I asked. Interior Alaska river rats run an annual race called 'The Yukon 800.' A race 800 miles through the wilderness. For twenty years, outsiders, specifically engine manufacturers, told us it wasn't possible to attain sixty-five miles an hour with a fifty horse engine. We shrugged our shoulders 'whatever,' and ran our race. We designed our own boat with 'air traps' long before anyone else ever heard of them. The guy who won it more times than anyone else is a friend in Nenana. One thing we understand, is boats and water. Speeds increase to over eighty miles an hour.

I hope the moose hunter is behind me. I'd told him to follow exactly in my track, and not be out by as much as a foot. I slide left, I slide right, I get readings in the fraction of an inch below the prop. *two...three...five...Leveling out at six,* We are through the crossing. I feel the engine back off of red line a few rpms, as the water pump gasps on sand. The shimmer of the water changes to that faint 'shimmer, shimmer' where the current starts to come in from the main channel around the Island. Like the beaver in the swamp that leaves a trail of disturbed leaves behind, long after Mr. beaver swam past. I spot a trail in the water—*Barge half an hour ahead of us.* "Yup." The barge has left a trail in the water and I feel it, but do not know how. I think a slight flat spot in the current.

The moose hunter following me, comes up alongside to yell, "How'd you do that!? How'd you know where the water was? I spent an hour here with a pole and couldn't find a channel!"

I shrug my shoulders and think. How does one explain to civilized people, the world of instinct, gut feeling, leaving your body. It's all a bunch of nonsense. I smile, remembering the days before I could read water.[1] "Experience" I reply.

I started out my first ten years of boating at ten miles an hour with a sixteen foot boat and twenty horse motor. I spent the first 10,000 miles going five to ten miles an hour learning. I'd put the nose into every sandbar there was, ease off, and try again. Like this guy, I'd come to a place like this, stop my motor, tilt it up, get a pole out, and even then, give up in frustration. Then some old timer would come along at sixty-five miles an hour, usually a member of the Burke family. Sometimes Dim, sometimes Moonshine, laughing at me as they'd zoom by and get through. I'd follow and try to fathom what they are seeing, and wonder why they swerved this way and that across an unreadable surface. I assumed they were crazy.

I've never got hurt on the river, and never been so high and dry in the shallows I couldn't easily get off. I don't see myself as taking foolish chances. Anyhow, after twenty years, and wearing out five engines, anyone with the aptitude would know how to read water. One day I knew I had arrived. Yes. *I was goosing my steeds into a tight sideslip turn. I could hear all fifty horses whinny, glad to be alive, manes flying through a shortcut, twisty shallow slough of the Tanana. Up ahead I came upon the Burkes stuck on a sandbar.* I smile, remembering. There was Pat, Weedz, and Dim. To miss hitting them, I had to take the boat over a log. The boat would make it, but the propeller would not. I slowed, went into a side slip, leaned the boat enough the edge digs in the water, which gives the boat a lean. Now the prop is higher. The prop clears the log and I drop the boat back down. I come to a stop next to the Burkes. They'd missed the eye of the needle by two feet.

I calmly tilted my hat back, "Need any help?" All mouths hung open. Course back in those days, I was a cocky arrogant punk kid! (Said with a proud grin). As ability goes, I'm only about average. I have a little too much flash-dash and razzle-dazzle to be the best, or impress anyone in the know. Many Nenana river rats could teach me a thing or two, but there are no secrets here, and everyone knows I'm not the listening type, and at least half the time I'm full of salmon giz. (Thinking I'm Indiana Jones). I shrug my shoulders. Pobody's Nerfect.

The river, the wilderness, a small community, this lifestyle, it's in your blood or it's not. That's not what 'all this' is about. (The wilderness life). It's the hairs on the back of your neck standing up when a Yukon 800 boat goes by, or stopping what you're doing when the swans fly over. It's the simple things, like checking fish nets in the rain, eating moose jerky by an open fire in the frosty fall, northern lights over-head. It's hanging out at the local cafe, listening to Buster talk about the best way to carve Diamond Willow, realizing the reason the mechanic shop across the street is 'closed' is because the owner decided to go fishing today. Nobody's in any special hurry, and you can run your business as you want. Maybe it's running into Martha at the post office, getting caught up on the latest gossip, but really, everyone knows 'the little cabin' has the best gossip in town. For some, it is a chance to be a big fish in a little pond, or a good place to do nothing at all, lost in a back eddy—the main current of civilization a long ways away. Many come here after some dream or other. Some achieve the dream, others had to come to terms with their shortcomings, and stayed anyway. For 'River Rats,' it's threading the needle through Caribou Crossing, with God as your copilot. You have 'arrived' when you don't ask 'why,' or 'how' anymore. When you realize this is your life, this is your home, and these are your people. You don't have to explain it to anyone.

I sigh, guess I am feeling more like part of the community now. *Is that safe?* To care, I mean. In a world where you cannot depend on anyone but yourself? I wonder as I run the river. Yes, this river guy was glad I helped him through, but he wondered how I knew where to go.

"It's called a high Jesus factor" as the quick easy one liner reply that doesn't say anything, and ends the conversation.

I meet Seymour in Manley. As he said earlier, I'm to meet him in the river community Tanana tomorrow morning. He will fly his plane, and I will boat the bulk of the equipment. There are no roads to this village. This allows me to camp at

Fish Creek, one of my favorite stops along the way. There is even a certain tree that hangs over the bank I tie to each time I am here. There is the same flat spot against the river bank between two trees where my tent fits. Before I do anything else, I cut wood for a camp fire, and get that going. In this way, no matter what I do next, if I get cold or tired I have a warm fire. A nice bed of coals is one secret to controlled cooking of food.

Once the fire is going, and my bow saw hung up, I get out my tent, sleeping bag and camp gear. Setting up the tent is the next project. If the wind comes up, a rain squall, or any weather issue, I can dive in the tent. I also need to verify I have a usable tent so I can choose other options if I discover my zipper is broken, or the tent got moldy or torn since I last used it. I can decide to leave and press on, or build a simple shelter of some kind with a tarp and brush. I need to verify my sleeping bag is dry, and that I have the other basics for a good camp. If weather looks nasty, I sometimes choose to put the tarp up over the tent with poles and rope as the tent is lightweight and sheds minor rain, but will not stay dry in a serious downpour. If anything touches the tent, the rain will come in this spot where it is touched.

Necessities go in the tent where I can find them, in a specific order and spot. This holds the tent down instead of tent pegs. I have a self-supporting dome tent with fiberglass poles. I turn the entrance to face the water and my boat, so at any time in the night I can look out and check on the boat. Also if a bear visits, nine out of ten times he will approach from the river. I get my pots and pans out for a meal. Fresh water from the creek is one reason to camp here. I now have a canvas folding chair I carry in the boat that saves having to find the right log to feel comfortable sitting on. A fresh fish is cooked with rice, and dry turnip leaves are added, along with pepper and garlic. Crackers and peanut butter on the side, with hot powder drink mix. I relax as I eat. The entire process between stopping the boat and sitting here eating, takes only half an hour.

The boat is looked over before going to bed, to make sure everything is put away that might get wet in the rain. A five gallon plastic bucket with a lid goes under the steering console with many items I need when running the river. Dry gloves, snacks, a flashlight, window scraper, a map—things like this are in the bucket where I can grab them up without stopping. In the tent I put a flashlight in the same spot each time so I can find it, along with a pee jar. My clothes are laid out exactly the same each time so I can find everything easily. There is a stocking cap and sweater if I get chilly in the night.

A bald eagle has been sitting on a dead tree branch watching me make camp all evening. This must be a good spot for the eagle to catch fish. He shifts from one foot to the other quietly scowling at me. I know well enough the eagle is not happy with me here. I do not need scientific proof. I frown as I get in the tent, thinking of the raven expert putting me down as a teller of tall tales, not to be listened to. No proof animals or birds have feelings, or know how to think, reason, or work together. *If I only pretend to interact with nature and wildlife, so what. It seems a cold, pointless world without jokes, laughter, and interaction with my surroundings. It could indeed all be an illusion. Maybe life with people is too! Just an illusion.*

In the morning a grouse flies up and startles me as I stick my head out of the tent. *Darn I could be eating him for breakfast!* I watch the bird go across the creek and out of sight. Sometimes a grouse will stop and land on a branch and feel safe. I have left over fish for breakfast after a quick fire, then put some hot fish rice mix in my thermos for later if I need a hot snack. I am only two hours or so away from where I met up with Seymour.

SEYMOUR COULD LAND his floatplane on the river. He decided instead to fly with wheels and land on the Tanana runway, because he can haul more wight in the wheeled plane. The runway is next to the river so it is easy to meet him and transfer the load as he ties up his plane off the runway. This a normal routine for us.

Seymour and I decide to camp out instead of staying in the village. Sitting around the camp fire waiting for dinner to cook, we talk. "Miles, I'm thinking of retiring in about two years. You and I have been at this a lot of years now. Eve and I have been saving our money and could live off the interest in a couple of years," He has told me previously he expects to have $200,000 in savings.

"I guess that works out for me as well. I have wondered for years if my art work could support me. I have never had time to give it my full attention, with us working off and on all summer. That's the tourist season for selling art. It's a little scary to go for it on my own with no back up. But my back injury was a wakeup call in a sense." I explain how Seymour has always said our job is like being in the Olympics or something. Very physical. "Well here we are at fifty years old, and this work is for the young. I could push myself till I drop. End up wore out and broke in five years. Or I can pace myself, and be healthy, and stretch my health out for another twenty years."

"Hard to change lifestyles, Miles." Seymour has said this before. He thinks I'd have a tough time without the extra funds from surveying; I'm not sure myself. He implies I could not make it selling my crafts, that's wishful thinking. We both know a lot of broke artists. Over 90% seem to be hobby artists, not depending on the money. Yet I also know it would be foolish to think I can live forever running a chain saw for a living. I'm lucky enough I have had twenty or more years doing this without an injury, till my back gave out. No saw injury. Never wanted to wear the safety stuff either. Gets in the way, makes me hot, tired, and that makes me accident prone. I admit I am an odd build; short, short legs and arms, big biceps and calves, large muscular chest. Very few clothes and very few safety devices fit. Wearing those chaps on a job where it was mandatory contributed to my accident, in my opinion. Chaps were a good six inches too long. I was stepping on them, tripping on them, to where they rode on my hips and lower back.

Being 'safe' to me, is mostly keeping your wits about you, not working when exhausted. I have never worn a life jacket in my boat. Nor safety goggles anywhere on any job. I stretched barb wire as a kid on my first job on a ranch I was sent to at fifteen, and never wore gloves. I stand before you, as healthy as any man, well, my back had nothing to do with any of that. I recall when 'safe' was a personal issue, not a legal, government issue. I recall the first change – drivers and passengers being ordered to wear seat belts. At first 'asked'; at first 'suggested.' At first a lot of statistics shown us about how much more safe you will be. But then mandatory. Arguing it affects us all because it affects insurance rates. Creating public anger towards those selfish folks who want to make up their own mind and not be ordered by the government. Same with smoking. I still consider this a personal choice and none of my business. Or yours. Same with drinking. *It is only my business if your behavior effects me. It is the behavior that is the issue, not the drink, the smoke, the beliefs, the gun.*

"This is the government, we're here to help!" Seymour and I laugh. "Could you imagine Tarzan in knee pads, a helmet, all decked out in safety equipment swinging from vines? Or Indiana Jones or Rambo or Clint Eastwood or Crocodile Dundee or…" Seymour is silent, which means he does not agree. He believes in 'safe.' It's one reason he believes in the sure thing and putting all his money in the bank with guaranteed interest. I think nothing is guaranteed safe. Not even banks[2]. "If I had 200 grand like you do Seymour, the last place I'd put it is in the bank. It pays how much interest? I can take that kind of money and double it in a year." I do not say much to prove that, but the numbers show me that money I invest, I double and triple fast. No, not the stock market! I buy moose antler from the locals for $3 a pound, and in a week sell it for $6 a pound, or hang on to it and retail if for up to $10 a pound, and it's gone within a year. I can buy fossil walrus ivory in about any amount I have money for at $30 a pound and sell it all at $50 a pound in a few days. I just do not have the capital to make big time deals. Still, my business is growing fast. My annual income is doubling every year, and has been for a bunch of years.

I started at two grand a year. It took hanging out in civilization. Next year was four grand, next year was eight, this year is sixteen grand, and no reason it should not double this next year. I understand that making money is like pushing a bullet through the air. It is not hard to go from 400 feet a second to 800 feet a second and then 1600 feet a second by adding more gunpowder. After about 2,000 feet a second, there is a point of diminishing return. You double the accelerant or force applied and only gain a few hundred feet a second increased speed; the rest of the energy is consumed in friction and heat. Faster, faster. This is a maximum at about 3,500 feet a second. I do not think it is possible to reach 4,000. In theory, till supposedly you approach the speed of light and pour in infinite energy trying to go faster, but gain no speed. *Making money cost money, with more and more friction and heat. Till at some point you burn up and gain nothing, even start slowing down.*

Seymour brings me back with a question. "Miles, your lifestyle is changing now that you are in Nenana! How is it going?"

He is getting a feel for my ability to retire along with him, and if I will be ok. He does not want to leave me in the lurch, and wishes to change the subject now. 'Safe' and 'money' are big topics when discussing retirement. I'm not putting Seymour down for not sharing my views. It is nice to hear a different perspective. We show respect for each other.

I explain how some things have not changed a whole lot. I still do not drive. I still spend about $300 a year on food. I still produce about a plastic bag of garbage a year. I have still never paid for a haircut, have no credit card. The thrift stores and garage sales are still where I buy everything I need. Or dump or transfer station. I like to recycle. Even my craft business is made from 90% other people's garbage. Teeth, claws, horns, bones are so valued in civilization, but in the village, they are garbage acquired at dumps. Beaver teeth and moose leg bones I get from dog racers' dog yards!

"Foods ready, let's eat!" Macaroni with chili dumped over it, all we can eat. His wife no longer makes her special sauce for us. I do not comment. Less time and energy these days, I assume.

We sit on tree stumps by an open fire, our tents set up in the background. Seymour is a little worried, so will stay up late going over the numbers for our job and getting ready for tomorrow. I have no worries. I usually drop right off to sleep. So which of us is richer? Seymour has his airplanes, his nice home, and a fat bank account. I admit that is pretty nice. But is it worth the price? Seymour worries much more than I do. I have memories of my father struggling hard to get ahead. Guessing we all have to come up with priorities and our own answers! Anyhow, I'm off to sleep. The Pic coil I burned in the tent to kill the mosquitoes has dissipated enough for me to go in and get out of a buggy environment.

We have our usual, "How many mosquitoes can you kill in one swat?' He won with forty- six. All squished on his knee. We did not kill any squirrels this evening. Our powerful pistols are handy though, just in case. We are dying to test out our latest rounds. Eve got Seymour a new Taurus titanium forty four magnum that he proudly shows me, as not weighing much. I heft it, and compliment him. I would not carry it, too short a barrel, not enough energy, and I cannot afford the thousand dollars it cost. I still have my used pawnshop purchased $200 Ruger 357 Blackhawk I swear by with custom fossil ivory grips I made that Seymour admires.

I'm curious how accurate this new pistol is and want to see if Seymour can hit a squirrel with it. This is survival knowledge in our lifestyle. "What will it do on a bear?" Is the bottom line, accuracy matters. *If he cannot hit a squirrel, can he hit a bear in a vital spot?* "Yea, that's what matters."

I'm usually the first one up, so get a fire going, coffee started for Seymour. Over coffee and breakfast, he lays out the plan for the day's job. "We'll data collect using the level rod. Just try to walk straight parallel lines about two feet apart. Pick up a few spot elevations if the terrain varies, like a hole or a raised spot."

"You want to start off doing a perimeter and ground level elevations?"

"Good idea, Miles, that helps me write the code in the computer and not have to keep changing it." We begin our day at 7:00 am.

The gravel pile looks to be about two acres big. Sort of boring, collecting hundreds of elevations. Stop and turn, every two feet and 'got that,' then do it again all day long. Even so, it still beats working for a living. Other than getting stung by a yellow jacket because I stepped in a ground nest, it is an uneventful day. We work until 6:00 pm. It takes an hour to get to camp, get the fire going again and get settled down from the job before we relax as dinner cooks. We sit around a few hours talking. Apparently this village has an issue over gravel used for a local job. We are to resolve this dispute, and tell our client how many yards of gravel there is now. Apparently the village knows how much they started with.

"I'm not sure when I first went to Tucson, Seymour. Couple few years ago now, I guess. I stopped keeping a diary on my calendar. I suppose in my early years everything seemed exciting and note worthy. When things got more normal and ordinary, I quit." I explain what I remember about the first Fossil Gems show trip to Tucson. Reputed to be the biggest show in the world, held each year in Tucson, Arizona, running for a month, beginning the end of January. The first time I went, I was not sure I'd consider this an annual event. "It cost me half a year's wages to go, Seymour!" I explain that my mother lives in Tucson, so is one reason to go. We are not close, so it was more a free place to stay. But sure, secondary or somewhere on the list, is an honest interest in seeing how she is.

I explain to Seymour the serious reason I had to go. "I found a nice mammoth tusk. It was brought to the local dealer/buyer, Tusk. I was happy enough at the time to get $2,000! Exciting for only three days of work! Or so this is how I saw it." I explain how I watched Tusk get on the phone while I was there, and in five minutes had a buyer for $10,000. I thought at first it was a bit rude to sell it for such a profit while I am listening. I thought he ought to be pleased with the high price, and toss me an extra grand, or few hundred anyhow. I am used to folks in my kind of business doubling their money, maybe a little more. Maybe at best, triple the investment now and then, when lucky.

I inquired of others selling to Tusk. Someone heard the guy who got my tusk took it to the Fossil Show in Tucson and sold it for $26,000! This seems impossible. We have all been trusting Tusk, selling and being happy. But this kind of money it fetched at the show is a couple of year's wages to me. For this kind of money I'd charter a plane and hand deliver it.

"Heck yes, Miles, that's a lot of money. But how do you know it's true?"

"I met the guy who bought it when I went to Tucson!" I fill Seymour in on the details. "So I decided I'd take my ivory down to Tucson, and get the big bucks, cut the middle guy out! If I bring my ivory here, I may as well bring all my art!" I have at any given time 500 or so art pieces in inventory. Maybe $50,000 worth. As I ask, and hear stories of the big show, I heard of all kinds of fantastic happenings. How people sell out the first day and come home. 70,000 vendors and a million customers. I repeat in awe, "The biggest show in the world."

Some buyers I am told, if they like your work, say, "Box it all up, I'll take everything," As in, Dang! With wide eyes, thinking *would that be awesome or what!* I am getting actual names of people I have heard of in the villages who took Eskimo art and sold out before the show opened.

"I'm all ready to hit the big time and get rich quick, Seymour!" Seymour chuckles because he knows me. The big break I have been waiting all my life for! My ship is coming in. I line up a room at the Howard Johnsons at the show where you sell out of your room. The guy who had this room last year was an Alaska Eskimo who was one of the lucky who sold out! Obviously a good spot at the show. So I'm committed to spending $7,000, with the potential of selling $50,000 worth of art plus any ivory I have.

"I know you, Miles, so what happened, what's the rest of the story, the truth, not your dreams!"

Seymour is one who thinks I exaggerate too much, a bit of a bullshitter. He puts up with it because he is my friend, but does not take much I say seriously. He is entitled to his opinion. I do not argue or take offense. I wish it were different, but keep reminding myself, *Respect is earned, not demanded.* Oh well!

"So I went!" I say with the same excitement and awe I felt at the time. I had not been outside Alaska in years. Never done a show bigger than the Fairbanks fair, mostly little bazaars with a hundred people showing up where you pay $10 for a table. From this, cold turkey, to the biggest show in the world! Cut out all the middle steps to get there. I show up as a complete unknown. A country bumpkin. I was warned by Alaska friends to be careful of getting fleeced by the city slickers.

"It's a shark frenzy out there, Miles!"

I did not even know how to get in my room! A maid had to show me what this silly card is for, "Where is my key?"

But luckily this show involves people from many countries. Some vendor and buyers know even less than I do. I notice when you pay seven grand to be there, people treat you with respect, and show you how to get in your room, and do not laugh and tell you to get lost, or call the police. Money talks, all right. This part of the show is two weeks long. I do not start off with a bang. No one wants to buy me out the first day. No one wanted my ivory. I find out 'the best' ivory sells for top dollar. The interest and the money drops fast with a number two grade product. One tiny scratch or crack and that's $1,000 off. Nothing I have is perfect. That $26,000 tusk was a once in a lifetime find. By the end of the show I had not sold any ivory. I ended up selling it 'cheap,' for less than I'd get from Tusk in Fairbanks. I sold some art. I traded, and bought some good raw materials. I think I about broke even on my trip costs. I saw all kinds of opportunity, and ways to make money. It just takes money to make money. The guys who bought my ivory had a plan, well thought out.

They spot greenhorns. They wait till they suspect the seller is in panic mode, trying to earn the cash just to get home. They move in for the kill, ten cents on the dollar. I never let myself get in such a bind. I'm never down and out. I always know how to get home and recover. I had a round trip ticket, and did not go in debt to be here. I was able to smile calmly and reply. "I don't think so," And "I'd rather not haul all this home, but I can. I didn't sell it here and so ok. I'll sell it cheaper now, but not at a steal. How about…" and came up with a breakeven price I could live with.

I told those selling around me. "I didn't come here to break even! I came here to get rich!" I thought I was never coming back. *What a joke.*

The other vendors smiled, they had heard it all before and told me honestly with a chuckle: "If you broke even your first year, you did really good. Few do that well." I looked around me, heard the stories, and saw it was the truth.

I had to understand, and replied."Well it is like when you guys come to Alaska with your gold pan dressed in new jeans, and ask me where all the gold nuggets are! I have to explain there is no free lunch!" We all laughed about that together. No free lunch. What a bummer. One guy came up to me trying to sell his expensive watch so he could buy the gas to drive home. He was that broke. It's a cruel world.

"But Seymour, I realized more and more how much I learned doing the biggest show on earth. The very best people in the world at what they do, set up here to sell. Over half of all the gem stones in the country, in all the stores, get distributed and pass through this show. The guy in the room next to me does million dollar deals selling sapphires, for example. The knowledge here is amazing. I felt I learned more at this show in two weeks than in the past ten years talking to Nenana locals.

I'm learning on a world scale what is happening with the market affecting my business. I suddenly understand international marketing. If I'm to be a wheeler-dealer trader going internet worldwide? Tucson fits right in with a new direction to go. I already knew the local tourist market is not great for individual artists or small time suppliers like me. The local shops treat vendors with a great deal of disrespect for the most part.

The camp fire is dying down so I take a break and toss a big log into the embers to brighten the world and add some heat. Day temperatures can be hot yet when the sun goes down it gets chilly! The night Alaska sounds are familiar. I go on explaining how selling is in Alaska.

"Make an appointment with a store or gallery and they are an hour late, act bored, in a hurry, cannot make up their mind, make you wait again, make you get more stuff out." They may or may not buy anything at all. If I do not like it, there is a line of vendors eager to take my place outside the door, hurting more than I am. I learned this traveling, selling with Crafty. Also talking to other sellers. The big tour companies control the flow of the majority of customers. They make deals with the gift shops. Deals I'd call kick backs. It's hard to get an in. It's a rigged game.

"One incident I recall explains what I mean, about so much to learn at the Fossil-Gem Show!" I smile remembering. One of the materials I use for my art is amber. Much comes from Russia, and Russia used to own Alaska. So sort of a local material, connected to Alaska. I proudly show off my amber work in Tucson.

Several customers said, "Nice art work, too bad you put it on plastic! Why did you do that?"

I indignantly reply: "No! This is amber!" They give a polite smile and walk away. No sale. Till someone asked more questions and I say, "Well, sure it is amber! I sell it in the galleries in Alaska as amber! I bought it as amber! Here, rub it, see, it smells like amber!"

There is a polite reply, "That might have been true twenty years ago, but fakes, replica and copies have come a long way in twenty years. It is easy to put amber perfume in plastic."

I say: "Ok, then put a hot pin in and see! It is resin, not plastic!"

"Copal, new amber that is really just fresh resin, is mixed with the plastic. A hardener is added to a little real amber to make new amber. It's legal in the same way calling blue plastic mixed with turquoise dust legal. Turquoise is now a color, not a material." They tell me. "See the bug in this piece you offer? See the bubbles coming in a trail to the surface? This is where a hole was drilled, a bug inserted, and the hole sealed shut again." There in fact, is no fool proof test. "The bottom line is, nothing is as pretty as real amber. That is the only true test," I was shown what real quality amber is. I am seeing it for the first time in my life. It is not available in Fairbanks, Alaska.

"So, right here, Seymour, what is that worth? One of the few in Alaska who knows most of what we buy in Alaska as amber is garbage. Maybe good for the tourist industry, not for galleries and discriminating people of the world. I can tell the difference, and now, the only one who has the real product in the state."I am now able to explain the difference to others, and build up my own credibility. Just as I am able to explain in Tucson what a real wolf claw looks like, to those dealing in coyote or plastic, and not knowing the difference. "So a real turning point in my life, Seymour."

I get the impression mine is not a lifestyle Seymour can relate to, though. Except, weird, I saw my Christmas gift to him on display, the fish cutting board I carved, and my watercolors are proudly displayed on his wall. Could be his wife's doing though. Yawn. We are talked out, time to end another day.

The job ends. We can give an accurate gravel volume of what is in the pile. The village supposedly knows what they started with and there is a dispute over how many truckloads were removed. That part is not our business. We just crunch numbers. Well, Seymour does. I just hold the level rod. More important, I show up on time, sober. Only one reason I would not show up. I'm dead. That's how I feel about work ethics. Once long ago Seymour gave me the day's assignment, and I turned aside and vomited, turned back and continued the conversation, saying yup, it'd get done. Seymour never showed concern I might be sick. There is no such thing as being sick. I ran the saw all day and stopped to vomit when I needed to. I got over it.

I head home, with a stop at the Kantishna River homestead, about forty miles out of my way, total of eighty extra river miles round trip off the main Tanana River I run to get home. If I stay at the homestead long enough, I can get in on moose season. Usually I cannot get a moose early in the season because I have no way to preserve the meat in the subsistence life without electricity. I'd have to wait till after the sport season when weather got cold. Or even get a moose off the trapline in winter. Now I have a freezer, so can get an early moose if I have the chance. I probably would not plan a special trip to look for one, but while I am already on the river in good moose country and headed to the homestead, *let's look for a moose!*

There is a cow with twin calves hanging around the cabin and creek. Tracks along the river look old, and indicate the calves are not this year's. This means she has had them over a year and will be kicking them out soon and coming into season, attracting bulls. The bulls may already have the eligible cows staked out, and might be beginning to hang around the general area in anticipation of the rut, due in two weeks.

In the past it has helped me to step out the cabin door a couple of times a day, especially early morning and late evening and bang on the trees with a stick like a bull hitting trees with his antlers. I may not get an answer, but it does no harm. I think all moose hear this and get curious, or respond, and begin coming into the area from miles away. The bulls not in rut yet could still be angry that one of their kind is beginning everything early. As in: "Hey! What's this all about! You can't start early, it's not fair! Someone needs to go over there and smack that bull around a bit!

You go! No, you go! Ok, I'll go!" While I keep quiet and snicker. *Who knows what they think? Who cares? As long as it works, right?*

After so many years hunting here, I get a sense of where the moose will hang out, and what direction to expect them to come from when they hang out locally, or come to investigate. There may be a stray bull just passing through this time of year coming down out of the hills. The cows have been in the low swamps all summer. Bulls and cows are just seeing each other now. At some point the bulls move the cows around into groups they hope to manage as their harem. I see no evidence from the tracks this is taking place yet. Cold nights are a big deciding factor. No cold nights yet.

I bang on trees a few times and get no reply. I try to keep it quiet around the homestead in terms of human sounds, not disturb the natural order of things. It is best if the wildlife does not know I am around. But after two days I need to split some firewood. I think the sound of an ax is not so bad compared to running the chain saw or banging on metal. I get the wood split and come inside to heat the cabin and cook on the wood stove.

While drinking Labrador tea I picked and steeped, I am looking out my five foot picture window. A big bull moose walks right past the window looking around suspiciously. There had been no sound. No response to my calls in the early morning. Possibly he heard the wood being split and responded to this. I have heard this sound can attract bull moose, but have never witnessed it before. I have to wait till the moose is a little farther away before I can open the door unnoticed. The .270 rifle is next to the door with a bullet in the chamber and safety on. I only leave a bullet in the chamber when I am alone. I have in the past had to make shots in a hurry and without making a noise, like now. Even inside the cabin I think the moose could hear a gun bolt put a bullet in the chamber. *Many moose know what that means. Ha!* I laugh, remembering the expression of a bull when he heard that sound. He got away. His head snapped up and his eyes got big. He made a mad leap forward in under one second. Or, faster than I could lift the rifle and fire.

Anyhow, all is ready for this situation, just not expected. The bull looks to the right and the left, with a look of frowning. Wants to know where that moose is he heard that dares move in on his harem. *And we shall show him post-haste.* I quietly open the door as he heads for the creek out front, just fifty ft. away. I have watched moose enough to know when he gets to the bank he will pause, and look up and down the creek before stepping into the water.

He steps to the bank and looks to the right, offering me a perfect heart shot. My .270 goes off, loaded with 130 grain bullet moving about 2,900 feet a second. I doubt the bull even heard the shot. While starting to sag, he steps forward into the water. *"Oh no!"* "Oh no!" We both say at the same time. Neither one of us wants to butcher a moose in the creek, or try to drag a moose up the bank. *What rotten luck.*

I try to eject the shell in case I need another shot, and the bullet case is stuck. The bolt comes back without the empty case. It might be a reload problem from long ago. I had the cheaper reload equipment that does not full length resize, so is only good for five reloads or so, then the base of the case has stretched too much and can get stuck. I have since learned, and bought the full meal deal for $300. *Only we paid like $45 at a garage sale right?* "Yes, thank goodness for garage sales!" But no, not on my mind now as the bull staggers around in the water. Dead on his feet.

My high Jesus factor kicks in, and the bull makes it twenty-five feet to the other side, gets up the bank, and falls over. Actually more perfect then on my side of the creek. I can leave the fifty gallons of gut pile there, and not stink up my yard, or bring the bears to the front door. Not that I mind, but if it happens after I am gone, bears might want to get in the cabin. Now we can put the rifle away for another year. Yes, that's about the size of it. A 1,500 pound bull like this will have a good 900+ pounds of meat. I could eat a pound a day every day for almost 3 years. There is no need to study what the bullet did upon impact with curiosity as I used to do. After probably forty moose in my lifetime, I know how the bullet preformed.

I will probably give some meat away to the needy. My freezer will not hold all this meat. As I speak, flies are already moving in on the kill, wanting to lay eggs. I often wonder where flies hang out, that they suddenly appear out of nowhere when there is death nearby. Being near the cabin helps. I have a plastic bag handy for the liver, heart, tongue, and any fat I want to save off the guts. I may keep the kidneys, but this is my least favorite part. Still, I do not want to be wasteful, so often eat parts I do not like, out of a sense of responsibility and respect for the animal. To be legal I only have to save the quarters. All the rest can be left behind. I do not know why the law is so lenient. I will for sure save the ribs, and the back strap.

As I cut the hide, I peel it back to have something to set the meat on. There are low willows and alder trees all around me, so I have to cut them out of the way to make room. This thick forest is about ten ft. tall, with trees one to two inches apart. Colors are just beginning to change from dark greens to yellow and soft reds. Not a breeze stirs in the almost record heat. It would be impossible to keep this moose without owning a freezer. In earlier years, I would not have shot this moose for this reason.

I no longer gut the moose first. I get all the meat off one side and organize it on the clean hide till I decide what cloth bags to put meat in. It is good to let the blood drain, as long as I chase the flies away. Before trying to roll him over I gut him, to lighten the load. In this way, no matter what, there will be no gut contamination of at least this much of the meat. I found if I gut the moose first, I might accidentally step in the guts, or get some on my sleeves and accidentally transfer that to my edible meat. I am not the most dainty person on the planet, so tend to get covered from head to toes in anything I engage in. *And proud of it.* That's really being a hands on person!

Being older, I have to take a break and notice my back hurts. There can be no break till the meat is in cheese cloth and in the bottom of the boat where it will be cool. Even half an hour break will allow flies to lay eggs. I do not consider the work 'hard' as some describe it. Maybe time consuming. Four hours. I think about all this meat and feel blessed. Like taking care of a huge gift – figuring out how to unwrap it and where to put it. It would not occur to me to call it 'work.' That might even be disrespectful, or insulting to God.

If the average person were given as a gift, 1,500 pounds of groceries the reply is, "Thank you, thank you, you are so kind!" Not "Geeze what am I going to do with it, it's so much work putting it all away!" To do so would mean never being offered a gift again! So I have a big thank you smile. *God loves me.*

First, the meat has to go in the canoe to carry it out to the river where the boat is tied up. I can only bring 500 pounds at a time. It is a challenge paddling in the heat. This meat has to be lifted again to be transferred into the boat across the beaver dam onto the river.

The liver gets eaten right away. It is not my favorite, but if I do not eat it today, it will not taste worth a darn in only a day or two. I made liverwurst once, but did not have a recipe, and it was only ok. Actually, it was pretty lousy. There must be a secret to it.

The river water is colder than fifty degrees. It is glacier water after all. In the bottom of the boat below the water line, under a tarp, the meat can be kept fifty-five degrees. Much better than the seventy-nine degree air. Fifty degrees is a critical temperature. Much above fifty and bacteria multiply fast. Below fifty, and decay is much, much slower. Without blood, decay, and heat, even flies are not as interested.

I'm all bloody head to foot. *Imagine that!* "So what are we going to do?" *Like we did last time!* "Oh yes." We go look for a pond on the sand bar. The river level is dropping leaving ponds of water on the vast sandbars. The silt drops out of the water within hours. The sun heats the shallow water fast. The water is still fresh, with no algae or bugs yet. This is like being in a sauna it is so hot. So with towel and bar of soap in hand, I head out with my boat to track down such a puddle of water. There's this green specked goo on me, that I surmise must be 'guts.' Me and goo seem to have a fondness for each other. I sigh, soaking in the hot water, resting my sore back. Laying naked out in the great alone under a blue sky with birds flying over, is peaceful. I am wistfully reminded of my old life. There would be sled dogs jumping in the water all around me. Fish hanging, drying on the rack, on a sandbar near the boat, like this.

Not much use hanging around the homestead now. It is best to get the meat to town, and in the cool shop to hang a while, and stop reminiscing about the good old days. This meat in the boat will attract bears if left over night. I sleep in the boat to protect the meat from predators. The boat is tied to an overhanging tree so it is out in the river. Any predator will have to swim, and then have problems getting up the side of the boat. I'd wake up before they got in.

A bear does in fact come around. I wake up to the sounds on shore as the bear tries to figure out how to get at the meat, pacing the shore back and forth and making moaning sounds.

"The gut pile is across from the cabin!" I yell at the bear and go back to sleep. A trip has to be made back to the cabin to close it up and grab more supplies I brought in with me. The bear could break in the cabin or be waiting for me.

In the morning I am careful, and armed, as I go the canoe and paddle to the cabin. The bear has indeed found the gut pile, and is already reducing it back to its natural elements. In a week there will be no evidence anything happened here. I keep an eye out as I am vulnerable near the thick brush and walking the path back and froth from the cabin back to the canoe. I have no reason to look for the bear, or bother him. I'm glad I do not see him.

MY BOAT ENGINE has trouble getting all this meat up on step in the water. I decide to forget getting on step and back off the throttle to idle downriver to the Tanana, forty-five miles away. There are flocks of geese along some of the sandbars. Not the big flocks as I used to see, but twenty to thirty birds. Swans are in pairs in predictable spots. They like to be at the tips of sandbars, facing into the wind so they can take off over the water if disturbed. They are big heavy birds that need a lot to get them airborne.

It is nice to have a good boat, with an engine that actually runs and is reliable. Ha! My early years were about fixing engines, having adventures (read 'mistakes'). Knowing I will get home with my meat is a good feeling. I have a good spare engine. My thoughts trail off... *I wonder what day this is?* "Yes, I notice it takes about two days to forget how many days I have been gone, and what day it is." *There seems to be great joy in not knowing. Like it does not matter. To eat when I am hungry, sleep when I am tired, work when work needs doing. All this seems so natural and part of the basic 'tradition.'* The word 'tradition' is being used more when defining who qualifies legally to be called a subsistence person. *What is a tradition, and how do you know when you have one?* Interesting legal questions when applying for a special permit. That piece of paper that says 'yup, you're subsistence all right.' A piece of paper that says I can live my life as I wish, or cannot.

I smile as the engine purrs, and I eat up the miles deep in thought. I get into this state of mind, and keep referring to this 'Zen thing' zone out. I can run my boat ten

—fifteen or more hours, and not get bored, not give up, not get cold. An internal radar pings the environment in the background. I refer to that as my unconscious working, and taking care of things. I do not have to use conscious energy to take care of everything. Trusting my instincts might be another way to put it. Like my computer in rest mode. As soon as the mouse is moved, the screen lights up again, icons begin to load. The computer does not need a complete boot up. Just like me and I.

The Kantishna River is very twisty, filled with sandbars that change by the day. Lucky for boaters, this is soft mud like consistency, and not rocks. It is actually rocks though, that have been ground by glaciers into fine pumice like powder, like chalk. With a little soil and clay added. The main channel in the river is about four feet deep and averages twenty feet across. It wanders from bank to bank, sometimes over a quarter mile wide. To the novice, the quarter mile across all looks the same. Water. But experience teaches where this twenty foot wide channel goes. It is not just a random here and there. The channel moves for a reason, and experience teaches what those reasons are.

I used to have to use my full concentration, study and stare hard to see where to go! Now it can all be handled almost unconsciously. I'm traveling faster speeds now than when I first came up. I'm usually averaging twenty-five miles an hour down-stream, when I used to average fifteen miles an hour. The engine is the same horse-power, but the biggest difference is the modern boat. The old wood boats looked nice, but when wet and water logged took on hundreds of pounds of weight. The old, long narrow pointed boats that look so nice were made to haul loads slow, and will not get up and plane well.

I reach the halfway down the Kantishna point. I see where an old cabin used to be that fell in the river. Around the next bend, and on the opposite side, is a tiny creek, hard to see unless you know it is there. Most boaters will take the inside turn, while the invisible creek is on the outside of the turn. Tall grass hides the mouth.

I nose into the mouth, and shut the engine off to drift in a little. The fishing pole is out. On the first cast I have a nice pike. Since I have lots of moose, I do not need the pike, so unhook it and let it go. I look over the engine and gas level, change the load weight a little to adjust for the weight of gas burned. This stop allows me to stretch, focus my eyes close, far, and wake them up. I'm not hungry yet. I plan to stop at Rock Creek where my gas stash is, and eat there.

A boat comes towards me. Someone I do not know headed upriver to moose hunt. In earlier years I would know everyone headed upriver; it would be odd to see a boat I did not recognize. *The country is getting more crowded all right.* "It used to be unusual to see anyone at all on a trip. In fact it would be rude to go by anyone without stopping to chat." *Now it is polite to merely wave.* We wave at each other, and neither of us slows down. I have to turn my boat into the wake the other boat made so I can cross those waves head on. A wind is picking up. I know the wind will be stronger on the Tanana River. There will be two river crossings to be careful of in the wind.

At Rock Creek I make my stop. While gas is being siphoned into the running tank, I make sure there is nothing loose that will blow out of the boat, knowing there will be heavy wind ahead. The tracks I made stopping here on the way down are still here. The only tracks to be seen, so no one else has been here. Possibly a year can go by and I will be the only one who stopped here. My meal is hot moose stew in a thermos. My life vest is hung on the back of my chair, since I will be out in rough water with a heavy load. Assuming I can grab it if the boat goes down. I never wear a life vest. I tried once and got it hung up in the motor rewind rope, and it almost tossed me in the river. Other times I got hung up on all the straps and strings as I moved around the boat in a hurry. I decided it is more of a hazard then a help. Looking around at people I know, very few wear life jackets. Mostly those who are scared of the river and do not know what they are doing. Nor have I heard of drowning on the river where a life jacket would have helped. 90% of drowning involve drinking. A life jacket might even help a person get hung up on a snag under water. But anyhow.

My thoughts wander in this direction as I travel. *In all my years of boating and adventures I have never fallen in the river. No more often than a city slicker has fallen off the curb into traffic.* Will told me there is some new law being considered that requires everyone in a boat to wear a life jacket and you can be arrested for not obeying. Sounds impossible. *Who would put up with rules like that? That would be like me telling a civilized person I, and my friends, determined road traffic is dangerous to those walking on the sidewalk only three feet from speeding cars.* I finish the unconscious thought, "So I and my friends get together and decided to keep you safe." We pass a law requiring you to wear a protective device which you must buy from us. The average city slicker would burst out laughing. As I am doing now.

"You and who else, is going to make me buy this from you, and wear it?" I design some stupid looking florescent device, that resembles a military bullet proof vest, that might protect you if you got hit by a car after falling off the curb into traffic. I grin at this image of you, as I ride my boat. Alone out here with God. My planet has not been invaded yet. *Thank goodness.*

The Tanana River is three times bigger than the Kantishna River. The water color changes a little to a more reddish hue, with mud color. The Tanana runs half a mile an hour faster, six miles an hour. Fast enough to cut into the frozen ground, and cause the banks to cave in. Trees on the bank fall in, or hang thirty feet out over the river, waiting to fall, only a few feet above the surface, even right at the surface. This would be the most likely dangerous issue, to stall the engine near such a bank, and have the current take me into these sweeper trees sideways. Sometimes I must travel near them, as this is where the deep water is. If I get sideways, the boat will roll over. I've never had it happen, but came close once with the houseboat, with the old engine that would barely run. *I think it burned as much oil as gas- ha!*

It is nice to have a reliable, almost new engine. *Still under warranty!* "Yes, years ago we gave up on warranty because we were in the wilds for a year." By the time we got the product under warranty back to civilization, the warranty had expired. I also used goods for jobs not intended for the product, voiding the warranty. Like using my chain saw for a garden rototiller. Or taking the boat engine apart with a crescent wrench, and moving parts around, then running it. But just leaving civilization voids most warranties.

Last year, I guess it was, I made some extra money with mammoth ivory. I decided to put some of the profits back in the business, and actually brought the engine in for routine maintenance. "You know, check compression, change the oil, do a water pump test, make sure it is running good" Is all I said. The engine was running fine. The shop pulled the prop off and decided to replace the seal on the drive shaft. The mechanic found a bearing going out. Because they saw it, not me, they covered it under warranty and rebuilt the whole lower unit. As in Wow! I paid $200 for the look over, and other things done. $500 worth of warranty work is done, but more, if the engine had failed on the river, the cost is much higher.

I think of this as I eat up the river miles. *Time to rethink life. My world is getting too complicated to understand every single aspect of all I do. At some point, I need to trust someone else to do a professional job.* "I used to just do it all because I was so remote." I'd fix radios, saws, work with wood, metal, bone and plastic. I'd make parts. *Very rewarding when it works! Often though, it works, but not forever. Or it works, but took 100 hours, when a pro could do it in half an hour.* "So how much is my time worth?" I have these thoughts as I ponder the mysteries of life. It may have been fun and exciting to spend twelve hours designing and making a snare lock worth less than a dollar all in the name of 'I did it myself!' but what else could I do with that twelve hours? I had nothing else pressing at the time, but that was a lifetime ago. During that lifetime, I was married, had a son and lost them. I was never told why, but discussions revolved around money.

I figure out a ballpark amount I am worth an hour. I find out what a pro charges per hour. I calculate if I enjoy doing this particular repair job or not, and give this a monetary value. This is not as hard as it sounds. I say, "Do I like it $100 worth?" Long ago it was a no brainer. I'm worth slave labor—fifty cents an hour as a trapper. As an artist, who knows? I once needed all that money for minimum survival, not paying some shop $100 an hour! Even surveying, I do not work all the hours I want. I am not sure how much I want to trade a day's wages for an hour of someone's time in the shop. $100 is a lot of money to me! Still, being smart is also having equipment that works, and getting older is supposed to be about smartening up, and getting wiser! *How many times did I try to save $100, and ended up floating the river to some remote village, having to fly to civilization for parts, and paying hundreds, even thousands of dollars because I would not spend that $100?*

Now I make a little more money in civilization. It is sometimes worth paying someone to do work for me. I also see the problem from the other side more now. I have customers with no money, who want me to go look for something for them, but do not want to pay extra. In fact, they ask for a discount. Want free advice so they can do it themselves. Need a deal, but want me to invest my time like it has no value. Tell me they are my friend, smooze me. Run a guilt trip. I have to learn how to deal with these situations. Some situations I use myself when it is me with a need!

I now reply, "My shop time is $65 an hour. How much of it would you like to pay for? The best deal is to order it without any questions or involving my time." But this outlook has taken a long time figuring out. And tends to irritate a lot of customers. I assume there must be a nice way of saying this in a polite way. Perhaps just ignoring them and never answering? A simple, "No thanks, have a nice day." or "I'm all out of what you want, sorry." Lie like that? Is that what civilized sellers do? Most sellers I ask roll their eyes up and tell me they just put up with people. But this is being an enabler. It lets people know they can be rude. If I ignore them, I am not teaching them anything, nor letting anyone explain themselves if there was a misunderstanding. When it is we as the buyer I hear.

"Yes! I'll get right on it!" Then never hear from them again.

Now and then a customer says, "$65 an hour? No problem. I understand good product and good service cost. I do not mind paying, thanks for being up front and honest." Others say, "Why that's outrageous!"

I can reply, "Then I suggest you do not shop with me, have a nice day," Some customers find that rude, others refreshingly honest.

The hum of the engine is hypnotizing. The chop on the river makes a rhythmic sound on the hull in tune with the engine, like music. The boat flexes going over each wave. I've known more than one person who had boats break in half in rough water like this. It's got to be hard on the boat. I know I am trying to outrun a weather front. If the weather gets too rough for safe travel, I can pull over and camp. I have a tent and all I need to stay overnight. Near the old village of Minto, in the flats, I see the waves ahead are too big to take on safely. Even though it is 3:00 pm, and I am only thirty-five miles from home, under two hours running in good weather, it is better to stop. There is a creek and long lake not far, Tosjacket Slough. A good place to camp. I am able to go far enough up the creek to be out of the wind, protected by willows.

I drilled four holes in the edge of the boat in the bow that fit my dome tent poles and set the tent up on the bow. I had taken a sheet of plywood and bridged two boat seats, put hinges on and a clasp so I can lock goods underneath. This is exactly the size and shape of my dome tent.

I wish to protect my meat from bears, so will sleep on the boat tied out in the creek. I can cook right in the boat, no need to leave it at all.

A small open can is filled with alcohol and paper. A folding rack is set up over the can with height adjustment. A small pot with fresh moose heart, liver, rice and herbs, is set on the rack and the can under it lit. I was going to transfer gas, but with the open flame and gas fumes we might have a lift off? The boat slamming on the water has caused gas to splash up through the caps on the tanks, creating enough gas fumes to smell. Anyhow, time to transfer gas after I eat, or later on. This creek is calm and out of the wind. There are ducks, two pair of swans, a bald eagle in a tree overhead, and just a lot going on here today.

I bring my cooked food into the tent and squat down out of the mosquitoes to eat. A good book is in my survival gear. I consider something to read a necessity. It gives me something to do while I wait, instead of being impatient, and maybe taking off when I should not. So I lie on a sleeping pad in the tent and read. The wind and waves die down in a few hours as evening approaches. Plans are changed. I decide not to spend a night, but to press on so I can get this meat secure. About 7:00 pm, I take off again.

The first Nenana fish camp is passed. Then the first fish wheels. All the landmarks I am familiar with go by in order. I am glad to be approaching Nenana and my 10th Street parking spot late. I'd rather not have anyone around. I do not have registration numbers on my boat. Not yet required, but headed in that direction. No steel shot is in my shotgun. So far, local officers agree it is a dumb law, not relevant in Alaska, and is being ignored. There are a lot of disadvantages to steel. I have little safety gear in my boat. There is talk of requiring life Jackets, fog horn, running lights, an anchor, and who knows what all. It's all nutso. I'd rather not have to answer questions about my moose. I think it's legal, but the book of regulations is as thick as a phone book. So who knows? I might have been on the wrong side of the river. I might have killed it on the 3rd Tuesday of the month. The moose rack might be an inch too short or too long. Oh yeah. I am supposed to bring his balls back with me. In certain management areas. To prove it's a bull. Yeah, right. With all the things to take care of, I'm going to remember to go back for the balls? In 400 miles of travel I am supposed to know all the management areas I cross in and out of? I smile as I pull into Nenana quietly in the dark.

My three wheeler is parked with a small cart where I keep the boat. I am able to get half the load up to the house and into the cool, fly free, shop. One room in the shop has a rope down its length, just for hanging moose meat each year. It's fort-five degrees in here. Newspaper is on the floor to catch any drippings. Before midnight the moose is all taken care of. There is no dirt, sand, or leaves on the meat, nor fly eggs. How the meat is handled is a huge factor in how it will taste later. I sometimes wonder if those who say they hate game meat, have eaten meat not taken care of right.

I have an email waiting for me to reply to. My first book is about to be published. Some people, mostly women, are nervous. A second email is a sort of famous artist I email who has done duck stamps, and offered comments that help me with the book.

Email

Hello! Sheila

Thanks for your long communication on the book and your thoughts about it. Hm, ya, well, maybe you are right about having some Alaskan do the illustration, or do it myself? Do not be concerned about 'publicity.' Our friendship means more than your name used in the book. Maybe I will have you read it, and you will know the substitute name I use, and you tell me how you feel about using your name. I'd not make it so people who knew you would recognize you, even with another name.

One of the situations I find myself in, or wanting to ensure, is 'credibility.' The story is about me, my adventures with very few ways to prove or verify anything. There are some magazine stories, but again, I wrote them (or a lot of them). It would be good to, somewhere, have a few people who are 'real' that I know, that makes me more 'real,' so readers feel what they have is not a totally made up book.

As for our understanding of each other, you may be correct about both statements, possibly I interpret how I wish, to suit how I'd like it, and partly I do understand, but not fully.

The dog incident? Hmm. You feel I may lose a large portion of the audience with my vivid stories of violence and such? I have to consider this, yes, but I know I was raised on Walt Disney, and the standard 'Mountain Man' books. They almost got me killed...

I still remember "My Side of the Mountain," for example, that so affected me when I read it—about a child who ran away and lived in the woods and had a pet something or other, and how wonderful it was. But it isn't always wonderful, and I think people need to know that...

I certainly wish to do a positive upbeat book, full of fun, humor, entertainment, beauty. But also life, from one extreme to the other, pull at people's feelings from one end to the other.

I am not wishing to be pessimistic, discussing the negative, however, most civilized people are puzzled by two opposite things. One, is why anyone who has a good life in civilization would want to go live a life of hardship in the wilds, and then call it a good life. Second group, those who hate civilization, can't get away, and envy the free life of the wilderness person. So, I want to show the reality of both civilization and the wilds from the viewpoint of someone who made the choices I have.

Not want your name in lights? I smile, yes I sort of know this about you but 'forgot.' I get enthusiastic about something, and get tunnel vision. It's my excitement about it, and I can't believe someone cannot share that excitement! What I focused on was something else about you… that you would like to 'make a difference,' have an effect on the world, and the way things are etc., to do something positive. It's a little about what your art means to you. I do not know how compatible that is with wanting to be 'unknown.' Your art is a statement in itself I think. But many people need a name, a life connected to this art and artist. They like the story behind the story. Yes, I tend to forget your personality is more shy.

Sunshine, Miles

This famous artist is an environmentalist. A bunny hugging, tree kisser of the first order. Interesting that we are friends at all, and on speaking terms. We get into interesting discussions. For example, who Audubon was and what he stood for. *There is a preservationist society named after him. Amazing.* He is quoted as saying, "If I do not kill at least 100 birds a day, it is a bad day," Here is a guy who killed things, propped them up with sticks, sketched them, then left them - by the hundreds. Being held up as the best example of conservation. *History is an interesting thing.* My friend paints duck stamps. This is a stamp issued to hunters so they can go kill ducks. It's not a stamp about kissing our feathered friends. She accepted the money to create such a stamp, but detests what it stands for? I think, in the, long haul, we'd be on the same page.

I am learning that emotions may not have reason behind them. I assume I too have emotions not founded in logic or reason.

Another Email

How many personal ads have you placed?

And one more thing…I'm not sure why you wanted to live the life you did. It seems you almost abused yourself… why with freezing and being hungry and all… I can understand wanting to get away from the city and people and live in the wild and remote, but to jeopardize your life?… when it was not necessary… difficult to understand… talk some more to me about the

WHY.

Here are some excerpts from my reply, as I glance over what I write before sending—

So you ask 'Why'? You didn't read my poem "12 answers to what for?" On what level do you want an answer? There are economic reasons, psychological reasons, social reasons…

I found something I was good at. I found someplace I belonged.

I didn't seek out trouble or pain or a rough life. I didn't enjoy the troubles I had. I saw it as the price to pay. You want to dance, you pay the fiddler. If it was free or easy, everyone would do it.

Nothing great is accomplished easily.

I could have gone out with an experienced person? And why would an experienced person want me along? I had no money, no skills. I was not strong; I was a soft city kid. I had nothing to offer. Also, would I recognize a skilled person? It was 3-4 years before I met another trapper. I didn't know where to find them. I didn't know how to find them. Any more than a tourist could find a real trapper. Wilderness people don't hang out where tourists do. I met a person or two like at the Salvation Army who suggested we partner up together so they could teach me. No serious outdoor person would have anything to do with me. I was a Moony eyed, sensitive artist who would have said "Gosh, golly are you a for real trapper?" And a real trapper would have said "Go away—you're bothering me kid! Ha ha" My first real advice by decent folks was "Why don't you stop talking about it—and **go out and just do it kid."**

It may not have been worth even replying to this person beyond,

"Lots to do, pretty busy, I'll be in touch when things slow down!" If anyone looks at my life and has to ask why, they will never get it.

So yes, there are all kinds of views and ways to skin the cat, many roads to Rome. Not everyone will understand what seems so obvious to me- whatever it is we do, live for and dream about! I understand why there are so many people passionate about whatever it is they believe. All the jobs that need doing by society to make a herd function are desired and coveted by the ones who take on the various task. We each play our part. I have met truck drivers who think they are in heaven because they can drive long distance trucks. I met a garbage man whose whole family thought they had died and gone to heaven to have access to all this cool stuff. Others might say, "I'm glad it's you and not me!" Ha. But yup, someone has to do it, so sure is nice that someone wants to! It might be with me and my work. Someone has to break trail for civilization. *Not everyone understands what needs to be done, or even why.*

Trying to come to terms with civilization and its ways is still hard. *This darn computer and internet stuff!* It is hard just to sit still and stay in the house. My whole life has been spent as an outdoor person. Most of my life, from the time I got up to the time I went to bed, was spent outdoors. Hours at a time at the computer drives me nuts. I explain it to Will when I see him. He asks how things are going with my back and all, and the changes. He cannot picture me with a computer! We both laugh.

"Will, I got forced out of a lifestyle by the law. So what can I do for a living to take care of myself?" I explain how I can still live in a remote village and sell my art if I can do so on the internet. I do not have to drive, or travel, or be that plugged in. I only need access to the post office. He asks about that first computer he gave me a ride to go get.

"It only lasted a week, Will." I thought I was doing the right thing to have a custom built computer just to fit my needs. A computer shop built it for me. But when I had problems with it, no one knew what the components were to work on it. The geek in the shop who built it was already gone. I did not know enough to figure out what was wrong, or what part to replace. I had a bunch of pirated programs. The idea I buy something, and it is not mine, is new to me.

"It is like buying a car, Will, and getting told only you can drive it, and if anyone else does, they need to spend $500 for permission from the car company. You have to use our wheels. No others fit. Burn our gas in it, not anyone else's. If you get caught, the contract says the car will be confiscated. The manufacturer can go in it, fix it, tweak it any time they want, without your permission or knowledge. So can their advertisers. 'We will put ads in it for you to look at and we have our own set of keys to get in.' I said, "I don't think so!" and looked for ways to do it another way. But without enough knowledge to do so. "Even my second computer was the same way."

"You wrecked a second computer!?" He sounds shocked, like this is incredible. Or that I could say so, with such pride, no guilt, no shame. Or go through two computers and not give up on them.

"Yes, I bought this cheap version of Word from a guy, on a disk with no label. The installation code was written in magic marker. And I only suspected he hacked into or stole it or something. But the price was good, and screw Bill Gates, ya know?" This program worked, so a happy thumbs up! "But after a while, the computer tells me the word program needs to be upgraded, or it will not work anymore." *Oh, oh.* Should I try to update it? I had to, or it would not work anymore. "I held my breath when I was asked for the installation code." I tell Will how the computer sat thinking for a long time; doing nothing. Then all of a sudden it made noise. It made up its mind, and the screen went blue, and then all my words on the screen turned into boxes and dashes. Someone at the other end hit a button and fried my computer.

No "Would you like to purchase a legal version of Word?" Or "Are you aware…?" No accusation, no opportunity to tell my version of the story, or go in front of a jury of my peers, or make restitution. I was tried, found guilty, convicted, and punished. Oh, the computer sort of worked, but without Word, what can I do with it? Word cost about as much as a new computer.

"Come on Miles! Who do you think you are, to be messing with Bill Gates?" Said with a sarcastic deadpan tone.

"I think the question is worded wrong, Will. It is more like, who does Bill Gates think he is, messing with Wild Miles!" We both laugh.

"Anyhow, Miles, it's the new world order. They call it 'the web' for a reason. It belongs to everyone. If it belongs to everyone, no one can have it."

"That's called communism ,Will, in case you have never read the Communist Manifesto by Karl Marx. But yes, a concept all right, but not new. You buy something, but never own it—only rent it, lease it, and the real owner controls it. Interesting concept from a business standpoint." But we are off the subject. "This computer I have had two years now, and seems OK. I understand the people who designed the programs better."

Will asks me about my book. "How long has it been now? Twenty-five years in the writing?"

"Soon now," has little meaning.

"Well at least you do not give up…" he says, words trialing off as the only thing he can say.

I do not have one of these new CD drives. My computer has a slot for an 'A' drive floppy disk, "that holds almost a megabyte of information. Will!"

"How much is that, Miles?"

"Almost the whole book! Well… all the text but not the pictures. Pretty amazing, huh!"

"A whole book fits on this little flat cracker looking thing? Wow!"

"I have to use a zip disk now, and just got an external driver to run that. The zip holds about 700 megs!" The printer in Germany is set up to handle zip drives, but the book has to be in the right format.

I AM STILL TRYING to understand what all that means, how it works, and how to accomplish it.[3] There are a few computer geeks, but this is a new term being coined, and in my village of Nenana, 300 people, I know about as much as anyone. I'm the one exploring the cutting edge of technology. It is me others are turning to for information. I may have to understand something called PDF, a new format with no program for it easy to buy, but maybe I can just use Word. "Raak in Germany is asking me what version of Word. I may have to upgrade to Windows 98."

I can tell I have totally lost Will in all this computer terminology.

"Geez, Miles, it was not long ago you never had electricity and were doing your art with hand tools by kerosene light. Here you are teaching others about the computer age. Too confusing for me. Why all the changes? I thought you liked the old ways!" He sounds let down. I am his symbol of dreams come true. Someone who made it over the fence. The one who flew over the cuckoo's nest. Why would I come back??

I give a lame, "How could I get my book done without a computer, Will? Look what it takes to have a computer." I sigh and try to explain better, since Will looks so disappointed. "It is not simple, and no one reason, Will!" I explain the biggest factor. "The government does not want people spread out, off on their own, not plugged in, nor someplace where they cannot keep an eye on us and know what we are doing." I've had countless encounters that convince me of this. I was forced out of the wilds. It is easy to think, "Who cares what the government thinks! They do not run my life!" That is not quite true. The government has ways to make life miserable. That alone would not stop me however, if I wanted to do something badly enough.

I was lonely and hoped to find companionship. I sort of hung around Nenana more to get to know, at the time, a certain woman. I was partly depressed and bummed out over having lost a wife and child over my lifestyle. Maybe the off chance my family might come back if I was in civilization. Maybe the chance to have my son sometimes.

"The economy is changing, Will!"

He talks about that a lot, so should understand. Those good old pipeline days are over. That was a decade of good money we both enjoyed. "The days I could come to town and sell a year's worth of art in three days and head back to the wilds!" Will nods in agreement about those days. "Well, now it takes three months to sell the same amount. I miss three months in the wild. There are issues like, what do I do with my sled dogs? How do I raise a garden, or fix the trapline cabins? Where do I keep my boat?" My back is injured. What would happen if I had to be on the homestead hauling wood to keep warm? I'm on high blood pressure pills now, where would I get them? The VA will not just authorize a year's supply. They got me by the short hairs, Will. I have to get a doctor's approval to get the pills; I will die without them.

"Ya, well, Miles, you would not need those stupid pills if you lived the good life!" I tend to agree, but am not 100% sure. My doctor told me it is 90% heredity. I can only have a 10% effect with stuff like diet, exercise, and getting rid of stress and such. I read other opinions that differ, so who knows?

"Ran out of pills once, and my blood pressure went through the roof. Maybe it is possible to slowly disconnect, but my father tried and had a stroke. Once again, if this were the only issue I would not let it stop me. Other potential health issues can also be expected, now that we are over the hill, Will."

Stuff like needing a dentist or glasses all require exams, trips to town, and more money. Money I can't make in the wilds. There are more land disputes with Native claims being filed. Mental health, university land, timber tracts offered, and it all affects where I can go, what I can do, and trapping areas available. Making a living trapping was hard enough when young, able to go almost anywhere unrestricted, while fur prices made a small profit possible. Price of fur is getting lower each year, I'm not as young, and am restricted by both laws and my own physical abilities.

Laws changed. Now it is important when hunting to know what month it is, and a radio to keep track of changes made by the day as harvest limits are met. Like wildlife is a crop. Again, getting meat is something my life depends on. This is not a sport or recreation to me, though the law treats it so. Subsistence laws are becoming a 'native only' issue.

Will nods, and sees that too, and adds, "But I do not get it, Miles, isn't discrimination illegal?" I do not get it either. I change the subject. I also want my art to grow. There are changes I am excited about seeing happen that require electricity. I'd like to market better. The internet may offer a new opportunity.

"Anyhow, Will, this is not a set in concrete permanent change. It might be just temporary. I'm still headed out trapping this winter. And I keep track of internet changes. If this new satellite thing comes to pass, I might be able to access the internet from anywhere, even out on the homestead. If so, I could maybe run a web business 200 miles in the wilderness. It's almost possible now, but the price has to come down. I have to see how my back is when it is fully healed. So I may move back out in the wilds, Will." He understand we need to be adaptable. He is out of work due to a bad back.

"I'm on unemployment now, Miles, but it runs out soon. You going to collect this winter?" Sometimes I work enough days in enough quarters I can qualify for unemployment. But not this season. I hesitate to collect, since I do not like the idea of abusing welfare. However, I think unemployment is about getting back money I put in, and my boss paid in.

With a healing back, I am unsure if I can trap this winter. It would be nice to collect unemployment if I can't work, but I do not qualify this year. "A little scary, Will. Nothing to fall back on. No insurance, no big grub stake."

"Know what you mean, Miles, thinking of going back Outside to see if I can find work."

I still think the best work is right here in Alaska, but Will and I have discussed this before, no use going there again. Will likes to cut his firewood in summer, and tells me he has all his winter wood already cut! He knows I like to go out with the snow machine and get a week's worth of wood at a time, as this gets me out in winter.

"I sometimes get a rabbit or grouse or something while I'm out cutting wood. This gives me something to do. Hopefully I will be out trapping though, Will. But the trail is getting grown in over the years. Growing in faster than I can keep up with the cutting. It's fort-five miles, just to get to the homestead. That's a lot of cutting. Especially as I get older."

Will had followed me out to the trapline one winter, and fell through the ice at the Kantishna River and almost lost his snow machine. I came along and there was a big hole and a wet Will with half the snow machine under water.

"Anyhow, Will, I need to get back to work. Hope to see you this winter. Watch your top knot!"

"Yup, keep below the horizon." As Will leaves, I notice a chill in the air, and recognize it as winter trying to arrive. I hand Will a box of wrapped frozen moose meat. I know he is seeing hard times. Some moose meat will mean a lot to him. *Do not forget how Will helped us in those early years! We took advantage of him, and he never said a word about it!* "Yes," a reminder from my inner self, maybe we can help pay Will back for all that help giving us rides, when I had nothing to pay him back with except fish stories.

I have only a very few childhood memories. I therefore have few facts to go on. Facts concerning why I am the way I am, out of sync with the rest of the world. Neither my mother, father, sister, nor I, tell the same story of our family, covering the same exact years living under the same roof. The stories are so different, that I wonder what the truth is. What is reality, and what are facts?

I think my parents did the best they could with what they had. Which may not change anything, but hate and anger is not a good path to go on. As I learned along the way. The stories my parents tell of their own childhood reads much the same. Even my grandparent stories. Each of us has our own version, our own story and our own memories that do not match. So who is right? What is 'truth'? I do not think any of us are lying. Do I remember any good stuff? Sure! Dad used to read me the funnies every Sunday, me sitting on his lap. It was good times. The family used to sit around the radio listening to 'Dark Shadows.' "The Shadow knows," mysteries on the radio before the days of TV. I still remember that part of the 50's. Camping with my Dad is one big factor in my choice of lifestyles.

I was not cramming my ideas down anyone else's throat, forcing anyone else to live like me or with me. I was not asking anyone to hire me if they do not want to, or be my friend, or help support me, or help me in any way. I was in fact embarrassed society had to rescue me my second year in the wilds. I felt bad about that. To have cost society that money I could not pay back. I tried hard not to ever have that happen again! I'm going to pay my own way. I didn't want society's handouts, any more then I wanted my father's. In fact I try to pay back society, by way of thanks for paying for my rescue.

The lifestyle I chose was not called 'subsistence' when I was growing up. It has been pointed out to me, the 'sub' part of the word means 'beneath.' Meaning some sort of lifestyle that is beneath other lifestyles. I feel a different lifestyle than what most are used to does not make it 'beneath' any other option, just different. People who lived off the land were my heroes. I name and quote them numerous times.

Possibly I created my own world to live in. I crashed and burned. Out of the mess, I arose from the ashes, as did Oz. Humorous, interesting, funny and weird. But not dangerous and illegal. In many people's minds 'different' is the same as scary, unwanted, not trustable or believable.

Mother Nature is like this, testing the new, strange, and different. The herd shuns such. Maybe 'different' is contagious. Different can represent a mental defect or disease. Not always good! So the 'strange' must prove itself, and be tested more than the normal. The good news is, sometimes it is the strange and different that adds something special to society or the herd, in the long run. This is where change comes from. Some of my heroes were nut cases. Hemingway, Einstein, Poe, Picasso, Benjamin Franklin, Howard Hughes, Joe Meek. Lewis and Clark, were all very odd people who changed the world in a good way. Oz was a humbug all right, but he did the best he could with what he had, and in the end good came of it. He helped Dorothy find her way home.

So I went off to live alone. But was not left alone. The census people I recall, twice spent hundreds, maybe thousands of dollars to find and interview me. Not just count me. There was a warrant out for my arrest because I had not got my mail in six months.

Problems with time. A survival tool. A world where time does not matter. Where time stands still. Like the title of a favorite book, one of the Tarzan books, 'The Land That Time Forgot.'

I can joke, "Who cares!" be the clown, tell my jokes. Even come up with reasonable answers for why, that sort of make sense. The clown is often the most serious one in the circus. Obviously I'm a criminal, why else hide? But being viewed as a criminal, is still better than being a nut case. I could end up like my sister, a lifelong terror. When you get carted off, they even take your shoelaces so you can't hurt yourself. So there is no way to stop a torture worse than death. My sister, banging her head on padded walls, screaming her head off, being laughed at and raped in a mental institution. I feel bad I did not kill her when she asked me to. I recall we both took what we thought was an overdose of aspirin. I think I had decided out of guilt to go with her, so she would not be so alone in Hell. But the will to live kicked in, and I had to walk away so I could save myself. And watch her be tortured for the next fifty years. Life is like that sometimes. So maybe it was God, or my unconscious, or Mother Nature, who went in my head, and pulled some wires loose and rearranged things. It's no big deal. I have no memory. What memories I do have are, whatever I want them to be. What a perfect condition for an artist-story teller! Made to order. A blessing! To turn what could be a deficit, into an asset! Why wouldn't that be good?

We have to make choices. I was determined not to be taken alive. So I had to come up with plausible reasons for everything. Plausible and sane. I could pull it off pretty much but... but suppose not totally.

I was kind of well-prepared though, when I got to the wild. Crawling on my hands and knees in the snow, starving and freezing to death was easy compared to what I had known in civilization. *And we were good at it, so darn good at it too!* I smile. "Yeah." The kind of guy who could be pinned under a log, take out my dull rusty Swiss army knife and cut my foot off and crawl 200 miles. *Like Joe Meek!* We're good at something! Yeah! So I turned a mental problem into my friend! Into a way to make a living. Something to be proud of. Without drugs. Without being a burden on society. Without experts. Without help. To end up actually productive, an asset to society. Thus, why should I be ashamed of having some wires loose? I am not the one who unwired me. Nor are my parents. There is no blame. It is only 'life.' I hold my head up, and feel the equal to anyone. But no. Why am I going to tell some curious woman I do not even know, all about family secrets? All about 'stuff,' that if she told the right person, would get me carted off screaming. Create an investigation. Getting to the bottom of what ? Solving what?

One of the Yukon 800 boats going eighty miles an hour, hydroplaning with only fifty horses, supposedly impossible. Nenana bridge ahead. Nenana is one of the race checkpoints on an 800 mile river race through the wilderness. This is the last road for 750 miles.

CHAPTER FIVE

GRANDMA, DIM WALKS OUT, TRAPPING SEASON, ROBERTS RULES, DOGS, INTERNET WEB

I am not interested in a sob story or excuse. No time, nor patience for it. I see it too often, folks crying in their beer telling 'if only' stories. I'm determined not to be one of those people. There are those who take drugs to escape, to forget. But once down that road there is no coming back. Brain damage is done, and if the healthy brain can't fix you, how could a damaged brain help? So Rah, Rah, Rah and all that stuff , let's go get it! Out of the huddle we (me, myself and I) break, and charge forward to greet life head on! Out of chaos, pollution and dust comes the dandelion, the weed that splits a cement sidewalk, greets the sun with a mellow yellow smile. *Donovan! Mellow Yellow right? Hey I remember that!* Our reverie of Golden Oldies is interrupted by the phone. *Phone? Yuk! Our first phone call! Rats.* We could just pick it up and say, "I don't want to talk to anyone, go away, have a nice day" and hang up?

It's Josh, my buddy. "Hello?" Pause "Is this really You, Mr. Maw-tin?" Another pause.

"This is the answer machine, please leave a message at the tone—beeeeeep." I wait a second. "No this is really me." But Josh is not sure. I got him a good one the other day. Our answering machine message worked. *What a fun machine!* "Fun all right!" I had to leave a recorded message, so I began, "Hi! How are you, good to hear from you! What's up?" Pause ten seconds "Oh? Interesting." Pause another ten seconds. "Wow!" Pause another ten seconds. "Actually, this is not me, but the recording machine, please leave a message."

For some unknown reason, Josh did not find it hilarious. *Oh, brave new world that has such things in it!* "We cannot tell the machines from the people. Fascinating." I'd love to perform a series of experiments..."Ask me a test question, Josh."

"Is this you or the machine?"

"How about if I just come over? You are only a couple of blocks away." It would not surprise Josh if I never showed up, and he was talking to my machine the whole time. I changed my message. Josh is amazingly shook up.

It is not my intention to scare anyone, hurt them, give them nightmares, any of that. I'm just, oh, 'fooling,' testing stuff new to me. *I wonder how long we could keep someone going? An hour? If one of these telemarketer gizmo guys calls, could I pretend this is the answer machine? "Miles is not in, please leave a message," and gently hang up? What fun!* I answer myself, "Yeah, reminds of me of experiments I read about where scientists replace bird eggs with rocks, to see how long they will sit on them, trying to hatch a rock! Or just how many rocks you could put in the nest before the mother bird got suspicious! Three? Or ten? And for how long? A week? A month? Forever?" *Yeah, how long cold we food people with a machine? What could we get people to do?* [1]

"Hey Josh! I got a good solution for these telemarketers! I've been getting these crank calls you told me I might get." I explain how it works. "I have a tape recorder handy ready to hit 'play' when I set it by the phone mouthpiece."

Josh is curious, so I tell him that the message on the recorder says,

> **"Hi!** I'm so glad you called! Obviously you believe in selling things over the phone! So have I got a deal for you! If you go to my web site at www.milesofalaska.com and let me know you were a telemarketer, you may have a free batman whistle with orders over $100!"

And it goes on and on forever talking about deals and prices for half an hour. I come back to the phone later, and of course the caller has hung up. No mess no fuss. "Civilization is kind of fun Josh!" *I turn the victimizer into the victim! Cool huh!*

Josh changes the subject, "Do you think I should wait between shots for Kennel Cough? It seems like it might work better to wait only two days. Runyan did that and had good results." Josh does not trust the vet, thinks the vet is getting paid off by either the top dog racing competitors, who all share the same vet, or the drug companies. It's not to the vets advantage to make your dogs healthy.

"Well, my guess, Josh, is there is an incubation period for this cough to hatch a second batch, and the second medication dosage needs to be after the second batch hatches." He needs to figure out how long this is. "Maybe a book at the library?" I do not have enough knowledge to look it up on the internet. Information on the net is not that organized yet, anyhow. Not a lot of data has been entered. But maybe a good way to verify what the vet says. Josh has been training the dogs with a cart he built so he can run the sled dogs in the summer. "How has training been going?"

"OK, but some are too young, and I do not have a really good leader." One of Josh's big issues is, he has dogs hot to trot, but not all there upstairs. "The reason I called was, I know someone who has another dog for you to put down." Ah yes. Josh knows people who love dogs and cannot put them down when they get old, or when they do not work out as sled dogs. I suppose, I am known now as the guy who takes care of that problem. You got an animal that needs putting down, see Miles, he's the local lead dealer. *What movie was that? Clint Eastwood hands out his card that says he is a lead dealer by profession.! I need a Clint Eastwood poncho!* "We have one, did you forget?"

I do not especially enjoy it, but it seems better than the alternative. Some folks drive the dog 100 miles round trip to the pound and pay a fee to have the dog put down in the socially accepted method. Unwanted, sick and lame, get turned loose to fend for themselves in the street to become a nuisance, bothering people, and suffering themselves. Lean and mean. It's hard to live that life and be a nice dog. Someone has to take care of this 'problem' and no one else wants to step up to the plate. I usually charge $5. I get handed $10 for two dogs. We all know the routine. There is a place by the river with trees to such leave dogs. I show up after they leave, shoot the dogs, dump them in the river, and give back the collars and chains.

I am, in fact, a little resentful. But yes, someone has to do it. I am the one left with the visual images and memories to deal with. I try to be humane, quick and easy. Even so, I have to get the collar off the bloody head and get close and personal. For those who cringe and find that gross and horrible. *They should!* But, hear what it is like when things do not go so smooth at the river! *Yeah, just go see the movies Chain Saw One and Chain Saw Two.* Yes, something like that.

If I were such a dog? I'd rather go in the river I know, understand and love. I'd rather be taken out on my home turf, surrounded by the familiar, taken out by a dog musher. I usually say a few parting words. "I hope someone wants you in your next life!" If I were a dog, I'd hate to get dropped off at a shelter. It smells like medicine, filled with other scared dogs, unfamiliar, strangers. A smell of death, comprehending I have been abandoned. I do not want dogs to go through that. *We know what it is like.* "Spare me the details."

When I get home I see my shop door is open. I do not recall leaving the door open. I frown and approach. Two little girls are in my shop giggling, talking about a box of toys. Judy sold me the house. She used to do carnivals, sell balloons and kid's toys. I recall there are boxes of such toys still in the shop. Some are over twenty years old. I sigh as I step into the shop. "Can you two tell me what you are doing here?"

Two very happy cheerful voices say, "Where are the toys? They used to be right here." One points to where the toys used to be. I therefore assume they have been here before, helping themselves to toys. They are bubbly, cheerful, and seem to have no clue as to where they are, or what they are doing. Much like the town loose dogs. How am I going to handle this? I do not have the social standing that I can scream for them to get out and never come back and call them thieves. If they went running and crying, I'd be the one in trouble. A single weird guy alone in his shop with two little girls? Besides, these two children have no clue what they are doing is improper in any way. The problem is with the parents.

"So how long have you been coming here for toys?"

"As long as we can remember! We used to come with our parents! They got some really cool stuff!" They show me the back of the shop where the wall was ripped open and set back in place so the family could come and go. Originally this was a shop full of tools, guns and walrus tusks. So I heard. Judy had nothing to do with the shop. Hated it for some reason. I assumed her ex had built it, and there was something about the shop as a problem between them. Why he left all his stuff behind and never came back is a mystery. I heard he lives near Fairbanks now. *Interesting. A free for all, come and help yourself.*

"Judy is gone now, you know. So if you want anything, can you remember to come see me? The house is over there across the yard. Knock on the door and ask me if you can have a toy. Ok?" I pause. "Do you know what stealing is?"

"Yes! That's when you take something that belongs to someone else!"

"And so who do these toys belong to?"

"No one! No one cares anymore about these toys! They are old and no one wants them." Both children smile and nod happily. *They're doing the world a favor by putting unwanted things to good use! There is in fact a basic truth in what they say. What constitutes ownership? Do we own something if we do not care about it? Do we own that which we do not even know exists?* In truth, I bought the house and land. All the rest was 'stuff' to simply deal with, as either a gift, or something to dispose of. *Judy refused to even acknowledge the shop existed, much less its contents. Judy loved kids, and if children came and helped themselves to outdated toys...* is interrupted with my words, "Judy is gone now. Do you miss her?"

"She was nice to us!"

The other says, "Sometimes she'd invite us in the house and we'd play house, or bake cookies!" Well, yes. Hmmm. My mind wanders. *I wonder how the parents justify breaking in and taking guns and tools?* "Same argument I suppose. Who cares?" *No one.* I did not buy the shop and all its contents. Judy who had a say so, is gone. The owner of the stuff is never coming back. Anyhow, I send the kids home with a handful of toys.

I later give away all the toys to the local elder who does something like Judy did. He knew her, and will appreciate some free stuff to sell to kids at the fair, cheap. The kids can learn to go to him. I fix the hole in the back wall of the shop. There is a well beaten path going in and out and across the back yard. I heard rumors that all the dishes and furniture the neighbors have came out of this shop. Judy and her guy were regular pack rats. There are still truckloads of goods in the shop. It gives me new insight into what it means to enjoy collecting, as I do. I understand better, how it might be when I pass away. Of course, all the good stuff is gone now. There are labeled boxes that I open, and wonder what in the world anyone would want this for—used clothes that are not even good for rags. Boxes of vinyl 78 records. Judy Collins, Elvis. Some might have an antique value, but which ones, and to whom? You'd have to be in the business. A pawn shop might give me ten cents a pound and cover the gas hauling them in.

There is a 300 pound, four foot crane gear—brand new packed in grease. There is a drill press that weighs a good ton and may not run, but looks like it would dim the lights of all Nenana if it ever was turned on. The power supply cord is the diameter of my arm. Some items I can sell cheap to make room for my own junk. Some has to get carted off somewhere, somehow. I am only now beginning to focus on what I have. There are seven rundown buildings, some of which I have not even been in yet. A perfect situation for a pack rat, as soon as I clean out someone else's junk. A scrap metal dealer in Fairbanks buys three truckloads of metal for scrap, for a few hundred dollars.

I seem to have a sense of ownership not felt by others here in the village. Or whatever. I have not figured it out. I decide to put an alarm in the house and shop so I know when it is broken into. I have enough knowledge to rig a mercury tilt switch to a relay, then the relay to a solenoid and high voltage fog horn. The tilt switch is hooked to the door and the fog horn set up inside. When it goes off, it will be impossible to enter the shop without being thrown to the floor by the sound wave, and have blood running out your ears. I think people need to know when you go tip toeing around other people's property anything can happen. You do not belong there. And even if polite tolerance of thievery that goes on seems acceptable because nothing can be done about it, think again.

Yup, only a few days after installation, the alarm goes off. I am not home, but halfway across the village I hear it. No one but me cares, much as in the city when car alarms go off. The local police are far too busy dealing with drunks. I head home. Standing in my driveway looking confused is my buddy, Josh.

"What's this, Miles?" He refers to my alarm system, waving his arms towards the shop. The alarm is off now. I have it on a timer.

"It's a way to let me know someone who does not belong in my shop has entered it, Josh." In truth, if I had my way, it would be a gun set. You break into my shop, you'll be lucky to live. I have the right to shoot you. So what does Josh have to say for himself?

"I just wanted to borrow your lawn mower, Miles, mine broke." I'm curious how this works. *So he breaks his and borrows mine? So he can break it too, because he does not know how to take care of his equipment? Would he buy me another one? Would he return it when he was done?*

"You'd return it then, Josh?"

"Sure Miles, eventually. But if you need it, you just come get it."

"And how would I know where to look, Josh?"

"How many friends do you have? You just ask around, like I do when my stuff is gone." So I hunt around for my mower and find it in Josh's yard, rusting and broken. I follow this logic and see how it works. It's a very interesting cultural study of ownership. Someone buys a new mower and uses it once. Then it's gone because a friend borrows it and mows their lawn once or twice. A friend of that person borrows it and the mower makes the rounds. By the time the original owner needs his mower again, it's not available. Broke. Wore out. However, twenty lawns got mowed. Now, no one in the group has a working mower.

Next time someone else buys the mower. Repeating the cycle. If the mower cost $200 and twenty lawns got mowed, that's $10 per lawn. I suppose that's reasonable and workable. The fellow who lost his new mower, borrows the other guys mower, till his turn comes around again to buy a new one, in maybe ten years when he'd need a new one anyhow. Fascinating. *In other words each person spends about the same amount of money as if each of the ten friends bought their own mower, kept it, and never lent it out. It's just a different way of distributing the goods.* "Interesting."

This happens too, I suppose, with toys, wrenches, cars and trucks. An interesting version of communism. Everything belongs to everyone. Except, if anyone 'borrowed' one of Josh's sled dogs? He'd kill them. So there must be some sort of social understanding about what is acceptable to borrow without asking.

"Miles, I thought you wouldn't mind. We're friends. What's with the alarm?" I had this same exact response from another Native friend in Galena over a gun years ago.

"Well, Josh. Sorry. I guess my alarm does not know the difference between my friends and thieves, huh?" I make light of it, but Josh now knows he can't borrow my stuff anymore without asking. *Stupid white people, go figure!* "At least we do not have to argue or even discuss it." He just has to accept I'm weird. I want to know where my lawn mower is when I need it, and I want it running. He can fix his own, or buy a new one. No. I do not want to lend him mine. Because Josh and white - man- stuff, do not get along. If I ask if he checked the oil, he goes, 'Huh? Oil?' Followed by a concerned 'It's running isn't it?' There is a long list of stuff of mine Josh borrowed that came back wore out, or broken beyond recognition.

I have heard this logic often from Natives. "It's working, right? So why should I mess with it?" I have seen this go so far as, if it even runs out of gas, it is now broken. "No run no more. Come look, White man!"

I ask, "Did' ja' check the gas?" Like when it runs, it is magic. Magic makes it run. White man magic. I noticed this in the past the most with guns. I do not know even one Indian who is a good shot, or takes care of his gun. None I know reload, or study ballistics. I now understand better, It is White man magic! It has nothing to do with talent or practice. The animal gives itself to you, or it does not. The bullet connecting to the target, has nothing to do with the gun or ability. It is a spiritual matter. The one selling you the gun, is a Shaman.

'Friends' is when you accept each other's faults. So here I am in civilization, learning how to be civilized. As the plot thickens.

Past Flash

I am with my grandmother who has come to Alaska to visit. I am thirty-five years old. I have not seen her in twenty-five years. She wants to know about me and my life. I wonder why? No one else in the family ever expressed an interest. It's awkward and embarrassing. I had told her "Grandma, what if you don't like me?"

Did she ever consider that? But no, she didn't care, so, Oh well. Here she is. I'm not going to play games and pretend I'm someone I am not. Our whole family is about guilt, cover ups, secrets and such. I see where that leads, and I refuse to be part of it. The people who associate with me know who I am. She reminds me how she flew to Hawaii from Maine when I was born to help take care of me while my father was on a submarine. She asks if I have any memories from Hawaii?

"Yes, I recall crawling up to the window sill and seeing this lizard and being able to look through him and see his guts inside." I am not sure it is a true memory or just imagination. But she confirms she thinks there is such a type of lizard there. "And I remember screaming my head off because my feet are burning up. I can't talk yet, so have no way to let anyone know."

Grandma goes into shock. "Oh, my God. That was me. I took you for a walk and you were barefoot! I wondered why you were screaming. You were usually so quiet, happy, and easy to take care of. I feel so bad!" She begins to cry.

"Good grief, Grandma. It was a million years ago. You think that's the worst thing that ever happened to me? It's just life, Grandma, no big deal. "

"Yes, Miles, life hurts, doesn't it?" She pauses. "I never approved of how you were raised. I arrived to try to help. Some of the things I saw broke my heart. But what could I do? Your mother and father used to lock you and your sister in the closet and leave the house to go swimming. Once the neighbors called the police because you two were screaming."

"I don't remember."

"No. I suppose a person would not want to remember that, would they? I often wondered if I'd read about you in the paper. One of those kids who slaughters their family in the middle of the night."

"Yes, well. I suppose that is not my destiny Grandma. Everything has a reason. I am who I am today as a result of all the factors that made me. My blood line, my upbringing, my own personality, all coming together to define who I am, and I am happy enough. That's the bottom line isn't it? The details can be forgotten, of how I got here." I pause. "I used to have to answer the phone before I was old enough to know how. I'd get beaten for doing it wrong, getting a message wrong or forgetting a number. To this day, I can't really deal with phones, nor remember numbers or names, times or dates. I do not suppose beating all that into someone works very well."

"My husband fell apart on me during the Depression. I had to work in a time when women couldn't find jobs. My husband became an alcoholic. He started to beat on my children, including your mother! I had to leave him in a day when women didn't leave their husbands. I could not feed my children. I had to put them in an orphanage. We would have all died if I hadn't. But there was a price to pay all right."

"Yes, my father's story is not much different. I know you never liked him, but he did the best he could, considering his own background. None of it is worth all the pain, Grandma. I'm fine." I smile and show her the planet I created. A safe world where no one can touch me.

"Miles, when I was young, I used to dream of marrying someone and living in a lighthouse, as a lighthouse attendant, out on some remote rock in the ocean." So Grandma fit right in here in the wilds. She thought it was sane, healthy, a good solution, a good choice to make in life.

"I should have kept in touch more over the years, Grandma…" I trail off, what can I say?

"Oh, you did fine. Those beautiful water colors of yours say it all. I save every one of them. I bet I have hundreds!" Yes, it's true, I have painted hundreds and thousands of watercolors since I was maybe six years old. I could not talk with words, so I did so in the only way I could. Beauty and peace. Flowers, birds with beautiful skies. Grandma adds, "So often with water, often weeds, and single blades of grass, free in the breeze." Yes. That's me.

"Yes, for someone who has few friends and doesn't like people, I end up sending out over eighty watercolors every Christmas." My contribution. About the only social thing I know how to do well. With art, there is no argument. I'm not even there to hear it. Art soothes the troubled soul.

Grandma adds, "You have an IQ of 135, but can not remember names, follow the most simple instructions or know what time it is."

I grin, "Isn't it great!" We both laugh.

My past flash ends

Who do I think I am, indeed. *"I'll pick door number three for $1,000 please."* "Yeah? What's behind door number two?" *Do you think we'll survive civilization?* "Well. Hard to say." We don't have any choice. Our planet as we knew it has been invaded and destroyed. We have to bow to the conquerors, I suppose. Figure out how we can fit in someplace. I do not mind. What good would it do to mind? There are some exciting aspects. But I am not ready to give up. Trapping season is coming soon. I have a good snow machine, and look forward to getting out.

THE NENANA RIVER freezes before November. The day after, I am, as usual, the first one across. Most people wait a week before crossing, and it is suggested there be at least four inches of ice. I know an inch of ice can be crossed if I keep moving. There is only three inches of snow on the other side, so hard going. There are creek crossings I have to bank up with snow, using a shovel I always bring for just such situations. A small chain saw gets fallen trees out of the way.

There are lots of wolf tracks, and two places wolves killed moose. A pack of wolves can kill a moose every three to four days all winter. Spots where moose are killed make good places to set traps. Dim has not been out here trapping in ten years, yet claims this stretch of trail. Now that I run this stretch so often it might be worth talking to him, asking if we can work something out. It seems unreasonable to honor someone's trapline when it has been unattended this many years. It's a burden on me to have to run this stretch and not be able to trap. Oh well, it is not good to trap within twenty-five miles of the village anyhow, let the game build up a little bit. There are always recreational trappers, children learning to trap, those desperate to make a little money, with no snow machine, who must trap on snowshoes and can go after the fur closer to town. By the time I get to Eight Mile Hill across the flats, all sign of civilization disappears. No one seems to fool around even this short distance out.

As I travel, I day dream, think of solutions to various issues. Dim is kind of a friend, at least someone I respect. I want no hard feelings. His family has had a hard time over the years. His father died out here on the trail. Broke his leg and went out again with a leg cast to check his traps. I think the cast hit a tree along the trail, leg swelled, maybe got infected and he didn't make it. Dim's brother, my friend, Weedz, was killed by a lunatic in Manley Hot Springs. Another brother, Pat, went through the ice, shoved a companion up on the ice saving her life, while he went under. Other family stuff leaves Dim with a lot on his mind. So I just never address the issue about whether I can take over this section he dreams about.

Once I get to these hills we refer to as 'Eight Mile Hill', the trees get big and game populations increases. I'm always glad to get here because there is no more swamp to wonder about falling through. I keep thinking of the statistic, that 90% of all snow machine problems involve water. I am averaging about fifteen miles an hour, twice as fast as with sled dogs. In some stretches I can go up to thirty miles an hour, but other places down to five. I have about 100 pounds of gear in the sled this first trip. Emergency gear that goes with me every trip is about thirty pounds. I have some new traps, bait, extra food to drop off at line cabins, kerosene for lanterns in the trap cabins, more fiberglass insulation, books to read, and other odds and ends. The insulation is the bulky part of the load.

I miss the sled dogs, but not to where I am sad. It is simply not in my nature to dwell on a past I cannot change, or on the negative. Part of a spiritual belief I have is to honor life as a gift. Life feeds off life. Things have to die so I may live. This is not something to take lightly or forget. Honoring life is to live it well. To be unhappy is an insult to the gift of life. I want a 'thank you I am glad to be here' outlook. That, to me, is the bottom line of spirituality.

The snow machine is still new and exciting, with much to learn! Like I am at the airport in only two hours! *We named this little shack the airport back in the 80s, remember? A strip was bulldozed out for a plane to land fuel for the bulldozer when they were looking for oil.* "It used to take four hours in these conditions with sled dogs!" Can I be at the homestead in four hours?! *Amazing!* I enjoy the heat coming off the engine as well. The machine is designed to have engine heat blast in the face. There are electric heated grips to hold on to.

I built a food heater that clamps on the muffler. I have hot food at the airport as I take my usual half way break here. It is time to look over the snow machine and make sure the load is tied in well. I check nuts and bolts on the machine, and make sure everything looks good. If there is a potential problem it is wise to work on it here. If I have to stay due to unexpected fix it issues, I have a warm cabin with a few basic supplies locked up in a barrel. Once I found a cracked fuel line, and was able to use extra hose from the tool box at the airport to patch it. Now and then I find a loose ski, or a bent part that I can fix. Usually not life threatening, but the parts are there for a reason. If parts are loose, broken, bent or missing, it has some effect on the performance of the machine. If I had not caught the fuel leak and run out of fuel, I could be stranded.

Everything is fine today. The store bought pocket bread was just the right size to fit in my muffler heater. This gets eaten with gusto. I put snow in the muffler oven can so as I travel further I can have hot water for tea anytime I need it.

Rats! I think we lost our tea when we hit that last bump! I stop to check. Lift up the snow machine engine cowling and, yup, we lost our tea. "Rats." *A sealed container next time?* Hmmm, "Well you know it can't blow up on us, so has to breathe." *A breather hose on it?* "We'd have to build it. I can't think of any such container that already exists. Like a small pressure cooker that holds a couple of cups." And I'm off thinking of the next invention/gadget, *that we can patent and will make us our first million dollars!* Thoughts are interrupted off and on by trail conditions, something interesting to view, or some event unfolding in nature.

Tracks are in the snow where a lynx jumped a rabbit. They twisted and turned, knocking snow off branches, as the lynx gets his daily meal. Taken in a glance as I zoom down the trail. All are scenes mankind has lived with for 50,000 or so years. *Except for the snow machine.* "Yes, for that I have to use my imagination." But I have to face it, much is about imagination. Primitive man had no matches, no down sleep bag, no chain saw, no set of clothes from the salvation army that cost a few dollars (representing one hours work in trade). Clothes used to cost mankind a week's wages!

I often wonder what it would be like to go back in time, and bring all the goodies with me. *Whip out a Bic lighter as others hunker down with a bow drill and piece of wood to start a fire.* "Yeah! As others got out a hundred pound buffalo robe, I pull out my three pound fiberfill that is even warmer and stuffed in this tiny bag. Show the chief a bullet." *Yes, yes this tiny thing in the end will kill a grizzly bear from here to across the valley we are in. I know! I laugh too, sounds impossible doesn't it?*

Moose ahead, pay attention. "No, you pay attention! Let me know what you find out." I depend on and trust my unconscious. It is so nice not to have to do all the thinking around here. *Yes, it's good to be friends with your unconscious. Otherwise, there is an enemy within us. Split personality, schizoid, all that psycho stuff.*

Not much fur sign this season. Tracks of young marten, not so many elders. Not as many traps are put out. I need to help the population, not trap so many this year. *Voluntarily accept less wages in order to help the environment.* I shrug my shoulders. I'm not thinking what it means. Lots of otter tracks, so maybe I can focus on surplus otter. Not as much money, and more work to catch, but I can make some money. I'll need to have more shiny objects for otter as they do not go after bait much. Otter like to catch their own fish.

After a week out on the trail, I turn around and head back towards home, 200 miles away. Near one of my line cabins I have a wolverine I had not expected to get. *I've had some amazing encounters over the years with wolverines! Gave us religion!* "Yes, I recall." Living things that will not die cause one to ponder the Higher Powers. But this one died without much of a struggle. Nice light stripe on the back, which is always desirable when selling.

I stop at Two Map Cabin for the night and skin the wolverine before it freezes solid. I've lost track of what day it is and how many days I have been out. The new electronic age has allowed me to buy a digital watch that is reliable and does not need winding like the old watches. *We just forgot to bring it, right?* "I'm much happier not knowing the day or time." Time is a stressful subject. As I skin the wolverine, I think about this subject.

Growing up, my sister and I had to be quiet so Dad could study. He had a deadline, a test coming up, he seemed always behind and working overtime. There was never enough time. Maybe later. But later never arrived. Time became kind of the enemy, not a friend. There is time here in the wild! Just not time as civilization knows it. Things need to get done all right, and there is a time for it. But not to the nearest minute, or even hour, and rarely to the nearest day. Fish need to get caught, but within the next few weeks. There are no appointments. A day planner is not needed. No alarm clock is needed. No getting fired for being an hour late. No failing and not getting the gold star for skipping a class for the day. It is an important aspect of this lifestyle I like to hang on to. Sleep when I am tired, eat when I am hungry. I do not know many people who can live like that.

I do not answer myself. It's not a question, just a reminder. All my line cabins have propane lights now. Just two have kerosene. The ones furthest out. I forget now how many I have... *there's camp one - fifteen miles out; camp two - twenty-five miles out. This one, on Two Map Lake. Going further out, Hang a Left Lake, Square Lake, Hansen Creek, and the Federal Homesite.* I comment, "Kind of hope a trail will go from there on down to Hansen Cabin on the Kantishna, the old stomping grounds, but we never seemed to have time to get down that way. I run out of traps that direction." I answer myself, *About the time we get traps out, it is time to turn around and check traps on the way home!* "Yeah."

It would be nice if each camp had some snow machine tools I can't haul everywhere I go. All the extra dog stuff at each camp is not much use. There are spare dog harnesses, eating dishes, (used car hub caps I got at garage sales) dog foot medicine, etc. All unused for a lot of years now. *In case we ever get back into dogs!* "Looks like we never will."

In the morning, I add to my list of things to get such as hinges for the door on one of the cabins a bear broke into, more squirrel traps or poison as mice and squirrels always get in. They can eat holes in critically needed blankets, felt boot liners, and chew into packets of food. Wildlife can do a lot of damage during summer months when I am not here. I am no longer optimistic, that one day I will have all the cabins squirrel proof.

Sourdough pancakes with blueberries and honey, with moose meat is my breakfast. I could have propane stoves if I hauled them in, but cooking on the wood stove works. I need to get a good hot fire going in the morning to warm the cabin, so may as well cook at the same time. Same when I arrive, the fire has to be hot so I can cook dinner.

I pack up fresh bread that I made in the wood stove for my lunch today. I learned how to bake bread inside the stove on top of green logs. The bread has a wood smoke flavor, but this does not seem to harm how it tastes. Or I am just used to it. I can do a moose roast, but rarely need that much meat, or a baked potato, only potatoes is not a food that travels well on the trapline. Frozen potatoes do not taste good when thawed. All my cookware is cast iron. To do the dishes'I just put the frying pan in the stove and burn off the leftovers, then blow off the ashes. When still hot, I add a little grease to season the metal. Cast iron cook ware is common at garage sales. Maybe it is considered camping gear? When folks want to tune down their life, cutting camping out of the picture seems a first thing to do. So tents, sleep bags, cast iron cook ware, Coleman stoves, lanterns, and such are very common to find for a dollar or two.

My yearly food bill is still down at $300 a year. Getting a moose saves a lot. Add a few big salmon, some garden stuff and I'm set. I buy whole wheat flour as I always have, in fifty pound bags pretty cheap, and corn meal at the animal feed store, still fifty pounds for $10. $60 for a five gallon bucket of local honey lasts me two years or more. Whole rice and beans in fifty pound bags is still cheap. I'm amazed at what people tell me they spend on food. But, oh well. That's their life. *Ten times my income and they tell me they are struggling. Me telling them how rich I am. That's hilarious!* "Yes, hilarious."

There are new bills coming I never had before, like land taxes, $350 a year, and an electric bill. Water and sewer is due to arrive next summer, no more private well and leach field. Now I am on my own well, with an electric pump and my own septic system. I think about money, and new bills as I head home.

When my trail hits the fork where other travelers branch off, I see foot prints in the snow! Coming from the wilds, headed to civilization, looks like Dim, walking. I stop and look close. Then come upon his snow machine—broke down. I inspect it and see the problem right off. He has burned up his drive belt, and then his spare. He is hauling three huge beaver in the sled—too heavy a load for this depth of snow.

I have a load headed in, but have room for these beaver even though it is an extra 150 pounds. I can help Dim out by hauling them in for him. If left, there is a good chance wolves will eat the beaver before Dim can get back. As I travel, Dim's tracks look steady, but close together like he is tired. The snow is a foot deep. Not horrible, but slows a person up. I hope he is OK. I continue on with the snow machine, and eat up the miles following Dim's tracks. I feel for him, as I have walked out too! Too bad I had not come by first so he had a broke trail to walk in. My incoming snow machine trail is here, but drifted in and with new snow fall, not a good trail to walk. *Maybe I will run into him along the way and give him a ride.* "Let's hope, huh!"

Ten miles, twenty, and now the tracks weave and falter. *I do not want to come across a frozen body.* "Me neither." A few steps. He stands and rests. I've been there, know how it feels. Turn around to check, and realize you have only gone twenty feet since the last rest. Time stands still, every step an effort. Every foot a challenge. A mile is forever.

I see here, where Dim got cold, must have been getting dark. He stops to build a fire. Must have been a couple of hours rest for him, maybe a nap. I see he laid down, but not for a long time, just a rest. The tracks leaving seem stronger. Mile after mile.

Look, weaving, stopping a lot, he is tired for sure now, exhausted, getting to the end if his limits! Five more miles to go yet. "This reminds me of the Minto story from last year." Trapper walked in, got tired, crawled the last mile. Found frozen on his own doorstep. Could not get the door open. Wife and daughter just on the other side of the door. *Yes, sometimes two feet is forever.*

I get to the Nenana River and cross it; looks like Dim made it. There is Josh ahead. I can ask him.

"Hello, Mr. Martin. I just took Dim home."

"I followed his tracks! Is he OK?"

"I think. He was babbling and walking in circles. I'm not sure he would have made it home. I got him in the shack here and warmed him up." Josh pauses a moment. "You came in walking once the same way, remember?"

Yes. More than once, but one time was rougher than the others. Seymour, my survey boss, put it well. How what we do is like top athletes training for the Olympics. I see this best when looking around at ordinary people. I know quite a few city slickers who can't walk 100 feet in a foot of snow. A mile would be a great accomplishment for the average person. Twenty to fifty miles in a foot of snow is the equivalent of qualifying for the Olympics.

"What's in the sled ,Miles?"

"Oh, got Dims furs. I'll run over and drop them off."

Dim is in bed sleeping. His girlfriend greets me with a thanks, and tells me I can drop the beaver in the snow out front. She is the one who usually skins his furs. Sometimes I think they have such a great relationship I envy him. However they both drink, fight, beat each other up, end up in jail and such.

I GET HOME and my new phone rings. "Hello."

Whoever it is repeats "Hello, can you hear me?"

"Miles here. Can you hear me?"

Whoever is calling says, "Turn your music down so I can hear you!"

Pause while I think, then reply, "I'd rather listen to my music than you. Call back later."

"What?"

Click. I stare at the phone. I can't believe it. The audacity of some people. A stranger, telling me what to do in my home. Turn my music down, indeed. How about an, 'Excuse me you sound busy, I'll call back later.' *I can't believe how rude people are!* The call is forgotten, till I check my morning emails. I tend to leave the music on all the time, even when I am gone. I live alone. I guess I like the human sounds. The talking/music greets me at the door when I come home. Instead of "Honey I'm home!" I have a substitute machine answering. Anyhow—emails to check.

Hello Miles. I almost gave up trying to order something from you! I called and you hung up on me! Are you running a business, trying to sell things or not!? Anyhow I'm interested in some wolf claws, let me know if you are in business or not . **Peter**

Reply

Hey Peter! You call me at 9:00 pm to conduct business. You are lucky to get a human being to reply, and not an answer machine…

Wolf claws are listed on the… and I tell him where they are listed. It's a $3 item. Try to keep in mind, my low prices are because I am the source, no middle people. There are more wolves than people where I live. The downside might be, I'm lucky just to have electricity and phone. I have one computer, one email address, one phone and one phone number. I try to explain on the website. I understand, you do not have time to read it! You want me to have time to personally explain it? If you like normal businesses through normal companies you can pay more, and buy from the people I sell to who live in civilization, for three times as much money. Low price = dealing with off the grid…

So many things I need, and only so much money. I need to work with what I have. "Yeah." Customers, even friends make fun of how many mistakes I make. A lot of people calling from 1,000 miles away do not comprehend the time difference, or do not care. I sometimes get calls at 3:00 am.

"Hello, I'm comparing prices…" Many customers have questions they wish to discuss for as long as I am willing to talk, maybe hours, concerning my $3 items. Gravitating to "Oh, you live in Alaska? I always wanted to live there!"

Occupying another hour if I let them. They are ecstatic, and I'm making a penny an hour. Learn to say, "You might enjoy my book! It's all about this!" For only $15.95.

IT'S SUMMER AGAIN, time flies. (or is that 'fly') Into the same routines. Not much changes.

"Miles, how in the heck do you water your greenhouse when you are at the fair? I have been meaning to ask you that. I do not see anyone going over to take care of things." A neighbor is inquiring on the street. What's his name. *You know, one of the Burk boys.*

"Everything is on automatic."

"What do you mean, isn't that stuff expensive, complicated and unreliable?"

"I wouldn't know. I built it all myself and I'm happy with it." I explain the two important factors, temperature and watering, that the greenhouse needs regulated. For temperature I have a fan that turns on if it gets overly hot. I bought one of those cords at the hardware store that turns on to run a heat tape in winter. Costs $3. They do not make one for heat, just cold. It turns power on at 32 degrees. But I took it apart, and saw it operates using a bi metal strip. Two metals back to back that warp with temperature change. I'm familiar with the concept. All I had to do was flip the plate around so it goes off at 32, not on. I bent it a few times so now it operates within the temperature range I want, turning the fan on at 80 degrees. About a half hour job. I just plug a regular fan in.

I also have a window with a wood door that drops over the window when cold. I bought a piston that opens attic vents in houses based on temperature. It is a gas cylinder with an adjustment. As the gas expands from heat, it pushes a plunger that operates a lever.

"The lever pushes the window open."

"But what about watering, Miles?"

"I tried one of those auto-watering devices that run on batteries and they are only OK, not great. They turn on based on time alone. But if it gets cool or rains, the plants get overwatered." I designed an on/off moisture electric tilt switch for $2. You can buy one, but they want $300 and I think mine works better. Or is more fool proof. All it is, is a mercury tilt switch on a balance rod with a sponge on one end and adjustable balance weight on the other. When the soil gets dry, so does the sponge. The light sponge is offset by the adjustable weights that slide on the balance rod about two feet long. Weights overcome dry sponge—rod tilts—which turns on the battery valve in the $15 garden water box. I interrupted the battery contacts with the tilt switch. I just tapped into the positive wire on the battery water timer with the interrupt switch. As the sponge gets wet, it gets heavier, moving the rod down, activating the mercury tilt switch. It might be five times a day if it's hot, or once a week if it's cold. It's an on-demand system that's simple, and does the job. I was gone for a month one time and came home. "All I had to do was weed."

I have drippers, misters, sprayers and soakers, so different parts of the greenhouse get different amounts of water for different kinds of plants. But it is not perfect. The well water I use has rust in it that plugs up the misters, gets rust on the greenhouse plastic that is about impossible to remove, so cuts down on the light. I'm still perfecting the system. I'm supposed to get city water maybe next year. I'm unsure how I feel, as it adds to bills and costs I do not have now. Everything is ongoing.

"I often spend as much time fooling and adjusting gadgets as I do simply doing the watering and opening the door manually!" I say this mostly so I do not come across as bragging, or having my nose in the air being smarter than the average bear. I get a nod of understanding. But he understood what?

My neighbor asks me about gassing up my boat. "I tried to get Shaw to deliver gas but he does not have time. I'm not sure how to get gas. My boat is on the river and I don't have a truck to get gas at the station out on the road. I used to get it at the river bulk plant! Just pull up in our boat and the hose would be handed to us, and we'd buy gas pumped right in the boat."

"Yes, I notice that too. Once I had to roll a fifty-five gallon drum a mile from the gas station to my boat in Manley Hot Springs. I used a wheel barrel here in Nenana before. Or I get Josh to make a trip for me with his truck. But that requires having a friend who will help. I wonder what the homesteaders who come in for gas do."

"I heard the reason the bulk plant stopped is about safety and oil spill issues."

"I heard that as well. Insurance, regulations, EPA, are so hard on the gas company, they gave up. If they spill so much as a thimble full of gas in the river, they legally have to fill out a report. It's nuts."

"Ha. I know. Only last week I had a barrel on the river bank, trying to siphon gas into my tank on the boat with a hose. The bank caved in and the whole barrel went in the river. I lost the barrel and all the gas. Much more of a spill than a possible thimble full if the fuel company makes a mistake filling my tank."

My neighbor explains. "The fuel company is set up to deliver fuel. Those of us at the river bank are not set up for this, so there is more chance for an accident."

Yes I know. I have had this discussion many times with homesteaders. I lost twenty gallons of gas in the river before, the same way this neighbor did. My neighbor thinks the rules are not about being safe, but about control. Jobs for people who regulate such things. I have no answer for him.

"Geez, Miles, I wanted to take off today downriver. It's going to take a full day just to get gas. I have work to do at fish camp."

It is spring once again, and 'Fish Camp' is a way of life. The time to get out on the river and think of the fishing season, the cabin on the river, the fish nets, firewood at camp, clearing brush, maybe see if bears tore the place up. I want to get to the homestead. Just need a break in my business.

MEANWHILE—

I got a web program to do a better job on my web site. It's a $50 program. There is frustration dealing with a dial up internet connection. But that is all we have in our remote village. High speed might be years away. There has been some help here and there, understanding the internet in general. Perhaps it's slow progress for me becoming more of a social person. I am now head of our community Chamber of Commerce. We meet once a month, but there are things to get done all month. Sub-committees that meet, decisions to make, people to contact and consult with, which involves social skills.

I explained to Josh, who does not understand, "Getting along; survival, depends on understanding and dealing with your environment right?"

"Sure, Miles, in the woods you have to understand the weather, bear behavior, where food is and things like that."

We agree, and have talked about this a lot over the years. "So, Josh, I'm saying that in town the rules are the same, only the environment involves people and understanding them."

Josh has sled dogs chained up. Some are worth thousands of dollars. He does not like loose dogs starting fights with his dogs, or mutts breeding his $5,000 females. It's worth getting involved in the dog leash law for example.

One main reason to 'get involved,' is not liking the fact the community comes to me to kill loose dogs as a solution. I want to change that. The Chamber addresses many issues of concern to the community. Usually financial issues, or in my opinion, that is what 'Chambers' do. But we sort of took over the functions of the disbanded Lions Club. I am not happy about our role. Many of our functions seem more suited for the disbanded Lions Club, or a church group. Like putting on children programs, doing a Xmas event, and Thanksgiving dinner for the community.

I go along with the consensus of the group though. One of the reasons I had such interest in the first place was, I feel many business people in Nenana push for volunteerism, and the citizens feel used and burned out. Major local businesses encourage citizens to give of themselves for the good of the community. Yet they themselves are not setting examples. It comes across as a scam, a way to make money off other people's free labor, and sense of community.

So my thought is, *Let's talk about making money, getting paid, and taking care of ourselves by paying our way!* I thought making money would be an exciting topic to have as a priority. "I feel a Chamber's role is to look out for the welfare of the business people who are paying their dues. Only if there is left over time should we put energy into the community at large. I agree we need to concern ourselves with the business people's relationship with the community, but in so far as it reflects our business." *Church groups, the school, Lions and other such organizations can look out for the community in general.* "Yeah!" I'm not going to say this to the public. There is politics involved, and I'm aware of this. We need to create good relations with the community in order to exist. There are not good relations for two main reasons.

The first is that there are some businesses in Nenana that have been here a long time, and have a monopoly on their line of business. They feel they worked hard to get where they are, so are not inclined to want to help stimulate competition, driving prices down. Those businesses who join the Chamber, pay dues, and show up, tend to be the ones who have a need. "Do something! Help us!" But they can barely afford dues, and tend to not show up to do much. "Too busy!" Those with political clout, money, knowledge, who are in a position to help, tend not to join because they feel there is nothing in it for them. They are not in favor of change.

The second issue is the bars, the sale of alcohol. It represents a lot of money - a huge and major portion of the community's income, and thus political focus. The bar owners are not chamber members. There are drinkers and non drinkers. The two groups tend not to mix. Most of the Chamber members are among those who do not drink. The bars make a lot of money with pull tabs. They want the backing of a Chamber of Commerce with a gambling permit. There is also Chamber talk of restricting bar hours.

I hear, "Sober people make more money, spend more money, and provide a better, safer work place for the community." And - "Tourism and drunks in the street do not mix well. Drinking and stealing go hand in hand."

The local cop tells us, "Drinking is 90% of our community's police force and volunteer fire crew costs."Over time, money for local police comes and goes. At the moment we have a local cop. Our present mayor is one of the town drunks.

The Chamber, when reflecting on the community, also thinks of the future and the message we send to our children. Will the message to the young be, 'Hang out at the bar if you want a job, influence people, be respected, and make money'? If the Chamber and City Council are not on the same page, it is hard to see the Chamber being effective. The City Council has the political clout, and is the source of a lot of the business discrimination, being responsible for laws, codes, and enforcing them. Permits to do business can be given or denied. Tickets handed out and enforced for drunk driving is council controlled.

Recognizing this, my personal reason for giving of my time, is to help create some equality where a strong Chamber has some political clout to be a force to be reckoned with when facing the City Council, compared to one business trying to get things done. I also say to the new Chamber, "It would cost us all less to advertise if we could work together as a unified force. With community adds, working together for half a page, instead if each of us with a business card size add." I'm referring to travel magazines, Alaska magazine and other outlets we advertise through. "Also radio ads." I'm certain half a page adds get more viewing.

THE CHAMBER, it appears to me, is allowed to exist, as long as we replace the Lions Club, feed the community, and do not rock the boat. We are thus, in my view, very limited on what we can effectively do as a Chamber for the businesses. I'd as soon fix the issues with the bar owners. Maybe work on the laws, so bars may be legal and avoid fines, a high cost to the bars right now. Offering a safe place to hang out for non-drinkers might increase bar revenue.

"A village bar could be a social gathering place for us all. A place where people gather to shoot darts, play pool, watch the football game together, and eat. Where not everyone drinks, or drinks no alcohol." Taking the idea from English pubs. I have no problem with gambling as a way to raise revenue, such as pull tabs, raffles, auctions. The majority of the community supports this. However it is a lot of work someone has to deal with - voluntarily.

I'm told as well, "It puts us, our community, each of us under the limelight from bigger government, keeping close track of how we do things!" There are reasons not to be under Federal scrutiny. I am in favor of running ourselves, far away from our King. *Our country had this issue ages ago and is why we broke from England.*

Meanwhile, the Chamber meets. We decide who will play Santa and use Chamber money to buy toys, as is the wish of the community. But in so doing, indirectly I am getting known. What I stand for, what I do beyond just talk, gets noticed by some who pay attention to such things.

I donate art to the school for fundraisers, spend time putting up posters, setting up chairs and discuss community issues with maybe a different class of people than I have dealt with in the past. Shop owners, the magistrate, the gal who owns the newspaper get to know me, not just homesteaders. Few pillars of the community see much use for homesteaders. This has been so throughout history.[2]

I write regularly for the paper as well, and donate articles. I think I was always like this, only I had some setbacks. I had started out back in Canada, in the first community I settled in, back in '72. I got the ice rink opened up, donated time at the library, and eventually would have attended city meetings and stood for something. Hopefully something positive. Getting deported soured me on wanting to get involved. How many years later can I overcome this? Thirty years? It takes a long time to heal sometimes. So here I am trying to make a difference in a positive democratic way. But one price for getting involved, taking sides and being active, is to make enemies.

Many of my ways are odd, according to society. I have weird personal habits from living alone so long. I still get all my clothes at the Salvation Army. I still like to fix things, rather than go buy new ones, and my fixes are not for looks, so there is duct tape and baling wire hanging from many projects that is not socially cool. I eat 'weird stuff' like lynx meat. As was so with many in the olden times. I used to sell it for human consumption to the elders. I cut my own hair and do not do a good job. It all takes away from being credible, when I speak or do anything. This also makes it easy to attack, discredit, and otherwise render me ineffective. The word I'd use is 'heartbreaking'.

The issue over loose dogs comes up off and on. A little girl in a panic stops me on the street crying and scared, "I lost my dog a few hours ago. Barbie got away dragging a chain; you didn't kill her, did you? Why do you hate dogs so much? I hope I find my dog before you do!"

I sigh. "I do not go around looking for loose dogs. If I know who the dog belongs to, or if it is wearing a collar with an ID tag on it, I try to get hold of the owner. If I see your dog, I will let you know, OK?"

Poor kid, thinks I'm hunting her dog down. Who else thinks that? Who tells such stories and why? It seems odd to me that my thinking is not understood or universally shared. I had an 'incident' long ago this reminds me of. *Yes, Canada. We were 23 years old. We made a sculpture of a wolf in clay supported on a pole. Locals asked why I am stringing up dead dogs in my yard.* "I felt complimented, that the clay sculpture looked like a real dog! Wow!" The community set me up and I was deported. Partly because, maybe they thought I was weird, or 'not like them,' and into the realm of 'threatening.' So what people say and think can matter. Survival can depend on it.

I bring up the subject at the next Chamber of Commerce meeting. "We have talked about this before. I do not like to be the one who takes the brunt of the problem. If we as a community agree we do not want to tolerate loose dogs, we need to make a united stand and address the City Council. Maybe instead of just speaking of a problem, let's offer a solution. There is a leash law on the books, why is it there? " So we as a group agree, and discuss various ideas to present to the city. One idea put out is to offer a reward for picking up strays paid for by the one who owns the dog. The money collected supports dog catcher costs. Or the cost of taking the dog to the Fairbanks Pound.

One member points out, "Miles. So then what?" Personally, I think word will get out that dogs end up at the pound and people will keep better track of their dog. I realize. however, that some families do not want a dog, but the children do. The parents are not strong enough to say no. If the dog is simply 'ignored' it eventually disappears, problem solved. Not 'problem solved' if there is a cost to take the dog to Fairbanks, or a fine. We could require name tags on dogs like in some communities.

"Yes, how can you care about a pet and not want it to be identifiable? I know it is the first thing I do, put on a tag with name and phone number so anyone who finds my pet can get it back to me!" It is understood in the old days everyone knew everyone, and whose dog belonged to whom, so there was no need to collar dogs. It seems an unnecessary law in a world filled with rules and laws. We want our freedom of choice to put a name on them or not.

"Those who do not choose to have her dog be identifiable can pay the price!" But in the end, it is the dog that pays the price. Or the community through fear of loose dogs, those getting bitten, none of which is fair.

Balanced with my words, "I have seen children knocked off bikes by dogs chasing them. Every one of us knows someone who got bit. Joggers get bit all the time. I believe it is inevitable there will be a serious encounter. There are now pit bulls running loose. If a child or elder gets injured, we will all be in shock and wonder how that could happen. Worse, I fear some sue happy tourist will get bit. Princess Tours could stop offloading its tourists, hurting our economy, even sue the community for being irresponsible." I know elders who will not walk certain streets because they are afraid. I think this is not the kind of community we want. These concerns offset an individual's right to allow their dog its freedom.

Most agree with me. I go on to explain that I do understand our dilemma. We have important people in the community who are among the offenders with loose dogs, like the village Indian Chief. If the Chamber has anything to do with his dog getting reprimanded, it will be called prejudice, discrimination. Maybe a lawsuit. There are also dogs many do not mind running loose.

One board member adds, "Blackie, everyone knows Blackie, food is put out for him at the store and Post Office. He has been around forever. He would never bite anyone!" So that's a big issue. We want to pick and choose who among the dogs needs to be tied up, and who can run free. How, and who, decides? We are not in agreement.

The same issue with our village children running loose, "My child would never do that!" Followed by, "How dare you accuse my child of smoking pot!" *Your child who you rarely know where he-she is, not even at mealtime or bed time.* "Nothing I dare say out loud." I'm a little socially inept. I am not suicidal.

Then, added to the issue, are the people around here, who, if you kill their dog, would burn your house down or kill you. Few want to go there. So the solution appears to me to be, the community makes up a law we do not enforce. A law is randomly applied at will with discrimination, saying "Well it's the law!" Yet is not applied equally to everyone. It comes across in my mind as a way to railroad people.

I seem to have a personal issue about this dog thing. First, I spent time in the wilds, have wild habits and smell like the wild. Many dogs do not like this strange wild scent, so get more aggressive towards me than some people. I deal in furs, meat, bones, teeth and claws and smell like it. Second, I have a thing about my rights being lower than a dog's. I already have social status, authority issues. It will be a cold day in Hell when a dog tells me what to do or where I cannot go. Likewise, I resent the dog owners who enjoy their dog keeping everyone off the entire street, and enjoy the fear their dog instills. The dog does their dirty work; work that they can not do themselves, but the dog can. I see the owners in the window scowling as their dog attacks me. I yell at the dog to shut up. The owner comes out furious,

"Stop teasing my dog!"

If I reply "Well, your dog stared it!" That sounds rather childish. I can whisper to the dog "You just come onto my turf away for your owner protector, you blankety blank mutt and we shall see who is in charge!" *I'm resentful of feeling this way. I begin my walk smelling the flowers, listening to the birds with a smile on my face and good word for all I see. Now I end up taking out my feelings on the next person I see, or the whole community. This is not doing me or the community much good.* "Not much we can do about it."

Jack Corncob is on the City Council. I talk off and on about laws, what they are for, how they get made, how to change them, who is in charge, who can enforce laws, why we have rights. Questions like, "Do we all really have equal rights?" Stuff like that. Jack helped write the Alaska Constitution. I never forget that. I'm on the Library Board, and so is Jack. I get to see him in action sometimes. We just had a library meeting. We are trying to change our bylaws to allow a process to take place that meets requirements for us to have an organization called, 'Friends of the Library' that would allow us to do fundraisers for the library. As things stand now, all funds the library raises go to the city general fund. The library loses control of the funds. We want to sell or auction off collections of books. While we are rewording the bylaws, we are fixing some minor wording issues. It should be a small thing now, after weeks of work, now taking a few minutes to approve. We will then have the long wanted organization, 'Friends of the Library.' We hope to get started right away raising library money!

One board member who likes to be particular, can spend hours over tiny details, and is about to point out an error. Nothing that changes the meaning, but would require a review, another meeting and another open for discussion. We have already dragged this on for months. We all inwardly moan. Here we go again. This protester says, "Let us refer to the Roberts Rules of action... " She has this book of rules in front of her. But before she can touch the book, Jack reaches out and grabs it. We are six country dressed folks sitting around an old wood table with folding chairs.

Jack says, "You know what this book is ?" We all listen to what he has to say on a midwinter, pitch dark, fifty below northern lights evening. "This is all about getting along and being nice. If we get along, and can discuss things, and agree, we do not need this book. Do we get along and are we all in agreement?"

The protester stops, blinks a few times as if waking up, and coming back down to earth, saying, "Yes, everything is fine."

It is agreed we do not really have a problem here and so, no, we do not need to look anything up. So smooth, how Jack saved the day. I try to learn from him. It is said he has been a hard man. *You would not want to be on his bad side. Very complicated man.*

"You must be referring to the Gene murder." Jack was mayor of Nenana for five straight terms. Before my time. I take it, he ran things much like a Wild West sheriff. He is not interested in being on the Chamber board. Jack sides with the bar owners. The Chamber has the reputation of being a church group. One of our members refused to go put signs up in the bar. I personally think the smart business people in town who like things as they are with their monopoly, will use any excuse to make problems, and jump on a subject, and use it to their advantage.

A small incident became a major problem, on purpose. I may not agree fully with the thinking or behavior of everyone in the Chamber or on the Board. Yet we all have one thing in common. We put our actions where our mouths are. We stand up to be counted, we pay our dues, take the time to show up at meetings and do something, with no excuses.

I have said to the bar owners "So join! Get your friends to join. Become a majority and run the Chamber how you and your friends feel it should be run." I neither drink nor go to church. I try not to be involved in that fight.

"Why bother, Miles, we already run things."

Another chamber member is our magistrate, who I am getting to know, Dale. He is the one who denied any kind of action when I reported Gene Graham trying to kill me. "Not enough evidence." I have never brought that up, but wonder if Gene would be alive today if anything had been done about that, and he had gotten help. I honestly think the guy was going off his rocker. Maybe medication, or just temporary time out, or the reality of a short stay in jail, might have gotten him back on track. But, whatever. Dale seems to be someone who cares about the world and how it is run. He has some good ideas on how to deal with issues, so is a good one to listen to. Being a magistrate, he knows the law better than the average person might.

His idea is, we – the community - should simply focus on the good stuff we are trying to do, and not fight back, or even address the negative things said. I wish we had a more evenly distributed representation of business in the community through the Chamber. Get at least one bar owner to join, for example. Some members do not have a business, but simply want to help out, I guess the community, not necessarily the business people join. We have about twenty members and a board of seven. In a community of 300, that is not so bad. There was no Chamber a few years ago. I helped from the ground floor to get one started.

I'm meeting with the barge people, the restaurant owners, gift shop owners, people connected with the school. I seem to not have as much time for the homesteaders, trappers, bush folks I once spent time with. Maybe it is a new game. Something different to focus on, like this art business and web site. I'm challenged and intrigued by the various issues involved in a web business. (!)

I notice right off that I do not know where a customer is from, what race, color, age, or sex a customer is by the email address, or communication concerning business. I talk to Dale about 'business' in general."The internet might eliminate prejudice. Also cut out a lot of the middle people one day." I have this vivid image in my head I relate. "Dale, I imagine a kid in the Amazon with a laptop computer in the jungle." I think 'Amazon' maybe because of 'Amazon.com.' I explain how this kid sees a parrot in the trees. He grabs it. Hunkered down under big leaves in a rain forest, in a loin cloth. He gets on line with his lap top computer and types, 'Have parrot'; someone in New York types, 'Looking for parrot.' He can make a deal. This rich lady in New York pays $300 for a parrot, direct to the kid who found it. Impossible to do a few years ago. This kid would have gotten five cents for the parrot, if lucky. It would have gone to some dealer, then to a distributor, then to a vet, then to a store, with everyone along the way doubling the money, collecting and paying for fees, insurance, inspections, etc., ad nauseam till the lady would get it in a pet shop for $1,500.

What happens with the internet, is that the middle guy is cut out. "Now, this kid can run his own business. I think it is cool, and a huge change in the world, opening doors between countries for equal commerce around the world." This sums it up simply. In general, we cut out lots of middle people and deal much more directly with the source. There can be much less slave labor, with folks being between a rock and hard place, and no choices. Much more direct business between countries and much more communication, a so much better reality about the world at large.

"In theory, Miles,"

"Yes, in theory." That term 'educated idiot' comes to mind that I was introduced to when I first arrived in Alaska. I understand what Dale was getting at. He's a lawyer, almost a judge. Will laws keep up with the changes? Will big business allow this Amazon kid to get paid for the parrot he caught? Will countries allow their people to meet, trade, mingle, get to know others around the world, and view us all as equals with equal buying power? Is 'equal' to any government's advantage? Will there be restrictions due to the possibility of importing disease? Will that be an excuse for denial; control? Will the internet end up with rules interfering with free trade, for no other reason than, so organized crime gets its cut? In the name of looking out for our best interest?

Future Flash

In 2013 I have an internet web conversation with a friend, employee, of a big Fairbanks store. The subject of all the rules and regulations comes up.

"Telling us what we can import and not! Stopping free enterprise!" I snort. My friend, without anger tells me of another side of the story.

"A year ago our store accepted a shipment of imitation Christmas trees. They were made of pieces of shaved wood imported from overseas. There is an exemption in the import law, if the plant product is not considered raw, but a finished worked art item. Untreated wood has a spruce tree fungus in it, not present in our area, or anywhere is the USA. Customers put these trees outdoors for decoration. The bugs spread. Now the entire hillside south of Fairbanks is covered in dead spruce trees, with the bug and death to trees spreading. Because of this imported bug arriving through our store, sold to us on the internet with no inspections." I'm not educated much on this side of reality.

Future flash ends

I sigh, offering my viewpoint to Dale, "We, in the U.S., often talk of equality and fairness. We speak of a world without prejudice. Equal pay for equal work, no matter if you are black, a woman or any minority." I pause and add, " How lovely." With sarcasm. "It is easy for the winner of the race to be in a good mood, have nice kind words to say about the race officials and racing in general. But the measure of character is seen in the one who comes in last. Ask this one about the officials and the sport. The U.S. is top dog- living high on the hog.

It is easy to say, "Halt! Stop this fighting and complaining, let us have peace." Peace means the status quo, no change. We would then remain high on the hog, living well. It is also so easy to tell others to change. See what it is others need to do, so there may be peace and equality." It has been Dale himself who has helped firm my beliefs.

How many small business people come to me, the head of the Nenana Chamber and suggest things we need to do to make things fair, right, and stand up for something? Usually, maybe even 'always' it is the small business owner who needs help of some kind. Usually this is not even a member, saying "Can't afford dues." Does not show up at meetings, saying, "There is no time!" But wants help, wants others to come up with the time. So I have been learning to ask for a solution to be proposed. A solution that involves them. An appropriate reply might be, "Good ideas! I'll put you in charge of a committee to investigate this. You can give the group a report of your findings and the results at our next meeting."

If I hear, "Oh, but I thought that is what the Chamber is for, to take care of stuff like that!" *Yes, well, who is the Chamber exactly?*

Dale reminds me, on a related subject, "Alaska just sent tons of salmon over to Russia, who is having a hard time this season."

I recall this, because I was not allowed to fish. Told, "Not enough fish in the river, Miles. We have to give the fish a chance to spawn!" I am not very trusting. I do not know for a fact any fish at all ever reached the hungry in Russia. Nor do I know for a fact, Russia did not have to pay one way or the other for this 'gift'[3].

"Well, it's a valid view, Miles, all we can do is keep at it, learn, and do our best.

Hang in there." I noticed, without saying he agreed or disagreed. *Spoken as a true politician.*

"Yes, well, it is only a mood, one view for now." *Is war really about the poor having a need?* Actually, I speculate not. As I get older and wiser I see the poor very often as a group, being content enough with their lot in life. I have seen many fairly happy poor people - even more than happy rich. Is war about those who have, trying to squeeze a little bit more from those who do not have enough to live to begin with? But squeezing five more cents per person out of a billion or trillion people is a lot of money when given to a handful of people. Thus, I am not actually indignant and full of righteousness. I do not know what is going on. Or even what the right answer is. It all began with a single pure dream of some kid in the Amazon and a parrot, and the possible wonders of a future internet. This is my vision.

Based on this vision, I set up my internet business accordingly. I wish to be open minded to new opportunity, especially worldwide. I understand there will be cultural differences, so set up my web site explaining how I do business, what I stand for, who I am, and define terms and words, so there will be the fewest misunderstandings. I try to do so with humor if I can, such as explaining selling raw material: 'Raw to me means dead, but still twitching, or out of the ground wet and still muddy.' Because? Many customers deal with shops who call a raw wolf claw, one that has been cleaned, the bone glued back in the hull, polished, a hole drilled in it, and all you have to do is put a chain on it to call it your finished product."

A customer who expects 'raw' to mean, 'ready to sell as is,' may well feel 'ripped off,' if they get what I call raw. Replying with words like "Yucko, it still has fur on it!" Or "How do I get rid of the smell!" I begin standard cut and paste replies, so I do not have to keep repeating myself.

"You get what you pay for, and the price is low because it has had no work put into it. I offer this to those who know how to clean it, prepare it, and want the good low price. The price is not low because you got a killer deal and I'm stupid. You may want a 'further up the line from raw' product? I sell this on the same page. As you can see, for twice the price. Either you get it cheap and clean it yourself, or you pay me to do that."

I would think all this is self evident as in 'business 101.' As in 'what planet are you from.' I struggle trying to be kind and understanding. In truth, I buy the wolf claw raw, meaning still on the frozen carcass. That's the best price of all. I've already done a lot to it by the time it is offered to the public as 'raw.' I also have to deal with what is the legal definition of things! Such as what may I legally ship in the mail? Obviously, not a frozen wolf carcass, but at what level? I do in fact get frozen wolf skulls sent to me from the villages. Bloody, thawed out, dripping and smelling by the time they arrive. No big deal to a villager, just a way of life. His whole yard smells like this, so he is puzzled at any distress this causes.

More than once the Post Office has called me. "Miles get over here right now and pick this package up. There's something dead in it! I refuse to bring it in my post office, it is on the back steps!" Luckily, the Post Office is run by Martha, my buddy Josh's wife. Grin. Most of my customers, I'm discovering, do not have a clue what 'raw' means. So I tell 'em raw stories and ask, "Is this what you want?"

I tell Martha when I pick up bloody packages, "Oh this is nothing, Martha. I had a teacher once who had a beetle tank for cleaning skulls as a school project. She asked for a wolf skull raw, frozen for the beetles. Being open minded to all sorts of new concepts for business, I sent her a frozen skull. Figuring it would get to New York in three days, as usual. I figure it would stay frozen for five days before it began to drip. But the package got lost in the mail. I think lost for three weeks." Martha smiles and rolls her eyes up. She knows all about this, maggots and dead things, as Josh drags all kinds of stuff in for the sled dog cooker. So yes, the rules change when leaving the village, and assume different parts of the country, then again for different countries. I need to know what those rules and expectations are where you live, and get a feel for where you are coming from as a customer. This affects the legal aspect. The issue can be way more than a misunderstanding!

I explain further, "Yeah, Martha, when store owners had physical stores in the old days, the customer could make an easier assessment of the kind of business they were going into by the address, the condition of the building, the number of cars in the parking lot, how the owner is dressed, what color the person is etc., and it all gives information on the kind of business, like if the owner is doing well or whatever.

We, as customers, decide if we want to go in or not. If we are looking for a diamond ring, we may not go into a shop in an unlit back alley, next to a dumpster. Yet that location might be what we expect when buying raw wolf claws." I explain it is also true for store owners, looking for good customers! "How do I recognize various customers? It is amazing the information we gather and make decisions on that might even be unconscious! The age of a person, how they walk, dress, talk etc. all give us information. When I get an email I often have to begin by asking stuff like, "Are you nine years old or 90? Is this for a school project, a scientific lab, a craft project?" I can often 'guess' the answer to these questions, if I can see the person. I can make a decision, and have information that affects what I show the customer, or how much time I spend. If I saw a ten year old in person, I might show them cut glass, not a diamond. It's quite a challenge, Martha!"

"This new internet thing, you can have it. It's beyond me. I have no use for computers!" Yes, I can understand this view. As for me, I'm seeing a way I can move out of the wilds, still be a free man, live remote, and make a living. What are my skills and what am I qualified for? Martha points out that I gave a talk at Kantishna

Roadhouse last year. And Moose asked me to be a speaker on his upcoming tourist paddle boat. I shrug my shoulders.

"Maybe, Martha. But the Roadhouse only let me stay there for free, they did not pay me to talk. Moose talked about paying as much as $10 an hour on his tour boat - basically minimum wages, and wants me to move to Fairbanks." The Park and Princess pay tour guides minimum wage, hire outsiders, give them a crash course on Alaska, and send them off to speak to tourists with authority. There are ways to get paid more, but it takes work, time, and is a way of life. It's not what I'd be happy at. I'm not patient enough, and I tend to… well… not follow the rules. I'd be off telling the Gene Graham story in three part harmony. Shocking the poor tourists. I'd be saying, "You call that raw? Here let me show you what raw is!" We both laugh. I'd be whipping out a raw bloody paw with tendons hanging from it.

Martha adds, "Or one of your maggot stories!" She gets my point. But a lot of customers do not! It is common to get an indignant, "Well, all customers should be equal, it does not matter who or what I am!" But equal to me does not mean the same. *Try to imagine a car dealer.* "Yes, exactly." I know what my unconscious means. If you were a car dealer, what does equal mean? Are all used cars equal? Could anyone be matched to any car? No, that would be ridiculous. A sixteen year old, an old woman, a rich man, a welfare worker, a farmer, all have different needs. To be ethical, it would be good to try to match a car to a need, by asking questions.

"I need a car." This is not enough information for a car dealer, and is not enough information for a wolf claw. For the same five dollars I have a huge record size wolf claw that is damaged, a tiny one that is perfect, or a rare tiny white one; ones that look good, or hold up good, or have a cool story behind them.

"Does a customer want all those qualities or just one? Not all for $5, dream on!" I'm an expert on the subject, and wish to verify what you say you want, with the knowledge I have. As I feel any reputable person in any business would.

I also exercise a personal view selling personal one of a kind raw items. Martha understands, being married to a Native and being from a small subsistence village.

"I feel if you cannot handle the reality of the item you buy, like what a raw claw is, where it comes from, how it is acquired, you do not deserve one!" Martha snorts, "See how far you get with that attitude, Miles! Ha!" *So a solution is to spell it out in the web site, ask what level you want to come in on and here is the price break.* "This should work!"

I make an entry in my computer diary. I'm intent on understanding my computer so I can run a business better.

Sunday—Mastering Windows 98

Three days—ten hours, forty-two minutes, fourteen and three tenths of a second. I slam my fist down on the desk, and look up at the clock. I stand, with hands raised over my head triumphantly, as the crowd up there in the balcony roars. The spotlights are bright upon me, but being blinded by them is the price one pays for the hall of fame. Reporters from all over the world rush forward with microphones—all asking questions at once.

"Is it true Mr. Martin, that you lived twenty-five years in the wilderness without electricity, only got it two years ago, and today have set the record for mastering 'Windows 98?" I smile modestly in this direction as another question overlaps, but of course I have to face the crowd; bow to the right (the crowd roars); bow to the left (more, louder roars. Crowds like to be acknowledged—) "…That you know all about Word 2000, looked up every program, document, file, have mastered Photo Deluxe, Zip Drive, Publisher, can reformat, get on the net, upload—download, and in short can do anything your computer offers?"

"All true, yes, all true." Spoken with the right amount of shy modesty, facing the camera 'just so,' with my 'Wild Miles famous mountain man' look.

"But isn't it true that in erasing the games program you lost important data and 'remind exe.' in 'win.ini' cannot be found and an important message saying so, now shows up every time you boot up?" Microphone in the face for answer.

Ignoring this silly question, I smile and nod at the parting crowd.

"And the Zip. Is it really zipping like it should? Didn't you get a 'full disk' signal when the Zip was only 1% full? Isn't that so?"

Annoying microphone in the face again. look around. (Will my body guard whisk this guy off?) I'm still smiling at the roaring crowd; wave. Another microphone in the face, reporter posed with notepad to record my every word for all time.

"You cut and pasted the Juno email along with all its files from the old computer—Windows 95. into the new computer—Windows 98—without the 'install' disk? How is that possible? How did you bypass the 'illegal operation'?"

"There is 'illegal,' and then there are people like me, who don't understand the meaning of the word 'can't!'" I smile and wink. The reporter scribbles furiously. Is that a woman swooning in the background? The pretty one with the bright red scarf?

😊 :) ?

My shy smile turns her direction, but no, she only slipped on the ice. Smile goes on by without pausing. We didn't see that. Oh, the price of fame, setting records, being so great.

"Stayed up seventeen straight hours at the computer till you solved the printer hook up problem?"

Someone in the background: "Did you hear that? Seventeen hours, amazing." The voice drifts off but is repeated down along the line as I walk.

When alone at last, I sigh, all that attention, all that noise, all those sponsors wanting to hand out money, if I will only say I drink milk as I work, wear Spock bunny boots, Google glasses. I let my agent handle all those details. Agent, agent,

agent. I still have that smile as I stare out the window of my log cabin, chickadees at the feeder. Rub my eyes. A break from the computer, which I haven't left. There, of course, is no crowd, no reporters, and no fanfare. I shrug my shoulders. It doesn't matter, not really. I came out of the wilderness and wanted to understand the computer. And I did. It's all inside me. That's what matters. No one else has to know. Perhaps down the road. If there is a book? Someone might ask how I did it. I might open my mouth to explain, and simply shrug my shoulders. It would be a long story. I would say what?

"I had a dream!" "There is no substitute for work!" "It took me twenty-five years!" "There is nothing else in my life—I live and breathe the dream, at the cost of everything else, look around, I don't even bother to wash my dishes, nor care what I wear, what I eat, everything but my work is 'minor details.' Hours I work are measured in the thousands."

There are no weekends. there are no holidays. Say, "It all comes with a price, it wasn't 'free!'" Do I let that sink in? Would anyone really and truly want to know about the life of a manic depressive? Would I sum it up so neatly with one simple word? "Insanity." Probably I would smile my smile, nod my nod, wink my wink, (that I always do), that tells it like it is, "If you don't love what you do, you haven't lived. Dare, to follow your dream. "Or my one single word standard reply?" "Magic!" Or "Talent!"

My diary entry ends

Fall comes around at the end of the year 2000. There has been much thought given to the mammoth tusk that sold for $26,000 in Tucson, that I only got $2,000 for.

"Mom? Yes, I got my ticket to come to Tucson for a visit. I can use my Permanent Dividend Fund money to pay for the trip. You know, the oil revenue money all Alaskans get, like I used last year? I will set up at the Fossil Gem Show at the end of January. I suppose, take the same spot, even though it cost me half a year's wages! If I remember right, $5,000 to set up at the Howard Johnson's " The phone connection is not great so we have to speak up.

"Goodness Miles, that is a lot of money! Have you found more tusks to sell ?"

"No, mom, it's a once in a lifetime find, probably. But there is other ivory and other artifacts I found I might get top dollar for. Who knows, my art made from animal products and fossils might sell too!" I have to speak up: "I said my art might sell too!" I try to explain how an Eskimo I heard of went to this show and sold out all his stuff the first day and came home! I have to end the conversation due to the bad connection. I can phone back with the details later. I have not seen mom much in my life. *My sister told me she was dead.* I saw mom for the first time in twenty years. The visit was only OK. We hardly knew each other. She does not like change, and her routine was interrupted by my visit. I was busy at the show anyhow. She and her boyfriend and I and her sister went on a day trip to Tombstone and had an OK time. But the trip is 75% about going to do the show. While in Tombstone, a vendor stops me, and asks if I am Miles. I say yes. It turns out this vendor knows me from Alaska. Mom was in shock anyone here might know me! It is common enough for me, but I could see mom sees me in a new light. People know me, her son!

Different from twenty-thirty years ago, saying, "Headed out into the wilds, Mom, never to see another human being again, bye!" So, what happened? This doesn't sound much like the sort of person anyone would know about.

I decided I can go visit Helm in Germany as well. He has been inviting me, and the invitation seems genuine. Maybe see my son in California. Germany first. There is a direct new flight from Fairbanks to Frankfurt. Helm is sure I can sell a lot of my art work in Germany. I agree, because so many of my customers are German tourists, and seem to love my showy style of animal art. Helm also tells me his friend at Raak can handle my book, that is ready now to print. I understand the computer well enough to put the book on a Zip Drive, with all the pictures in place, cover done, and ready to print. There can be a chance to actually meet with these people one on one, and discuss how to do this. I've explained to friends "Cutting edge technology, not yet offered in this country, print on demand."

Helm tells me this is a million dollar machine; no other like it in the world. It's a little scary to actually print the book. It is one thing to tell your friends you are busy working on a book, and build up their anticipation and expectations. What if the book is no good and I am not a good writer, or the subject matter is of no interest to anyone but me? After all, I did poorly in English in school. At one point I flunked English. So what makes me think I can be a writer? Besides my own warped ego? My own inflated opinion of myself. This might be like proving to my parents I'm worth something and can make it. Yet, like some horrible nightmare, the harder I try to make my point, the more I prove their point. How much in my life have I been laughed at, made fun of. You'd think I'd learn, give up, and accept my lot in life as an incompetent idiot.

If I get the book printed, there will be physical evidence, some object to hold up to ridicule. Still. It's me. It's my story as I see it, through my eyes as I live it. For better or worse. It represents certainly hundreds of hours, even thousands of hours. Now thirty years in the making. People might talk badly about it, but did they write a book?

"Oh yeah, good idea, I think I'll do that,"

I hear a lot, "If Miles can do it, anyone can do it." Partly true. Anyone can do it. "If" and it is a big if. If you do the work. It may require thousands of hours. Anyone who puts thousands of hours into anything should have something to show for it, even if they are an ordinary person or below average. Even a complete moron who spent thousands of hours at one thing, would have something worth seeing. Thus, I keep motivating myself with such thoughts and review my quotations on the wall. Quotes from Einstein, the Beatles - 'wits of wisdom' I call them. Chinese proverbs, poems of inspiration. One of my favorite is from a book 'The White Dawn" supposedly a quotation from an ancient Eskimo shaman, "There is one thing and one thing only, to turn your face from the dark night and greet the white dawn. Arise!" Yes, taking that first step in the right direction is the hardest.

Once we have decided, "I can do this!" solutions begin to emerge. A way to get something done will present itself. So it is with the book. I meet someone who has a friend who owns the only digital book printer in the world. Meaning? Well, on demand printing means I can print one book, look at it and make changes. I can economically print as few as 200 books to see if they sell. In the USA today, with offset printing, a writer must commit to a printing of 5,000 books before it is economical to sell them, an upfront investment of $25,000. A big risk, and beyond the means of the ordinary person. *Remember how we started, with pencil and notepad? We then transferred the notes to typing, with manual typewriter and carbon paper so we'd have one copy?* "Yes, I recall sitting in a six by six cabin at fifty below zero, with frozen fingers, my thoughts for the day." Whole tablets had to get copied again after the houseboat sank, then again when the cabin burned. I worked with wet and burned penciled notes.

Raak, if all works out well, can allow me to invest $1,500 or so. An amount the average person might be expected to risk and survive, if it is a failure. I can recover from a loss of this amount. So while I am scared, I am also excited as well.

😊 :)

How cool is that, to pay for my vacation as a business trip? It's a good feeling to say, "Yeah, going on a business trip to Germany," with a sigh and sad look. "Hate to go, but someone has to do it." Not everyone likes my sense of humor.

Will laughs and replies, "Didn't you make a trip outside last winter, was it Tucson? That fossil gem show you told me about?"

"Yes, got to see my mother and set up at that big show."

"So how'd it go? You never told me?"

I had to do a lot of thinking after this show. I learned a lot. It was not as I expected. I have to admit I did not know as much as I thought. So I didn't really want to talk about it a lot. "Do we tell Will this? Instead I say, "I told you about the mammoth tusk, I think?" This was the big motivator to go to the show. I figured I'd make a killing and bring like 200 pounds of mammoth ivory. Get at least $100 a pound. Make twenty grand easy, just on ivory. But also have my art work, maybe fifty grand retail value, with a good chance of selling out at such a big show.

"The potential to make 100 grand." Will leans forward to hear all about it! Wow! Just to be able to dream that big, to even have that as a possibility in one's life is awesome beyond imagination. Especially when I am in the 'under $10,000 a year' income bracket. I tell Will how I ran into a Native who went last year with all his handcraft Native stuff that looks a little like mine. He sold out the first day and came home!

So I get a nice selling spot at the Howard Johnson, where the show started in the beginning. "The show takes up the whole city, Will! There's bunny huggers out there, that if you wear your normal fur hat? They will spray paint you! Tar and feather you! Terrorists! And no one will stop them either. Who will get arrested? You will. For creating a problem. Monsters. All kinds of horror stories about the big city. An evil place. I'll be lucky to even return alive. Enough to make an ordinary person give up!

"Road rage, Will! I could be walking along minding my own business and these city people will go out of the way to run you over and think it's funny. It's in the news all the time." Will nods in understanding. "I tell you, Will, and you can't even shoot them. Can't defend yourself. It's not polite to defend yourself."

You are supposed to dial 911 if you live. We all know what that produces. Nothing. Endless useless paperwork when the law does arrive. So that is a bit scary to be a victim, a sitting duck in a shooting gallery of crazy people.

Will understands all right, "I wouldn't do it, that's for sure!"

But city people have a way of surviving. They must. Some actually get to be old. There must be some secret. I'm gonna figure it out. Some not only stay alive, but are happy and successful! Hard as that is to comprehend. "I'm going to figure it out, Will" So there I go, spend half a year's wages to go get fleeced by the big city.

"First thing is, I can't find my mother's place."

Will nods at how hard it is to get around in the city compared to the wilds. I tell him how I meet this cab driver, John. He wants to hear all about Alaska. There's some issue seeing my mom right away, so I have to find a place to stay with all my stuff. Mom does not have room. John invites me to his place outside of the city. Kind of a Mexican neighborhood. Poor folks, but nice enough. I was surprised. We cooked food out in the yard. I need to get all my stuff over to the show first, before seeing mom. It's a lot of stuff.

"This cab driver John, is willing to lend me his dolly to move displays around. He says, 'I'll come back at the end of the show to pick it up, Miles.' He did not think I was going to steal it. As hard as it is to imagine Will, city people can be nice if you give them a chance. So the way the show works is, everyone sells out of their hotel room. There are maps, guides, and free shuttles all over the city for the show. The mattress you sleep on gets leaned against the wall. You lay out your stuff on tables. You can lock the room up at night. It's pretty slick."

I quickly realize, that there are folks here from other countries who know a lot less than I do. Some can't speak English, come from a small village in a far off place. I end up helping them out. I helped out one vendor from Russia make a dollar sign.

One customer did not trust banks, so carried all his cash in a suitcase. I was nearby when an event unfolded in front of me. A street person looking for someone to rob, grabs the suitcase and pushed the customer into the street!

Will wants to know what happened, as we all worry and wonder what a person can do when such a thing happens besides being a victim.

"Well, this vendor nearby leaps over his table and catches up to the thief. Another vendor drags the shaken customer, yanks him back up on the sidewalk out of traffic. The poor customer cannot even speak English. Other vendors including me chase after the thief to make sure he is not getting away. Some guys I would never recognize again, force this thief into a little empty storage shed." I pause to let this sink in as Will leans forward to hear how the show takes care of its own.

"Everything is vague Will, I cannot recall details" Will understands and nods what a shame it is that memory can be so horrible at a time like this! "Yeah. So when the cops finally arrive half an hour late as usual, there is this person laying on the sidewalk, all bloody and beat up. No one knows what happened. The thief seems to have a different view on life now. The customer got his suitcase handed back to him with an apology this sort of thing happened. He also had a different look, more like he is willing to trust those around him more."

Will says: "So maybe there is a way to survive in the city and folks actually care, and help each other? I never heard of anyone in the city being nice, Miles. I wonder if they are human then? Maybe good stuff like that just never makes the news, only the horror stories."

"That's what I wonder too, Will." *In the same way the city gets warped news from the wild and its inhabitants.* I think. But do not tell Will that. I go on, " I also sort of have memories from when I was a kid in the city and met some ok people." Hard to believe. Anyhow, I change the subject to the money side of things. "Will, the big money I hoped to make just did not materialize." I'm bummed out to have to say so because I had hinted to everyone how this was my big break and I expected to come home rich! Ha!

So I'm a little in trouble here. All this overhead costs! I could have got the same price for ivory in Fairbanks, right at home. In fact, none of the ivory is selling.

Seeing my mother was also only OK. We did not know each other. I was an intrusion on her daily routine. She had no room for me to sleep or stay. She does not drive. It cost her money to come see me at the show, have extra food for both of us to eat when I was with her. But I handed her some money to help out, more money then it cost her. She saw big wads of cash. She has never seen that much cash all in one place in her entire life. I tell her "Yes, it is why I live as I do. One reason. It is fun to have wads of cash like this. Feast and famine." She can see the thrill. We are, after all, blood. Somehow, someplace, we are similar. She tells me of a few adventures she has had, and we laugh. Mom gets out poetry she writes. I wrote more poetry when I was younger, but here is mom being a writer, and also doing crafts, quilting rugs and making cards! She also likes used things, and living frugally. She reviews some of what happened in her life since I last saw her. "I married Joe after your father left me. He was good to me. Very handsome, a ladies' man. Not smart like your father, but he could fix anything!" Yes, I recall the tall French guy who built a car engine from scratch, from a block of metal. He made his own bearings even. A twelve cylinder power house. He surrounded it with an old looking, rusty nothing body. You had to touch two wires together to get it to start. I was a child, and we pull up next to some teens in a hot sports car. Joe revs up the engine, and nods to the kids who take the challenge. I will never forget the surge of power and burning rubber as twelve cylinders kicked in. I bet burning a quart of fuel a second. There were air rammer jammers up the ying-yang. The front end left the ground. What a hot car! *No way in hell my real father would get near such a thing.*

I like to be alone a lot. Here I am fishing on an unnamed creek off the Kantishna River.

"Well," Mom tells me, "One day, he and his friends got drunk, went out in a speed boat, and robbed some lobster pots! He came home with all these stolen lobsters and I was furious! But what was I going to do?" Yes. Do indeed, what a dilemma. I already understand my Mom and keep a straight face, asking,

"What did you do, mom?"

"I cooked them all up, of course!" And adds, "Now I know how many lobsters it takes to get sick. I ate ten lobsters in one sitting. We had to get rid of the evidence you know, forty lobsters!" She says, with a twinkle in her old eyes. It occurred to me then, how very different she is from my father. My father would have turned this into some boring moral lecture, having nothing at all to do with reality[4]. It occurred to me that my mother and I have the same twinkle in the eye and same sense of humor. *I'll be darn.* I could feel comfortable around her. Be at ease. Be myself. Be human. I could picture her getting rid of the evidence, and the appeal of this hot rod driving, handsome devil. Lord knows, she paid one heck of a price for her personality. Joe, the one who ran off with and raped her daughter, my sister. If she can find a way to smile thinking back, that is amazing.

And I think she also found something in me she could connect to. Despite her grumbling about no room. I think too, not wanting to think about the past. The fact I look just like my father, I'm guessing, is not a lot of good memories there. Her first words to me were, "How come your father left me!" Not, "Good to see you, how are you, how has your life been, son?" I'm not my father. I never left her. I imagine what it must be like to have that on your mind all these years, to blurt that out forty years later. But anyhow. *Make the sign of the cross.*

Covering the entire bed with piles of bills, running out of rubber bands, making bundles of $500 gives a whole new meaning to the word 'money'. $10,000 in small bills. A lot maybe, but this is only one of two shows I do all year. Half my year's income. But we need not talk about that part. We cling to the moment.

Just like we can't focus on all the horrible things Joe did, we focus on all those lobsters and what a fine meal that was. It is a way of dealing with life, with problems, and how a mind works. I see now, I got that from my mom. She sees herself in me, I think. It's not about being poor. It is about that one time of the year when you cover the bed with piles of money. Whoever gets to see that in their life?

"I'm going to have trouble fitting it in my wallet, mom," I say dead pan. We both burst out laughing. I do not recall my father laughing, ever, not once in his whole life. So odd, my father raised me, but we were never close. My mother was not part of my life, yet here we are, laughing.

I fill Will in on a lot of these experiences in Tucson. Adding, "I don't know if I want to go back to do the show. It's a lot of work and time just to break even." I could see improving some, but as I was told, it is a way of life and it takes a while to get ahead at it. You got to love it to stick it out and make it work. As fun as it was, I have not decided this is what I want to devote my life to. But, here I am making plans for a return. Mostly because I'm going outside to Germany. "I may as well extend the trip, doesn't cost that much more."

I'm a tad nervous about trying to be close to mom as she has not been a part of my life. She left my sister and me so long ago. It is hard to feel trust. However, time changes many things. It is easier to understand what was going on way back when. We kids were supposed to stay with mom after the divorce. I was eight years old. But mom changed her mind, and refused to take us, left us with dad. Dad had a girl-friend, his secretary. They were getting married. We kids were not part of the deal dad made with his new love. Mom was hurt and furious. Maybe scared. How can she make a go of it in life with no trade, no money to speak of, and burdened with two kids to take care of? Mom had already spent much of her youth taking care of her younger sisters!

Dad had all the money and a good job. He gets off scot free, a new life, with a honeymoon to look forward to. When he's the guilty one who cheated on mom.

She says, "I don't think so buster!" and "You keep them and see what it's like to raise two kids." Wanted to put a crimp in his style. Break up, or make the new love more difficult. Understandable. I think it is common to use the kids as pawns in marriage disputes. Not that it helps the children any. But life goes on. No one wanted us. It's fine to intellectualize this a lifetime later. It does not change how growing up was during the time. The clock cannot be turned back.

Still I see mom's pain. I reply to mom's question, "Why did your father leave me?"

Sure I understand why. It might help if she understands as well, so I say, "You were both young. Dad especially, did not know what he wanted out of life. He thought he wanted a family and kids, but did not know what that meant. As he gained his education, he saw something he wanted more. Status, prestige, respect. You assumed he would be happy working in the shoe factory you and your mother had worked in, as simple lower class workers."

I have trouble picturing my father being happy living like that. I am a lot like him in this one way, and see him in me. In that, he gets bored easily. He needs a sense of importance, like what he does matters. He wanted to bring important people home and look good. Serve them special wine of a certain year, fancy meals with napkin rings at each place. He imagined a good looking wife in modern dress, being sophisticated and intellectual. His new woman was in the newspaper with an article on the proper etiquette of fixing a meal properly (for the educated and rich).

Mom is a meat and potatoes, no nonsense woman. No frills, no pretense. She always hated to wear shoes. She told me of one of her first dates with dad. She is all dressed and waiting for him to pick her up at her mother's house. He arrives. They head out the door to go eat out someplace and she is barefoot; forgot to put her

164

shoes on! My mother is perfectly happy going out for ice-cream at Dairy Queen. My father is suit, tie, and proper. He has never been to a garage sale in his life. He does not like used things. He has only bad memories of his own youth being poor in New York. It is easy as an outsider to see the differences and upcoming problems between mom and dad.

Mom was very beautiful and naïve, being raised by her mother and having to stay in and babysit the younger sisters. Her mother abandoned mom by putting her in a convent. She grew up there—beaten and abused. Dad met her in Maine where he attended college for a short time before joining the military, wrote her from Hawaii. A young pretty girl in cold Maine, might well dream of life on the beach in Hawaii, far from her present problems. Looking at a sober man with a steady job, that her mother had approved of by introducing the two. The Prince, who will rescue her.

Dad is far from home, from people and ways he understands. Not much self-confidence having been raised by a strict father who did not understand him. How nice it would be to be with a beautiful woman from back East. And, it's the thing to do. You get a job, get married, and start a family. This is how to blend in, look normal, get accepted. Dad longed to be normal, due to his own past, to the extent he became an over achiever. It's as far as his vision could reach, given the information he had at the time. Who could fault either one?

"It does not make you a bad wife, mom, or bad person. Just not suited for dad. Or being a mother. So yes, dad ended up with a sophisticated woman who was well educated, could serve proper wine, and cook fancy meals at a table set with napkin rings. But in the big picture, how did that end up? It did not last. He married for prestige, not love. You probably truly loved him more than anyone."

Dad told me he thought mom was still young and beautiful when they divorced, and it is better to part early, "So she can go find someone else while she is pretty and adaptable." A very thought out intellectual answer. Dad felt she'd recover and get over it. But mom is not intellectual; she is emotional. She never really recovered. She believes in forever. Blames herself. She was devoted to dad. The rest of her life was never the same. But what did either one know about love and happiness?

Mom tells me, "I always thought happiness was the lack of pain. If you were not in pain, you were happy. I was seventy years old before I knew what being happy was about." How can I feel angry or bitter about such a past? Forgiving is not the same though, as feeling a bond. She is upset the house needs to be rearranged when I visit. I move things and disrupt the routine. She is used to her life as it is. We can understand each other without having to be close. Without pretenses. It is good to talk openly about how we feel. It is nice we do not offend each other with our honesty. I actually enjoy mom; she is fun to talk to. Her words are not hurtful, merely human. If I know what the issues are, I have something to deal with. I can accept it or not, and make a decision. When there are unspoken issues that are not understood and I can only guess at, like with my father, this is hard to do anything about. *This effects how I choose to deal with others. Tell the truth as I see it, and then it is up to you to deal with it or not. It is not me lying, keeping up a pretense, or insulting you with promises I have no intention of keeping.*

Something has come up changing the trip plans; dad had a stroke and has recovered, but is not the same. It might be a good time to visit him. Dad had just come to see me for a visit a year ago. I forget—I'm not good with time lines. When my back was out—whenever that was. I had not been comfortable with him, even though he meant well. He has always been a 'root hog or die' sort. Not very compassionate when folks are down; never passed it on to his children. I learned from him, things like, "Do not put your hand out; if you need help, go get a job!" There is no such thing as 'can't work' or 'no opportunity.' If you fall, pick yourself up. If you need a helping hand, look at the end of your other arm. If you are sick, get well or die. So of course, why wouldn't I be embarrassed that I can't get up? Go away, let me die, or, if I can get up, then I will live. Either way, it has nothing to do with him. He feels obligated to see me, and there is no reason to feel that way. The time to need him was long ago. After all these years, I accept how it is.

Now he is down for the count. What am I supposed to do about it? I can't do anything for him. He has a wife to take care of him and loves him—I assume. My presence only reminds him of his failure in his mind, of being a bad parent. It's not true, in that I am a product of my upbringing, and I am not unhappy, I consider myself successful. Partly thanks to my father. He has taken life harder than my mother. He just does not let it show in the same way. He has money, insurance and all that. I can't help him financially. He should have a pile of caring relatives and tons of friends if he lives his life right. I'm only vaguely aware from observing others, that life is supposed to have something to do with this word called 'Love.' I do not know what love is. Or, not as others know it. Seeing dad is a necessary obligation. I feel bad and guilty for that. But… oh, well… get that part of the trip over with. The entire plane trip – dad, Germany, Tucson, maybe my son, and then back home is going to be $1,500. About the price of my Alaska oil dividend check.

Mom and Joe—picture of a picture, old timey, when young and beautiful.

CHAPTER SIX

VISIT DAD, IN GEO MAGAZINE

W hen thinking of my upcoming trip to Germany, something comes to mind. GEO Magazine had the big story on me. I am an inspiration to some people in Europe. So it might be good to go over there to try to sell my art. One of my customers, sort of a friend, Stephan, has been trying to get something going with GEO and my book. Stephan reminds me GEO owns some big publishing companies, so it would be great to get GEO behind my book, and have help with the marketing. I am unclear what Stephan is up to. He has been vague and evasive for a long time.

At first he had been optimistic! Telling me GEO acknowledged owing me money. Figuring out how many tapes sold, my friend thinks in the neighborhood of owing me $40,000. After that I did not hear much. Helm, also in Germany, thinks this Stephan is not my friend, and might be taking my book and running with it. Maybe he is getting my book published in his name, or selling it in pieces as short stories. Or received and kept the $40,000, acting as my agent.

If I come to Germany, Helm will help me with a lawyer to get to the bottom of this, since Stephan is not cooperating and answering me.

I found another mammoth tusk over the summer, and figure it is worth about $10,000. I'm not sure if I want to get it to Germany, or try to sell it in Tucson. It's heavy and awkward to ship. Helm has told me of a group in Germany that is an Indian-Cowboy group that meets, and does kind of a reenactment of the American Wild West. He knows people in this group; and thinks if we go to one of these meetings we can sell my sort of 'Wild West' art. The Alaska cowboy.

I have a black powder Hawkins rifle I built with lots of metal scene inlays. Helm already thinks he has a customer for this rifle for $3,500. There is a necklace I made with huge fossil bear fangs, and other teeth and claws worth another $3,500. I have about $50,000 in inventory. I suppose, as well, I will have a good time. (?) But to me, selling and doing business is 'fun' and a good time. Maybe because it is new to me, so fresh and exciting.

My mountain man dream is adapted into kind of an Indiana Jones concept. A modernized version of the frontiersman. Or Crocodile Dundee or Grizzly Adams, there are many to choose from. I'm aware it is common for people who had a dysfunctional family, to be driven, to seek public attention. Possibly create an alternate fantasy life, as an escape from other realities. I see nothing especially wrong or bad about that. Just a psychological motivation explaining a personality type.

I unexpectedly got a little attention from my success in the wilds, written up a few times. This was rewarding, but did not think 'addictive'. I still was motivated by doing my own thing, with any attention being secondary. Now though, attention, business and profits, might work together and complement each other. Part of a marketing strategy comes about by accident, but at least a little contrived. Teller of tall tales, man of mystery and adventure. This is an important move to test it out. I went to Tucson first. *Was that a bust? I only broke even!* "Focus on the positive."

I explain it to my friends Josh and Martha when I am over on one of my rare visits talking about the changes in my lifestyle. "I only broke even when it comes to the money. My trip to Tucson was written up in Gem Magazine. They wanted a colorful story. A story about following your dreams, and how I got there." I did not mention I think they chose me because I am colorful and meet the image in their mind of what readers might expect. I had my mountain man hat, cave bear claw necklace...

"Did they pay you ,Miles?" Well... no... they did not pay me. But my name is out there over and over. More and more people have heard of me as a result. It may help sell my art and my book.

"No money, just advertising. Actually the magazine wouldn't let me place an ad in the issue I would be in. The reason stated was because I was not a member of any gem organization." There is a pause as this sinks in.

"Sure, Miles, and I have the same thing happen as a Native American and dog racer. I'm good publicity, but have to go to the back of the bus as a member of a minority race."

So yes, I also thought it was interesting. Good enough to have a story done, but not have an ad. I feel a lot of gem items that jewelers work with are not certified in the same manner as gem stones. There is a grade of mammoth ivory we refer to as 'gem grade'. The grade where a pea size is worth big money, so extreme in color, its value is that of a gem stone. Other fossils like saber cat teeth, are considered gem material when used in jewelry. Without going into the subject further, I simply do not agree gem magazine readers would not want my product. It's just another example of the snobbishness, inequality, and how the fossil people are treated by the gem industry and high society.

I did learn a lot at the show. *I learned a lot from the best vendors in the world.* I'm not sure I can explain world level trading and how the money moves to Josh and Martha, who are not into big business. Josh knows at least a little about the mammoth ivory business, as he has heard me talk and seen what I find. After all, it is Josh who is one of the natives who has given me permission to look for fossils on his native land, one of the legal places to find fossils.

"I found out a lot about the mammoth ivory business worldwide, Josh." I explain how the Russians are just now getting their ivory out of Siberia to America and world market. Fossil mammoth ivory was available in the past, but am told Russia had a fifty year economic setback they are just coming out of. The market is being flooded with this new Russian source making world prices on the low side. The Russian government has not been keeping an eye out, nor taxing the export of the ivory because they did not recognize the value. Now they do. More and more the mafia runs the government. More and more the ways to get ivory across the border and avoid the high export costs are getting stopped. High export costs will be reflected soon in higher prices. Russia controls about 75% of the world mammoth ivory market.

I continue, "On top of this, China is trying to buy up much of the ivory, and may well have a monopoly soon on the major sources. Much of the Russian ivory will be bought in St. Petersburg before it ever leaves Russia. What arrives in the U.S. will already have been high-graded by China."

Martha and Josh look puzzled. "This is all an interesting story, Miles" They are amused. *Miles telling tall tales as usual.* "Is that what they think?"

I add, "This will affect the sale of Alaska ivory. There is not enough quantity to interest the Chinese… yet. If I find it myself, I have a chance of some high quality." Getting that to Tucson will mean some high quality material, in a high-graded market. I never would have known any of this if I had not figured it out myself, by talking to the Russians and Chinese in person. This has a big effect on how much money I can make, knowing what to bring to Tucson, why, and what prices to ask. I'm not going to learn this second hand here in Alaska at the bottom of the totem pole. Now it is me in Alaska, who knows more than the other Alaskan ivory dealers. "I can play Crafty; buy low, sell high. Knowledge is power and money." *Not rip off, but fair deals I understand.* "I hope so."

"But it's all just your opinion, Miles."

"Ok, well then, I'm enjoying myself, the bills are paid and I'm just Miles being Miles then!" We all agree to this with a laugh. My unconscious thinks *Part of the laugh we wink and agree to is Miles is nuts. Where me and I simply think this explanation is over their head and more complicated than the average person not in the trade can grasp.* Few think I have any answers, or am especially intelligent, or are interested in my opinion, unless I have a lot of money. Only money talks. So I smile, nod and play along. I do not have a lot of money. Watching the chess board of life. Making my moves, planning out my game strategy. I have said many times, more to convince me than you, it's to my advantage to be seen as an idiot. *People give out a lot more information if they do not see you as competition.* I smile.

So I'm going to Germany and writing it off as a business trip, pretty slick all right. I play that role. Pretend the trip is to fool the IRS, a scam to have a vacation. That's the easiest to understand. That's the mentality of the average person I talk to. Wink, wink. Slap on the back and a "Good for you, smart move! Good luck! I hate the IRS! Wish I could pull that off!" There is little point in suggesting in a huff, that I might be a writer, or half way decent artist, or that I understand business in a world market. Put another way? If I showed everyone the wads of cash my mother saw? I guarantee someone would call the IRS and whisper in their ear they think Miles made some cash and did not report it. Someone else would break in my home and look for it to steal. There would be only a small percent who would say, "Good for you Miles!" and mean it. There is a thought out plan going on. This is not an impulsive trip, all about needing a vacation.

I have seen over and over again very fine art not selling, created by starving artists. Not selling for any reason other than the artist does not understand marketing. It will not sell itself. The average customer will not recognize it because it is good. Humans are sheep. Followers. Herd animals. They need a shepherd. Someone to guide them, steer them in the right direction.

"Hey, Miles, heard you might be headed for Germany! How can you afford that? Last I heard you were poor folk like the rest of us."

"Yes, well, someone has to do it, it's business. I'll stay with friends, visit some castles, get some business done and write it off my taxes. You know," wink, wink.

"Ah man, I'd about sell my soul to be in your shoes! I haven't had a vacation in twenty years, much less a chance to go overseas. Good luck man!"

"Well, you just have to work it out right. Play the angles, figure out how to turn what you like to do into what you get paid for. Your vacation can be your work." It's a way of thinking. I hear so often; like from a friend not long ago.

"Miles, I'm headed for Arkansas for my daughter's wedding. Can't really afford it, but that's how it is."

"Arkansas, huh? There are crystals that come from there that I bet you can get cheap." I say by way of a hint to pay for the trip.

"Sure I know where that is, got friends who mine them, others have rock shops there."

"Well you make the connection and buy a few hundred dollar's worth. I buy them from you, and you can pay for your ticket in profits. I know enough people who need good crystals. I think I could move them. You buy them for $1 each. I pay you $2 each. I sell them for $4 and they retail for $8. I could move about 500 crystals."

"Naw, this is a wedding, I'm not gonna' have time." I think, *Then quit bitching to me about being broke!* This is a common conversation.

TIME TO HEAD off for Germany, to Frankfurt to meet Helm and Anita. On the Concord jet, there are comments over the speakers at intervals telling the passengers how fast the plane is going, how high we are, and our updated estimated time of arrival. I smile and assume Germans are into numbers and statistics. Helm meets me at the airport and takes me to his very impressive home. A private gated property in the downtown city. An old cobblestone home, the equivalent of a city block with a garden and apple trees, all fenced in. Old in Germany is different than old in the U.S. We are talking roads built before the time of Christ. Homes from the 1600's, stuff from before Columbus discovered America. Helm has a bell off the Titanic and other cool artifacts around the home. He is semi-retired, does not need to work hard, and can take off anytime for as long as he wants. He seems self taught, and had worked hard in his youth. We have an appointment to speak with Raak about my book printing. I'm excited about that.

I AM SHOWN the multi-million dollar machine. It looks like a huge copier with a conveyer belt out the back. I am shown how it works, on someone else's book that is already set up for the computer. The book is on one of these new CD disks. A button is pushed. There is a whirring sound inside. The belt turns on. In ten seconds, a book comes out the other end, ready to read.

"And you can do this with my book?"

"Sure, but it has to be in the right format, and set up a little, maybe an hour's work. I need to look at it in the computer first. Is it in PDF format?" I had tried, but did not know what font imbedding meant. My program I think did not have font embedding.

"No, I had to stick with the word program, running Windows 95." Raak nods; he understands. He is not sure how this will work, but he's a computer geek, so will look at my Zip Disk on the computer. After over thirty years in the making, my heart is racing. I get a tour of the place while the computer work is being done. I get undivided attention now because Helm is a good friend of this Raak. I think to myself, *That's what it usually takes, an inside connection.* My computer to me is brand new, being just a year old. Yet it does not have one of these CD drives in it, just a floppy drive and external Zip Drive. It's the fastest on the market, with a whole gigabyte of storage space. Amazing. The book is only three megs at the most. I forget how many zeros are after the meg to make a gig.

I know more than the average person, but not as much as a geek. Geek is not really a term being used much *yet*. In the middle of talking, we are interrupted. We are ready to put the Zip into the book machine. Just like the sample book; ten seconds, and here is my book on the conveyor belt! Wow! *It looks like a real book!* I'm suddenly an author. Here is my book. I thumb through the pages. At first glance, it looks like a book. There are pictures in it, a front and back cover. I read the front: 'Going Wild' by Miles Martin. A wilderness survival story.

Raak wants to know how many I want, and talks prices, time frame, shipping and such. I want to know if he is interested in being a publisher, or just a printer. No, he does not want to pay me. He wants to be shocked I'd even ask. Very cheeky of me. Yet he is polite.

"Miles, why would I invest in your book?"

"Geo is interested. My story has made the New York Times, and Alaska Magazine has carried my stories five times. Survival and reality is in style at the moment. It's a hot subject with a large audience. I spent a long time working on it, not just throwing this book together." Raak seems impressed with at least my confidence, and the logic of my words. He nods and concedes I have valid points. But still, he is just the printer and wants to keep it that way. OK. We end up agreeing on printing 500 copies to be sent to me in Alaska within a month. I pay half now, up front. I will be billed for the rest when the books arrive. I shake hands with the owner of the biggest book printing machine in the world, as a business man. The book printing is $5 each, but with shipping to Alaska makes the total cost to me $6 a book.

"Do, the math, Helm, selling at $18 a book!" We do a high five.

Helm takes me on the autobahn highway with no speed limits. The average speed is about eighty. Semi-trucks are doing ninety. Some sports cars are doing over 100. It's an experience to behold. I note hawks on the electric poles along the highway. There are fields of hay that have rodents for the hawks.

"Miles, I want to take you to the Rhine Valley for the day." Helm explains the importance of the castle we are looking at on the cliff overlooking the river. "This castle guarded the entire valley and protected it. Invaders had to arrive by boat. The river is narrow here, so arrows, rocks, fireballs, could be tossed down on the invaders, driving them back." The cobblestone roads we walk are Roman roads from before the time of Christ, cut and laid by hand over 2,000 years ago. Still being used. Very amazing, all right. Helm shows me the vineyards from Roman times, still growing grapes and producing famous wines sold all over the world.

We stop for lunch at a small outdoor café overlooking the river. A modern barge hauls supplies, much like where I live. At docks up and down the river in view are motorboats. We drink good local wine, with fresh sausage and Swiss cheese.

"Helm, this wine is OK, but not as good as your own apple wine!" Helm has apple trees in his yard, and big wooden kegs to put the juice in he squeezes to make his own wine. *How can it not be good!* "Indeed!" We are very relaxed, not in a hurry, on a perfect warm sunny day in a post card setting.

"I appreciate you taking time to show me around, Helm."

"Miles, it is no different than when I am in your country and you take Anita and I on the river in your boat for the day on one of our picnics. We have been on expensive cruises that are the rage! But you cannot buy such a river trip as you give us Miles. It is among the best vacation times we ever have any place in the world. A local who shows us the nice places to stop and look for drift wood and rocks where no one else goes." I can understand then, that what I do many times is normal for me, but a big deal to someone else. Helm comes here pretty often and enjoys it, but to me, it is new, fresh, and something to remember the rest of my life.

Along the way in our travels I see a sculpture of a man on a horse. Well done, bigger than life stone carving. But the rider has no head! "Helm, how come this guy has no head!?"

"Well, during the war much was destroyed in Germany. Here, two young American soldiers were drunk and walking along. They decided to use the head for target practice." Helm does not sound bitter or angry about this thoughtless destruction, but it gives new insight as to the sorts of things that happen in war. I suppose any war, anyplace. The news and history is mostly about how America saved the world with its allies, against a horrible Hitler and the evil Germans. Evil changes its face, once Japan or Russia or China. All were faces of friends that may well be friends and allies again down the road. 'Enemy' is a relative word and in some countries it is we who are the enemy. If we hear the whole story, maybe we can see why.

Events and information like this help me formulate an outlook I am developing, or being aware of. I wish to associate myself with, and call as my allies, those who behave in a certain way, who I agree with, and do things I approve of. Wherever they live, whatever religion they have, whatever color they are. There is no such thing as belonging to a certain group with that alone making a person good, or evil.

Helm and Anita want me to finally meet with the Cowboy-Indian group."Miles, there is a meeting tonight, and I told them I would bring you! So you might make some sales." I am curious what an Indian-Cowboy group in Germany looks like! This German group is excited by this time period in American history of the Wild West, freedom of the plains, life of a free trapper and buffalo herds to live off of and such things.

On the wall of the lodge is a picture of Sitting Bill and Sioux Indians in head dress. These Germans have never heard of Athabascan Indians in Alaska. I'm called The Alaska Cowboy. Their dreams and expectations are not connected a lot with reality. I am expected to ride a horse, have a cowboy hat. There is interest in some of my art and raw materials, but it does not fit in with the image of the Wild West. Of more interest would have been antiques like spurs, rusty guns with a story, old blankets reputed to have been made by Sitting Bull's relatives and such. Talk of 'snow' drew a blank stare. Homesteading was also not on the agenda. About everyone wore feathers or cowboy hats and wanted to look like either John Wayne or Sitting Bull.

Helm and Anita have a table set up to sell things. They, too, have a few leather goods and cowboy/Indian type wares to sell and gave me a space on the table. I made about $700 in a few hours.

"Helm? Where is your blacksmith friend who is interested in the black powder rifle? You have emailed me about him quite a bit. Does he come to this gathering?"

"Sometimes, but he is pretty busy right now. I think we need to go visit him." The black powder rifle is nicely inlaid with scenes. One side has a string of bears made of copper walking up the stock. The last bear is rearing. The story is: 'You are walking along in the wilds and all is peaceful. Suddenly the peace is broken by an angry bear rearing up. You have one chance, one bullet in the gun. Your life depends on this gun you now carry.' The other side has flying geese of silver, copper and brass. The story on this side is: 'Beauty is nice, but this is dinner flying over and it takes this gun to fetch dinner or you do not eat.' The trigger guard is etched with rabbits, the ram rod has flowers and leaves all along its length. The big octagon barrel is impressive. It shoots a 500 grain chunk of lead the size of your finger that makes a hole the size of a bowling ball out the back of whatever it hits. The overall look was taken into account when I built it. There is a pleasing flow of color and lines. I'm asking three grand. The blacksmith talks me down to $2,500.

The blacksmith has a friend or a friend of a friend, I forget. Well, it's a situation best not to recall the details of. 'Somebody somehow,' introduces me to a professional diver. He dives for treasures in harsh conditions. His home is tall. There is a waterfall in the house. Around this waterfall is a chair to sit in with plants all around, with tropical birds flying around. It's obvious this guy has money. He shows me pure gold statues from Egypt. King Tut era. He is a diver, and found these in the ocean. Selling such items is worth millions.

"Miles, would it be possible to dive for the mammoth tusks you speak of coming out of a cliff, and falling into the Yukon River?" Many people think there is a pile of tusks at the bottom of the river, if anyone could figure out how to get on the bottom.

"I think this is a diving challenge all right. eighty feet of whirlpools. I saw whole trees go under and not come back up again. Silt you cannot see in. If you need a boat anchored on the surface and you need a line going down to you, I do not see how this is possible." I pause and add: "But, if you knew how to go through the ice in winter? The water is not as deep, there is less current, the water is clear, and there would be no debris coming downriver like trees to snag on."

"Yes I know how to dive in ice water, I have gone down on wrecks in the Arctic."

"The next big issue is the legal part. Any time money is made, officials want their finger in the pie, true all over the world This best place is not a place I can legally go." Possibly this could be a scientific expedition.

Mr. Egypt replies "Yes, you understand this right. Any time there is big money there are legal issues. No one can make big money without paying people off. Basically, buying permits is the same as paying the mafia for protection. So who do we pay and how much?"

I would not know about such things, as I do not have the kind of money it takes to grease the hands that let the deal slide through with the proper stamps. I'd be more inclined as an artist to make fake stamps. I tell the short story: "When I was a child, I once needed a stamp to mail a letter and did not have one. So I got out my watercolors and painted a stamp on the envelope and it went through. I might have been nine years old and had no idea what forgery was."

Details are gone over, on how we might acquire a hundred tusks off the bottom of the Yukon River, worth an average of $10,000 each. Things like, how many people would need to be involved as a crew, how transportation would be taken care of and such.

"Miles, I will keep in touch, maybe come to Alaska to look over the area and find out who to contact to take care of the permits."

Helm tells me he knows several gallery owners we can visit to see if they will buy my art work. If so, this might be a business for the future. *Maybe just send art to these galleries from Alaska. But if all goes well there is a possibility of more trips to Germany doing shows.* "Regular trips to Germany? We need to make sure we can afford it! " The first few stops are very disappointing. No interest. Helm is perplexed and feels as badly as I do. He collects my work and thinks it's fantastic! I give my opinion.

"Helm, in theory, good art should sell itself. Yet I have seen very good art offered by poor artists on the street, cheap. The artist can't sell it. Often the public has to be told it is good. It does not sell itself. Even galleries need an introduction. It is hard to come out of nowhere and make it big time."

I think of someone I look up to, Einstein, who was German. The most gifted scientist of all time was not listened to for ten years after he figured out how to split an atom. Because? He was a nobody. A librarian, not a fellow scientist. All he got was a "Yeah right!"

So Helm may know these gallery owners, but in a different setting, in the context of parties they both attend. Not the same as being a respected art critic. Helm is not familiar with the gallery owner mindset and proper protocol, is what it looks like to me. Not his fault, he means well and is my friend trying to help.

My mind is on Mr. Egypt and is unusual lifestyle and offer. It sounds exciting. However, my guess is, this is exactly why governments all over the world have laws about grabbing valuables off the land. I also suspect it would not be me making any money, splitting it all 50/50. *I'd be the flunky informant…*

Helm interrupts my thoughts, asking about art galleries. "I have been to galleries, and what is expected is to chat, name drop, create an introduction; create a time to size each other up, before discussing business."

Walk the walk, talk the talk. If we can't, then the deal is not as great. In this case, a polite 'not interested,' or 'busy' or 'no room'. Helm expects to get right to the point, no nonsense. That's crass. I know how it is done and what to do, but do not look or dress the part. Or I do. I look like an eccentric artist. A typical gallery owner thinks, 'Deal time! Ten cents on the dollar time'. Artistically 'eccentric' is a difficult move to pull off successfully.

My father is on my mind, since I will be seeing him soon. I have had dad's version of rich, his version of 'having arrived'. I was born into his world. If I had stayed, there are privileges, doors that open, for no other reason than the class you are born into by birthright. I knew how to dress, how to talk, how to fit into that world. I might have got a job through a friend of a friend and through the connections, arrived someplace 'important'. Oh, partly based on merit. There are people who, by nature of their class, can never even get through the front door. I believe there are other worlds operating on similar principles. *To be accepted by trappers, there is a way to dress, a way to talk, and sets of required knowledge, just to talk to a trapper as an equal. My first few years I was not going to get any help. I could not talk the talk or walk the walk. I had to prove myself first.*

"Miles, are you listening? Here is another place I know. Anita sells here, special designed clothing sometimes."

We stop at a kind of high fashion clothing store. I sell a few stick pins for scarves, and a few pairs of earrings, but I hear a, "Well we can try it and see, no promises, we have a lot of things here, but we will try to make room." They take my card and will get in touch if they need more. I did not hear, 'Good work, I know we can sell this!' So like they said, we'll see. I try to cheer Helm, who seems more discouraged than I do!

"Helm, at least they bought outright!"

"Yes, and this friend of the Egyptian, who wants to buy many wolf claws for a new line of belt buckles, this looks good to me!"

"Maybe Helm. Only maybe. This customer seemed to me to be looking for rock bottom, dirt cheap, and he wants several hundred. That's a lot of dead wolves, Helm. It's just a product line to him with no concept of the wolf."

"And why does this matter so much? Does the car salesman wish to control how the car he sells is driven? How can he stay in business?"

I explain to Helm as we head down the autobahn again. "I gave some thought to the wolf claw business. For about $10,000 I could control the world's supply of wolf claws, have a monopoly."

"There are a lot of trappers, Miles! How can you control them all?"

"They all sell, or 90%, sell to the fur dealers. Wolves are concentrated in Alaska, certain parts of Canada and parts of Russia. That's 80% of the world's wolf population. There are fifty major buyers for wolf. These buyers sell to one of only a dozen furriers. I have connections with half of them. It would not be difficult to discuss an arrangement whereby I buy up all the wolf claws at a flat price, under a contract." I explain how there is not a huge market, and the fur dealers are not that interested in this side business. It is the fur they want. It's a pain to hunt around for claw buyers who might buy a few dozen claws here and there, or sell dirt cheap to a place like Moscow Hide and Fur in Idaho. Such places pay fifty cents average. Maybe $1. I could offer $2, twice the going price. I then clean them, grade them, and sell from $5 to $15 each, retail; wholesale for half that. In this way, sell 200 to your friend, and if he does not like the price, guess what. I'm the only game in town. I could set the world value on wolf claws if I control 60% to 75% of the raw material.

"So Miles, Vie have you not done gis?" Said in Helms German accent.

"First, I care about the animal, at least to some extent. It's about respect. Second, I see laws changing, and I would not want to tie up a market, have a huge inventory, then have the sale of wolf claws made illegal.

Future Flash

In 2014, I go to Federal prison, with one of the charges being the illegal sale of wolf claws. Wolves got added to the Federal endangered species list only temporarily and fall under protection laws, for now. Hides are legal to sell, in some states like Alaska, against Federal law, but need to be tagged. I ask a friend on the game board at the time the law changes are being proposed,

"So, there is one tag for one wolf; what happens when claws, skull, and teeth are removed and offered on the market? Where is the necessary proof of legal harvest? The tag remains with the hide." There is no answer. Being arrested is the answer. I'm lucky I did not stake my occupation on having a monopoly. I think the Federal government, backed by animal rights groups, would have made an example out of me. I'm glad I saw the potential of this in the past.

Future flash ends

"It's just a thought, Helm, if all I cared about was money and I was a typical ruthless business man." *Just because I have a flash of insight and see clearly how to make a pile of money, doesn't mean I'm going to do it! The fun is in thinking of it and knowing it would work.* "I'm just not that interested in selling 200 wolf claws at rock bottom prices to someone who has no respect for wolves, and it's just a marketing scam." *Flash and dash with no substance.* "Advertising slogans about the majestic wolf. It's about being responsible, Helm. I suppose that is what I mean." If I show this clown a live wolf and say, "Go kill it and save the claws," he would not know how, and would wet his pants. So OK, I can pass on one claw to someone who wants to understand wolves, who has no clue, but wants to learn, or is even misguided and does not have a clue about the wolf. It is only one claw. There will be a percent of sales like this I cannot control, that just happen – hopefully made up for by those who do understand. But not to the tune of 200 claws; 50 dead wolves. Hundreds of square miles of territory totally disrupted by the imbalance. "Will this man comprehend the price?"

We talk about responsibility and control. Summed up,

"Helm, all I can do is have my beliefs and behavior based on what I think is the best information I have, and act on it according to my own conscience. It does not have to be right, or how everyone else does it. I am not going to try to stop this guy from trying to acquire his 200 claws someplace else." I am not outraged. I am not interested in creating laws to stop him. I am saying I will conduct my own business according to my beliefs. *Discrimination. I decide who can buy from me, and what they will pay.* "Do not get caught, that's probably illegal." I think before speaking. "So does everyone have the right to own anything, as long as they have the money? Is everyone to be denied everything, if they cannot pay?" *This defines 'free enterprise'.* "Does it work in reality?"

Helm understands. He reminds me of the strong animal rights groups. Those who feel it is wrong to have a wolf claw, unless you personally killed the wolf. I get asked a lot when I wear my art. "Did you kill the bear?" Or the wolf? or the alligator?

I wonder, *Did any of us grow our own carrots? Did we raise the cow that our belt is made from? Did we catch the fish we ate?* My point has to do with the fact it is easy to point a finger someplace else, ask what someone else has done, how they have behaved, asking someone else if they were responsible. It is easy to want someone else to feel guilty and take responsibility, but what sacrifice has the accuser personally made? *Is it rude to ask someone if they harvested the diamond in their wedding ring?* "In a tone of accusation, do not forget that." *Yeah, as if it's wrong.*

After some inner thoughts, while we eat sausage and cheese at an outdoor café along the Rhine, I continue trying to express myself to Helm, "What have we personally given up to support the talk we dish out? How much income are we personally willing to sacrifice to back up our noble words? That is what I want to look at." I like to think I'm willing for my income to be less. I'm willing to live with less class, so I am not as huge a consumer as I could be if I wanted. "One big reason, Helm, is because I care about the planet."

"Others besides you care, Miles. We each show it in a different way."

"I may not have killed the wolf, bear, or moose. Usually I know who did. I try hard to acquire materials from simple subsistence people, like the local natives who ate the animal, trapped it for basic needs, or killed it in self defense. They did not kill the animal for the primary purpose of selling me the parts."

"This is nice and noble of you Miles, but the law does not care. You can either sell claws, or not sell claws. To everyone, or to no one." *Not totally true, there are restrictive permits on limited items and other ways to* control *who has what.* "But no, let's not argue. Helm is set in what he believes."

Later.

With this new internet selling, I am losing some control of where things come from. It is not the animal parts I tend to acquire at the shows. However, instead of buying rocks and fossils, I try to trade my animal parts, since I did not buy them, or got them at the source, cheap. From an environmental standpoint, I strongly believe in recycling, repurposing, trading, doing add on value, bartering. *Yes this seems easiest on the planet.*

"Yes, Miles, I think you are an ethical person all right. It is one reason we like you so much!"

My visit comes to an end. I have made enough money to pay for my trip, but not much 'profit'. *What a wonderful time though!*

Time to see my father.

MY FATHER IS on Lake Champlain, dean of Burlington Vermont College. Sort of retired now. But tenured and well off. It is good to see him. He is glad to see me. After a few hours, we are caught up on what each of us has been up to that is of interest to the other. The world through rose colored glasses version, good weather, blue skies.

Dad thinks it's a good idea if we all go to a Pequot Indian museum. Maybe the biggest museum of its kind in the world, newly built on Indian casino money. Dad is tired and slow, but manages. Certainly my memories of him were younger, when he had it together a lot more. His wife has to help him along. She is quite a bit younger than he, about my age. Dad has always had good looking women around him.

The museum is interesting in its concept. The great outdoors is duplicated in plastic under glass down to creeks, trees, bugs on the trees, birds and squirrels on branches. There are plastic deer in plastic foliage, with plastic hunters sneaking up. So real, a photo does not look fake. I'm sure it cost millions of dollars to do. Dad points out a grass hut the Indians live in. A sick Indian is inside with a medicine woman nearby mixing herbs. You can see how the sleeping bench was built. There is a fire in the fire pit. Narrow paths through the trees keep us on the correct trail through the plastic forest.

I enjoy the Ice Age section the most. How ancient Natives lived around here during the Ice Age with caribou, is molded in plastic. They are wearing furs and such. I look close at the weapons, the knapped spear points. There were special three pronged ones for getting birds. There were ones similar for getting fish. It is time for dad to rest.

There is an auditorium with a video to watch about the Pequot life. "Let's rest and watch the film here, son." Some modern natives tell their history on film. I was only a little impressed. *Well, no. I am very disappointed.*

An overall, 'Poor Indian, feel sorry for us' story, a, 'How the white man messed us over' story and 'How the white man needs to feel guilty and give us money' story. And 'Here is how to donate' story… *Uh, huh, yeah. Well, the guy telling the story is wearing a white man gold watch so he can tell time and wears his white man hearing aid. In the good old days, he'd be dead now.* "In his old Indian lifestyle, if you can't hear, you don't live." *He wouldn't hear the mountain lion closing in on him.* "His wife next to him in this video wears white man glasses." *Same deal, in the good old days if you can't see, you don't get to live.*

Elders in Alaska tell me few people would want to go back to the old days if they knew the truth and reality. They did not even name their babies for the first two years because they usually died before then. Starvation was common; such as if the caribou herd did not migrate the path the shaman predicted. One close native friend, Josh, tells me of his childhood. Recalling fighting for rotten fish on the beach with loose dogs. Sleeping in one of the dog houses, barely able to stay alive. He was glad enough when the white man arrived, and put him in school.

But I suppose different tribes in different areas fared better or worse than others. Still. "I get tired of how much I owe the Indian." I'm not into 'Feel sorry for me, you owe me' stories. All races could tell them. All races had problems with other races, went to war, and at some point lost a few, or flat out got ripped off by a more powerful or devious corrupt race. How were the Irish treated when they arrived in the New World? Or the Mormons or the Chinese? Indian tribes treated each other horribly, even before whites arrived. If whites had lost the war with the Indians, I think we would have been wiped out, not been in existence on a reservation. Yes, there were some stories of adopting the enemy into the tribe I loved to hear when I was a kid. Some tribes never went to war with us at all. I'm sure it is complicated. I'm sure bad things were done, unfair things!

"I'd have been a success only if! And it's your fault I failed." It's a special sore spot with me, dad does not have a clue about. This irritates me perhaps. He buys into this, what I call crap; guilt trip stuff, and smiles and nods. He is ready to write a check to help the poor Indian who has money to build a billion dollar plastic replica of the outdoors. An outdoors that already looked like this, even better, before the casino was built on it. For those who do not want to get bit by a real mosquito, or risk getting rained on in the real world, we have the best parts under a bell jar. It is, in fact, fascinating to me. But not for the reasons everyone else is fascinated and impressed. *This is Indian money and what they chose to do with it, no different than any other race, it's all about greed, so what makes you so special?* "Am I sore because I bought into the Indian myth, and am trying to live it, and finding out the truth?"

We stop in the Indian gift shop, advertised to be selling authentic Indian crafts made from authentic natural materials from the land. I'm especially interested because there is an Indian on site who does demonstrations. This is a museum promoting authenticity with the backing and sanction of expert scientists. If I can get the artist's attention, I might be able to supply him with natural material he may need. Sinew, moose leg bones to make hide scrapers, stuff like that. Stuff I know how to get, use, and my life has depended on. It's harder these days to get the real stuff.

The gifts in the shop are a joke. I'm so shocked, I think the shop should be sued for false advertising an outright lie. Dolls with plastic faces are dressed in factory tanned cow hides sewed together with white man thread colored with white man dyes made by white man tools and electricity. Feathers are all dyed chicken feathers. They are no more authentic Indian than Kmart products. The correct term is not even replica. I know what the real thing looks like and this is not even an attempt at a copy. It's tourist trap crap geared towards white customers. Dolls look like Barbie dolls, only with a chicken feather in the hair. Now it's 'an authentic Indian doll,' for three times the price.

But no one else is concerned with the scam, and seems eager to get in line to buy. It is sad to me, realizing how little hope there is trying to offer anything close to the real thing. Only confused eyes and non-comprehension when I suggest this is not how the Indian lived, or what the Indian had before white man. I have a better understanding of the problem I run into all over. Such a disconnect from the real world. I can understand if this is understood to be a tourist trap. But this is a museum, owned and run by Indians who say they wish to be understood, claim the purpose is to educate all of us about who they are, what they stand for, that we may respect and know them as a race. Do these Indians understand who they are? Treating us and themselves like such idiots?

The demonstrator is showing something or other about his people. "Sinew sewed the hide. We take pride in the work and have a ceremony to bless it with a sage fire, honoring our grandfather." I talk to him a little in an aside, and no, he has no use for a source for authentic materials like real sinew.

"It is all supplied through a budget, a purchase order form, using Federal grant money." *Read, white man's tax dollar.* "Through an Indian crafts source in China." White man plastic beads surround him. White man music is in his white man ear phones. "Screw the white man," is on his lips. I know 100 times more about how his people lived in the past than he does. I don't say that. Why bother?

"Screw the white man?" The Indian race says. *With what?* "Yeah, He has nothing Indian to do the screwing with." *His screw gun and all his screws are made by white people.* "No, it is not his fault." *There does not have to be any fault.* "But if he truly screwed the white man, what would he have left? Can he really go back to how it was before the white man ruined it all?" *Can any of us?* "It's not just the Indian who got screwed. Wake up! It's the entire planet!" My emotion is not anger. Just incredible sadness for all of us.

My father is beaming. "Wasn't that great! I love this place! It reminds me of you, son!"

"Yeah, dad. I'm glad we came here!" And I mean that, it gives me a lot of insight into how my lifestyle is perceived by the world. Or by some people, not all. I wonder though, *what percent?* "Sadly, it appears to be a majority."

Dad says, "We need to visit each other more often!"

How do I get out of this one? "Would it be better to be honest and tell him what a joke I think all this is?" *Would it help to tell him if I had to live like this I'd weep, and die of heartbreak at the loss of our beautiful land and connection to it?* But why tell him. I begin, but see he has no comprehension, no perspective to go by. People are born into a plastic world and know no different. Nothing to compare it to. I described my first steps off the airplane in Alaska as, 'A duck finding water for the first time.' Imagine being a duck, and never in your life seeing water. With clipped wings never able to fly. I understand well enough why the Savage in the classic book in a 'Brave New World,' hung himself.

Dad came to visit me last time instead of me seeing him. As usual he would not stay in my home, and did not want to see my pictures, but insisted on taking me on a tourist trip, and showing me the tourist post cards. "Have you thought of going to school? You could stay here with me. You could get a job like this guy has, doing demonstrations to the public." It does not occur to dad I could teach the teacher. Does not occur to him because how could I possibly know anything without a degree? How can anyone possibility know anything without a degree? We have this same conversation over and over followed by, "Do you drive yet?" I suppose it would be hard to get a degree if I cannot drive. One needs to drive to class. I assume.

Dad does not seem interested in the art I sold in Germany. I made a few thousand for all my effort. How pathetic. Put another zero on that and he might be interested. Might tell his friends, "I have a son, he's doing OK." But, he does like the custom knife I made for him with his name and mine on it.

"It's a boat knife dad, for sailing, for when you are on your boat."

He smiles; he loves his sailboat. The one thing we have in common, boating and water. Dad had once told me he had considered writing a book, but saw how much work it is when he watched his woman write a book. Part of getting her doctorate degree, I think, is a requirement to write a book, but I'm not sure. I read it. Well done, a good read. Insight into Salem witchcraft. Proof through land transfer records that witches were burned, not so much because of spiritual issues, but for land takeovers. Call someone a witch; help burn them and get their property. Pretty slick, all right. Told in a good style. Sold a lot. But oh, heavens no, there would be no advice, or help finding a publisher from her.

I hand Dad a copy of my book, now in print after twenty-five years of work. His first comment is, "It needs editing." No congratulations, or glad you got it done, or "It must mean a lot to you," or anything like that.

"But..."

And before I can add anything, he angrily, stubbornly says again more firmly, with a scowl, "It needs editing!"

I am about to open my mouth to defend myself and stop. Been here, done that. I'm too old for this now. I smile and say, "Thanks for your opinion, dad." Without sarcasm. With as much warmth, kindness and forgiveness as I can muster. And we never say anything else about my writing. It's true. I do not have the money to pay a professional to edit the book—it cost ten cents a word. I have had ten friends try, and not improve it much. A few others who have read it, tell me they consider the way it is done a unique and workable style - like reading someone's personal diary. The whole book is in quotes. But, hey... maybe these are friends trying to be polite. The proof will be in how many I can sell. I do feel though, that if the misspellings interfere with the flow of reading, it breaks communication. The truth is, I do not see the misspellings. I have written it my way so many years in personal letters, I see it as correct. It is not lack of caring. Or an oversight. I honestly do not see it. If you showed me the misspelling I'd give a puzzled frown,

"Really?" Spell check does not know the difference between "to" and "too," or "coarse" and "course."[1]

If I sold a million of them, my father would not likely say, "Good job." He may think being a writer is no way to make a living. I do not know. He did not tell me it needed editing kindly, or suggest he knew someone at the university who could edit it for me, or a student who needed some money. He is retired and bored and could edit it for me. I even asked him if he was interested before it got printed. A chance for us to do something together, to bond, get to know each other better. But no. I think it is not about needing editing. I assume it is about me, living a low life in the wilds as a dumpster diver, and having no shame, proudly writing about it. *How mortifying for my family.* It's a slap in the face to hold my head up, act proud, and takes gall, to actually hand my father an autographed copy. Maybe I wrote something about my family, or him, that he feels I had no right to speak of. The truth is, I am proud of my father for what he accomplished. Just that it was his dream, not mine. I should have known better in hindsight. The book should have remained one of those family unmentionables.

Photo Section

This New York Times article about me is an example of an embarrassment
to the family.

My 1916 Nenana home in winter. Custom made gate is a mountain range with the sun coming up over it. The roof of my home is the hull of an 1800's steam paddle boat turned upside down, made of hand whipsawed Sitka spruce.

Same view of home, but in summer with all the flowers I plant.

A wolf track the size of my hand. Guessing an over 200 pound wolf. Up the Kantishna River, near Toklat.

A mammoth tusk twelve ft. long 180 pounds, and about 60,000 years old. Found while fishing on the Kantishna River. Worth $20,000.

Boat loaded with mammoth tusks. Just, 'out there in the wilds someplace.' If I told ya where, I'd have to kill ya.

Tripod up in Nenana. There is a lottery, guessing when the tripod moves in the spring, and stops the clock the flagged wire is tied to. Worth over $300,000.

Tied up for the night with the boat. Sometimes there is not much to tie to! In this case an uprooted grounded tree root wad. Note my 1950's fuel tank that holds just enough gas for a day run of twenty-five gallons.

Alaska Trapper

April 2004

Don, my longtime friend, fur dealer, boss at BLM, makes the cover of the Trappers magazine with his life story.

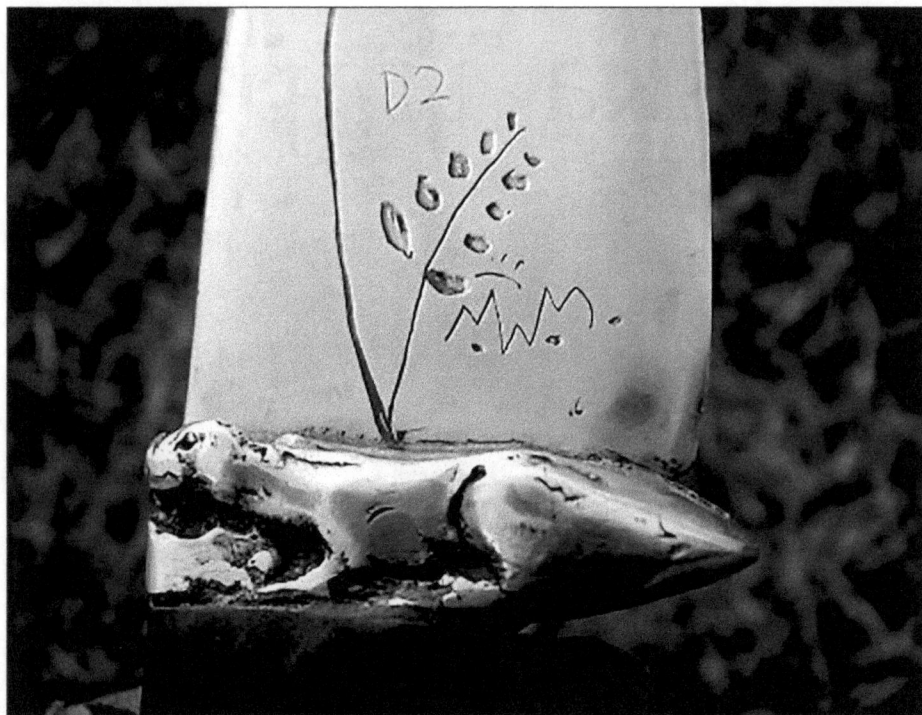

One of my custom cast bronze knife guards. Cast from barge propellers that went up and down the Yukon River for half a century. Acid etched steel designs are on the blade. The signature mwm run together with the sun coming up over them, designed when I was eight years old.

Above, moose leg bone as a set of custom knife handle. I try to use everything off my harvest.

My son and I in the early years, visiting my buddy Crafty

Me as a young teen. Around my neck, my first lost wax casting art, a ring made in school.

My acid etched knife blade. Freehand drawn.

Blade covered in resist wax with design drawn, ready to etch.

That same blade after etching and resist wax removed.

Taking a bath, miner style. Fire under the loader bucket full of water. I work a lot with remote miners. I show up this day to look around for fossils they might have dug up, and show up on bath day.

Frost on the window at 50 below zero.

Nenana has dog weight pulls in the street during winter events. As head of the Chamber of Commerce I am involved in organizing such events. Such dogs can pull 1,500 pounds. Events are put on as community fundraisers.

Mountains in Denali Park, not far from home.

My art on whale baleen. All hand cut, soldered, pinned copper brass bronze and silver.

CHAPTER SEVEN

TUCSON TRIP, MOM AND SHOW, CULTURE CENTER, BUYER EMAILS

E ventually it is time to head to Tucson to see my mother and do the biggest show in the world. I made $7,000 in two weeks in Germany. But the trip is costly. Much is invested back into the business, like the books. I certainly do not want IRS problems if they think I made all kinds of profits. Nope, nope, no indeed. All gone, all money gone, all spent, all on business, yup, yup. I had told Helm, "I think there are many environmentalists here in Germany as well as the U.S. Many who will not buy art made from animal products. Even though I meet many German tourists who love my art, the Germans who love Alaska, and the Alaska dream, are the ones who will take a vacation to Alaska! The others, the majority who do not come, will not buy my art. It is something important to learn." It was really nice of Helm to invite me, put me up, take me around everyplace and be my guide and friend. This is a rare person to do this. Certainly not like the friends I had earlier in my life. I re-think my opinion of mankind.

I'M AT MOM'S.

Mom's boyfriend, Les, picks me up at the airport. He is in his late 80's, still drives, and is alert. He lives a couple of blocks from Mom in the 'Friendly Village' off River Road, near the Tucson Mall along a wash. The wash has a nice walk path mom takes every day. She walks five miles a day. Les and mom have not decided if they should move in together or not. *Geez, at their age they better decide!*

Mom wants to see the art that I will be showing. She seems glad to see me. She looked forward to this visit more than the first visit. It is not awkward, like with dad. Les will take me to the show each day, and bring me back to mom's at the end. This year I did not spend the $200 a day for the hotel spot. I get a table by the pool for $100 for the whole show!

Many vendors remember me, and greet me with warm words. Mom and I take the cab driver, 'John,' from last year out to dinner and to a swap meet. This is a thank you for the kindness he showed me when I did not know my way around. I spend $2,000 in two days buying materials to take back to Alaska. *I need to slow down! It is easy to get in a buying frenzy at the show. So many deals, so much offered, so much to see!*

I meet up with Eaa, my Mexican Mayan friend who calls me his northern brother. We set up selling side by side at the pool. He has long flowing white hair with bright blue eyes to contrast. He wears a Mexican robe, hat, sandals, and looks the part of a Mexican out of a Clint Eastwood movie. He sells crafts his villagers make, like jade masks in the old Mayan tradition.

"Eaa, I got some Alaska black jade for your masks if you are interested." Of course he is interested! He has some Mexican opals to trade me. I can cut and polish the opal and use it in my work more than I can use the jade. Besides, I trade up. I never trade straight across. I got the jade for $3 a pound and traded it at $10 a pound. Fine. Eaa probably traded up to! Ha! As long as we trade retail to retail. Still, I'd have to pay his price cash if I had to buy it!

There are about a dozen people who emailed me that I have appointments to meet. I have some gold nuggets from a miner friend, and meet with at the Alaska Tanana Fair. Eaa buys some gold for cash. He needs it in Mexico. I offer him the deal. "I got a friend who gets gold someplace he can't talk about, digs it up himself in the mountains. I do not want to know where. But he does not want to declare it or sell it on the open market. He sells it to me cash; no receipt, so I get it kind of cheap. Nice jewelry grade nuggets for well below spot." Eaa nods in understanding. The story is only partly true, or maybe true. I have no direct knowledge. It simply makes a good story. I know miners who want to sell gold on the open market, rather than through an assay office because the office takes a percent like a middle man. *Why not sell direct to the consumer, cut out all those middle people ? Legitimate and legal.*

Sometimes I feel overwhelmed with oppression, feel like the world is an evil place, with the government at the bottom of it. Do I only imagine people have a way to be free, beat the system, get ahead, and not be slaves? I think there is a reason the Tucson show is so successful with timing at the end of a tax year and people in need of dumping taxable inventory. The timing is no coincidence. Cash talks in days of distrust of the government and banks.

Many of the deals in Tucson appear to be shell games of the goods of the world[1]

As Mr. Egyptian put it,"Buying permits is paying off the mafia." Basically crooked. Or no. Not quite.

My understanding of 'the situation' and how the mafia got started was an OK concept. It translated, 'This thing of ours.' Taking care of us, our oppressed minority neighborhood. In theory, if you needed to borrow money, there was someone to go to, and someone to protect you when no one else would. The interest rate in theory, and in the beginning, may not have been outrageous. In the same way the government concept of 'taking care of us' may have started out with good intentions.

Before the show is over, I've traded Eaa's opals for Russian ivory. Eaa has traded some wolf claws he got from me for a place to stay.

I had learned from previous experience here, that I create my art in one of the highest economies in the entire world. $10 an hour is minimum wage, when the national standard is $5 an hour, and international standard is measured in pennies. Getting anyone to actually care and do anything where I live, cost $20 an hour. It is difficult to offer products under such conditions. I must compete on a world market —against third world countries selling art every bit as good as mine, but at one tenth the labor cost because the artist overseas works for a dollar a day. It looks like a buyer's market for me in Tucson, more than a seller's market. I think if I deal in Alaskan raw materials that cannot be found in very many places, like wolf and lynx claws, mammoth ivory and Alaska jade, this cannot be duplicated in another country. If you want it, you pay the price. Except much of the same is coming out of Russia, much cheaper. But many do not know it, and prices vary from one show area to another. Russians seem to not know how, or where to set up, or sell well, or understand the dollar. Money can be made in buying at the show, then going to another section of the same show, and selling at twice the price. If you know your product, this can be done.

So I buy then resell, sometimes only an hour later, and double my money— which is fun. In some ways, fooling myself into thinking I'm really making money. I know myself enough to know I will never do well selling. I tend to buy to high and sell too cheap, being more concerned with everyone being happy than with making money. A friend at the show who does well told me it takes about $50,000 to start with, to make real money here. I can see that to take advantage of deals you see, the few thousand I can invest isn't going to do much. It is just fun to 'dabble' in things I understand and know. I love to talk to others with a shared interest. Extremely exciting. It motivates me for an entire year. I make a little on my art work, but know to do so I have to have a name, art unique to me and desired, that people will pay ten times as much for it as art from other countries. That's not easy to pull off. I practice in front of a mirror *"Because I'm the man!"* I turn another direction and grin again, *"Because I'm the man!"* I'm all psyched up saying, "It's show time!" (out of 'All that Jazz')

I'm meeting Africans and exchanging close encounter stories—subsistence stories. Talking to Russians about the world's mammoth ivory market. There are mine owners from India to Australia, and I am hearing news direct from the source. Life doesn't get much better. I feel very at home and at ease here. I'm 'one of us' as far as we are all concerned. Almost like an elite group few understand. The latest tools, the latest products, the best dealers in the world. Million dollar deals, closed here on a handshake.

Room here also, for a craftsman, myself and others, looking for one perfect stone for a project. Searching out a few choice items for an exclusive customer. Whispering in the right ear, "Hey, got some grizzly claws..." and the eager, 'How many? How much!?' Eyes light up, finding a place to set and trade. I love it very much. I cannot get a scene from the movie 'Star Wars', out of my head. A market place. Aliens and creepy crawly looking creatures selling who knows what mixed in with who knows who, the police, thieves, and our main character, Yours Truly, looking for a star ship —no questions asked. I smile.

I cannot get a recurring image out of my head. A woman I lived with when I first went out into the wilds in Alaska. She must have been a creation in my mind, because she showed up out of no place. A very primitive woman from another time. I called her Squaw. She liked animal parts jewelry, and would fit in with all these odd people dressed in strange ways, talking funny, offering weird things for sale. Odd smells come from rooms I walk past. I assume things being cooked for dinner. I assume foods I am just not familiar with from around the world.

I smile again, the fleeting image from Star Wars and the notion of... not just creepy crawly weirdness, but a variety of times in history, as if I were time traveling. Hand knapped arrowheads traded on the left, between barefoot hairy people in leather robes. Right next door, meteorites, diamonds, new cutting edge minerals. "Seven stage rock-saws sold here! want to see?" I move on. Laser cutters, 3D printers, all sold by people in the latest futuristic plastic designer clothes I never saw before in my life. *The past and the future. Who really knows where all this cool stuff comes from, so out of this time!* I smile to myself, "Are you suggesting time travelers meet here to do business?"

Future Flash

2021. Working on books nine and ten. *Is this a new direction?* I need to call it 'science fiction'. Even though I call it 'A continuation of my life story". There are even more books yet unthought of. It gives new meaning to all these years of meeting weird people from all walks of life. Being groomed to understand and accept. New meaning to all these experiences and odd rare things for sale. A world of fake permits, import/export shell games, political pay-offs, 'now you see it now you do not'. People arrive, people leave, vast amounts of goods appear, disappear. Suitcases of money move around. Hairy people, furs, turbans, capes. *Who are these people?* "40,000 years ago, 40,000 years ahead? Who would know? Or care?" *Yeah, Make a pile of stuff, trade it for another pile of stuff. No words exchanged.* "Where is it really going? How are these people paying??"

Arrowheads, Bit-coins, credit, odd looking stuff that reminds me of paper, but is not. What is it really being used for? *What is this stuff?* A fake Latin name given to some glow-in-the-dark metal, shown with a wink. I used to say, "Far out!" "So out-of-this-world!" Only to find out, it really is! ha!

I tell Eaa, "You look like you could be right out of the bible 2,000 years ago my friend." We have been looking around, commenting on the weirdness surrounding us. Curly hair, dark skinned people in hippie cloths, setting out rugs in the dirt at exactly noon, and bowing down, wiggling hands, saying something that sounds like 'Ala!' This does not look like the planet either Eaa or I know.

So he dead pan replies, "And, Miles, you could pass for a cave man out of the ice age. How do I know you are not my friend?"

I only smile. His 'story, is about as unbelievable as mine. *Mayan carver indeed.* Eaa gives me a look like he is thinking, *Runs sled dogs, eats moose, fights off bears. In present time? Who really knows, who could verify his story?* So we both smile and decide it does not matter. If we need cover stories to protect 'whatever', it's all good. I do not care, up-time, down-time all here to mind our own business. *We get our goods and back where we came from, across time and space in our starships, or dog teams.* Eaa and I agree, for sure, the truth about what is going on is not as it appears.

Now I get it! But it was all a bit confusing in the beginning! Much of the weirdness going on in the world, begins to make sense. Once you get accepted as an insider. But as Cider and Universe tell me, (40,000 years ago.) "It would be best to not be a nutcase. I think it wise to be just a strange forgetful person, with time/name issues. Eccentric, a tad of Alzheimers. You know the drill." Indeed! I do know the drill! *What a bunch of nonsense!* "Time travel, isn't that hilarious?" It just takes a lifetime to listen. Well, also a lifetime to build up my credibility and alias. Eaa and I agree, it would not be good to be taken seriously! My Mayan friend, with long white hair, deep blue eyes, in an out-of-this-world robe from the time of Christ. A flint knapper, stone carver, speaking with a Mars accent. Both of us, pretending we are present time humans. *Hilarious all right. A long list of weird, 'trying to be people', explained.*

It is said everything happens for a reason! I get it! I continue with my dog and pony show. Incognito. A secret recruiter. Seeking out enlightened people. Well, in truth I am too old now. However, The Squaw…

Future Flash ends

Eighty degrees under the palm trees. A nice break from the dead of winter in

Alaska where the sun will not rise yet for another month. Eaa laughs. Humming-birds flit around us. "I thought you were the tough Mountain Man, Miles!"

"Well, I once wanted to be for sure, maybe even thought I was once, twenty years ago. I enjoyed the dark and cold much more when I was trapping. I do not trap as much now. The cold just makes it hard to keep the shop warm to get much done. The cold increases my costs to live by a lot. This is OK, because I understand if Alaska had Hawaiian climate, it would be New York City. It is the cold, dark, and mosquitoes that are the guardians of the wilderness and life I love." So... yes, they are my friends... the dark and cold. "I do not see as much fur out in the wild as I used to Eaa, so do not feel as motivated to go trapping. I'm not interested in catching the last marten or lynx. I care about the wilderness. It is different when I feel I am catching the surplus and not hurting the population much. It is also different when trapping is all there is to do to make a living in the wild. Different when I am dirt poor. Now I survey and have my art, so there is less need to make ends meet by trapping."

"And big brother forced you out of the lifestyle, Miles!"

Yes, well there is no need to focus on that. Also, one can get in trouble badmouthing the government overly much. People can be made to disappear... or more often... simply made to shut up. "Some of this fits in with many vendors not being eager to pay taxes or import/export duty and such."

Someone says, "It's not so much anyone sees themselves as a criminal or selfish, or not wanting to pay their fair share to take care of themselves! I donate more money then I pay in taxes, to causes of my choice where I know the money got there to where it was supposed to go." Many do not like what is being done with the tax dollars; like buying fake sinew from China for authentic fake Indian Barbie dolls to help the poor Indian understand his heritage.

Eaa laughs the loudest. He lives in a remote Aztec community and promotes original handcraft. He represents his people selling the village goods. *So he says.* However Eaa sounds convincing when he talks about the whole village being set up to accept high level company people who burned out on the job and whose insurance pays for them to come to his village to become sane again.

"Called a retreat, Miles." He goes into detail about a valley with a waterfall at the end, a simple camp with Indian teepees, campfires, flute music, basic whole foods. "People pay thousands of dollars."

While we are talking, Eaa's friend from Bali shows up. I forget his name, Jay, I think. He sells carvings from Bali, and is the one to see if I have a design I need made out of bone or ivory cheap. He has a fleet of carvers working for him. He may pay twice the going rate and give $2 a day to his carvers! I dealt with him in the past on a small scale. I had him make me carved ivory caps for crystals I put together. I make molds from the carvings and copy them in bronze. A way to compete with cheap and even cheaper.

I buy an ivory rabbit, a wolf head and a few eagle heads all delicately carved in every detail for $10 each. Easy to sell for $30 each as is; seen as high as $100 each in galleries. But I think I might be able to include them in some of my art designs. Maybe as caps on top of claws instead of crystals.

"How do you get the rabbit to stay on top of the crystal, Miles?" I'm beginning to learn about lost wax casting. I think I could cast a cap for the crystal, and that same cap can take the impression of the rabbit while the wax is wet.

"Basically, I make a connector between the rabbit and the crystal out of wax and lost wax cast it into bronze." Another idea occurs to me. "Or put a pin in the bottom of the rabbit and use a diamond drill to put a hole for the pin in the crystal. Two pins so it cannot pivot." We discuss techniques we have tried, heard, read about, or seen others do. Jay knows a lot from his travels and selling his carvings. My mammoth tusk draws a lot of attention. Jay trades ivory for finished carvings.

"How did you get it here, Miles?" He is interested in large amounts, by the hundred pounds. I understand he is fishing for how we could work this out. He does not have good relations with the Russians, even though they control the world market. "Alaskan fossils might work Miles."

I would not have to sell my own finds, I might work with Tusk, who gathers up almost all the Alaska material. "Shipping would kill us."

"My mother lives here, so I am able to send things ahead to her." But before I can explain, Turquoise Penny shows up to do a trade as we had talked about by email. She usually sets up here at the show to sell Arizona turquoise. She had emailed me about needing more wolf claws. She arrives with five gallon buckets of turquoise in her car. We do a nice trade. Nice looking gal. Me, Eaa and Jay stare as she turns her back and bends over, ever so gracefully, to reach in the buckets. All legs. Tall and thin, long, dark straight hair. Dark skin like she lives here. Maybe part Mexican or Native American. When she turns around, we all snap to attention with the same guy 'blank expression', frozen 'who me?' smile.

She mumbles, "Men."

I say, "Just looking in your buckets."

We all nod, 'Yes' at once and Jay adds, "And examining your exquisite turquoise." We all agree, with uniform affirmative nods.

"Exquisite turquoise. Quite extraordinary." Anyhow. If women didn't want us to watch, they wouldn't bend over. Right? *Makes sense to us! We're guys!*

Turquoise loudly says, "Do I have 'screw me' written across my forehead?"

I say, "Well no." *Maybe* "Just stare and drool, but do not touch." I mean, *We guys were here minding our own business, talking, and suddenly we all get the same exact thought at the same time.* "Is that by accident?" Is she giving off pheromones, whiffy things like flowers do that, say 'sniff me' or something? The exact stuff they put in perfume mixed with jungle cat sex gland extract that women rub behind their ears?

Turquoise Penny admits, "Ya' well, Steve and I just broke up. I'm pretty upset"

Steve? *Oh yeah, he was the guy with her last year selling turquoise with her.* "There. See. We knew it. 'Lady in distress' scent in the air." We all grin, and wait for her to turn around and bend over to show us more of her turquoise. But she doesn't want to, so I help her out with a polite, "Here, let me get that for you."

She steps aside so I can get the buckets of turquoise out. I give her cash for turquoise I only marginally want because she needs money after the break up. Life is like that sometimes. Acquiring things is not always just good business with lots of profits. *Yeah, ten years later I still have most of the turquoise, but it is going up in value, better than money in the bank. Yeah, I keep saying that. Along with 'beats working for a living'.* I promise to email her. She is not doing the show this year, but selling off a lot of the inventory she shared with what's his name.

JAY and I talk fossil business, how to best move goods great distances in an afford-able creative manner. A private conversation.

I have a list of things I want to look for this year here at the show. The whole city is the show, so I need to go to one of the other sections of town to the African village. It looks like rain, so decide this is a good time to wrap it up for the day and go do more buying. Eaa is calling it a day as well. It's nice to be small time dealers no one will miss. It takes just a few minutes to pack up what we have on the table into a suitcase, and leave it under the table with another vendor to keep an eye on. And yes, it is amazing how we all stick together; help each other out. People from all over the world helping each other. *Too bad the whole world can't do that.*

I look up the African guy I did business with before. I kept his card. He has African lion claws and teeth. I'm offered elephant ivory by another vendor, but do not think it is legal, and do not want to get involved with that business. All elephant ivory is controversial. Well… so is the walrus ivory business, I suppose, but it is near home, and I have a better handle on how it is acquired. I can rest assured it is a byproduct of subsistence food taken, not poached for the ivory. But anyhow, I turn the elephant ivory down.

The lion claw guy I trust, because we talked a long time, and he seems to walk the walk and talk the talk of a subsistence person who deals in byproduct as I do. Lions are killed in his village in self defense now and then, as it is with bears where I live. He is not connecting with guides or trophy hunters. He's a barefoot, illiterate poor person from a small village. He's hard to find, way in the back, not one of the prominent dealers. This time he has a few fossil fangs from ancient times. I know I will do well with these, so buy all he has. I tell him I will be back every year if he looks for these for me, I will buy them all. I pay his price with no haggling, even though I know the price is inflated, I also know I can at least double my money, and know this is a rare item hard to put a value on. We shake hands on a long term agreement.

He's dressed in long desert robe, barefoot. From a remote African village. We had talked in the past, and he told me lion stories. How getting water digging a hole in the sand is a big issue. I laugh and tell him bear stories, and how getting water through the ice is such work. He and I have more in common than either of us has in common with the other vendors! We both laugh. Me - white; him - black. We had done a trade with claws. Now I can just buy them outright. Is the deal legal? I have no direct knowledge that it is not. Possibly a gray area.

I do not think the African government cares if this man lives or not. His life has less meaning politically than the lions. The lion has more rights than he does. The government does not care if he or his whole village is starving. So he looks out for himself as all his people do. He gets to the U.S., how? I suspect a group gets together and works together. Somewhat like the mafia. A group who looks out for you; cares about you. But, of course, wants a cut of the take. Even a big cut. In return, all is taken care of - tickets, permits, show fees, set up tents.

Proper hands are greased high up to make it all run smooth. He and I are peons. At the source where he lives, a piece of paper and pen for a receipt and permit would be more rare than the lion. 'In writing' means nothing. For all I know, he can't read or write. As is true with many remote villagers I deal with in Alaska. It would be rude to ask for a receipt. I have his word. But who needs anyone's word? I have my product and he has his money. *The deal is between us. If both of us can cut out the mafia for a little secret cash to buy rice and beans with...* I have no direct knowledge. Like him, I'm at the bottom of the food chain.

I suspect for the first time that these are not really lion fangs, but cannot place what they might be. I was once sure they are lion, and my customers know less than I do for the most part. *Baboon fangs?* "I'm not sure." *Really fossil?* "I doubt it." *All the same size and same looking age? Not likely.* I, also, have been exploring the wonderful world of, "Now it is new, now it is old," *Nothing up my sleeve.*

I buy a few strands of African trade beads, but not many, as this item seems common all over the world, so hard to mark the price up on. I can use a few in my own work though, especially the ones that are the same kind of bead made in Italy that were also called Russian trade beads. Same as African. Same source. Just that Russia got hold of them and traded them to the Eskimo in the 1800s. I like three kinds—white hearts, Russian blues, and Dutch Dogons. Skunk beads and padre beads are offered, but I do not understand the value of these, so shy away.

There are a lot of fakes and scams going on, so I do not bet into another man's game if I can help it. I try to know already from another source what something is worth and what to look for. That's why chatting with trusted vendors is so helpful. More than just the money here at the show, is the vast wealth of knowledge represented here. I may in time be able to inquire of my lion fang source, "I suspect, but do not know, these are not lion and not old, probably better that way from a legal standpoint. I want them anyway, but would like to know, for my own information, what they are and how handled." A very few buyers would want to know. I cannot indignantly reply they are real. If it is all magic, one of the definitions of magic, is not being included in the reality of the trick. Then it is not magic anymore. Most people tell me this is a poor attitude they do not want to be part of.

"Fine." I'm not going to argue. However these same people are usually part of the ninety five percent who do not care if I make five cents a day, and am starving in the street. So how much would they like, or expect me, to care about their needs? Is this a 'treat others how you hope to be treated' situation? *Give back ten-fold that which you give to me.* "I'm not upset, just realistic, facing reality." I try to care more about the customer than the customer cares about me, but there are different levels of care.

Most of my customers care the most that the fang is not plastic. Getting a real predator fang of any kind is a big deal. If it is lion, bear, or wolf, it's awesome and they do not care so much, so long as they remember when they show it off,

"Yeah, lion, I think the guy said. I forget." The price reflects reality. *You are not going to get a real diamond for five cents out of that bubble gum machine.* "But yes, trying to upgrade; be knowledgeable, credible; eventually knowing for sure; being the expert." This is the goal. *Meanwhile making a living, in the game.* Where would we learn this stuff? Not college! *Some black illiterate, barefoot African village guy, is a world expert on killing lions with a spear.* "Or... so he wants me to believe."

EACH NIGHT I am with mom. She has been going out of her way to cook nice meals. She had complained about change at first, but now enjoys it. She lives on a fixed social security and retirement from her previous husband. I know it is not a lot of money, so I give her plenty of money to buy food and some extra.

"Oh I do not need all this, Miles!"

"I know, mom, but look what it would cost me if I had to find a place to stay! I do not mind passing some of the savings on to you. I feel better about it anyhow, knowing I can help out a little." So the financial burden of having a guest is off her mind. She has cable TV, which I have never seen before. We enjoy the same shows,

BEYOND WILD

so sit and watch bait car and cop shows. We like all the excuses people come up with for being in the stolen car. There is a hidden camera in a car. Often it is stolen within a few minutes! Repo is also fun. The crew shows up to repo cars. Sometimes, the wife does not know the husband has not been making car payments. I begin to suspect, "Mom, this cannot be real and must be staged, nothing ever goes smooth. Mom and I laugh together while eating her home cooked meals.

"This apple pie is good, mom. I remember it when I was little. You must make it the same way!"

"Yes, it was my mother's recipe and I think she got it from her mother." Mom peels and cuts the apples, rolls out her own pie dough. Real butter, no imitation, sprinkled with cinnamon and sugar and other stuff. Most women I know, when they say, 'home made' mean open a can of spiced apples and dump it in a store bought pie crust. Who rolls out their own dough anymore? Who would bother? Who even knows how? Can you even buy rolling pins in the store anymore?

Les usually eats with us, then drives the few blocks to his place to watch his own TV shows. He wants to sit in his own chair. For some reason, he is not comfortable at mom's and she just accepts that. Sometimes she walks up to his place to spend the night, and walks back home at 5:00 am.

"That's weird, mom, that you are an early person just like I am. I do not know many people who start their day at 5:00 am."

"You get that from my side of the family!" She sometimes gets out old family albums and reviews with me who is who in the pictures with some new story of my Grandpa or some aspect of her childhood. We get up together early, and go for a walk along the wash. There are hummingbirds, cactus flowers, and once I saw a coyote run down a rabbit. We get to watch the sun come up over the Catalina Mountains against a backdrop of palm trees. Mom seems to enjoy nature.

"I sometimes miss my garden in Oregon, Miles. I used to have the best strawberries! It is hard to get anything to grow here, but I do have some Swiss chard growing. I have to protect it from the rabbits." She has a lot of flowers out along her drive that she tends to every day. She makes extra money taking care of the elders. She does not consider herself an elder at seventy.

As part of our routine, we get back home for breakfast, which is grapefruit off her tree. Grapefruit is not something I'd normally eat at home in Alaska, but it sure tastes good right off the tree here. We chat over her morning paper and at exactly 8:30 am on the dot every day, her boyfriend calls. If he is even five minutes late something must be wrong. She'd call him, but she never has to as he has never been late.

And every morning at 9:00 am sharp, he leaves to go have coffee with the boys. They meet at McDonalds for coffee for half an hour. Maybe twelve guys. So each day I am part of this routine. We head over to discuss the ailments and cures of the

217

world. No women allowed. After coffee and donuts, Les gives me a ride to the show. I'm there by 10:00 am—about when we open and people start coming around. It's a nice enough routine. The guys at the coffee shop remember me from last year. Most are retired. A couple are retired military. Les was a salesman all his life, mostly selling shoes, but off and on, cars.

One fellow of interest is a good friend of Les named Jeff, who makes a living on Ebay selling paintings he buys at thrift stores! I find that interesting. He recognizes certain names of artists around here who do the cowboy or southwest art. "Some of the thrift stores are in rich neighborhoods. People throw out all kinds of good things. They do not want to be bothered with a garage sale, I guess."

Since he is successfully selling art on the internet, along the line of work of interest to me, I talk to him about how to make it work. "One reason I do not like eBay is, I can't navigate the pages. I have slow speed dial-up access to the internet. Sometimes I try to download things, updates, fixes, programs I buy. They will not download. I think now, it's because I time out."

"That's possible, all right. You can usually order the program on CD though."

But still I do not want to wait fifteen minutes for each page to load, looking around, or listing anything for sale. I explain: "I use my web program and build it off line. When done I upload it. Even though it takes forever to upload, I can walk away and come back later to preview it and make sure it went up all right."

I also have this idea that I want to stand out. I want my site to be different and noticed. If I used standard format like Ebay, it is hard to get noticed. All the pictures are the same size, in the same place with the same spot to describe the item. Few are interested in my opinion, however, because it is just an idea so far. I cannot say I am making a living off it. Talk is cheap. No one says it is a good idea. All the questions and focus is on how to use Ebay. As is so often in my life, I'm out there in left field? So far, I'm not even in the same game. I'm used to that and it is OK, or nothing I can do about it. I can talk about Alaska.

I hand out business cards that say I have a web site, and encourage people to go there and look. I have cards printed that tell you where my spot is at the show. When the cashier takes my money for coffee, the eighteen year old asks what I sell. I hand him a card, and tell him about the teeth and claws. He is interested, and might come look me up. The card will remind him how to find me, and increase the chances he will show up. Or encourage him to contact me in Alaska.

I'm a one man show with no helpers. One advantage is, I do not have to split or share my profits. I set up, clean, open and close each day; I do all the talking and run the till. It is not so bad this year with a single table to pack and set up each day.

A couple of other Alaskans are around. We get together to talk prices and trade some product. One gold miner brings the tusks he finds in Alaska to sell. Ed Lap buys a few of my minor bones and teeth. He has a kid working for him. I watch how he runs his business.

The kid goes out as spotter. He sees vendors who are in a bind. Kid reports back to Ed, they discuss the reason for the bind. Often Ed decides to show up and buys the vendor out; moves the inventory to a new location with a mark up three times what he paid, and sells it. *How can we sell it when the previous vendor could not?* Various reasons include, vendor cannot speak English well, cannot make dollar sign and numbers clear. Poor display and location. Poor salesman who looks scruffy and disreputable. So this becomes a learning experience for me. Same is not selling. Price has a lot to do with... well a lot of factors. Only one of twelve factors is the value of the product. The poor schmuck who got ten cents on the dollar, and lost his shirt had a fast learning curve experience in the shark infested waters of free enterprise.

This country bumpkin, me, does not fall into any of these traps. I'm one of the predators... kind of. But wait... sigh. The Russian gal next to me can't sell her beautiful Charolite purple stone, new out of Russia to the American market. It should be a killer stone, selling fast. She has had no sales, and looks depressed, scared, and vulnerable, ready for someone to move in for the kill. Cute, little damsel in distress, too. Dang. I stroll over to see what is going on. Oh, yes. It is obvious. *She does not know how to make a dollar sign.* She has made it backwards. I try to tell her.

I point and say, "The dollar sign is backwards." She thinks I am trying to buy product. She does not understand English. Sigh. I pause, then walk away. I come back with a sign I made for her: 'Charolite = $20 a pound'. I show it to her, then take away her sign and put mine up. Within five minutes she gets sales. Now she understands. *Yes. Ed would have simply showed her maybe $500 in cash and loaded up her entire 500 pound inventory. Sent her home crying.* "Unless she was interested in trading pussy for a place to stay." That's how to get rich and get what you want. I guess. I suppose. Or I nod and say "Cool!" Being nice is not going to get me any money, and might even get me on the soft touch sucker list.

It seems the Russians all know each other. The Charolite gal is not stupid. She tells the other Russians I helped her without asking to get paid. Without knowing it at the time, this is a move in a good direction when dealing with the Russians on coveted Siberian mammoth ivory. About all the other dealers tell me "It is impossible to do business with those communist Russians!" Well. Whatever.

All the other ivory dealers were scared when the Russians first showed up with several tons of mammoth tusks. We all thought we'd be out of business. Dealing with them was not a fun experience. The rest of us know buying a tusk is about the experience, the story, the magic of where it came from. The Russians frown and stand cross armed, guarding their tusks distrustfully. When a customer asks how much a tusk cost, they get a cold stiff answer, no smile, no greeting, no sit down and sip tea and lets tell stories. If someone is going to spend ten grand on a tusk, it is worth half an hour of storytelling and schmoozing.

One customer spreads the word that went around like fire. "Yeah, I got one of the Russian tusks last year. Looked nice, cost me eight grand. I got home and found out it is two tusks put together with a rod and shoe polish in between to blend it. I bring it back to point out the fact, and get my money back! The Russian I got it from is not there. This other guy tells me to see Peter.

"Where is Peter?"

"Back in Russia."

"But the company owes me, not Peter!"

"No, go see Peter." The rest of us sigh in relief. Few customers will buy mammoth ivory from the Russians this year.

However. I am not stupid; nor do I think the Russians are. They want to do business; make money. Maybe they are just unsure how. Maybe they just do not understand what is expected and why. One Russian ivory dealer not far from me seems like a nice smart guy. I stroll over when things are slow just to look. I take one of his cards. 'Igor' is his name; that I want to remember. 'Siberian Fossils.' He can speak only a little English. He shows me on a computer set up in his room, his web site, and where he gets the ivory and prices in English.

I see major flaws in his web site addressing American customers. Everything is metric. The weights and the lengths. The story is not with pictures westerners like to see. I keep the card and email address. Maybe later I will send him a copy of his site with some corrections that appeal to western culture. It would take me half an hour and help him out tons. I can see he does not have many western friends or help. Partly, I am just being nice. But I think in terms of just good business.

If kindness and trustworthiness is offered and received, the plan in the big picture is to gather around me like minded people. Customers and vendors who enjoy what they do, are proud of who they are and what they do, and want to do honest business with others who feel the same. Even if we are a minority. 'Legal' is not even a major priority, but 'ethical' is. In this way, business should be fun, rewarding; not just watching your back and taking people's money. I cannot prove this works, but it is a long term plan I want to try out. It is not even the only way I do business. I sometimes go by how I am treated. 'What you give me I shall return tenfold.' Igor does not say anything. He may be waiting for the punch line, the scam. I'm setting him up. Let him think and let him figure it out. We can be nice, try to trust each other and do business, or we can try to scam each other.

The Russian Charolite gal comes over and to give me some stone. I take it, get out my calculator, figure the cost and hand her the money. She shakes her head and does not want the money. This is a thank you for helping her. My thinking is, making the sign took me no time and cost me nothing. It is how I would hope to be treated if I were a visitor in another country. I know she is grateful and appreciates it. I do not want her to think I did this, and she owes me anything. I did it to be nice, not to be owed a favor. *Pay it forward. Isn't that a new term I hear? When you help someone out for no other reason than because you can and want to. The person is not in a position to help you in return. They in turn, help someone else in the future, because they recall how someone helped them and how much it meant.*

I know she is scared and hurting for money. I pay her a fair price; I can still make a profit off what I pay. There is no reason to take advantage, not in this situation, anyhow. Other times, other situations and other places, yes, I have been known to go for the gold. I have my own sense of ethics to follow that may not make sense to anyone else. I put the money in her hand, smile and will not take it back, and ignore her so she cannot return it. She knows I am not up to anything. I am glad she is making some money and able to smile and do well. It is a good feeling to have helped. She does not understand English, so I turn my back on her, cover my ears to show her I do not want to hear about it, saying, "Bla, bla, bla, bla" to drown out her words. She laughs because this gesture would be universal worldwide.

I forget about it. We both have business and customers to tend to. I take notes on what is selling, what to buy, what to bring next time. I am not 100% happy with this spot. *Too many tourists, not enough serious buyers.* I get a great volume of people, almost too many. It is hard to get anyone to stop to talk. I tell Eaa, "I heard there might be a spot by the Vagabond in the grass under a tree instead of here on the cement." The Vagabond is set up more as a fossil part of the show. "High rollers show up there who buy entire dinosaur skeletons for a million dollars. I'd like to cater to this guy's wife and kids when he is making his big deals."

"It's an idea, Miles. I'm kind of expected to be here. I have regular customers who look for me here."

I'm just asking around, looking, figuring out my best options. I settled in here the first time without knowing what is going on because other Alaskans are here. The show manager seems a little shady to me. There is major construction on the road, so many visitors are bypassing this show. As I talk to Eaa, there just seems like a lot of low end customers here.

"The Vagabond does not have vendors setting up free along the street like here." I think the hippies setting up free along the road and soliciting business, lowers the quality of customers this show attracts. I understand better, when it was me looking for free space and being among the riff-raff horning in on a show others have put together. But we can learn and change. I had little choices back then. I was dirt poor with no other options if I wanted to sell. I suppose vendors who set up without paying would say the same thing. "Who can afford these show fees?" Still, it's only $100 for the whole show, minimum. For that I get listed in the Show Guide. Anyhow, just toying with some ideas here.

I buy one more fossil Megalodon shark tooth six inches long from Florida Fossils. On my list is some Peru opal, if I can find a smallish piece I can afford. I find the main seller direct from Peru. He is about all packed up. It's the end of the show.

"You got a small piece of robin egg blue I might get, in the $45 range?" I did not want him to go out of his way. I understand he is busy.

"Most of my material is put away. Trying to find room for this one big block that does not fit. You want this?"

It is a nice piece all right, and I tell him so, but it is twenty pounds. I can't afford it. I only have $45 to spend. He acts grumpy, or like he did not have a great show, or is tired and wants to leave. Maybe he had a good show and just wants to get home. He's frustrated. He can't find room for this football size gem stone. He has blue opal, and sells it by the hundreds of pounds during the show, as the main source. He owns the mine. My $45 interest is probably nothing but a pain for him. I am about to apologize and leave.

"OK, hey, you can have it for $45. I need to get rid of it!"

I give him $100, because this is a $2,000 rock or more. I'm grateful, and will remember to look him up in future years here. It's hard to figure all the situations that can be run into. Play it by ear, I guess.

I lose money here and there along the way. It is not all about deals. I had a lady keep coming back for more turquoise, and wondered why. I had traded for it in the past with Turquoise Penny. This lady got several hundred dollars worth. I wondered what was going on, so asked a turquoise vendor. I find out I do not know the value of what I have very well. I sold it for about a tenth of what it is worth. Penny had been nice to me, given me some real quality natural untreated, as good as it gets turquoise. She assumes I'll appreciate it. But I didn't. In all honesty, I did not deserve the quality she sold me.

I got a deal on some trilobite fossils that turned out to be fake. I bought some amber with bugs in it I was excited about, only to find out it is really copal with some amber mixed in, melted on the stove with bugs inserted. I paid three times too much for my phantom crystals before seeing the same product someplace else much cheaper.

The main thing is to keep on going, without giving up or getting discouraged, to try to learn, and to look at the big picture. At the end of the year, am I arriving or leaving? Is my income bigger then my outflow? If I'm ahead, the rest is just little details. So much like at the Tanana Fair. I go around and try to offer encouragement for the discouraged.

"I'm selling wheel barrels, are you interested?"

"What do I need a wheel barrel for?"

"All the money we make here. Don't you need something to carry it out to the truck with?" We both laugh.

"So where are you going for vacation to spend the million dollars you made?"

A common answer is, "Headed home back to the grind stone. I have a shop. This is a nice break from office work, selling is about being on the phone, going to meetings, mingling with representatives. Put my suit and tie back on. This is a fun show that puts me in touch with the customer at the grass roots of my business. It helps me understand how to advertise, what to spend, what products are in fashion and for what price. How about you, Miles?"

"Not like that for me. I'm a one man show. I find a lot of my own materials. I'm also the artist who does all the work I sell. I do not carry anyone else's work. In this way, I have total control of my business. I'm never in a suit and tie, do not even own such clothes. I'm not getting rich, but I like what I do a whole lot. I agree with you, there is a lot to learn here."

"That's what it's all about Miles. It's a pleasure to know you, hope to see you back again." This is a typical conversation with the more high-end sellers. Some of these prime selling spots go for $1,000 a day. Way out of my league. But still, such people respect how I run my business and why.

This gives me something to think about when I am back home, when those who are not in the business make hurtful comments. I can have less of a chip on my shoulder, less of a need to prove anything to those not worth impressing. Or, as I say to Eaa, "Not so much 'not worth impressing' I guess, as 'not worth all the energy' to change someone's opinion, when they do not want their opinion changed. "

"Most of us run into that, Miles." He tells me more about the other aspect of his business - the retreat. Apparently some companies insurance covers such 'medical' costs. "When you and I, Miles, are already well."

Along the same lines I point out something I observe. "I know a few people who make over 100 grand a year. They go and buy expensive exercise equipment, pay big fees to join health clubs. All so they can do what we do for nothing, or even get paid to do. Go swimming, lift weights, and jog. I often wonder when they are done spending, if they end up with as many toys as we do, and enjoy life as much. Some do, I'm sure. But only when the money is part of the fun, the game, and not the overall purpose."

"For sure we can't make money our God!"

"Still, money makes the world go around. Money solves a lot of problems!" We both laugh. We were both here to make money for sure. I've met too many people in my life that had no money, despise money, but then are a burden on others as a result. Such people seem especially happy to me. Nor do they contribute much to the world that is good and positive. I do not look up to or admire very many of these people.

I chat with Eaa and others during the show about life. It is interesting to hear how basic issues are solved in different cultures. How to eat, keep warm, have shelter, deal with the governments, find a partner, find success and such. One rich gem dealer from India wants to come to Alaska for a boat trip with me. He has my card.

"If I had my choices of places to go, I'd love to go to Siberia!" I tell the guy from India, who is aghast at this strange, cold, inhospitable place I want to go to."It is much like Alaska, only hundreds of years ago." I envision much fur and mammoth ivory to be found, lots of room, with few roads or industry. Maybe an untouched wild place where the planet is still pure and safe. I wonder if the government wishes to go to Siberia and regulate, or care what a few people in thousands of square miles do. It is of no consequence. Moscow, like Washington, has better things to do. Perhaps it is only a silly dream, but I envision such an environment. Or, if I were younger! Ha! Find some remote village to be part of. Marry some savage who has no stress in her life. Who sits by the fire in a hut, and skins game I bring in. Live life as it was 1,000 years ago. Subsistence off the land. As I wished for in Alaska when I arrived. Or, even just to visit, see, learn and compare how it is across the Bering Sea. Study solutions to travel, and cabin building in Alaska. I hear the sled dogs are hooked up different, and even reindeer are used for transportation. I wonder what trapping is like.

"No, the tropical jungles of the world do not interest me very much for some reason. I'm guessing my ancestors were far north people." Someone from India understands the concept of past lives. I am not so sure I would call it that. I think many aspects of our life can be genetic. Predisposed for certain environments and situations. Over many generations people adapted to cold, lack of light; walking in snow. So much so that it feels like home, like we have been there and done this before, because our body likes it, and recognizes what it is built for.

It is possible for body and mind to be suited to certain types of problems, smells, habits of all kinds, the entire package of an environment. Just like I see tall lean Africans from tall grass country who can run well, and are far sighted. Other races seem more near sighted, dexterous with the fingers for seeing up close, opening seed pods, and such. It is difficult to imagine a tall lean runner being a meat eater. Likewise as difficult picturing a football player being a vegetarian. There are exceptions, and we are told stereotyping is wrong, yet we see, get a little information, and can predict or have certain expectations. In modern times what use is any of this, predisposed for certain lifestyles? I think to myself though...

If I had come to Alaska and settled down in a small remote village, married into a tribe, and lived in the old ways, maybe I would have made it, got left alone by the government. If I had lived a simple life of just getting by on minimum substance from hand to mouth. No government cares about that. It is not a threat, and is of no consequence. Perhaps this is not, after all, my basic personality? "Everything went wrong with that dream when I started to succeed and get ahead." When we have something, suddenly others are interested and want it too. Or want a cut from my hard work and gain. I do not speak these thoughts with anyone.

I am afraid. I do not want to end up on the 'person of interest' list. Or no, *probably am already on this list*. "I do not want any facts in my file." Is it true that on such and such a date you told such and such person you are hiding things from the government?

Anyhow it is time to head home.

"I'm going to miss you, Miles. It is nice having you around."

"I look forward to seeing you again, mom. I'll try to stay in touch more during the year."

It is nice to get back home to Alaska. The sun is gaining light seven minutes a day, almost half an hour a week of gained light this time of year. Spring is not so far off in mid-February when I get home. Or it feels like there is some warmth to the sun starting about now. I call this time of year, the melt down, Chernobyl. Spring is still two to three months off, yet I think of what garden seeds to order and start them in March.

I get back to Fairbanks at 1:00 am. This seems standard for the cheapest flights. To leave and arrive on the red eye. I have not asked anyone to come pick me up at this late hour, so I take a cab over to Crafty's. I still have my own key and let myself in. There is a room kept for guests, mostly me. There is no public transportation between Nenana and Fairbanks, especially in winter. Well, unless I wanted to pay $150 for a cab. I have to start calling around in the morning to see who might be coming into town from Nenana. Josh can come in 'tomorrow' so I settle for that. I will wait around Fairbanks a day. I have nothing horribly pressing waiting at home.

I have been able to check on my emails here and there along the trip. There was free internet access at the airport, so I have been telling my customers when to expect me home, and that I have a lot of new things. One of the things I buy is a new digital camera, so I can take better pictures of my art. I have always been interested in photography.

I started out with my father's twin lens reflex, probably from the 1950s. I eventually got my own camera and stuck with a Thirty-five mm Pentax Spotmatic. This was reputed to be a great professional camera for outdoors and rugged work, because the workings did not depend on the battery. The battery only ran the light meter. So I had been able to get some awesome wilderness pictures in my lifetime, some at sixty below zero when few other cameras would work. I had all the different lenses for this camera. A zoom, a portrait, a telephoto and a bellows.

The main disadvantage was the inability to edit or alter the pictures myself, and the time delay waiting for film to get developed. The new digital camera allows me to crop and edit my own pictures, and have them fast and cheap. All the years I spent just knowing what a good picture looks like becomes an advantage in the 'selling on the internet' age I am entering. Also, having learned to express myself through the written word is a big help. All those years when younger, writing my feelings to girlfriends is paying off. Out in the wilds, I got used to expressing myself through writing.

I meet Will in town, "Writing and photography makes up a good part of selling on the internet, Will. I can tell my stories through words and pictures."

"And did you get your book printed over there in Germany as you hoped?"

"Yup, should have them on the market here within a month, all paid for." Will is not very interested in art, but maybe custom knives and different fossils I might have found. "Like this six inch Megalodon shark tooth Will! This Shark was as big as a school bus, related to the Great White of today, like 'Jaws' from a million years ago."

"Did you get to the homestead and trap this winter, Miles?"

"Yes, but not like I used to. I will get out again before spring and get some trapping done before the season ends. It's a good time to catch lynx and wolves." The truth is, I just do not need to trap anymore because I have better ways to make money. This is not information that helps Will in any way, so I hedge a little with the reply. "I enjoy trapping, Will, but it's just not the same as years ago. Not as much game, more trappers with hot snow machines zooming around. It no longer reminds me of the mountain man days of the free trapper."

"You got that right, Miles. I miss those old days in the '70s, when we took care of ourselves without the government telling us how to be safe and taking care of us for our own good." I still smile at how slow Will talks with his farmer background accent.

"Will, you mean you don't trust the government to take care of you as good as you can take care of yourself? I'm shocked!" We all know how concerned the government is for our personal well-being. Will is referring to all the new rules about tagging furs including lynx and beaver. Who knows what else. Supposedly it is to protect the species. Make it easier on trappers. However. "It is not about a small fee, Will; it is about control. Tagging furs means keeping a good record of when, where, and how a fur was taken. In the old days it was no one else's business. Now there can be a withhold on getting something tagged.

If so, you can't get it tanned or sold without breaking the law."

"You can't shoot it. The fur cannot have a bullet hole in it. Or a snare mark if the law says it has to be trapped, or a leg hold mark if the law says a conibear trap. Telling us what to do, when to do it and how to do it."

One issue that comes up, for example, is that I am way out remote. I may not be able to get my furs to town till after the season closes and the cutoff date for getting furs tagged has passed. Or I have someone, maybe a fur dealer, fly out to pick up my furs on the trapline. Will this pilot get them tagged, and will it be in his name or mine? Does the pilot know the answers to where all the fur was trapped? What about furs I might trade for, or buy from local Indians that are fresh caught. I have to get them tagged. Maybe I have to make up where they were trapped because I do not know or recall. This makes me liable for a crime of lying. Or I was lied to, and there is some glitch to the fur I bought, like it has a snare mark and it should not, or some game management area got closed that I did not know about since I have no radio and get no news. Maybe I bought it and can't get it tagged, sold nor get my money back from the one I bought it from. Maybe I need a dealer's license to legally buy fur, even if I am an old time trader, and traded fur with someone. Maybe I bought it like in the old days, when fur was used as money. The worries never end, and build up stress.

The freedoms I once cherished are vanishing. The very freedoms that were at the root of why I would choose such a life of hardship. *To be free, that's why.* The rewards of being responsible for myself and what I do, without being told, or forced to follow, someone else's view of what responsible means. Many friends agree with me and understand how I feel. Like Will.

Will is not an example of someone I would want to be as he does not seem either happy or successful. He is not getting what he wants out of life. He wishes he were not alone; wishes he had a better job; wishes he had enough money to get by on, but usually does not. I admire Will for his dedication to friends, his kindness and will-ingness to do for others. But for solutions to life problems, I am inclined to seek out advice from those I admire along these lines. Those I think are successful, meaning they have what they want; are happy, productive, and get along well enough with others to be an asset to their tribe. I use the term 'tribe' to define the group of people we identify with - our peers, family, mentors, those we hang with and trust. I'm convinced this is basic need or how things have been for humans for thousands of years. So, while we force ourselves to live in crowded conditions out of necessity or choice, we resort to our basic nature, and only recognize a group about the size that would be called a tribe. My guess, between twenty and a hundred people.

"Will, pretty soon I think we will need an ID to fly."

"No way, Miles, who would put up with that?" The subject comes up because Alaska Airline offers a special flying price during our Permanent Fund oil dividend time, to encourage us to fly with the money we get. There are various deals, like get two tickets for the price of one, or special deals to far off places. To take advantage you need to give your name. Sometimes people trade tickets, or offer their deal to an Alaska friend because they can't fly this year. Give any name, no ID required.

"I saw Steve from Hippie Hill at the airport coming back from Tucson. He was flying under someone else's name on one of those dividend tickets. He's the one who said they will check ID next year."

"Lucky you got an ID then, huh?"

Yes I had not long ago got a state ID. I still do not drive, and it is becoming illegal not to have a driver's license. Will has witnessed a time or two when there is a situation where someone is suspicious I cannot show a driver's license, and he has to vouch for me. I want to change the subject to something better.

"The ability to take pictures and edit them on the computer has the potential of offering goods in real time almost. Within hours of taking a picture, an item can be seen for sale on the internet. Pretty cool, huh!"

After talking with Will, I need to check my emails. I have a typical customer filled with questions . I scan the email…

3. How did you come about these skulls, were they found or hunted, trapped or ?

I respond from far away, living a different lifestyle then my customer—

The skulls arrive to me by various means. I started out selling only the ones I trapped —a by product of trapping which supported a very simple subsistence lifestyle of rice and beans and propane lights etc. I moved to the village; I do not get out trapping as much these days; I am getting older. I know other trappers and the local fur dealer, so now acquire skulls, claws and bones from other subsistence trappers. A few are from dead animals I found. No one person supplies me with a lot, and it is not a big business. I may sell ten skulls a year. Usually there is no market for bones – skulls, so trappers simply toss the carcass in the river or dump them in the woods.

My intention is to supply local trappers with a little bit more money for a lifestyle that doesn't have a lot of economic opportunity. I also like others to have the opportunity to have animal parts they might not otherwise have access to. Many of my customers are Native Americans who use these in traditional religious ceremonies, medicine bags etc. Few trappers get more than three to four wolves in a winter; wolves are very smart and hard to get. They cover a lot of country and there is a lot of country here where no trappers go. All my skulls come **from the interior of Alaska.**

I end the email with a sigh, wondering if this reply really says anything. It's just words after all. Advertisers selling products often say anything they think will help sell the product. The only absolute truth I can reply is a short, "I buy them." Nothing else is a fact I can verify. Or, here is how I got one skull, *"OK, here's a story for you! It was probably where your skull came from! A now sober, soon to be drunk guy, who happens to be an Indian, sold me the skull. I later find out he stole this wolf skull from his neighbor. Hope you enjoy it. Life goes on. Not all stories are romantic and pretty. Wake up and smell the doo doo."* But why bother? He'd never buy from me again.

I sigh in frustration when I sell rocks and no one asks how I acquired them, how they were handled, whose land it came from, if it hurt the environment, was slave labor, chemicals or explosives used, or the packhorses used humanely, etc. The law would not punish me for mislabeling it and calling it jade because it is green, or turquoise because it is blue. *The difference between a coyote claw and wolf claw is ten years in prison.* "But animals are living things with rights, don't rocks have rights?" Only partly true. Retrieving rocks can be very destructive to land where both animals and people live. Responsibility and environmental issues involve everything off the land. Yet only trappers and hunters are interrogated, or asked rude, personal, accusatory questions. Likewise – shop-time is worth $65 an hour. If I spend ten minutes personally answering a pointless question from someone who is not yet a customer, I'm going to lose money.

Hello, I am looking for a piece of mammoth ivory to use as a paperweight. I would like to pay about $50. Please let me know if you have anything like this. **Thanks, Tom.**

I reply

Yes—$50 buys about a pound piece—a nice paperweight size. I will look over what I have and email a photo of pieces I think might make a paperweight. Later then —**Sunshine Miles**

More emails

Dear Miles; We are acquainted with Sandy Johnson in Alaska through her art work with beads and gems. She gave us your name and did send your business card. We have been browsing through your web site tonight. You are truly versatile. We would be interested in having you do some carvings on burrs supplied by us. Perhaps bear, mountain sheep, etc. on elk burr for buckles and deer burr for bolos. Also, would need a quote on prices in lots of twenty-four.
    Sincerely, Ike and Gayle Tadday

So the work gets interesting, diverse. Sometimes an interest in raw material or carving, sometimes a knife. Just after shutting down the computer, the phone rings. I'm not used to the phone. The phone and computer share the same line.

"This is Altina; your father had a stroke. He recovered and is stable but not out of the hospital."

Dad and I are not close, but he's still my father. I care about his health, quality of life and his being alive. I am not needed there, but this does not look good. Dad is for sure getting older. This news only adds to the sense I do not like answering the phone.

"You should let your sister know." I'm the only one in the family who knows where my sister is. I'm the only one she'll talk to, or in some cases who will talk to her. All the family stuff comes up to deal with. I'm here in Alaska, as far away as I can get for a reason.

"Hi, Sis."

"Oh, it's you, Miles; that is weird! I was just thinking of you! We haven't seen each other in a long time. I was thinking of moving to Alaska to be closer to you, maybe stay with you! Wouldn't that be cool!"

"Kind of, but neither of us has a lot of money. How could you afford a move?"

"Oh yeah. I never thought of that. Maybe I could find work up there or work for you!"

"Well, you'd have to get here first and I think that's going to cost too much. I do not have much of a business going yet. Do you know much about computers? "

"No, I only heard of them, they are too expensive. I guess I'm old fashioned; all this new technology is beyond me. But I have made progress with my beaded bracelets I told you about. I even sold my first one to my friend for $5!"

"That's pretty exciting isn't it, to have a first sale? Good for you."

"Well, I might be able to make a lot of money, and you could sell them in your web store! I know it will be a big seller once I make enough of them. I'm working on patenting my designs so no one steals them! "

"Maybe. We'll see. But if you do swap meets and set up at bazaars, this would be a good way to sell your products; test the market. Maybe I can send you some of my art on consignment. You may not have enough inventory of your own. "

"I'd rather do my own thing, and sell my own work if I can, or even better, get someone else to sell it for me! "

The problem here, is most all artists want that, including me. We all want to do the fun part! The creating! Let someone else have the headache of marketing, selling. *All we do is make it, and collect the money!* I have been looking and struggling all my life to get what she wants, an idea she just now came up with, on a single product I feel anyone can make, beaded work on a loom. Not exactly popular these days. *My opinion, let her see if she comes up with another option, and not put a pin in her balloon.*

"Sure I understand. I just have a lot of inventory." I tell her about dad and how I am. We avoid the subject of her moving in with me, or working for me. Partly, as she says herself, we each want to do our own thing the way we want to do it. We do not agree how that would look involving the other. She wants me to work for her, while she's on public assistance, having sold her first $5 item. I think she needs to be one of the worker bees, not one of the bosses. Deeper than that, I am scared to live like her and be like her. I'd rather be dead.

"Nice hearing from you, Miles, my big brother."

I mumble something or other that's appropriate and stare out the window at my bird feeder with the phone still in my hand. *It's amazing how a chickadee can live on those sunflower seeds. It looks like it takes him ten minutes to get that seed out of the shell, pecking away and twisting and turning it in those tiny feet. It's a wonder there is enough nutrition in the seed to cover the energy it took to get the seed open. Amazing. And how does something the size of a golf ball when fluffed up, ever keep warm at sixty below zero?* "I suppose." I put the phone down, it's not in my hand anymore, as I ponder the mysteries of life. Bird seeds, better put that on the list. Yes, we don't want the birds to be without food. It's important to take care of the birds.

I think of money for seeds. Seymour has told me there is not so much work this summer yet, but he will let me know. After my back injury, survey work is winding down for me. Maybe Seymour does not want me to mess my back up again, but he too is changing how he views work. He has said off and on for years, "Prepare for less work and retirement, I need to quit!"

The web site has its rewards, but it is taking a lot of learning. One of the locals who understands computers has offered to teach me some things in trade for art. There was the class taken on the basics, but mostly I just play with it. Will suggested I was not being smart by crashing my computer, destroying it as a way to learn. We had this same conversation about one of my early snow machines. Life repeats itself.

"Gotta go, Will. Meeting to go to for the Historical Society."

"Historical Society, Miles? Since when did you get so involved in politics and social events! Ha!" Will is not reprimanding, just being humorous, pointing out the change. I have no real answer.

"A new Cultural Center has been built on the Nenana water front. The plan is to have a paddle boat stop here. There is another building that is a Salmon Bake. Grant money one of our locals got for us. Big plans that are now fizzling out." The original grant came in two parts. The first part had to do with a building and salmon bake. The second part has to do with a paddle boat, river tours. The boat is to bring customers to the shop and museum. I explain how the paddle boat part is not happening. The boat is ending up costing too much. One of the buildings is now a culture center with gift shop. It has old historical stuff and local crafts. But it's hard to get the tour bus to come down to the river front on the edge of town. I head to the meeting at the new river front building with glass overlooking the river and Nenana Hill.

Some of the grant money has to be used to acquire art work. The board asks me if I want to be the buyer. "Miles, you can go downriver in your boat and buy from village artists. It's right up your alley!" It would in fact be a primo job and lots of fun. Combine river travel with getting paid for purchasing art.

I reply, "Yes, it sounds good. But for the good of the gift shop, I think it is not the best use of funds. Most village artists already bring their wares to the city to sell. Most go to Fairbanks. I might get it a little cheaper in the village, but the savings would not justify the travel costs. I also think there are enough craft people in the local area to fill the gift shop." As an artist understanding the concept of the grant, I explain how we could focus on interior art. "There is a lot of Eskimo art in most of the tourist shops and museums, but not much Athabascan work." If we became known as an interior Alaska art focus, it would give us a niche market for collectors. The tourists are glad to buy locally made art. "I'd be glad to help with that, but I do not want to be in charge because this seems like a 90% Native issue and grant. I am white. I'd rather see a Native who knows traditional work, like someone among our beaders." I did not want to be into the 'Indian -White' controversy with Native artists telling me I'm discriminating if I do not buy their work. Issues are already brewing. More than one Native artist is offering me half-finished items saying, " But you can finish it and get a lot of money!" I did not bring that up at the board meeting though.

There are six of us on the board and only one is Native. We have been meeting regularly, so I am involved and understand as much as any of the rest what is going on. Apparently there is separate funding for an art purchaser. Later in the meeting, the financial report is read. It can be boring as we all try to follow line by line, numbers we have heard before. Somewhere in the long list of numbers and dry monolog of reading I frown and pause.

I wait till the secretary is done, to ask her to back up a minute. "You said $10,000 for the purchase of art?" It sounds to me like this amount is blending in with part of the general fund, may disappear, and get reassigned to some other category. I am the only artist in the group. "That is a lot of money to the locals here, distributed among local artists. Let's talk about that." No one had brought it up, or especially wanted to focus on this, 'free money to give out to local artists.' I even think, *artists would not know about it if I had not brought it up and got attention on it.*

After the meeting, I make sure this is not forgotten, and spread word among the craft people, how there is $10,000 to buy our art outright for the museum store. So I guess that is how I got to be the buyer.

"Miles! I have $2,000 worth of art to bring over, I'll get it right away!"

Someone else, "Miles, I can make a bunch of stuff fast!"

Many want to be my good buddy now. There is an assumption there will be some discrimination going on that I will buy from my friends or offer favors and such. I could, and it might even be accepted as 'how it's done' around here. But I come up with a plan right off. This concept is spread, after approval by the board. I tell a group of local artists at a meeting, "I'm going to promise everyone at least a $200 purchase. Whatever you bring me! You price it, and I'll buy it. But remember, if it does not sell I will not buy more." In this way, every artist, or wanna be artist gets at least $200, just for showing up. There is no juried art, no group of people who vote and decide. Let the customers decide. Let the sales records show who makes more money and who did not make a wise decision by overpricing, or offering junk that does not sell.

Some locals bring me unfinished work. Some artists bring ' stuff' that in my opinion, is not even art. I say nothing, and gave them all $200. Call it a free gift. Others have items selling right off. I let these artists know, so they can bring me more. There are no arguments or issues. The money gets out there to the local artists as intended. I sold $200 of my own goods. My art sold, but I did not buy more, because it might be viewed as a conflict of interest, or that my stuff sold because it was being pushed, or put in prime selling spots. I do not get paid as the buyer. I donate my time to help out the other artists and the community.

"Miles. I need to sell this to you because the transmission in my truck went out, can you help me? I need $500."

"Miles, I need money to go to town for food, my mother is in the hospital, I have this beadwork that is not done yet but you could finish it up easy, just $30."

"Miles, can I leave this with you, I need $50, I'll toss in my cell phone. I want it back later, I got someone who wants to buy my stuff in a week, so I'll be able to pay you back." It's a good learning experience worth having, if I want to be serious about marketing. The time I spent helping Crafty at his Craft shop helped, and some of my internet experience. I had to come up with an understandable, workable answer to all questions like this. Answers go something like: "I hardly know you; it is not like I am family or a good friend. Don't you have family or friends who can help you out? I work for and get paid by the city. To do a good job, I need to make a profit. Explain to me how this deal you offer is going to make a profit."

Business people in town tell me, "Miles don't bother. Just tell them 'No'. Period! These same people come around my place too, asking for hand outs and loans. " I sigh. I'd rather take a minute and explain 'why,' because it might not have a good effect on some who do not understand, yet might if they thought about it. At one point in time, I think I was something like these people, and honestly just didn't get it, and wish someone would have explained it to me.

"Miles, then how am I going to get my truck fixed?"

"I'm glad you understand people with needs, Ed! Actually I too need money to fix the roof on my house before winter. How about if I buy your stuff for $5? I know someone who will pay $50 and I need the money to fix my roof."

"But that's ripping me off!"

"Yes, it is. How would that feel? I would not do that to you. So why do you want to do that to me, and the Culture Center?"

"I need a transmission, not your crap, Miles. All my friends are right, you are such a talker!"

So where are all these friends helping you with your transmission problem that you have to come to me, a stranger for help? "U- huh. Well have a nice day." *Next! And don't let the door hit you on your way out. Don't call us, we'll call you.* I learned better how to sell when it is me who is at a gift shop as the buyer - like not talk about what it is I need. It's not the shop's place to care what I need. They may not have time to hear a good story and visit. Now I am in their shoes. I grasp better all the costs of running a shop. It makes more sense that wholesale is at least half the retail asking price. I'm on the Board that has to figure out how the money gets spent and where it has to come from.

"So Jenny, I can't finish your beadwork and put your name on it."

"But I only need $15."

"I understand, but with your name on it as the one who made it, this beaded hairpiece is worth maybe $75. It's nice work. You just need to finish it. You are Native and Native work sells for more money, it's what the tourists want, authentic Native craft! I bet if you went home you could finish this in an hour. I'll give you $45 for it in an hour, when it's done."

"Wow, OK, that's a good idea. I guess I can wait an hour for my trip to town." Maybe she will take more pride in her work and understand her name is worth something. It's not just anyone's work that anyone can finish up. She is a talented artist. I meet a lot of talented artists who just can't seem to get ahead. For various reasons, I suppose.

"Miles, can you donate something of yours to the kid's auction? Trying to raise money for the band to compete." I usually donate my art as I have so much of it, and like other artists, I do not have as much money as I do art! Ha! I donate a wolf claw pendant, and later hear it sold for $35. I donate more than I pay in taxes! Ha! Seems odd. Well, that way I am more in control of who gets it and how it is being spent. *So many hands are out for my money. Donate to this, donate to that. I have trouble knowing who is for real and what is a scam.*

"Yeah, we fell for the Veterans deal, bought the light bulbs, and the special soap to help out the needy." I never heard the end of that, phone calls all the time, wanting me to give more, do more. I got suspicious and looked closer at the label on the soap. The label tells me that about 10% of the profits go to the disabled who do the packing. I have this image of helping war Vets in wheelchairs who put foam peanuts in boxes for minimum wages, while the company gets government points, discounts, tax breaks, for hiring the disabled. Meaning I'm not helping much. If the entire company from top to bottom was run by disabled Vets, that'd be cool. I'd support that! But this reality I read in fine print is a scam. Now that I am trying to blend in and be part of society, there is a lot to learn. The caller bugging me, calls himself a reverend; quotes the bible. That is supposed to lend credibility to the scam.

As I GET OLDER, the seasons seem to come and go so darn fast!

"Josh, where did spring go? It seems like I just got back from Tucson and it is June, and boating season already!" He is asking me when I am making a trip to the homestead. "Yes, I have a lot I want to bring to the lower Kantishna. Fiberglass to repair the canoe, and wire mesh to squirrel proof the cabin, propane, and the usual things a homestead needs."

"You like your new Mercury four stroke? I was wondering what I should get."

"Yes, it's OK. I miss the Honda, but I waited forever for them to come up with something between the fifty horse and ninety horse. Now they came out with a seventy, I think, but I already got the sixty horse Merc. Perfect horsepower for my new aluminum, long, narrow, al-weld boat. Pushes easy; like a dream, Josh, just not fast, but amazing on gas economy!"

I did not tell Josh or anyone I had already made an early May trip up the Kantishna to an area I thought I might find mammoth tusks or other fossils. There is a cliff I go by. I keep thinking the layers of frozen silt appear to be the right age to have fossil remains. I came home with some ivory and bones. A new room in the shop is now the fossil room, for drying out and treating fossils. I had got a duck and still remember how good fresh duck is after going all winter without anything fresh, but maybe a rabbit or a grouse now and then. I'm spending a little more money on food now, maybe $400 a year. I smile, as the potatoes I got from the Patty Wagon at the fair last year are just running out now, and it is hard to find potatoes among the vines growing in the cupboard. Potatoes are fine, just a little wrinkled, but not rotting.

"Miles, how is the art work going? You said you were getting new tools?" Josh is not especially interested in art, even though he builds dog sleds and snowshoes. He is into only practical things. I tell him how my casting is coming along, but he is not listening. Hardly anyone here in the village understands how casting is done, or would care. But the shop space is getting expanded and used more.

"All that stuff John had I am slowly getting rid of Josh, and making room for my junk!" We both laugh. John, who lived with Judy and built the shop, had been a collector of 'stuff'. There was a gear off a bulldozer five feet across, an old drill press as big as a car that does not run, scrap metal, valves, car parts, and simply truck-loads of things that to someone else would have value, but not to me.

"Yes, when you pass on, I suppose Mitch will feel the same, thousands of dollars worth of stuff is just junk going to the dump or sold as scrap."

Probably true, but not fun to think about. Why bring that up right now? Oh well. The main thing is something positive. I am getting room to make a living and set up shop, doing what I love to do, and finding new rewards to look forward to, with new goals to reach for.

Josh and I talk about money. "I have often felt, Josh, like it is good to be rich, also good to be poor, but not good to be anyplace in the middle. The middle class pays for everyone else. It supports the poor with taxes and does the work for the rich who have privileges the middle class does not have." It seems to me if you are poor, you can get a lot of free stuff, be taken care of, left alone. The rich make the rules and can afford lawyers, fees, permits, and have others who can do things, look things up, take care of details, so life works for them. "Yes, Josh, maybe I will skip the middle and go right from poor to rich, what do you think?"

He reminds me, "Same with business, Miles, big business rules, and small business is shut down. If you go out of business you can be taken care of, so you have to move up or move down. Or work for big business."

😄 :)

I think of something else to consider. *It is not good to be poor because you are stupid or lazy. Being poor works when you are smart.*

"Sounds good to me, Mista Maw-tin—the man with the golden pen."

"Hold on Josh – got a phone call!" I am still not used to phones. Josh stands waiting in the house while I take the call. I'm also not used to anyone in my home. I am always uncomfortable. No reason beyond just not used to it. The ceiling is low compared to most homes. The ceiling is seven feet, but by the time I hang lights and other stuff, it's six feet or less. Josh and I are short, so it is no big deal. Josh examines the ceiling while I am on the phone. Made of hand whipsawed lumber as the hull of an 1800s paddle boat, it was turned upside down to make a ceiling. The boards are a full twenty-six feet without a splice. Where the thick paint is missing, you can see tiny saw marks of the whipsaw, marks that do not look like mill marks.

"Who was that on the phone, Miles, you act like you need to go someplace! Important!" Indeed how many important places could there be to go to in a small village as ours?

"Culture Center called, says there is a tour bus unloading and they could use some help, only one worker there now. I volunteer to help when the busses come by, which is not often. You know how 'what's her name' makes sure she gets all the tour buses, and thinks she owns the town." By the front door, Josh notices a hole in the ceiling.

"What's that, Miles, looks like a shotgun hole!" I'd forgotten and have not fixed it yet.

"Ya.' Well. Your buddy staying by your dogs helping you out did that." I explain how he came over drunk, interested in buying my small .410 shotgun that hangs over the door. There to shoot rabbits and grouse that come in the yard and take care of stray dogs with. "He's drunk. I take the shotgun down and make sure it is unloaded. Hand it to him to look at. He examines it, tells me it's not really what he had in mind, and has not got the money anyhow. I load it and put it back where it belongs, with the safely on. It's a single shot, so there is a shell in the chamber." Josh nods, so I finish as I have to go. "He grabs it off the wall as we go to the door and before I can say anything he has it in his hands and drops it! Lands butt first and goes off! Blam! Just misses getting him under the chin by maybe three inches and there you see, blasts a hole in my ceiling." Another reason to not like anyone in my house. "What a mess if it had got him. Brain matter all over my ceiling, blood all over my floor." We are outside and I'm headed for my little Big Red Honda three wheeler to get to the Culture Center a few blocks away.

"I'd have been out a dog helper, Miles!" Yes and Josh knows how I feel about people so drunk they can't function. Nice enough guy when he's sober. Anyhow.

"I'm off, Josh—see you later!"

I get to the Culture Center in time to be of help. The old folks are just now all off the bus and inside.

"Hi, Miles!" Turning to the group of tourists, "This is Miles, one of our local artists and characters!" I begin talking about the Indian cemetery on the hill, the famous railroad bridge.

"Second largest single span bridge in the world. This is where President Harding drove the gold spike at the end of the railroad, see in the picture on the wall over here." I talk about the Yukon 800 race boat on display: "Run by a friend of mine who won it five times in a row!" I get asked the usual questions,

"What does Nenana mean? Does it really get that dark in winter? What do we do here in the village?" And such things. After half an hour, they all pile back on the bus. I ask the clerk. "So, how'd we do?"

"Eighty people and we made $4. As usual, the driver stopped here for our free coffee and a pee break. Used $10 worth of our stuff and left $4. Maybe we should just close the curtain when we see Princess coming!" Yes, it's very aggravating. We talk about it a lot at the Chamber of Commerce meetings. We are pretty sure the tour company tells its customers to only shop at their stores, that all the rest are rip-offs. *They want a monopoly on the tourist dollar, and about have what they want.* "Yet it seems to us, it is not what the tourists want." Tourists say they want 'authentic' and are tired of made in Korea (Japan, China or India) coffee mugs with 'Alaska' printed on them. Tourists say they want a real experience, want to meet real Alaskans. The shops do not offer what the tourists want, because the shops want more profit.

Reminds me of the American car manufactures who would not give the people a small economical car. The large gas guzzlers were crammed down the consumer's throat, no other option. It took the Japanese to offer us what we want with the gas efficient small cars. U.S. companies were then forced to go along. They lost control of the situation.

I overhear, "I was hired to remove the China stickers and put 'Handcrafted in Alaska' stickers on." The shop owner, Eagle, gets turned in. Pays the maximum $500 fine. Keeps on doing it because she has made a cool million dollars doing this.

A crafter in the know adds, "The laws are not on our side. To be legal, you only have to alter something 10% to call it yours. So many successful local craft people in the tourist business buy imports and alter them. Like adding one bead to an imported necklace. The crafter then puts their name on it, as handcrafted by them, and it's legal."

We discuss what we can do about all this. The bottom line being, not much. Even so, I still have a belief that there are some buyers who care. If our community can hang in there and get a reputation for having the real stuff made by locals, even if it cost a little more, there will be discriminating shoppers who will look us up.

I point out, "After all, even many of the tour busses do not want to stop at Eagle's shop. They ask how to get into the village by another route to bypass her place, in order to be offered something more authentic."

"She even jumps out in front of the bus, forcing them to stop, so she can get on and play her accordion, and lead them like the Pied Piper to her establishments."

As the head of the Chamber, I contacted the Princess office to find out what we, as a community can offer, and do for them. After the talk, I understand what we face better. I feel Nenana is a perfect tourist place. We are on the main highway, only an hour out of Fairbanks. We are an authentic native village, not a stage show filled with actors. We are a crossroads with a railway, a highway, a river and an airport. We have a colorful history with the railroad, homesteading, mining, trapping, churches and Indians. A lot happened here. At one time, we were the headquarters for Denali Park. For dog racers, we are the community where the original Serum Run began, that started the Iditarod 1,000 mile dog race. Some of the big name racers live here. It is beautiful, with good fishing and hunting around us. The Park is only sixty miles away. We have a lot to offer. Yet we are cut off, out of the loop. I explain all this to Princess Tours.

"You could come here, see Natives building fish wheels, skinning moose. You could see homesteaders loading gear on rafts headed downstream for the winter. Tourists could meet local craft people, talk to winners of the Iditarod, mingle with locals at the café and hear wilderness stories!"

"When? Give me a schedule!" I'm puzzled.

"What do you mean 'when'?" Whenever it happens! Whenever you get here.

You can't stage stuff like this! There is always something different going on. It's like asking when an eagle will suddenly swoop down from a tree in front of the bus.

But now I hear their side of the story. "We need to know when - down to the exact second. We need to know what and how long it will take. It takes twenty minutes just to unload a bus so people can take pictures. We only have an hour at the most to stop." He explains. There needs to be a place the bus can easily and safely pull over, stop, then turn around. The drivers need to make practice runs with an empty bus to make sure there are no glitches getting in and out. There has to be a place for everyone to have a potty break. There needs to be a routine, a schedule. If something does not happen exactly as described, tourists are unhappy, saying, 'You promised and I paid!' When advertising, people want to know what they are paying for, exactly! 'How many Indians? What homesteaders?'

I can see the point. Tour companies advertise. The biggest factor is price, so they need to pack the most cool stuff in the shortest time at the cheapest price. The one who wins, is the company whose package looks good. I can imagine the sales pitch: "For only $3,000 total we get you there, we feed you. You get to see the Yukon River, get a boat ride, see sled dogs, a moose, visit five museums, shake hands and have your picture taken with a real Indian, etc., etc."

When? "Promptly At 9:00 am on Friday the 15th, an Indian will step out of his wigwam and shake your hand—so have your camera ready."

Maybe fifty things you get to do - all for a mere set low price no one can beat. Tourist will have a checklist for all fifty events they check off one by one. Princess cannot hear, 'What do you mean the Indian showed up while I was next door having an ice cream! You promised 9:00 am sharp!'

How do you measure quality in such an ad? What number do you put down, and what price do you give it? So in all that packaged stuff they write, "And see Nenana and…" If it does not happen as advertised, 100 tourists want a refund on the entire tour. I see the problem. I see why Eagle makes money and offers what is desired. She can turn her motorized fish wheel on at exactly 9:00 am, set the bait, and the tourist trap gets sprung right on time every day.

Work with the Eagle? She will join the Chamber only if we use our status as a Chamber to get a gaming permit, and let her run all the gambling. Lottery tickets, pull tabs, raffles etc. A majority of the Chamber members are opposed to gambling. A majority do not trust the Eagle. A majority think she would contribute a penny on the dollar of what she is supposed to from gambling revenue. She could help us a lot with her expertise on tourism. But it would all be for her.

"Maybe we can target independent visitors?"

"Maybe, Miles, but the state stopped spending money promoting tourism in the lower states and around the world. The reason stated was, the tour companies already promote Alaska, so why compete with free enterprise? Yet the tour companies promote only their version of the state, selling their packages. There is little information on driving, places to stop, or communities to visit that are off the beaten path. And I suppose the state is not going to subsidize a small village. The tourist dollars will get spent in the direction of where the funding is coming from."

"Maybe so, but if people come to places like Nenana, and have a good time, it helps all of us, the whole state. Those people bought plane tickets, or gas and meals all over the state. And if we make money, we spend the money in the big city, it all ends up getting spread around." I mention a couple of good positive things the Chamber accomplished, that we can remind ourselves of, despite all the adversity we face.

ONCE A MONTH I meet with the Library Board as a member. The library does fund raisers to buy more books, and have a summer reading program for the kids. I volunteer to read sometimes. That too is a challenge. Kids get bored easily. We are all out on the library lawn on a hot summer day. About twenty-five local children gather around me as I begin reading the story about Little Red Riding Hood. Ya,' ya,' we all heard it before. Some kids are beginning to get restless and tease other kids, or want to get up and run off someplace. Hmmm. I'm reading along la, la, dee, da: "My, what big teeth you have" Only I read: "My, what a thick egg shell you have." No one said anything. I read on—La, dee, da, da, da: "Then Humpty fell off the wall and one of the three bears spilled the cold porridge on the wolf... My, what big eyes you have...." A few of the kids frown as I read on. Puzzled look.

Finally a, "Hey wait a minute. I don't remember that part!"

I act confused, puzzled. "What do you mean, I'm just reading the story here. It says...." And I try to find my place again. "Oh yeah, ...um" and I put my finger on the sentence and follow with my finger reading slow... "and the bowl of porridge hit the wolf..."

And more than one child says, "But, that's a different story isn't it? About the three bears?"

"Oh! Did I mix up my stories?" Now all the kids are wide awake and paying attention, as they help me read the story correctly. "Well, why couldn't the three bears meet the big bad wolf? They all live in the same place in the forest don't they?"

"But not Humpty Dumpty, silly!"

"Who sat down beside her, you mean?"

"No, that's Little Miss Muffet!"

"Who got eaten by the wolf's grandmother?" So we discuss what makes a good story, and see if we can keep our facts straight. We get back to the story at hand, but this time, everyone is alert to see if I read it right! Afterwards, we draw pictures from what we remember about the story. Later there are confused parents when kids show drawings of Humpty Dumpty, and Little Red Riding Hood in the same scene.

"But that was the story, mom!"

"No dear, you are mixing up your stories"

I come in with, "Yes, aren't you just a little confused, kid?"

All the kids laugh. "We know who is confused, Mr. Miles! You're silly!"

"My, oh my, what is ever wrong with all these children?" But it is obvious we all had a good time. The kids can't stop talking about what we did today. *What a blast kids are. I mean, compared to their parents- Ha!* I mean, um er… The children burst out laughing. As time goes by, the children know my name, know me enough to stop me in the street to say "Hi."

I hear so much how children today are so disrespectful, rude, do not want to work, have no motivation, and I, too, have wondered what will happen when the next generation takes over! *We are all doomed!* "Yet a majority of the children are polite, respectful, and seem smart." I ask how school is going for them, and they want to know about my garden or my boat.

"Mr. Miles, I'd like some flowers for my grandmother, is it OK if I pick some flowers along the road by your house?"

I put wild flower seeds in the ditch along the road. It is not my property, but it is a good place for such flowers to grow, and come back each year. I enjoy looking at them. Anyone could pick them since they are not on my property. It is kind and thoughtful for anyone to think to ask. I did not demand anyone ask. This child is not asking out of fear, but out of respect, and respect is earned, not demanded. So I am touched.

"Sure, help yourself."

While this ten year old girl is picking flowers, I go to my backyard where I have some nice big blue lupines growing. "Add this to your bouquet, it's very bright and one of my favorites. I think your grandmother would like this."

She spots one of her friends coming on a bike so waves. The two go off together sniffing the flowers and chatting about who knows what. I stare at them as they go off in the distance. All seems well in the world.

Yea, I have my own son, sort of. It would sure be cool to be a parent. My unconscious who looks out for me, shuts me up. *The ex has him, it's out of our hands, she has full custody, nothing you can do, so forget it!* "I know, I just wonder how he is sometimes."

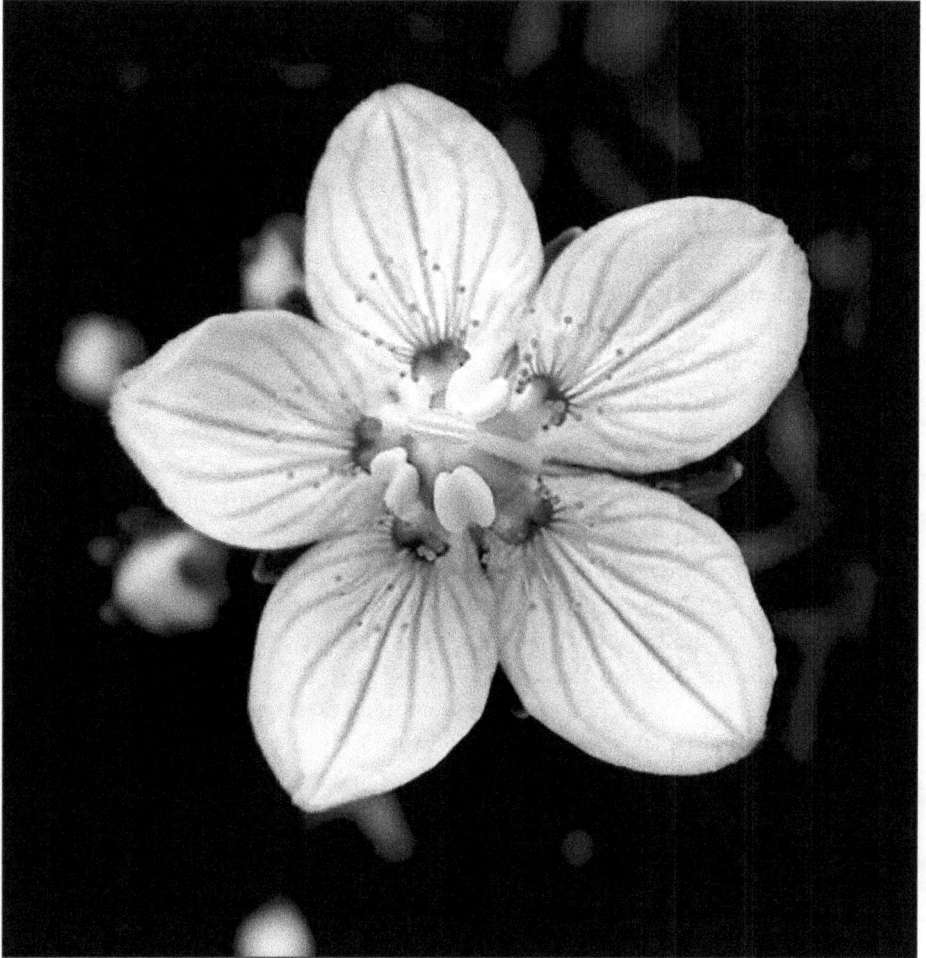

I grow a lot of flowers, and have taken flower pictures all my life. I was about twelve years old when a card company offered to buy one of my rose pictures. This is wild grass of Parnassus, much prettier in color.

CHAPTER EIGHT

DAD DIES, MOVE HOUSEBOAT, FIRE BURNS CABIN, BEAR STORY

S ummer is over. Snow is here and the usual, "Are you ready for winter yet?" gets asked around town.

Someone passing through who knows me, but I do not recognize, asks for an autographed copy of my book. "How did the fair go this year, Miles?"

"Well, financially, I seem to double my money every year, so that is a good thing! It's more time consuming. I do not have time these days to look around and enjoy the fair as I once did. But I'm happy."

"That is the main thing, that we are happy with our life. Hey, when is the next book coming out, Miles?"

"I'm working on it, but geez the first book took over twenty years to write. Hopefully the second is not going to take that long! Ha!" I collect $15 for the book. My cost is $5.50, so doing OK when I sell them. I am about sold out of the 200 I had printed. I'm unsure if Raak will do a second printing as the cost of paper and shipping has gone up a lot. It will cost me over $7 a book to print now, instead of $5. The internet and digital world are growing very fast. The U.S. is catching up with on demand printing. This is in the back of my mind at the Post Office as I get my mail and see my internet bill.

My Alaska Permanent Fund Dividend check is in. I have been collecting each year since the beginning, over $1,000 oil revenue money to each Alaskan every year, even babies! I can buy my ticket to see mom, and do the Tucson show. If I get the ticket early, like before the end of October, the cost is about half price. Many businesses have dividend specials to get us to spend our checks with them. I can let my mother know I got my round trip ticket, and give her the dates.

My back is feeling much better. I think I can handle a snow machine trip to the homestead and do some trapping… maybe. I have a new snow machine that should be a comfortable ride. Yamaha Viking 500. A big, heavy machine like a tank with reverse and high-low range gears. It's almost impossible to get stuck in deep snow. One big issue is that it burns an amazing amount of gas compared to the much smaller machines I am used to. But wow, what a comfortable ride! I could haul 1,000 or more pounds and hardly know it! As I have been telling friends, my income is growing, so it is nice to be able to afford new equipment.

The Nenana River freezes November seventh. I head out November eighth. I'm the first one across the river as usual. I have done this so many years I know the Kantishna will be fine for crossing. I cross at this exact spot each season, so have a feel for how the ice is. Floating ice pans jam, then the water in between freezes and holds the pans together. This new ice that is holding pans together is thin on the Nenana River, but no crack is big enough to fall through, or at least let the snow machine fall through. I just make sure I look for the biggest ice pans and go from one pan to the next. It's important to do this before snow covers the ice so I can't see. Given time, even a week, the water under the ice can drop and make thin ice sag, or warmer water upstream can come down under the ice, erode it and make thin spots, mostly where the current is. Certainly it takes knowledge and being familiar with the crossing to do this. The new ice cracks in one spot, but that is to be expected. I am on it, over it and past it before it ever totally gives way. The crack will fill with water and in a few hours be stronger then it was. It is important not to go under ten miles an hour or over about forty miles an hour and not at exactly thirty miles an hour. Exactly thirty miles an hour sets up a harmonic vibration the causes ice to 'sing' like a tuning fork to the frequency of the thumbing of the rubber machine track. This exact frequency can crack the ice just as the right frequency can break glass. *Everyone thinks we are crazy!* I reply to myself with a grin, "Yeah!"

I pull my old dog sled with an adapted snow machine hitch. I have traps, food, gas, emergency supplies, a tent, sleeping bag, and it all pulls like it is not there, not a struggle for the machine at all. The first two sloughs are crossed just fine. A beaver has made a dam across the slough that backs up the water and makes it deep, but slows up the current so it freezes thicker, which is good for me. Now just five miles of swamp to the hills.

Sometimes swamps can be more dangerous than the river, because decay in the water makes heat that keeps the water open. These soft places can be spotted and avoided though… usually. This machine has so much power that if I start to drop through the ice, I can give it gas and leap up and forward. Even on open water. The back wants to sink first. The skis are so wide, with so much floatation, this is the part that sinks last. As long as the skis never go under the ice I can punch the throttle and get free. There is one spot like this. The back drops, I punch it, rooster tail water out behind me, and leap forward into a more solid area. I have three to four seconds to react. *If I am ready*, this is about three times longer than I need. The exception to this is when there are obstacles in the way that stop me from leaping forward. Dead trees, logs, ice hummocks, and brush of all kinds can stop me from leaping forward to safety. Only experience tells me where to go, at what speed, and what the risk is. Looking behind me, small blackfish are being tossed up on the snow by my spinning snow machine track. Schools of these fish can keep the water open under the snow to get oxygen.

There is six inches of snow on the ground. Being the first one out means making the trail thorough the tall dry sedge grass that is four feet tall. There is a constant hiss of the frozen grass parting, then going under the machine. I travel twenty-five miles an hour… pretty fast for the conditions. When I get to ice, I either speed way up or slow way down.

Once I am in the hills there is easy going. I have to stop to cut a tree here and there that blew over the trail during the summer. I have the chain saw with me to cut debris out of the way, which gives me a break from sitting on the machine. I set traps out now. *Years ago, this was Dim's area.* I respected that and did not set traps till I was twenty-five miles out from the airport and beyond. Now I am the one with seniority in the area. I told Dim if he comes back to trap I will give it back to him, just let me know.

I see wolf tracks, lots of fox, some lynx, but no marten. They will be farther out. They do not like being near people. I get to the airport; a bear has broken in some-time during the summer so I have to fix the door and window. While I do that, I build a fire and set snow on the stove in a pot stored here so I have water to make tea and have my lunch. I take my snow suit off to let the body moisture out and get dried out in this shack. While I sit, I wonder how trapping will go, and about my cabin on the Kantishna. I have not been living there full time, so it is getting run down a little bit. The cache looks like it might fall down. The trees I used for support died and are rotting now. I have not had time to build a new one. In my new life, when is there ever time to do these things that I once had time for? Every choice I make has rewards, but also a price to pay.

The snow machine is still warm, so starts easily with a quick turn of the key. No more hand cranking like the old machines. A moose is in the trail ahead, and watches me approach for a while before deciding to run off through the woods. The stretch is filled with memories. This is the same spot the sled dogs caught a moose sleeping in the trial that I shot with the pistol.

Ravens overhead play, and follow me along the way. There is no cell phone, no GPS, no satellite overhead helping me out in any way. I am totally on my own, the way I like it. Because if I can't reach civilization, civilization can't reach me.

I leave the hills, make the sharp turn, drop off the bluff into 'Chicago' (the windy city) into the Kantishna River drainage. As usual, there is a fog. The temperature drops twenty degrees when I leave the hills. There are fifteen miles of twisty creek and swamp trail to go to my Kantishna River crossing. The trail is not marked, and could not be found unless you knew where to go. No stranger can show up at my cabin if I do not show the way with a snow machine trail. There are otter, beaver and mink here in the swamps. I'm guessing this area has looked like this for thousands of years, unchanged.

On the river bank, I pause and look close at the crossing conditions. I see snow on the ice so know that part froze before the last snow. There is a spot that froze within the past few days, probably safe, but I can go around. Going a further distance is no big deal on this snow machine. If I had the sled dogs I'd go right across. *The lead dog would decide if it is safe enough or not.* "Yes, something to miss, but the machine is ok as well." *We have no choice, the road to happiness is not a road of regrets.* I drop the machine off the bank ten feet and slam onto the river ice. The multi-thousand dollar suspension absorbs the blow, no problem. *Sweet.*

I cross, go behind an island, up over the beaver dam onto the creek my cabin is on. Nothing disturbed. I see my canoe is here as I left it. The cabin too is undisturbed. No one has stopped here in the past several years. I get a good fire going and unload the sled. The trip took five hours. With a broke trail I can make it home in three hours. *It used to take two days, remember?* I smile, remembering those days.

Next day getting old trails open to trap is harder than it used to be. I am no longer good at bending over to cut at ground level. Still, I keep it up, excited to see what I might come across... maybe lots of marten tracks! I hang around about a week, cutting open trail, setting traps and fixing the cabin up. I get out seventy-five miles. There seems to be enough tracks to justify trapping a surplus of the population.

The trip home is without incident. I can see it will be difficult to run the web business, and be gone a week at a time. I solve this by being honest on the web site, stating I am gone a lot, live remote and the good news is...

I am the source for much of what you see, but one of the prices is my odd time schedule. Not to panic if you do not hear from me. I request people not pay me till they hear from me and we have an agreement. As the source, I offer the best price with no middle people, have the story as well as the knowledge. Keep in mind though, wolves do not live where there is electricity and internet. I'll be in touch when I get back to civilization.

This should ensure I am not in trouble owing someone product who sent money and I am not even home to know. It is simply hard to do business. Customers are not used to it, some cannot comprehend it.

"What do you mean you might not be home for a week and do not know when you are leaving, or getting back?" But think this sort of irritation is much better than, "I sent you money, no hear from, where is my product, before I call the police?" I am still not set up with Pay Pal because the slow speed dial up is not working well with Pay Pal.

Some customers seek me out, find this way of doing business either cool, different, or refreshing. "Wild Miles, it adds to the value of the finished piece when I tell the story of how I got it! I love how you can't just go to Walmart to get this material!" I get a loyal following.

I HAVE a few furs to skin, stretch and dry. This keeps me busy. A fox, a lynx and three marten. I got a moose way out on the trapline, but think it wise to just keep the meat out at the camps. For a while, anyway. Just in case there is an issue about where and when I got it. I'm told verbally by officials if I live subsistence and need meat it is not a problem to take game if I am not wasteful. This is not in writing. This permission is not what the exact letter of the law says. I am distrustful, and feel the letter of the law ought to reflect what I am told verbally. I think it is better for both myself and the environment if I get a moose in winter. It seems wise to get a moose way out in the wilds where no one else hunts, where the environment can handle a missing moose well. This vast expanse of country is only accessible in winter. No one else hunts around here for fifty miles.

Anyway, lots of good meat for next year. Nice to think about as I skin my furs. I'm glad my Nenana home has a wood stove. It is hard to take care of furs properly without the dry, hot heat of a wood stove. The snow machine is used to haul firewood off the river. Many wood cutters go off in the pucker-brush and cut live trees, then season green split wood a year for the wood stove. I go along the river and find log jams of driftwood for my fuel source. This is wood the river took out and piled up. Often dry, with no bark or limbs. But sometimes with moisture and river silt in it. The silt is hard on the saw bar and chain. Still, it is much less damage to the environment. A sled-load gives me a week's worth of heat. I doubt I could work for half an hour and buy a week's worth of fuel oil!

Lots of extra work filing on the dull chain due to the river silt. Over time I have learned which logs in the jam are best suited for my needs. *Yes! I never pick a log below the summer water level that has either bark or cracks in it!* I smile. "For sure! Both cracks and bark collect silt." Smooth logs sticking up in the air are best. There are so many choices of thousands of logs in a jam I can be selective. I like spruce with no limbs for good splitting, but the birch for most Btu. Poplar wood is easy to cut but makes a lot of ash with little heat. Those are the main choices. Maybe a willow or alder now and then, but usually these trees are either too small in diameter or too much effort to get.

It is common to see locals headed out from Nenana, or back, with a snow machine. Often in the middle of an unplowed main road; sled in tow, rifle over the shoulder, and chain saw stuck someplace visible, and easy to reach. A load of firewood in the sled. Most of us heat with wood. The sight and smell of wood smoke in town brings happy thoughts of warmth and visiting. *Man has heated with wood for many thousands of years.*

Many trips out the trapline are made with nothing to talk about, that just repeat themselves as normal. I'm getting enough fur to pay for the trips and make some profit. Not a lot, but it beats working for a living. The costs to trap are astronomical. An $8,000 snow machine is required. A chain saw, traps, all the right clothes, various tools, an outfitted trap shack, sleeping bags, stove, travel supplies. I bet I have spent $20,000 on what it takes to go trapping to catch $5,000 worth of fur a year. In the four years it takes to break even, gear wears out and I need a new snow machine for another $8,000. It is hard to get a handle on the question of whether I am really making any money! It is true, I own many of these items as a lifestyle, not just needed for trapping. However, if a civilized person has the dream to become a trapper, this is what you'd need.

Even Don, the fur buyer, tells me he knows hardly anyone who is a full time trapper. Maybe a dozen people in the state. I was one of those dozen for twenty years. There was a time in my life, trapping was the only money coming in. But for that to happen I had sled dogs, and lived off the land. I was content to make fifty cents an hour for my time. Ignorance is bliss. As long as I do not dwell on it, or face it, or am aware of it, I am happy!

"I think even in the Mountain Man days of the 1800s there were few trappers who did well, Don. The ones who did OK were the fur buyers!" We both chuckle.

"Maybe, Miles, but it was not those in the position I am who got rich! Local store clerks bought furs from trappers. It would have been the Auction house, the big names in fur, the Astors and the Goldberg's back East, and those who ran the Hudson Bay Company in England, who got rich, buying from store clerks."

" Yes, I already had that part figured out a long time ago." Fur selling is a time to visit and get caught up on the latest news, have coffee with the buyer, trade stories. "The early Mountain Man trappers were romanticized by society in dime novels." I researched the truth. There is what was referred to as 'the free trapper' that was admired, but there were very few of them. Fewer, yet could afford a horse. Traps were hand made by blacksmiths, and cost a normal weeks wages per trap. Few could afford a winters worth of supplies to go off on their own for the season. Many of those who had that kind of money, had better things to spend it on because they had a trade, a way to make a living, that required they stay in town to keep the job. Mostly trappers were employees of a company. Slave labor *who owed their soul to the company store, like in the song about coal miners, who shovel sixteen tons and what have they got? Another day older, and further in debt!*

The Fur company owned the horse, traps and food. All had to be paid for from the upcoming seasons catch. Supplies were on credit, offered along with the big dream that you might be among the ones to pay off the debt and have enough left over to be rich! The big Fur Rondy was usually put on by the company, as a way to take the trappers profits selling drink, women, and gambling. It was normal for a trapper to sell his seasons catch, spend any profits after paying off last year's debt, and leave the celebration with a hangover, in debt again for next season.

"That's a far cry from the stories I read and inspired me!"

"Ha, true enough Miles, But you and others might have never headed out to the wilds without the dream, and never accomplished what you have!" We talk a little about the changing fur industry.

"Lots of new rules and regulations each year, Miles. People out of our state making rules about things they do not understand."

"Yes, Don. I mean I would never think to tell people in Florida what to do about their alligators. I'd say I do not have enough information to have an opinion worth hearing. So why would those in Florida feel they have a say so about what Alaska should do about wolves? " We discuss a proposal to outlaw leg hold traps, that will force trappers to use conibear traps. The conibear is a new style trap just out, reputed to be more humane as an instant kill trap. Laws about this are being made and enforced by people who do not trap, with no vested interest, beyond having stock in the company making them.

"Don, it would be like us telling a carpenter what kind of hammer he can use on his job. How absurd!"

"Telling us, and at the same time owning the hammer company." But one thing about Don is, he always likes to be positive and focus on good news. "It's still a good time to be alive. We are lucky to have the freedoms we do have." I agree there is no use complaining, or thinking there were better times. There seems little use in that, and not the road to happiness or success.

When I get home from one trip on the trapline, I have a message to call back East to dad's. I used to call more often, but I never did like phones much, and last time I called dad, my ex-wife answered the phone. Visiting dad all the way from California; I assume on his dime. Like last time, and the time before that. She was invited to visit, not me. She answered like she lived there. I was told none of it is any of my business. My father is raising my son, that's none of my business either. I decided, rather than argue and make problems forcing it to be my business, I'll just get on with my life and leave them alone to live their life as they wish. I do not need the heartache. Worse, I think I'd spend all my money and lose in court. *Society will side with the rich man and his university degree, before agreeing with the poor dumpster diver.* So I sigh, and guess I will call if I must, and hope the ex does not answer. All my own doing I am told. She told me previously, to shut up and quit complaining. *It's amazing how irrational and emotional people can get when the subject is children! She and dad quit talking to me, leaving me out of the loop.*

MY FATHER HAS DIED.

There is a funeral to attend. Everyone will be there. The transportation will be covered. Dad was seventy-two. Previously he had refused to take his blood pressure medicine, causing him to have a stroke that he survived. His wife thought he would not live. She sold, gave away, and got rid of, most of dad's stuff. When he woke up and came home, his world was gone. I can guess what effect that had. Now he dies on his birthday? I am guessing the odds of that being a random date to die on are slim.

But I do not know lots about his recent life. Still, it occurs to me I am the one who has known him longer than anyone else who will be at the funeral. That really stands out when I tell a 'dad' story at the gathering. How he and I took a trip in his sailboat, Curlew. An eighteen ft. catch. We took it from England, and got as far as Portugal after thirty days at sea without sighting land. We had no electronics—all navigation was done with a compass, sextant, and manual steering. No communications. Just us and the sea. I was seventeen years old. It is my greatest fondest memory. Dad and I connecting over the love of boats and water.

After my story I was told by more than one family member, "Oh God! I thought you were going to talk about that stupid Sea Gull outboard of his!" I heard more than one story of how they went sailing with dad, and had an awful experience, like getting caught in a storm! I think, *And your point is?* I mean there are storms. "So what?" It's part of the experience of boating. Why would a storm be dad's fault? Did the boat sink, or did you get lost, did dad show some kind of incompetence of some kind? No.

"It was scary, there was rain and wind."

Well then blame God! I began to perceive some of the issues dad faced. *No one here but me understood his love of the sea.* Knew of his dream, to single handedly sail around the world. All that got stifled, made hidden, private, not discussed. Because it was a stupid idea. Dangerous, selfish, absurd. Dad listened, believed them, because he wanted their acceptance and love. Tired of moving on, alone. He gave up all sailing. These same people would tell me how incompetent I am if I took them on a river trip in my boat and they got rained on. I'm sure the ex told them such stories of being with me, and would repeat such stories in court. *It's certainly no way to raise a child!*

His wife gave away the boat. Sold for a few hundred dollars, when it was worth many thousands. Just to get rid of it. Guessing how I'd feel if I woke up from a stroke to discover my boat got sold for nothing by my wife.[1] I dream I'd be buried in my boat like a Viking. Put me in the boat, light it on fire and send me down the river. *What do you mean the boat is gone?* Apparently in this household 'boat' is one of those unmentionable, embarrassing words. I'm very puzzled. I assumed he was happily married. He never said any different.

At the funeral and reception there were no fellow teachers, no former students. The handful of friends were a small music band he played with once a week. Kind of the only ones who cared, besides a few relatives. I'm confused, somewhat. There is this Russian kid dad kind of adopted. I never heard about this. Something about the son of one of the heads of a secret service in Russia. Dad had promised to get him out of Russia and take care of him. I did not understand the details. But. *How would dad know the head of Secret Service in Russia?*

Sort of secret family pictures indicate, and I was told there is a good possibility that dad has another family in Europe someplace. A woman, maybe even kids. No one knew for absolute certainty, or would not say. But here are the pictures. Dad was often simply 'gone' for who knows how long or where. When young, our family would suddenly pack up and move. Not exactly secretly in the middle of the night, but without much notice, and for reasons that seemed for no reason. I always assumed we kids were just not told the plan, but there was a reasonable plan the adults understood.

"Come on, we are going. No you can't take your toys." Leaving everyone behind. No communication with the last place, once we leave. As often as once every two years on the average. In the middle of a school year. Does that make sense, a college teacher leaves in the middle of classes? Why?

My ex used to joke, "Your father, the spy," and we'd laugh.

And here is a cool submarine medal. I examine it. "It is Russian, issued to my father, recently. Why would a medal be issued to my father from Russia?" My father was on the first nuclear submarine when he was in the navy, at the time I was born. I told the family I wanted that medal. *Alaska used to be owned by Russia!* The next morning the medal disappeared. No one knew where it was. Maybe the Russian kid wanted it? But just as plausible, the family did not want the family idiot, me, to have anything meaningful of my father's. Or it was more important to the Russian kid. Yet, why not just say so. It's not like it was a huge big deal or I would not have understood.

I toss the knife I made my father in the burial hole. A simple grave in a Veterans cemetery, someplace or other. I could never find the place again. I forget even what state I am in. Dad apparently died broke, maybe even in debt. Apparently, the IRS caught up to him, and he had some problem or other. I thought he told me, "When you have money, you are able to avoid taxes, you have lawyers. Your money is in a Swiss account."

This is when I put it together, that the rich and the poor are well off. It is the middle class paying for everyone else. Well no one is going to tell me any details about dad's money woes. I am the one incapable of mixing a pitcher of lemonade correctly. I'm only acting. I do not buy into this. I have my own thoughts. *I may not have a degree, but every business enterprise I enter I make money at. Not a lot, but I do not crash and burn like some people around here.* I play along with the role assigned me, on the level of 'barely able to tie my own shoes'. To whom you need to use third grade words, and speak very slowly.

"Seek and ye shall find," I play the part. It makes everyone happy. *Live here? Like this? I'd kill myself. Did Dad feel the same way?* Visiting for a few days makes me depressed for a year. One flew over the cuckoo nest and got away. I make the sign of the cross and count my blessings.

My son follows me around and wants to be near me. *Very strange.* He always wanted to protect his mother. Mostly from me. He's the man of the house. I'm competition. *Why isn't he following her around?* He and the ex were the ones close to dad, not me. My sister shows up with her girlfriend as her protector, but can hardly speak. She is stuttering. She gets dad's flute. I get the sextant he used to sail with. That's about it. I was told there is no will. No executor. The woman dad lived with who ran everything, took over. They were not married. I assume she got the house, cars, Swiss bank account if there was one. Who knows? I was out of the loop. No, I do not suspect her of running off with any valuables. I believe she was rich, and had no need of more money, in fact may have subsidized and took care of dad, who was flat broke for a long time. I think dad was just too tired and wore out to leave, after being with several women in his life, and nothing ever working out. I think he accepted his fate, did what he was told and expected of him. Easier than fighting. He may have never in his life had any money of his own to speak of, but lived off her. I heard school teachers made a lot of money, but then heard no, so I do not know. We were maybe poor when I was growing up, but am not sure. There was this pretense of being among the protected and the elite. Did we do so by being in debt? No. I think we just did without some things, so the trappings looked good.

There was another Miles about five generations ago we are all named after. My grandfather, father, myself and my son are all Miles. The Miles of five generations ago, left his wife and child, and with some other guys, stole a whaling ship in Boston and took off. Never to be heard of again. I wish dad had done that. I think he'd have been happy on the high seas. I'd like to picture him screaming, "Row my mighty mates, row! Yo-ho, yo-ho!" He was a gifted, competent sailor. He and I saw forty foot waves in a storm, and he was not afraid, handled the boat well, was calm, level headed, with a smile. Very 'in charge,' very happy, confident. We were thirty days at sea without spotting land, using just this sextant I now have, and a compass for navigation.

I hope he did have a secret life and wife someplace far away. Someplace where he was a hero, with a family who loved and understood him. Guessing I'm the only one who knows him, who wished this. I hope he was a spy. I do not care what side he was on, or what he stood for. As long as he stood for something he believed in; fought for with honor. I hope he had a secret life he took with him. No. I do not want any proof of it. Then it is not a secret. I would not want anyone to get in trouble who is still alive. Nor would I want anyone coming after me for information, to torture me, and all that movie stuff. I know nothing. Speculation. Proof is dust in the wind. The family idiot with a big imagination. *The jester outlives many kings.* I put on my father's sailor hat and prance round singing pirate songs till everyone laughs. *The Indian, the one who got away in 'one Flew Over the Coo Coo's Nest' pretended he could not talk, remember? The goofy one! Not the hero. The hero got the lobotomy.*

In the trunk of mementos belonging to dad that we are all looking over, I see about fifty letters I wrote him. All the envelopes are water colored with various outdoor scenes. There is a string around them. Upon inspection, I see most have never been opened. *How odd!* If he did not want them, why did he keep them? *If he kept them, why didn't he read them? Was he going to read them some day? Did he want me to someday know he never read them?* I open my mouth to speak, to ask. I pause with open mouth, with a puzzled expression, close my mouth, begin to raise my hand indicating, *'wait, a new thought,'* then drop my hand. No new thought. No communication. I let it go. Wipe it from my mind. If you do not see it, it's not there. *Survival 101.* Poor Sister did not learn, and did not survive.

"But, Miles, I don't get it?" Sis says to me.

There's nothing to get. "She says hello, and I say, good bye" — *from the Beatles song.*

Daron, my step brother from long ago, goes over the trunk with me and Sis. Someone decides it would be a good idea to make copies of all the written stuff, and distribute copies to all of us. There is poetry dad wrote, and grandpa stuff. Rent receipts from the '40s, green stamps, concert tickets. Just odds and ends. Things that meant something to grandpa and dad. I am the only one who remembers grandpa. I learn from this trunk material, that grandpa was a boxing manager in the Irish part of New York when my father was growing up in the Bronx.

Anyhow, we will all chip in $100. My ex will make Xerox copies and put them together so we each have a copy. The trunk with originals will end up in my care as I have the physical space. Sis is renting an apartment and could get put out. Dad's woman is not family in the same way as the rest of us, so none of us feel comfortable with dad's things in her care. Our concern is she may not keep in touch with us. Daron is on the move, not settled yet, and lives in another country. He and dad worked together as business partners. I never heard from Daron about IRS problems. *If they were business partners, how come Daron had no IRS problems? They were overseas a lot, and Daron now lives in the Slovakia Republic. There is a Russia story about Daron.*

"I must have told you, Daron? I have a friend in Galena, Alaska who runs the sporting goods store. Gordy Kruger." I sold him a lot of my art and furs and got ammunition from him and we just got to be friends. Well, he takes off on a trip to Siberia for some reason. Something about some archeologists. He had a lot of connections through the military base in Galena. Maybe someone wanted to go hunting, and Gordy was his guide. But they end up in the remote Siberian tundra alone, near the coast of Alaska. Someone comes out of the distance and approaches them. It turns out to be a white person! There should not be such a person around for 1,000 miles! Gordy and this guy talk, and it turns out this stranger knows someone in Alaska named Miles and is related. "It turns out to be you, Daron! Is that a true story?"

My buddy Gordy never got over that, out in remote Siberia, and runs into someone who is a relative of mine! What are the odds? Daron never does give me a direct answer. Instead we just talk about Siberia. "Yes, Daron I feel an attraction. If I were young with the new opened relations with Russia, I'd be in Siberia in a heartbeat. Like Alaska was 200 years ago. Sounds like Heaven." I do not know about the politics. I talk about maybe, way remote, "Why would big government care about a bunch of savages with nothing, out in the middle of no place! The government has other concerns, surely!" *Being a savage is a compliment, and being civilized is an insult.* I give such speeches often.

Out of the blue Daron tells me, "You would not live a week in Russia. You'd be killed." Said with matter of fact, unemotional conviction. Said like someone who knows about such things. So again, where would he have gotten such knowledge? What does he know about remote Russia that I do not know? Daron had said something earlier about us having much in common. I was puzzled. He'd said, "Danger, just a different kind." I did not know what he meant. As far as I know, and he says, he is a restaurant manager. What could possibly be dangerous about that?

And what the heck was he doing out in some remote place in the wilds? And for that matter, Gordy? Gordy has military connections. I forgot the Galena Air Force base is isolated, with a lot of top secret experimental stuff going on. We saw stealth helicopters when they were still experimental and unbelievable. Was there something happening there of interest, that these two had in common? A baker and a sporting goods store owner? And if our father and Daron worked together, what does all that mean? In the context of everything else going on. Daron had nothing to say, and only said how alone he felt, like me, implying he knew a lot he was not going to speak of, and how he had nothing in common with anyone here except me. *If so, why not stay in touch, say hello at Christmas? Because I have a big mouth? Would Daron have known dad's other family? So many family secrets.* Geez. I was pretty glad to get out of there and back home. I absolutely do not want to know anything, or be believed.

BACK home

There are traps to take care of, and trapline cabins to wrap up. May as well catch fur for a short time before closing it all up and going to Tucson. The snow machine runs well. This machine weighs over 700 pounds. It falls over on its side and I have trouble getting it upright again! I know an elder who had the same type snow machine fall over on his leg and he could not lift it up. Luckily his son was out with him and helped get it off.

I begin to carry a bumper jack in a holder I built along the running board. Bumper jacks used to come with older cars. I found one at a junk yard for a few dollars. Much like the heavy handyman jack, but lighter in weight, it can lift or pull the snow machine. I drill holes in the running board and put on wolf snare wire loops and two feet of cable. If the machine falls over I can reach down and find the wire loop, get the bumper jack in the loop and jack the low side of the machine up enough so I can roll it back down on its track again. Or if the machine falls on me, I have a good chance of getting it off with the small jack.

On the trapline, the machine freezes down to the ice overnight and the jack helps me break it loose. Lots of things to learn about running snow machines out remote. The whole way I trap changes as well. In earlier years, I wanted my trails to be cut out of the wind in the deep woods. I used to stay away from the open where snow drifts fill in the trail, or makes big hills I cannot get through on snowshoes, with dogs, or with smaller snow machines. This big machine will get through deep snow and likes to go fast; it is at its best thirty to forty miles an hour in the open country. I dip into the woods here and there to make trapping sets. The tight turns in the woods I cut over the years for dogs is not ideal for this big machine. Thus, nothing is ever done, settled, finished. Always there is some change that alters the entire plan I carefully lay out, thinking one day it will be easy.

Riding the machine got easy, but now the trails need changing! I now ride with electric heated hand grips, engine heat on my face, sitting in comfort, traveling thirty-five miles an hour in areas I used to think eight miles an hour was moving fast! It is easy to zoom out from the village 100 miles. Not so easy if the machine fails me. I reviewed in the past all the advantages and disadvantages between my various options—choices in transportation, costs and lifestyle. I had preferred sled dogs, but feel I am in a position of having no choice now, or the choice is between snow machine or not at all. I write an article for the trapper magazine comparing snow machines with dogs or snowshoe trapping that I got a lot of compliments on, and has been a useful guide for others for many years.

No one I know is trapping or living a subsistence lifestyle with sled dogs anymore. *Well, maybe the Collins twins?* I think of them at Lake Minchumina from the time I spent in that area. The twins are still there. I do not know them well enough to understand how they make it work. I know they write regularly for the Fairbanks Daily News Miner, have a book or two out, and sell crafts. They do not have trapping competition because of the unique situation they are in. They are grandfathered into an area that became part of the Denali Park extension. No one else can get in there to trap, not by snow machine or any other method. No new trails can be cut. I'm not sure of all the rules and rights, beyond it being a unique situation.

I had a trail once all the way to Lake Minchumina and wonder now if I can open it up all the way. *Maybe the new snow machine's faster travel can allow that to happen.* Yet here I am faced with a glitch, having to change where I go and what trails I can use. Some trails it looks like I need to give up. Trails that took ten years to cut. It is still exciting to look at maps and various places I might go. I wake up and it is dark. But it is dark all the time this time of year. I forget to bring a time piece. Or more, I dislike civilization's sense of time to the nearest day. I enjoy my wilderness life of eating when hungry, sleeping when tired. I am awake and alert, ready to start my day.

I head for Nenana. In the snow machine's headlights, I see glittering snow crystals on overhanging willow trees forming a tunnel. I feel like a surfer in a wave tunnel. *Beach Boys songs come to mind, and lyrics from 'Pipeline,' 'Surfing USA,' and 'Wipe out,'* twang and reverberate in my head as I lean this way, that way, dodging snow drifts, pretending they are waves. *Hawaii and Alaska have something in common!* Yes, Hawaii is sometimes on my mind because I was born there. Now and then I am airborne going over a hump in the snow. Behind me is a totally disturbed environment of swirling snow I have created. But ahead of me, pristine untouched snowflakes individually suspended in the time space continuum. A black hole sucks me into the alternate universe of string theory. The Theory of Cognitive Dissonance, a book I read, becomes rocket science here in a savage world. The beauty of chaos. It's as if I am pulled into a time warp.

I am in Nenana before most people wake up! It is 5:00 am. I've already put in a work day! Now I must plug into civilization's time. Before the world wakes up, I get on the computer to check my emails. I'm constantly getting facts and tidbits of information sent by people I do not know. Today's message is about the nation's wealth distribution. Apparently One % of the population owns thirty-five % of the wealth, while 80% control only five %. If true, I did not realize this. hmmm. *Are we more like India than I realized. I thought we had more equality than that.* Of course, just because someone writes it, does not make it a fact. Some of the jokes passed on are funny! I created a file to save them. I record my batch for the day:

5. IF YOU HAVE A BAD COUGH, TAKE A LARGE DOSE OF LAXATIVES. THEN YOU'LL BE AFRAID TO COUGH.

6. YOU ONLY NEED TWO TOOLS IN LIFE—WD-40 AND DUCT TAPE. IF IT DOESN'T MOVE, AND SHOULD, USE THE WD-40. IF IT SHOULDN'T MOVE AND DOES, USE THE DUCT TAPE.

7. IF YOU CAN'T FIX IT WITH A HAMMER, YOU'VE GOT AN ELECTRICAL PROBLEM.

No new exciting emails. I review my list of things I need for the homestead and enter it in a file in the computer. A list for the next time I am in town. This inspires some thoughts for my diary:

Computer diary Jan. 21st 2001

There is a change I notice in my lifestyle. I now have ongoing bills that never end. In the past I could 'hole up' at the homestead and all the bills came to a halt. I could stay and regroup. When I came back out, I'd have checks waiting for me from the art sold on consignment in gift shops. Now I have heat, electric, internet and phone bills that never stop, even if I do not use these services. This makes it difficult to run two homes, one in the wild and one in the village.

My costs go way up maintaining two households. Where will I ever get the money to fix up the Kantishna homestead and keep it in repair? The dozen propane tanks I have stockpiled at the homestead are now obsolete and can no longer be filled. I must buy all new tanks if I use propane. Who would have ever guessed they'd be declared unsafe. Laws get passed to outlaw their use! The design worked fine for fifty years. Well, the good news is, I am making more money than ever before in my life. So I just buy what is required, and so what!

Many of the supplies I worked so hard to acquire and store at the homestead could all be replaced with new stuff without a lot of burden on me. Things like twenty sections of used stove pipe acquired at a garage sale for $5 will probably never get used. I can buy safe new stove pipe. The weather is getting at my stockpile faster than I can add goods to it.

Diary ends

Another trip to the homestead is made hauling new propane tanks, and to check traps. *Time to head for Tucson.* "Time flies huh!"

THE CHANGE in weather is welcome. Mom is glad to see me; we enjoy each other's company. Her boyfriend Les invites us both out to Dairy Queen for ice cream. Mom is ecstatic and jumps up and down. She rushes around getting her best earrings on and fixing her hair. She's a pretty easy keeper. He is going to spend $6, and this is our big trip out, the big date, the excitement of the week. It is nice to see mom so happy with so little. Again I see myself in her as I watch.

The show goes well for me as it always does. I make twice as much money as the year before, which was twice what I made the year before that. I'm at the new location at the Vagabond. I may need more space next year. A table is no longer enough. There are regular customers who come to buy, and regular sellers who come to sell to me. Some items that I acquire, I know other venders have a need for. I sell what I just bought and double my money. This is especially true with mammoth ivory, a market I understand, and know how to grade.

I have a fossil ivory order delivered to Jay. This is a major sale. "But Miles, maybe my business is in trouble, Bali is not allowing any ivory of any kind to come into the country."

"Part of the crack down on illegal elephant ivory sales?"

"It looks like it. I think we can expect this trend around the world, so a heads up."

A trip is made with mom and Les to Mexico where I have my teeth cleaned and worked on for just a few dollars. We have a fun trip. When I get home to Alaska, I feel like winter is almost over. Even if it is only psychological. Alaska is gaining daylight about seven minutes a day; about half an hour a week. There is warmth now to the sun by mid-February. There is new inspiration from the Tucson trip and motivation to do art. There are boxes of new materials to play with and investigate. This new surge of excitement occupies me till 'for sure spring,' which arrives in mid-March, with a few days above freezing and beginnings of a melt. Time to order garden seeds! Time to look at the boat! The depression of my father's death, and over all family situation begins to fade.

BACK home again

I tell Josh, "Yes, it is one thing I like about Alaska, the feast and famine aspect, with big changes to expect. I was born in Hawaii, but would not like it there. Too much the same all the time. Easy to get in a routine, a rut, and not even notice. Here in Alaska, about the time I am disgusted with the snow machine, it is time to think of the wonderful boat! And by late fall, when I am cussing the boat, it is time to think of the wonderful snow machine again!" Josh laughs, knowing just what I mean. Everything changes. The clothes I wear, my job, what I eat. I think that's so great about Alaska. "It's good to see the sun again. Josh!"

As roads melt, I get the three wheeler out and put the snow machine away. There is talk of the upcoming Cultural Center Gift Shop season. There are Chamber of Commerce and Library Board meetings. A board member asks, "Does anyone want to revive River Days?" On most projects that succeed, there is a point person whom everyone rallies behind, who will do 75% of the work.

I say to the Chamber, "River Days used to be a big event here in Nenana. A good celebration of the beginning of summer with vendors, food, and activities along the river bank. The big attraction it all revolved around was the annual raft race, seventy miles from Fairbanks to Nenana."

Everyone agrees. We all know the event and how it used to be. The issue is that we can no longer have the raft race. Some organization or branch of the government decided it is not safe. Someone might get hurt. Someone who got hurt might sue someone. So just in case that might happen, we better stop. I personally do not think there will be another event to rival it, but am willing to see who steps forward, and with how much energy. I'm willing to make flyers and put them up, contact some vendors and get them interested, but beyond that, not willing to put energy into a cause I do not believe in. Nope, no grant money to pay anyone, or buy supplies.

"Is there an organization waiting with money to give to this cause?" No.

"But we could have a fund raiser!" I wait to hear if anyone else leaps forward with great ideas to raise money. I'm beginning to see a pattern here. Fund raising is as much a social event as anything. Done by those who are retired, bored, or somehow feel social duty or satisfaction in donating free time. Over and over I see a total of 100 man hours devoted to selling hot dogs to raise money. $300 is raised, and that is a success. Maybe as much as $700, which is a lot of hot dogs for a community of 300 people. I may have donated five to six hours.

I'd prefer to go to my shop and work on a money maker project, then give $300 to a worthy cause. It's cheaper in terms of dollars per hour for my time. It's even more fun and rewarding. This is more money then I pay per year in local taxes. If I gave the whole $300 needed, what would be the result?

"Wow, cool! That was a success! Maybe next year we can do it twice or make it even bigger!" Oh great. I realize there are fund raisers practically daily. The school needs to raise $10,000 to send the band to Hawaii to compete, will you buy our cookies? *If they got the ten grand, my guess is, the goal would be a hundred grand, to do even more trips!* So and so needs an operation they cannot afford. There is a fund raiser to buy

a new bike for Pearl, get a new carpet for the community hall, put a new roof on the fire station, buy a dough machine for the Senior Center. It never ends. If I gave $10,000, there would simply be ten times as many fund raisers for worthy causes of all kinds because obviously fundraisers work. So I'm guessing it has little to do with the money. It has everything to do with standing in the wind hawking hot dogs and being seen, for five cents an hour.

I used to set up and sell at River Daze. The fee is $25 for the weekend for a table. Crafty would show up with other vendor-artists I knew. We'd watch the rafts come in, and there would be a bonfire, a party, a celebration. I'd make a few hundred dollars. If I made at least $100 a day, I figured that was equal to working for a living. I might spend $50 with other vendors. Buy hot dogs from the Lions Club to support them; maybe a raffle ticket for a new rifle or snow machine.

Anyhow, "No." No point person for this exciting idea to revive River Daze. Summer begins with no celebration. Eventually it is fair time. The usual big exciting event of the year for me. Where I make half a year's wages in two weeks. It is a year with forest fire smoke. Sort of common. There is a huge fire on the Kantishna River. Some concerns! But the fire went by my place, so less worries now. Kristine, my German fair neighbor and I discuss how to sell, and exchange customer stories.

"Coming here to the fair used to be more of a social event for me than a selling time. I wanted to talk to people. I considered it rude to turn the subject to their buying something. I saw however, that I'd fill up my selling space with listeners, and customers had trouble getting in to look and buy. I used to put complete articles and stories written about me in the news and magazines up on the displays. I'd end up with too many customers standing for an hour reading the story and blocking my selling space, then leaving, and not buying. Happily entertained. They got what they wanted, but I did not get what I wanted."

So I changed, and put out titles, partial stories, just to let them know where I have been, to provide provenance. The customer can go get the article themselves, buy it from me, or get a free copy if they buy something. I learned to step aside when talking to friends, and still keep an eye out to take care of customers. It has been harder getting friends to buy something. That seems rude. Kristine understands the problem, but sees it more with her husband Gary, who does the woodwork. He enjoys talking, while she counts the money. At least there are two of them to work the booth. I'm determined to understand business.

My friend Heidi still brings her children by, and leaves them with me. But now they are older and able to be of help. Forest and Skyler now straighten out twisted tangled chains for me in return for ride tickets or trinkets I have. They used to play under the table out of sight.

"Kristine have you seen the labor people from the government come by? I'm told we can no longer have anyone help us who is under age, even if we are not paying them, unless they are family."

"Have you heard that?"

"Yes, it is a new law, or old law on the books now being enforced. I can be arrested or fined for having Forest help me. Also, any help needs to be hired and recorded with taxes and Workman's Compensation withheld and all this. Yeah right. What planet are these people from? I cannot even have a customer or friend I know stand here and watch so I can take a pee break without signing a contract with them."

"I know what you mean, Miles. This is only a two week event, the only time we need a helper, so why not have a friend or young person who wants ride tickets give us a break for an hour?" Now we have to be careful, lie and be criminals? But no, I do not need to focus on such things. It's too depressing. Or fills me with anger, and I want to think about the upcoming revolution. Time to throw tea in the harbor again. When America originally rebelled against England, there was only three % of the population that participated. I read that someplace and wonder if it is true. We focus today on that three % who were heroes! But at the time they were criminals! I wonder if three % of Americans are disgruntled enough to do something about it? No. It is not a thought I wish to hold on to. I want to believe in and trust in my country.

I am at the fair, and supposed to be having a good time; that's what fairs are for. *Step right this way for the magical mystery tour!* "It's show time! Be amazed. I am Oz, the great and powerful." I step aside for the inspector who makes sure I have a fire extinguisher that is up to code. He checks that my table covers are fire retardant and approved, my electrical cords are up to code—it is all about being safe! The costs are passed on to the customers who then complain about high prices! Complain? I'm puzzled. *Be glad someone cares and makes sure you are safe!* "Indeed. Least your child climb under my table and bite my electrical cord." *Don't worry, $5 of your entry ticket goes to insurance and safety officers salaries. Obviously you are incompetent to look after yourself. But have no fear, the government is here!*

"Oh Hi, Will! Good to see you. You got work for this winter?"

"Hey, Miles, looks like you are doing OK. I should be OK. My back bothers me, been driving a loader all summer. The work season ends soon and I can probably collect unemployment all winter as usual. That's what is good about seasonal work." I had done that a couple of times when I had seasonal work with BLM fire-fighting, working for the railroad, and other jobs in my early years. "You still got the houseboat?"

"Yes, but it will never float again. Josh and I hauled it to my Nenana place with his truck this past winter. No trailer. We just hooked a big rope to it and drug it. Some of the fiberglass came off crossing the highway, but the bottom did not rip out.

Now it is a storage boat. Actually it is the Chamber of Commerce storage shed now, Ha! We keep banners, party fixings, and stuff needed to put on events – Thanksgiving decorations and such. A strange ending for the life of such a houseboat, huh? Ashes to ashes and dust to dust, Will, just like us."

"You got that right. What have we really accomplished with our lives, Miles? We had such dreams in our prime." He trails off. I do not say much. I have lived out the dreams, and still am doing so. I accomplished all I set out to–well pretty much. *I feel like I am on a path, but do not know what that path is, as if I am driven or being lead—by what? Destiny? I am not sure.* Will can say the same. He gave up a lot to help others, mostly family. Was it all worth it? Only he can say.

"So, Miles, how did you get everything to the fair? You end up using that truck you got?" Will is extremely knowledgeable about trucks, this is his interest. He likes that eighty-six Ford 150 Crew-cab truck I got.

"Yes, Will," I say with hesitation. "I took a chance and came the fifty miles here early in the morning with all my stuff, and have the truck parked in the lot out back."

"You figured out how to get plates without a license or insurance, huh?" I do not say anything. Why bother? "It's all I use it for, two days out of the year, getting here and getting back home. Well, a couple times I use it locally going a few blocks to the river to get my boat in and out. I keep the river boat tied up at 10th Street in Nenana."

"Miles, you get anything good in Tucson over the winter?"

Will is not very interested in my line of work, so wonder why he asks. I think just to be polite, and knows this matters to me. He's just being a friend. I think of something. "Yes Will. The Russians are learning how to sell in the USA... fast." They no longer fold their arms and scowl and look like mafia. The fossil dealers did not listen to me, but they listened to someone. They are smart people. Adaptable. Igor is starting to sell to me and give me good deals. "Sometimes I need paperwork. Receipts." I shrug my shoulders. Will looks thoughtful. He sells cars built from used cars and parts. He understands the need for paperwork. "The Russians understand."

Will replies, "I bet they do." But he laughs because he knows how I like to act, pay roles, for effect, attention, make big things out of nothing. Pretend I am important. It's just one of the quirks my friends deal with. I say all kinds of goofy stuff. I like it like this. Will looks like he has more on his mind. Knowing him, he will get it out. Standing here, I am reminded again, how he looks like a farmer. I can picture this face looking in from outside, through a dusty tractor window. A blank accepting stare. Up one row, turn, down the next row. All day, every day for fifty years. He and I are not much alike. I could do that for about two days, then I'd be figuring out how to change something. How to grow something different that did not require plowing, or how to design the tractor to run on it's own… *In a circle, on a long cable, that winds up around a huge drum as the tractor runs a different smaller circle at each pass, that runs out of gas about the time the field is plowed…*

"Miles, I asked if you ever hear from Vicki?" I come back to 'now.'

I forgot. Will is interested in Vicki, finds her to be very beautiful. I had introduced the two. Vicki had only shrugged her shoulders after a short date. I did not want to say anything about it to Will. No, there had not been a possessive kind of attraction between her and I. The relationship was more like her job to protect me during the whole me being a murder suspect incident. *She is a 'take control-be in charge' sort. I do not think I want to marry such a person.* Will is just now reaching the point of being ready to hear my reply. It takes him a while to react to anything. He is not a fast person.

"No, Will. In fact, kind of odd. Kodiak is not a big place; it is an island. I inquired. It appears she is not from there as she told me. If not where is she from?"

"Yeah." His usual very long pause and… "I inquired as well. Almost like she does not exist, or is hiding something. What would she have to hide? I sure love that long hair of hers, the way she rolls it up and puts a stick in it." He pauses again before he sighs. I'm sure he is picturing her in his mind. Such a body! *He may not know her back is full of shotgun holes. She had said, a drug deal gone wrong. But has not mentioned whose side she was on.* Will is ready to speak again, in his farmer voice, he says, "Did you see her Glock, Miles? I know guns, sometimes I buy and sell. I looked hers up. I could not find it, almost as if it does not exist."

"It could be a model so new it is not on the market yet, or some custom item not available to the public?" *Or out of the future, yet to arrive.* I briefly wonder why my unconscious would say something so outrageous. 'Out of the future indeed! What an imagination you have Sir!'

Will does not hear the reply to my unconscious. He might still be processing what I had said before. I sometimes count the seconds waiting to see how long it takes Will to process. *Seven seconds!* And Will says: "Miles, If you need a ride someplace, let me know. Maybe we can go to some garage sales like in the old days." Sounds like a plan. Will is off to see his brother. I watch him take off slow with his head down, feet dragging. As I stare at Will's back, a Forest Service guy I know comes to my booth. I assume as usual, he is here to look at my work, maybe a custom knife?

"Check it out, Pete, my acid etching is getting better. I have electric now, and a new sander, so my finish work is improving, I think." Pete is one the of the office guys who helped me work out things over the Nenana homestead when there was an issue over the ex being a resident for long enough to qualify. He even has some personal knowledge about Gene, the guy I was supposed to have killed.

"Miles." Pete pauses. "I do not know how to say this, but your cabin on the

Kantishna burned yesterday." *No! He must be mistaken! Wrong cabin. The fire already went by a week ago.* There were sprinklers left at my cabin just in case. The homestead cabin is against a swamp and a river. The last place a fire could even get to. The expression on Pete's face tells me he is serious, is sure it was my place. This doesn't sink in. *If you do not believe it, then it's not true.* I politely thank Pete for telling me. For saying something. I forget what he said. Nothing important. It's fair time. The show must go on. Bills must get paid, money has to be earned. There is no such thing as quitting. I'm sure my place did not burn. It couldn't have. But after the fair I can take a boat trip up and check it out. I need to haul supplies in anyhow.

"MILES, YOU LOOK LOST IN THOUGHT!" A customer I recognize. My good friend, What's His Name.

"I saw you showing Pete that knife. Really nice. Sure can tell your work when I see it."

"Thanks! Yes, I am excited about having electricity. Sure makes the work go faster, especially when working steel, a pretty hard material!" I explain how I have a cutting torch now, and can cut my own steel blade blanks. Learning how to do my own hardening and tempering. "A blade still warps or cracks on me sometimes, but I'm figuring it out. I test each blade I make and they hold up better than factory blades." I sell another $350 knife. Some mammoth ivory I found sells, fossil bones sell. Russian ivory sells. It's different than Alaskan, harder, maybe less color. Even though I find a lot of tusk material, so much is not sellable or is, but is not highly in demand like hard Russian. I let people think it is all material I found. I do not lie, just do not say. My book is selling well. Life is good.

My tent neighbor Kristine comes up and hands me an envelope and card. I have known her twenty years, sort of like Heidi. We have been dance partners in the evening after we close, and the bands are still playing. Tall, German, brown hair, always in a long conservative dress and floppy hat. She sells necklaces she makes. She buys my custom necklace clasps and pendants sometimes.

"Sorry for your loss Miles, hope this helps." There is $500 in the envelope in small bills collected by the other vendors here at the fair. I'm touched anyone knew or cared. I know these vendors do not make much money, so it was a sacrifice for them. More than the money, is the thought and the feeling of hope for humanity. Civilization in general might be going to hell in a hand basket, but not the people. And after all, civilization is made up of people. Maybe the best revolution of all is to smile, be happy, and rise above the oppression all around us. *The message of the 60s hippie flower generation, our people.* 'You mean that produced Charles Manson?'

I think of my friend, Bill Underhill, from the Diamond Willow shop at Alaska

Land who made something of himself despite hardships in his life. Without anger, he forgave, and looked for the good in everything. I have not seen him in a while. He and Nora moved Outside. I heard he is a preacher now. How strange. But no, guess he always was a spiritual man and has the official title now. I just am unsure I like the idea of a best friend being a preacher. I do not think of him as getting in your face, telling you to repent or else. He's working with senior citizens now; a care giver to those who can't get out.

Nora passed away. I keep remembering Bill telling of it. "Among her last words were asking where Miles is." I never considered being important enough to anyone to be in someone's last thoughts on a death bed. Even more strange, I hear Bill is remarried now to the woman who cheated on him. The woman who hurt him so bad when he was young. The whole romantic story of how he met Nora is on my mind. Bill told me over the phone: "Well, some of the original attraction was still there for my first flame." I suppose, guessing, she somehow learned her lesson. Saw what a good man it was she lost. And he forgave her. Wow, that is amazing. How can that be forgiven? I mean... I can understand, OK, let the past go, no hard feelings, not wanting any harm to come to the one who hurt you. *But to actually love them again without being a fool? How is that possible?*

He had been off to war, Viet Nam era. Saved all his money and sent it home to his wife who was supposed to be saving it for a house they were buying. She was spending it all on another guy. Somebody 'of another race.' Bill comes home after serving his country for six years, almost getting killed, looking forward to a home he bought, a wife who loved him. He catches them in bed, with all his money gone. No house. Now he is a preacher and married to her thirty years later. Dang. I'm speechless.

My ex didn't do nearly that much, just left. Could I ever marry her again? Could even God smooth all that over? I'm a little misty eyed. It must be the $500 gift from fellow vendors. The only way to really thank everyone is to show the money helped. To do something with it, and get over my loss. To not give up. To see it is only 'stuff.' *Anyhow, what was I going to do with the place? It was getting run down.* I was torn between two lifestyles. Now the decision has been made for me. Maybe God said, "Here, let me help you decide."

Maybe a part of my life is ended, and there is a new phase to my life. I learned what I was supposed to learn. *Everything happens for a reason.* 'What I gained, I must now apply to 'phase two' of my life.' *More like phase ten!* I graduated. In terms of having a purpose. Even if that reason is selfish, only in my own head; within me and nowhere else. Maybe it helps to move forward with the idea I feel I am here on earth for a reason. Losing my home is just a test, part of a bigger plan. Certainly, I see no harm in a view that keeps me going.

Where lesser people might be inclined to give up. God does not give us tests we cannot pass. I must therefore be an amazing person, to have been given so many hard tests! God must know I will not quit or give up. God must be watching close. So goes my reasoning when I speculate on the meaning of life. Bill is one of the happiest, most successful people I know. He has had reason to give up if he chose to, and no one would fault him for it. Could have cried in his beer about how his wife took up with another guy, and spent all his war money. Everyone in the bar would sympathize, and buy him another beer. He would be just like another of the, 'would have, should have, but never did because' people in the world.

After the fair I will need to boat out to the homestead to see the damage, clean up, and see what I can save. It was only a few years ago my neighbor on the Teklanika River burned down another home of mine. I had struggled so hard to build and outfit a place for my wife and child. All done for nothing. Not good enough for them, and then burned down. Why had I even bothered? What would my life be like if I had said to my wife, "New home? I don't think so, dream on. Next!" What if all that energy was put into something else? No use speculating. We deal with what is.

I wake up in my fair booth in the morning to someone's radio blaring a song, and words, 'Building a stairway to heaven." Sandhill cranes are flying over. Fog engulfs the grassy fairgrounds field. Time to count the money total again. Last days sales, time to pack up. I make $6,000 in ten days. All my expenses have to be deducted. I pretend I am talking to the IRS and turn my hat backwards, *Sad, so sad, the poor economy, the costs of doing business. I just cannot seem to get ahead. Alas, I seem to owe you… let's see… nothing! But don't worry! I will try harder next year!* I turn my hat the other way. Big grin telling the same story, viewed with a rearrangement of the numbers and hat… *Dang this is sweet. I need a wheel barrel to get all my money home, it's just such a problem to carry it. Half a year's wages in ten days.* That, of course, assumes we can live on the twelve grand I make this year. *That you report!* I'm shocked my unconscious thinks I am not reporting all my income. I practice a few times.

"I'm shocked!" I turn the other direction to the jury of my peers, "I'm shocked!" I could live on half my income. So it's all relative, that term, 'doing good!' If I decide it is good, then poof, it is good. *Anyhow we get to write off that new snow machine!* Correct. It is absolutely no fun, totally all business, just like the boat!' *If it's fun, you can't write it off your taxes.*

The truck is loaded to the max inside the camper where goods will not blow out and can be locked. I make the hour trip to home in Nenana without incident and park the truck till next year. I wish I could use the truck to go to Fairbanks and fill barrels with boat gas cheap. Buying in Nenana cost fifteen cents a gallon more, just fifty miles from town. The trip to the homesteads will cost $15 more than it needs to. *Oh well. I'd rather not take a chance driving.*

I cannot go to the homesteads right away because I have been gone from

Nenana. The garden needs attending. There are emails and business to deal with. I spend a lot of days loading the boat, and checking to make sure I have everything I need. Now I decide to wait a few more days till moose season. *I can hunt while on the trip.* "I can too, not just you!" Maybe get my winter moose. Easier to get during the legal season, now that I have a freezer and electricity. I pack some game bags of cheesecloth in case I do get a moose, also some plastic bags. I have a metal detector and shovel to look for stuff in the house ashes. A tent is packed for a place to stay while there. All my usual camping gear is packed. With the gas, I have about 1,000 pounds to bring.

I can get the boat on step, but am only going fifteen miles an hour. Barely on step. The day is a little cloudy with choppy water making it hard to read the surface of the water for depth, and debris on the surface. This is normal, and just means I have to pay attention a little more. There are not as many boaters out as I'd expect with moose season starting. Possibly hunters are waiting for better weather. The old Indian village of Minto is passed, the usual landmarks go by, with just the constant purr of the engine.

Will would say, "No different than me running a tractor, Miles!" My conscience does not tell me, but keeps some secrets in the interest of us getting along.

Hot soup in a thermos is drunk to keep warm and serves as a lunch. There is a plastic five gallon bucket under the steering console that has things I might need that I can grab while running the river. My thermos, sun glasses, spare gloves and hat, in case I get a chill. I search for a chemical warmer for my hands, find the red pack, open it and crumple up the bag inside. Air activates the chemical, and this bag generates heat for four to five hours. They cost about $1 each. As gas is burned, I gain a little speed. The front of the boat drops and wobbles because it is happy. Shortcuts are taken to avoid the wind and waves—this boat is not good in rough water. There are about three spots on the Tanana River I know from experience, will be the hardest stretches. The worst is Tolovana, but I already paid that spot fine. There's Dim's old abandoned fish camp on the left and then, into the Kantishna. Four hours of run time to the mouth of the Kantishna. Doing about normal speed. Sometimes I stop at Rock Creek to see if there are fish to catch. But not this time, I'm anxious to see what the fire did, then maximize my time cleaning up.

In two more hours, I am at the pond off the river where I park the boat to get to the homestead. To get to the homestead, I need the hidden canoe required to go over the beaver damn that separates the creek from the river. Someone found my canoe and has been using it year after year. I do not know who. So I hauled in some aircraft cable that can't be easily cut with tools the average person would carry. I use two long pieces and small loops to accept a key lock. On the previous trip, I drove a steel fence post deep into the ground. No one has borrowed the canoe since. But always a concern this person would rather destroy the canoe than let someone else use it.

This is a canoe I built myself that has a lot of memories, a good twenty years old now. I use the paddle from my river boat for the canoe, so I do not keep a paddle at the canoe. I travel light the first trip to the cabin. There has been no burn here at the pond a quarter mile from the cabin.

I go about 300 feet, and see a moose in the water that just looks up at me as I approach. It is a cow and not legal to shoot. This looks like an older cow with no calf, so think she will attract any bulls that might be around—a very good sign for me to see. Leaving her alone and getting her get used to me improves the chances she will lure a bull within rifle range. Around a bend and she is out of sight. *Here is the first burned spot along the shore. It does not look like it was a hot hard fire. Only a few scorched trees above the burned grass. There is a lot of swamp around that kept the fire at bay.*

But yes, the cabin burned. All I see is ashes, then tin from the roof on the ground. The cabin burned hot, but dry grass fifty feet away did not burn. It looked like a small finger of the fire, twenty-five feet wide, wound its way around and came in right at the cabin, missing everything else around it. *What bad luck.* I sigh, because usually luck goes the other way. A fire hose and a pump is still here. The pump is in the creek, with sprinklers set to go on and spray the cabin. If the pump had been turned on, the cabin would be fine.

The guide who ran the boat hauling the fire fighters told me, "We thought your cabin would be fine with the swamp all around. There was a lot of smoke so it was hard to see or travel." This happened over a weekend, and half the fire crew had gone to town after the main fire passed and all seemed safe. They were under-manned when the wind shifted and blew the fire back. A series of small factors that added up to my home being the only one to burn.

Walking through the ashes I find the stove. It got so hot the steel legs melted and the stove fell. My pottery collection was re-fired and the glaze melted. That takes 2,000 degrees. My propane tanks blew up. My 300 gallons of stored gas went up in flame. I find an ax head and a splitting wedge that might be salvageable. Some drill bits are found, but have lost their temper and are soft. That's about all she wrote. Ashes to ashes, dust to dust. All the goods, all the memories, all the years of work, the dreams fulfilled. The ones lost. All the stockpiled goods gone. Here is what is left of a 55 gallon drum full of dry beans and other goods stockpiled against hard times. All the spare stove pipe melted. There is my melted 1800s treadle sewing machine, all the traps, the spare snow machine, the antiques I had collected. The tools to fix this and that, the generator, solar panels. There was once a ringer washer, bathtub, canning jars, pressure cooker, winter clothes. A two story house packed full of all I needed to live forever out here.

It's hard to grasp. If this were my only home, where would I be now? 'Heck no, there is no insurance.' *Insurance is like paying the mafia for protection.* What good would insurance do? Over a twenty year period I would have paid in enough money in insurance to buy a new house and goods. But if this was my only home I might have been here, and been able to turn the pumps on and save the cabin and myself. Hard to say. I'd have still been at the fair. Even so, the trapline is burned.

How could I live here and not be able to have a livelihood? I heard from pilots that tell me, for the most part, 200 miles of trail that took twenty years to cut is gone in a day or two of burning. I can follow the rivers and swamps to continue trapping maybe. Again, hard to speculate. It doesn't matter much. Not 'would have, should have, could have,' but 'did.' I'm pretty much in shock. Heartbroken. Not angry or puzzled or thinking, *Why me?* Just the overwhelming acceptance and understanding that a bridge has been burned. There is no turning back. A way of life is now gone forever. There is no way at my age I can start from scratch and rebuild it all. I gave this lifestyle and area my youth. It comes but once around. It cannot be given again. There is no way to lift twenty-five foot logs on my shoulder and carry them as I once did building this cabin. No way to recut 200 miles of trapline. Possibly a few of the twelve line cabins I built survived. No way to know without clearing impossible unpassable trails.

Anyhow. Sigh. I am wondering what to do. *I suppose I'd have ended up losing it all anyhow. To bears, the weather, rival trappers. One fell swoop dramatically, by fire, is more my style.* I'd rather have God take it all back. *Try to appreciate the time I had.* 'Try to dwell on the positive.' Be grateful I have a home in Nenana. The paddle back to the pond and river where the boat is, goes slow. Head down, paddle silently, dipping, splashing. There is a sound of a moose head coming out of the water. I do not need to look up to know what that sound is. I have heard it often enough. The cow again. I do not even bother to look up. A second moose head coming out of the water. A slow look up. A bull moose near the cow. I slowly work the paddle under the water noiselessly, till the canoe faces them.

I still favor my 270 caliber rifle, and keep buying the Savage Model 110 when I need new guns. The bullet is one of my reloads, not the biggest bullet I can get, but 130 grain that goes faster and flatter then the heavier, suggested loads. It performs well, and I have confidence in it. I like to sight it in at twenty feet and know this is the same sight picture in the scope as 200 yards. This shot is close to the twenty foot 'right on' sight picture. I slowly aim, just behind the elbow at a sideways bull whose head is facing me. The bull is trying to decide what I am. Moose cannot see well. They depend on hearing and smelling. He can smell me, but my scent may be here from the cabin, and all around my stuff stashed in the woods he has smelled before. *He has never been shot at before.* The sounds are normal to him, wood splashes in the water. My silhouette does not look like anything living, a long pointy thing like a log, with stuff sticking up above like a root wad. Knowing this, I can be slow, with no sense of panic or urgency.

I consider a head shot in the temple. But such a shot will drop him like a rock, right into the water he stands in. A planned heart shot will allow him to take about two steps onto the shore before he falls. *He will be dead, but his body will not know it. He will not feel pain, just puzzlement.* I take the heart shot. A single loud boom! Not heard anywhere around here in a long time. The environment is in shock. The cow runs off, a squirrel gives a tentative reply, ducks way off fly up, a jay screams. The bull moose looks puzzled. He never heard the shot. I have seen this look many times. The bull turns, takes two steps, gets on shore, sags down, dead on dry ground on the creek bank.

I have done this enough times I am not elated, filled with self praise, or adrenaline. I pause to quietly savor the moment. Honor the dead. *Thank you Lord for the bounty you have put on this table and the hands that prepared it...* "And so on and so forth," spoken as the Wizard of Oz, not necessarily out of spiritual conviction. I want God to know I am a piece of work. So I can wink and add: *And you forgive me right?* As God mumbles under His breath. I smile. I lost a home and a way of life, but here is my winter moose. I know what to do. Now the work begins. Familiar work.

There is a canoe to put the meat in. The meat needs moving 300 feet to the river boat tied up in the pond. I have a routine for taking care of the meat that works for me. I get the hind leg up on my shoulder and cut the hip socket connection that turns the hind leg loose, and keep pushing back till it is free and falls on the hide. The hind leg is too heavy for me to lift off the ground, so let it just fall onto the hide. My bad back will never be the same as when I was eighteen. There is room on the hide for some scraps I cut off, like neck meat, back strap, etc. I then cut the ribs I want to save, giving me access to the inside where I salvage the heart and liver. The heart has a neat hole in it where the bullet went through. The heart is about the size of a football. After I salvage all of the meat off this side, I cut the head from the body and salvage the tongue. I never have to roll the head over. I make a cut so the guts slide out easily, and this lightens the moose up so it can more easily be turned over. To turn the moose over, I have to roll it onto the hide. So now I have to get this half of the meat to the boat.

I always carry an extra clean blue tarp on the boat. This tarp has a lot of uses. It has grommet holes all along the edge. I have in the past, strung a rope between two trees and draped this ten ft x twenty ft tarp over the rope for a tent against snow or rain. I have done the same configuration higher up so I can set up my nylon dome tent under it for extra wind and rain protection. I have set it up over my head while I butcher a moose in the rain. The boat can be covered. My activities can be covered if I am concerned with what someone in a plane, satellite, or passing boat might see. I trust no one. Not even legal activities are seen.

In this case, the tarp gets cut in half. Such tarps are found at garage sales for $3 to $4. Half goes in the bottom of the canoe, and the other half in the bottom of the river boat. The meat goes off the creek bank into the canoe, and then paddled over to the beaver damn. I find I cannot lift the meat easily. The moose will take a lot of trips. My back is hurting. I get the tarp back out of the boat, and set it on the beaver damn. The meat is slid, without lifting, from the canoe to the clean tarp on the ground, then drug over to the river boat on the tarp, pulling with rope through the grommets. The beaver dam has a path across the top where the beaver and animals like otter keep it smooth and stick free. There is nothing to tear the tarp. The first tarp from the canoe is now bloody, so I rinse it in the creek, and set it in the boat. I only have to work the big pieces of meat up and over the side of the boat. If I maneuver it right, the bigger pieces are never lifted as dead weight, but raised off the ground and tipped into the boat.

I carefully write in '54 inches' on the right line of the permit that asks for the antler spread to be filled out immediately. I have no idea what day this is. But an armed agent of the government might stop by plane or boat and demand to see if my papers are in order. Anyhow, this is a legal moose. I just forget what exact day this is and did not bring a tape measure, so make up an antler spread number. It's not on my list as a priority to remember.

My tent is set up for the night. Over an evening fire, I cook moose heart and liver. I usually cook liver first because it spoils within hours, and will go bad probably before I'd get it home. There are always spices on board the boat in case I get game of any kind, and a pot, as well as dry rice. So I cook rice and toss in some edible greenery from the environment I find myself in. In this case, cattail roots. A starchy bulb that has a flavor for the rice and liver. Separate tea is made from rose hips dried on the bush nearby. There are a few cranberries and dried blueberries nearby as well. A boletus mushroom is spotted, but as usual, it is full of worms, dang. If I submerge the mushroom under water, the worms leave. Nearby is some coral mushroom that is only OK in taste, so I use just a little bit for texture. I toss it in the rice last so it will not cook down and be mushy.

Flies are out looking for meat. I forgot the game bags. But the meat is in the bottom of the boat, half below the water line, where the temperature will be close to 40 degrees. This keeps the smell way down. The flies are much less interested. Some of the scraps are in big black plastic bags twisted shut so no flies can get in. The bigger pieces I can wipe fly eggs off when I get home if I am careful. The meat will get rinsed at home. A little vinegar in the water with a rag helps kill fly eggs, stop mold, and does not hurt the flavor of the meat. There is little hair in the meat the way I butchered it, but no sand, dirt, or leaves.

There is only about twenty pounds of metal goods from the cabin to salvage. One ceramic pot with a lid that got re-fired, that is all lumpy, but is salvaged. I want it as a memento of what used to be. It is a favorite pot I have had for thirty years. Karen gave it to me. Her children I helped raise here loved this pot. Our dried garden turnips were stored here. This pot is on my mind as something positive when I drift off to sleep in my dome tent. Next to me are the things within reach I might need in the dark cold night. Laid out in the same pattern all the time so I can find everything. Always on my left, my pee jar with lid, and next to it, a pen flash-light. Shoes, socks and clothes, are all set in the same spot and on top of the shirt and pants. On the right is my pistol, the Ruger .357 Blackhawk. I'm sure the temperature will be way below freezing tonight.

In the middle of a sound sleep, I wake up. There is a rustling sound. Something large and secretive is investigating the meat smells around the boat a few feet from me. I lay quietly listening. Another similar sound from another direction. I know it is wolves, because, there is more than one. Maybe a sow bear and cub, but bears do not need to be quiet and secretive like this. Without even reaching for my gun I say loud, but not screaming,

"Don't even think about it!" There is a slight pause, followed by the sound of scurrying feet and crashing through the brush. These wolves are no danger to me under these conditions. They may want the meat, and might try to steal it. Their interest would not be in me. Nor would they fight me for the meat. Not this time of year in fall, when there is plenty of dead spawned out salmon on the beaches. There is the gut pile I left behind they can go dig into, their favorite part. I drift back to sleep.

In the morning I awake to new sounds. Louder. I know right away this is a bear. Sniffling loud and snorting, not caring who hears him. I hear the top tarp covering the meat being ripped off. There is enough light in the pink sunrise to see outside. I'm guessing the bear is fairly occupied, and will not pay attention to small sounds I might make. The tent is slowly unzipped and the hammer is eased back on the pistol. From the waist up I am out of the tent opening, leaning to get a view of the boat.

Yes, there is a big black bear in the boat about to start tossing my meat out into the mud where he can sort through it at his leisure. I have to wait for the head to come up. But no, I decide not to take a head shot with the pistol. If it is not a perfect shot, I might only wound the bear. Not a good idea up this close. It is good the bear does not know I am here. *His body is not in survival mode, full of adrenaline. If hit hard, even wounded, he will not know where the shot came from, and be puzzled, 'probably' we mean* certainly. "Enough to count on." But for some reason, a bad head shot seems to increase the chances of a bear being furious. Even spinning and charging. I have never seen this with a gut shot. I think a gut shot hurts more, and the bear focuses on his pain more. I want a heart shot. When his head comes up and turns to look out at the river, I fire.

Ka-boom! Louder than the rifle, with six feet of flame and a big kick, as my hot load leaves and hits the bear. I can hear the 'splat' sound above the boom. The bear jumps straight up, and stumbles out of the boat onto the shore. I fire again, Ka-boom! The bear falls over, and tries to get up again. I know he is dying. I need to just keep quiet and not move. *He will roll around for a little bit and die, unable to focus on where his problem came from.*

Only now does it all sink in. *Dang, I do not want a bear! Darn anyhow. My back hurts.* My boat is already loaded. I doubt I could have scared the bear off. The sounds he made were sounds of possession. This 'kill' was already his. If I let him know I was here, and told him to leave, he'd say, "You and who else is making me leave!"

If I said, "Me and Mr. 357!" He'd snort. If I fired the pistol for noise, he'd be scared enough to dash off a little way, but see nothing chased him. He'd probably overcome his initial fear and concerns, and come back. With new knowledge I do not want him to have, an informed bear is ten times more dangerous. He can see me, when I cannot see him in the dark. He'd know about guns, and I'm in his world. The element of surprise I have is gone, and I'm in trouble. Possibly he'd be back charging, before I could get the tent down and camp packed and out of here.

Now I have a bear to skin. My back already hurts. Halfway through the job I am bent over and cannot get up. I have to lie down, roll over, and push myself up. It takes hours to take care of the bear, with many breaks. I now have the bear meat and hide in the boat. I need to head home to make sure the meat will be OK, since there are flies around. There might be more bears if I try to spend another night. No bear proof cabin to stay in anymore.

Some wild rhubarb is spotted along the river bank. The upper green leaves are a mild poison. A pound of leaves is mixed with five gallons of water, to make a solution to cover my meat that keeps the flies at bay. This solution is lightly brushed on the meat and tossed into the bilges. A tarp over the meat helps contain the slight odor and any fumes this concoction puts out. This will not hurt the meat for my own eating. Mostly the outer layer of skin dries, and is cut off as part of the cleaning, processing. The poison is an alkaloid that disappears when cooked.

I could park the boat in the water on a long rope and sleep in the boat, but there is no room. In an emergency, I could sleep on top of the meat. But getting home would be better. About 2:00 pm. I take off, calculating take eight hours to get home, so about 10:00 pm., in total dark. If it is too dark, I can decide to stop and sleep someplace, maybe a cabin like Tolovana. Yet I want to protect the meat! I have to stay with the meat.

I zone out as I travel. I do not find time warps, wormholes, alternate universes, negative matter strange. *Very little is impossible.* I am able to travel in the dark without being able to see even the front of my boat. I only know I am concentrating on hearing and smelling. *Also a time line.* I know I am at Tolovana without seeing it. I ease over to the shore without running into any sweepers, and feel the nose hit the muddy shore.

I have a flashlight to see up close to get my sleeping bag. I see an overhanging tree I can tie the boat to and let the rope out so the boat is way out in the river where I bear is not as likely to be able to reach it. It would be hard for a swimming bear to reach up over the sides to get a grip to get in. His effort would likely wake me up inside the cabin. I do not hear as well as I used to so unsure, but I have no choice. My back is sore, I'm tired. Is this really Tolovana? My unconscious feelings are hurt.

Why of course! Trust me! 'Yes of course, here it is.' I smile as the door comes into my light beam. No one is here, and it is rare the owners are around. Friends in Nenana got a historical site grant to fix this old roadhouse up. One big central log room with potbelly wood stove, so dozens of people could sleep in caribou robes around the stove back during the dog mushing mail carrying days. Bunkbeds are against the wall. Kerosene lanterns are on the shelves. There is bedding, but it is polite to use your own sleeping bag and not dirty the linen. The door is never locked, and is not even set up so it can be. There is lots of firewood and food on shelves.

I get a good nights sleep. Or is it a days sleep? I go to bed at 6:00 am. Wake up at 2:00 pm. My back hurts. I go check on the meat in the boat. The temperature is still below freezing, and think it went down to twenty at night, so the meat is fine. I limp back to the roadhouse and get a fire going in the wood stove and go back to bed until the large room warms up.

Water in a pot on the wood stove is boiling when I wake up again. I add moose meat to noodles I find at the roadhouse. I write in the log kept on the table. Visitors are expected to leave a note. I look over who has stopped by over the summer. Moonshine stopped on a trip headed between the Hot Springs and Nenana picking up his wife Wren. He has a very young baby 'Cider,' with him in the boat. *Hard to imagine him with a baby*! "Ha!" A few other local river people stopped. I can guess how they are doing by when they stopped and what they write. I can guess if they are hauling fish to sell, are trapping, known by when they pass with a heavy load. *Skill we learned sitting on the bench watching boats go up and down the river with the Indian elders, remember?* 'We thought at the time it was such a waste of time.'

It is important to know what is going on beyond just gossip. I know who I can stop and visit, and who would prefer I do not. I know who might need their mail if I pick it up, knowing they are at fish camp. Well, the mail thing is the past. *Now you need ID, or you can't get anyone else's mail.* Oh, and have an idea who might be working undercover for the Feds. Like, "Hmm, just before fishing season, at a time you should be holed up at camp. Why such a light load? You should be hauling supplies." I know 'light load' by your record of how much gas you burned, or your time getting here. I know you left from Nenana, and know how far that is. I can determine how tired you are by your handwriting. I can almost write a book about you, based on several sentences in a log. One reason I write in the log is, so others know about me. My peers and neighbors. This is bush etiquette. Or, not writing in the log is similar in civilization to giving a fake name and not showing your Id when it's expected. I sigh.

In general, I am an open honest person. There is nothing I do that I am ashamed of or feel I need to hide. I do not trust my government, but am not prejudice, because if a neighbor robbed me, lied to me, hurt me on purpose, I would, by necessity, not give them information that would be used to hurt me.

I write,

Got my moose and then a bear. Going slow in the cold and dark, good to be able to stop here and rest up! Should be in Nenana tonight.

I smile. A book could be written about just those two sentences. Moonshine will read this one day and know my back is acting up again, I'm nervous about the legality of my moose. I do not need bear meat. I'm not getting back into sled dogs. I am probably not trapping this winter. I'm recovering from the loss of my homestead. No, I did not get any fossils this season. He will pass the word up and down the river. If the Feds ask? He will honestly say he knows nothing, has not seen me.

I GET a late start to Nenana. I can barely move, and groan as I lower myself onto the boat seat. A reminder this lifestyle may have to change. I arrive in Nenana in the pitch dark. I have traveled several hours once again, unable to see even the front of the boat. I focus on elapsed time and speed. Everything we ever saw, heard, or did, is recorded someplace in the brain, if we know how to retrieve it. Like the movie of this trip made many times, along with a time stamp. Oddly, I cannot negotiate the road from the boat launch to the cabin with my three wheeler. I have to walk to the house with my hands in front of my face so I do not get poked by a branch in the eye. I wander from one side of the road to the other. Because I have not walked this road much to have it memorized. Once I get to the highway there is light to make it home. I will get a couple of hours sleep, and then it will be light in the morning. I can go unload the meat. I am sure there are no bears around the village to bother it. It is cold enough at night for flies to be dormant.

Next day, a folding table is set up in the yard. My back feels better. I'm sure one reason is because I rested it when I needed to at Tolovana. I wear a back-brace today. The meat grinder is hooked up. The cutting board with butcher knife is laid out. I grind the scraps, wrap, label and put it in the freezer. The moose legs I hang in my cool shop to age at forty-five degrees. All the bear is ground into burger and made into sausage. Two days of work. Put into perspective, two years' worth of eating meat, 900 pounds, with 300 of that being sausage.

I write in my diary:

Monday, September twelfth, 2002 Cabin burns

Still tired and depressed, trying to regroup. Trying to count my blessings rather than my losses. During the Tanana Fair, the Forest department sent someone over to inform me my Kantishna River cabin burned in the forest fire. About two weeks earlier, there had been a fire out that direction, but not very large. Seymour and I had flown over the area two days earlier and seen no evidence of fire. I was told the fire went on by us three miles away—not headed our direction, so we seemed safe. I have lots of swamp out back. The river is on two sides, with a lake on the third side, so pretty much saw myself as an island surrounded by water.

My neighbor on the river, Tom, asked me for a ride up the Kantishna, saying they had work as boat operators for the fire fighters. Tom told me he could get me work if I showed up, as the firefighters wanted locals with boats who knew the river. Something like $50 an hour. Tom had his boat up at the homestead, so needed a ride there. I gave the ride, believing there was a good opportunity for work, and to check on my own place.

When we get to the homestead, the fire crew is using Tom's cabin as an outpost. Tom ignored me, never said a word about helping me being hired as a boat operator as promised. My interpretation of his behavior was that he did not care one bit about my concerns, me having any work. He got what he wanted, a free ride to his cabin and job. I was rudely dismissed. I felt hurt, to comprehend what our relationship was, after being neighbors for twenty-five years. Not that we were ever close, or visited each other a lot, but I assumed we respected each other. I left without work, Tom got a free $200 trip.

I did a little work around the cabin. I have a bear damaged cache to fix and clean up. This takes four days of work, just to pick up the garbage and sort the salvageable. The fire has already gone by. I do not see much I can do at this point, or need to do to protect it from fire. I pull some dead grass and brush around the cabin. My chain saw at the cabin is not working, so I am not set up to do any major cutting and brushing. The fire had passed by, way out across the swamp and water. All of us land owners gave a sigh of relief.

To later hear that my place, and no one else's, burned to the ground is quite a shock. The place I lived all those years. Sounds like all my trapline burned, and all the line cabins. fifteen or more years of hard work. Gone now are the generator, the treadle sewing machine, the solar panels, all my reloading equipment and lifetime supply of bullets. Gone are all the things I stockpiled and purchased when I was so poor, at such great sacrifice. Gone are all the things I worked so hard at hauling out there by sled dog. Gone are all my traps and trapping supplies. All these things gave me security. Believing if anything ever went wrong, at least I had my homestead and everything I needed to live the rest of my life in peace. The feeling was of something to fall back on, the old life I know and trust in case this city life gets too much for me. Now I have no back up, no choice. This place was the sort people wanted a picture of, postcard material. I will probably put up something on the land so I have a place to stay when I go out, but it will have to be some sort of small frame place—a kit or something. This is all I can afford, both in time and money. I can no longer go out in the woods for months because the bills no longer come to a halt when I leave civilization. Water/sewer bill, taxes, phone, internet, heating bills, (most of those in society know the drill and the trap), keep on going, while the money to pay them has to be coming in. This is an ongoing struggle. Well… not struggle… as long as I stay constant, but certainly always in the back of the mind. What's it cost? Must be $800 a month just to stay afloat. Much of my business would come apart if I was gone a month to build a place. The interest is just not here. The land will be desolate treeless ashes and destruction. Yes it grows back fast. But give me a break. It will be at least four to five years before the ground looks like more than ashes with weeds on it. The surviving trees are a fallen, crisscross, jumbled mess that takes 'forever' to cut down. How long before there are pretty birches and real game around? Still unsure what to do. Tom calls as I write this, from his cell phone on the Kantishna. He says the fire was two miles away and calm when last looked at and overnight moved two miles and one finger moved across my place- missing everything else. The fire was hot and burned everything to the ground—melting even aluminum.

Later, "Didn't you have insurance, Miles?" Someone who knows me, I forget the name who.

"Insurance is paying the mafia for protection. If you can survive maybe five years without needing it, the amount you paid in insurance would replace what you insured. Anyhow—maybe not for everyone, but when you do it all yourself your own way, how am I going to get insurance? Insurance wants a carpenter to build, an electrician to wire, a plumber to plumb, an inspector to inspect it all." *The cabin has to be certified and on the up and up. No used stuff, no duct tape, or baling wire. If you heat with wood, forget it. First off, you need special steel, special stuff in the stove pipe, shielding around everything nearby, a distance between anything flammable and on and on. Forget it, in a zillion years, I'd never qualify. I'm the guy who makes the rules, not follows them.* Insurance isn't for those who zig while everyone else is zagging.

"But what about insuring the goods themselves, Miles?"

There is an assumption I believe in and trust society and the system, which I do not. Insurance is based on enough people paying and not collecting. That's how they make money. Possibly even a Ponzi scheme, where the last one holding the bag doesn't get paid, where money from the new investors are paying off the old investors. It also means proving the value, recording the items. I get it all used without receipts, and pay cash at garage sales. How do you insure stuff like that? Do I really want to report to anyone what I have, and indirectly how much money I have, etc. I don't especially want 'records.'

I don't especially have anything to hide, but often feel like a Jew in the days of Hitler. How much information would a Jew really want the Gestapo to have for any reason whatever? *99% of that information is not for your good, but the good of those who like to keep track, for whatever reason. Insurance is like warranties, they're good until you need them.* But you took it out of the box it came in, so that voided the warranty. I have not had a lot of good experiences to base a feeling of comfort and trust on. I take things out in the wilderness where most things do not belong, and where warranties are voided by passing time. I used to come to town once a year. The time limit is out, even if the item failed the first day out. Besides, the item got wet, got plugged into a generator, got used in a way never designed for, etc., etc. I tell the insurance company what I do for a living, then I'm in the greatest risk percentile. It's like Evil Knievel getting insurance on his motorcycle. Insurance is even pricy for sheep. When you are not one of the sheep, it's like dealing with Lloyds of London. So anyhow, so much for that subject.

It is not so much the loss of everything by fire as the wonder if I have God on my side, so to speak. On the right path. If you believe in Karma, if you believe in everything having a reason. How can I not ponder the fact that I have lost at least four homes in my life?

In some ways this 'could' be a semi-blessing in disguise (depending on how I look at it). "Well, this is a loss—but the loss was already here, or quickly arriving." I'm having trouble cutting it. My back hurts, joints hurt, my heart is not what it was (high blood pressure). It is not as fun to do all this as it once was. Or—I can do it with my nice equipment; but I am not stupid, I know what it means if I break down. I think I can no longer walk out, or do things like lift my snow machine, or logs; do strenuous work in an emergency. I have trouble cutting trail. When I get off the snow machine I have trouble walking in deep snow even twenty feet to set a trap, or investigate something. Eventually that would cost my life. I know it, and it concerns me.

I have all these memories I cherish, and am reminded of at the homestead, which is great, but sometimes the memories are clouded by present reality. The reality that I have several trappers trying to take over and move in on the trapline and succeeding. I no longer enjoy trapping as much. In the past, I needed to trap as a way to buy supplies. I saw lots of game. I was harvesting surplus, not affecting the population by a lot. To explain—there was as much wildlife in my area when I quit seriously trapping as when I started over twenty years ago. I saw the population go down, I think, due to a natural cycle, so I backed off trapping and let it rest. While letting it rest, others felt I was neglecting the trapline, and that I had given it up. If the trails are gone now, access to the fur is gone, no one can cross the country or has a reason to. I am left with good memories, no bitterness that someone took it from me. I have a good excuse to retire from it without having to look bad,

"Hey, it all burned up" not "Hey, I can't cut it anymore." As it was, the land was slowly claiming it all back. I couldn't find my old trails. Bears were getting the weak spots in the trapping cabins. The cache got invaded. I was trying to patch it up, but how much longer could I patch as the trees and grass crept in, rot took over, and the cabin got hit by fallen trees, and things rusted. It seems very little is forever. A time comes to move on. Not giving up as such, simply being with the wind, moving in the direction of change, taking advantage of an ever changing environment. This is a secret to true, long term survival and happiness. Little is to be gained by being stubborn and hanging on to something that can't be. You can't make the animals come back. You can't stop a forest fire. This is all part of the cycle. And so a new phase I already saw coming. I can remember, do my art, enjoy other rewards, and not die with the last animal low cycle. I had my time in the sun. I saw one to three animal high cycles. Few trappers can say they trapped seriously for over 20 years. It is enough. I must be satisfied. My heroes of the 1800s were legends if they made it as a trapper for five years!

A brief, curious question. *What if someone burned my place down using the forest fire as an excuse?* Two potentials. Tom had acted out of character, cold and strange. Never said he was sorry to hear I lost my place, offered help, nor given an adequate reason as the fire fighter boat operator, why he did not boat over as part of his job to save the place. The sprinklers and pump were in place and never turned on. There are reasons he might want me gone. He and Jill run sled dogs and are environmentalists, who do not approve of trapping. They were sometimes concerned their dogs might get caught in one of my traps. They like space, not neighbors. After coming to civilization, I got to talking to others who knew them and had business with him. Some did not like how he did business. To put it mildly. The sort possibly capable of burning someone out.

Then there is Vern, my trapline rival. He just acquired his parent's homestead not far away. I hear he was at his homestead during the fire. He had said nothing about that when we spoke. Would he not want me to know that? Is burning me out a way to get rid of a rival? It's a common enough way wilderness people deal with 'problems'. It had been a bold, aggressive and insulting move to set a trap right in front of my cabin. It had been incredibly rude, to say the least, to put up signs along the trail informing the world this was all his and to keep out.

The fire pattern was odd; it fire passed behind the homestead a mile away and kept going on by. I'm told the wind shifted and a string of fire fifty feet wide snaked a mile across a swamp to hit my cabin dead center. Dead grass five feet tall and twenty feet away did not burn. So I propose the question. What if the fire went the other direction, and began at the cabin? And never went across the swamp. That would make more sense. Unplanned, just an opportunity for someone. Not provable.

The thought only adds to another pin in my balloon. Or put another way. I can only scan disk and defrag so many times. There is always damage. Residual data that will remain fragmented on my disk. Taking from RAM and cache memory. Put another way. It takes energy to forget. We sometimes call it, baggage.

It's a harsh life with harsh rules. I've dished it out. Can I take it? A rival trapper long ago tried to take over. I cut trees down across the trail while he was out. He almost died. If he had, I would have felt, "Oh well, that's what happens when you want to play rough" *Those who live by the sword shall die by it.*

Dear Miles, I just heard a mukluk message over the radio from Carver to the sister that you found out that your house burned in the fire. The house that we helped build, and May's cabin. I bet if we were still living there the fire fighters would have made a better effort to save it. What wonderful memories. The cabin that Bob and I built out at Mooseheart burned in a forest fire in 1990. This latest news hit me like a ton of bricks. So I can imagine how you must feel. I have not told May yet, but I bet she would love to help build a better cabin.

God has a way of simplifying life. Sometimes it is drastic. My sod house is really deteriorating from so many vole tunnels. Just last week I was in the house and a black bear was on the roof tearing away the sod. My big rifle was in the cache and so I just banged pots and pans and he left. Now my dogs are back and I feel safer. So I am sorting and throwing away, giving away and burning items as I scrub out Cleo's place, and moving a lot over there. His place is still not warm for the real cold winters.

Oh yes, Jean Klein at age 82 has just returned to Manley for a six week visit. I wonder if I am supposed to ever own property and a real home in Alaska.

I had a wonderful time at fish camp at the Rapids. I love salmon.

My sympathies are with you, but I suppose hopefully most all your important stuff was in Nenana. **As ever, Karen**

The woman I lived with for four years at the Kantishna. Memories of raising her two children in the remote subsistence lifestyle, Karen.

Hello Karen!

Glad to hear from you. Yes, I heard the news about Kantishna at the Fair. It really took me back. I had been there only two weeks earlier with Jill and Tom when the fire first started, and it looked like it went on by us and we were safe. I do not know if the fire fighters could have done any better a job. Hard to know. Tom tells me the fire was two miles away on a weekend and there were few crew members out, so were out near Twin lakes where the fire front was. The fire burned two miles overnight.

Yes, most of my things are here in Nenana, but all my traps, the solar panels, generators, the old treadle sewing machine and just years of stockpiled survival things like tents, sleeping bags, stoves and antiques I had collected are all gone. I wrote about it in my diary I will enclose for you. May heard. I saw her at the Fair, she just called me.

I may get a cabin kit from Gurtler to put together out there so at least I have a place if I go out to get away! Everything got burned to the ground. The canoe is saved (it was on the pond) and the steel stove. Yes, things do not last forever. I wondered how the sod house was doing. It was meant to last 10 years and it has been a lot longer.

Oh, vendors at the fair took up a collection and got $500 to give me to help me replace what was lost. I thought this is very thoughtful, and shows I have friends who care. Not that it takes money to show it, but it means a lot when a vendor at the fair trying to make ends meet will part with some of that hard earned money to help someone out.

Well, I am tired, lots of emails and just got home. Now off surveying, lots on my mind still, so talk to ya' later! Thanks for writing! **Sunshine Miles**

"Yes, my place burned and this is not the first time, so I wonder—because it seems to me few others have had such events in their life."

My Nenana friend What's-His-Name, "Miles, maybe you need to go to church more often!"

I think about this conversation. Many feel this way, I think. (That I attract bad luck.) Yet… *is it also true, not many ever end up with their picture and story in the New York Times? How many ever get the recognitions I have had in my life with international compliments? One in a million? How many ever ended up with four homesteads? Few ever prove up and build on even one. I just got back from the state fair and realize there are not many artists who can come up with the inventory I have. Over 300 one-of-a-kind, hand done by the seller (which I would call 'positive energy'). So, mixed in with all the good things, all the good energy, maybe it stands to reason it is not all going to be good?* 'And? Maybe a lot happens (both good and bad) to certain types of people.' Sort of like 'you put energy out, energy comes back.' Some, many, even 'most' people do not make a comeback after one disaster.

The man who burned my homestead down on the Teklanika River told me, "My parent's place burned

I got over it, as I will get over this. It never really set me back a great deal. It's only material things. That matters, yes, but often, when we build and buy, we learn. And if we had it to do over again, we would do it different, more efficiently, maybe not get exactly the same material things we thought we needed at the time we got it the first time. But we had to get it and see. Of all the things I lost that I stock piled and thought I needed, when I think about it, how much can I not live without, or will affect my life a great deal? A few thousand dollars will replace it all pretty much. The rest is just good memories I haven't lost, and a lot of things I was busy taking care of I didn't need to hang on to. Not that I am glad or anything.

But? We lose things in our lives all the time, especially as we get older. At some point, we cannot see well, so cannot see the things we have. At some point, I will get too old to take the trip out to the wilds! What will become of all this 'stuff' I spent a lifetime acquiring? It will do as much good as if it all burned up. No one else wanted it. It was my junk, with little value to anyone else but me. It was old, used, outdated, even at the time I acquired most of it at garage sales. It's so far out no one could get it anyplace they'd want it. The cabin itself? Oh, all I really need there is a place to sleep, eat, keep warm and keep my few survival items free from the weather and animals. A sturdy eight x ten place would work fine. (?) I guess, or so I tell myself.

All my life, the wilderness was the sanctuary—the safe place, the environment that I understood and related to. This is the environment I turned to if anything went wrong. This was the world that would survive if the shit ever hit the fan. I believed it would be civilization that would fail, collapse, become chaotic, unstable, unsafe, an unhealthy place to live, or depend on for security and stability. In the wilderness, I look over a lifetime supply of firewood. I looked at stockpiled goods with a sense of peace and confidence that this is what would see me through in hard times. In the '60s, I believed society would not last. I believed we were in for troubled times. I believed there would maybe be a revolution, or else our country would get taken over by a country that understood the concepts of survival better than we do. I saw fat, lazy Americans complain about hardships, who had no clue what real hardship was, while those in other countries were exploited by us. I am lucky if I can save myself. "This was my survival from the stress and pain of seeing my country fall." What could I do about it anyway, be Chicken Little, and go around saying the sky is falling? Save yourself? When I got sick, the place I wanted to be was home in the wilderness, where I could get well. Society was crazy, unstable, unsafe.

So, it seems strange that it is the wilderness that wiped me out. That it is society I turned to for sanctuary. That I did not run to the wilderness to be safe. A very odd turn around. I had put so much energy into stockpiling all the things I thought I might need in the wilderness. Stovepipe, propane, food, fish nets, guns, reloading supplies cloth, thread, matches, candles, books to read, all the ways there are to have light, food and shelter. I had ten stoves, tons of sleeping bags, snowshoes and on and on. All acquired painstakingly at garage sales with no money, over a thirty year period. I wasn't trying to be a radical but, 'just in case'. The signs seemed (and still do) to be there. The lemmings ready to go off the cliff, with me determined not to be one of them.

Then time passed. I thought I had reached an age where I had lived a full life. Past my prime. I have friends, am set in my ways, and would I really want to go on without my friends and relatives? I chuckle—I am not about to be among those who repopulate the world after new sugar gets added to the rotten sourdough jar. At this point in my life, how much does 'personal survival' mean compared to social survival. So whatever fate society faces, I may as well be part of it. My outlook was different when I was young, and had a full life ahead of me. And hey, I reached a point where, without my heart pills, I'm gonna die anyhow. That in fact, without society I'd have died of old age already.

Where would I have been when my back snapped and I was out 'there' on my own with no 'operation' available? I'm alive today because of surgery. Even way back in the beginning, that first year when I needed to be rescued, where would I be if the air force hadn't sent a helicopter out? I'd have froze right there. So how can I talk about survival without society?

"Oh well!" Survival, happiness, success, is about adjustment. Survival is about the ability to change, not making a last stand, and being foolish. I wonder if any of us 'end up' where we thought we would be in the beginning? So often we come full circle, right back where we started, after all our efforts, a lifetime of struggle, after trying to get ahead, get somewhere, accomplish something, but in the end, ahead of what? Many of us give so much to raising a child, and the child ends up where? Or a business, a pet, or a project of some kind, and it ends up? Oh yes, it usually is as well we took the project on I suppose, but still, It's all quite puzzling. Maybe the journey was not so much about the things we struggled to accomplish, but just the fact we made a journey. *The older I get, the less I know. The road to wisdom is a long, hard road.*

Hauling wood for my heat.

CHAPTER NINE

ADDICTS, COP SETS UP A BUST, ART TRAIN, SILVER HAND

I t is time for another Chamber of Commerce meeting. *Where did the month go?* Someone I hardly know asks me about the Nenana Chamber of Commerce. The Nenana Chamber represents many of our businesses. One gal owns the towing business. Someone else is in charge of Crowley Barge Lines. The one and only store has a representative. I remain hopeful we can be effective, make a difference, and do something that makes it worth putting the time in. There is a feeling in the community that we are some kind of religious group! Good grief! Try attending a meeting and find out!

"Miles, who would care, who would be opposed to the Chamber?"

"Several groups of people in town feel they do not benefit from a strong Chamber of Commerce. The drug dealers and their clientele, and that includes alcohol." I explain.

The bigger established businesses that feel they have a monopoly, would rather not see competition. Maybe a third of the community is low income, collecting assistance of some kind. Many in this group tell me they are not dependent on the economy of the community. Worse, some feel a good economy might hurt them. Property taxes could go up if the community improved. An effort to clean up the neighborhood would mean no junk cars, no garbage piles, no loose dogs, and all that means 'change,' they may not be able to afford. Several of our members are in fact 'church people,' but that is not a topic at our meetings. I do not say anything about it, *but it seems to me that spiritual people would tend to be the sort who would have life goals higher than themselves on their mind. Many churches encourage individuals to help others. These are not bad traits to have, are they?*

"So what is the church problem, Miles?"

I relate one story that seemed to have hurt the Chamber's reputation a lot, "The Chamber wanted to get some information out to the public about an event we are putting on. One of the church members volunteered to put up fliers around town. They refused to go in either of the two bars to post on those bulletin boards. There are a dozen public places notices usually go up at. The bars are not among the usual places. I will not go in any of our bars myself!" I explain how I went into The Corner Bar once to use the phone and see if someone I was looking for was in there.

The owner, and tribal chief at the time, said, "What are you doing in my bar, white boy?" It is primarily a Native drinking crowd. I was unaware whites were not allowed, and banned from entering. I apologized, and said I would never try to come in again. I was in the bar across the street another time, and sat down to have a meal. This bar serves a basic burger, and there is a nice cable TV screen. It was winter, with only a few locals hanging out. I thought it might be OK to hang out myself and have a meal, watch TV, keep warm, have a social life. No other place to eat was open. One of the local Natives sitting on a bar stool refers to me as 'the great white hunter,' said with sarcasm. I overlook it usually, but that day he was drunk, giving me a hard time, to the extent it might have turned violent.

"I heard you did some art work on bear claws, Miles. Bears are sacred to my people! You have no right to kill bears or do art work with the claws. You are not Native." Followed by what he would do to me if he caught me, and that maybe he should do so right now. I'm in the bar minding my own business, trying to watch TV and support a local business by buying a meal. I did not finish my meal, and leave. The owner did not ask the Native to calm down, stop bothering paying customers. I did not feel the Native had a legitimate gripe with me. He did not come across as having any spiritual beliefs whatever. Nor did I notice anything he did that was positive for him, anyone else, or the environment. As far as I know there is nothing disrespectful I have done. Many natives I respect thank me for the things I do, even concerning bears, claws, and my art. The drunk's attitude is an overall attitude among only some Natives. The bottom line being, screw the white man and the horse he came in on. A majority who think this way, hang out at the bar.

The local I am talking to about the Chamber comments, "Yes, Miles, we of the inferior race have to keep our mouth shut if we want to live around here."

I only partly agree. I have many Native friends I admire and trust. But I have heard this sentiment, and see no reason to take the conversation this direction. I understand why there might be white, and or spiritual folks who refuse to go into the bars, because the bars are not safe enough.

"Miles, I heard the Chamber took over the Lions Club functions when Lions went belly up."

"Yes, something we never seem to get past is getting viewed as the Lions Club."

Later, I am at the Historical Society board meeting I am a member of. The Cultural Center is looking for ideas to propose to get Indian grant money. I come up with what I think is an important matter. This topic also involves the Chamber and City Council, as well as the Wellness Group. I have my proposal in writing.

Authenticating Art

Proposal by Miles Martin

Introduction: 70% of all art marked 'Native Crafts' is fake, not created either by hand or by a Native. 'Hand Crafted' is a vague and dubious term. Legally, any item that is altered 10% can be termed 'hand crafted,' and signed by the new creator. Imported goods can be created so much cheaper than locally made that it is common to see imported substitutes. It is not hard to alter products or change labels. Punishment is minimal. Alaskan created goods suffer more than most, because of our high cost of living and labor costs. In order to get more money for Alaska handcrafts there must be verification this is a genuine product. Many people do not mind paying extra money for local handcrafts, but do not like to be conned. Two Alaska programs, 'Silver Hand' and 'Made in Alaska' addressed this problem, but both programs have issues, and have lost funding.

Proposal: Set Up a computerized program, starting in Nenana with the Cultural Center, that verifies who the artist is, and all critical data connected to the artwork. The non-profit Totchaket Corporation runs the Nenana Cultural Center Gift Shop. This shop sells only local (interior Alaska) handcrafts and represents over 100 artists. This set up would offer a good pilot study for a larger program authenticating Alaskan and Native made artwork. We seek funding to set up a computer program. All our artists would be entered, with a basic set of questions answered. This information could be accessed by automated phone or computer twenty-four hours a day by anyone calling an 800 number, or via computer email. Artists would be sold tags to use on their artwork, which would have this 800 number on them, or web address, and possibly their own verification number that the computer would respond to when the code was put in.

Goal: The goal would be to set up some system whereby a buyer could verify who the artist is, where they live, ethnic origin, type of work they do, simple biography, and any past credits. The overall purpose would be to get more money for local crafts with more provenance or collector value to the customer. This will benefit the artist, the shops, and the buyer. This also gives credibility to local art and the culture it represents, basically verifying a set of beliefs and lifestyle 'What Alaska stands for,' and cut down on replicas and fakes.

My write up is copied and handed out to the board "We will lose our culture if we cannot verity and authenticate it. If it gets imitated, copied, distorted, blended into a mix, it will disappear." I have another paper to hand out:

Sharing Our Culture Through Art The Delta Grant

Totchaket is in charge of Nenana Alaska's Historical Society. This is a non-profit organization running a free Cultural Museum. To help support this museum, Totchaket owns and manages a gift shop on the premises. This 'Wheelhouse Gift shop,' is in keeping with our main purpose of preserving local history, primarily Athabascan Indian. The shop sells only local handcrafted artwork. Over 100 artists are represented in this gift shop. Biographies of our artists are displayed by the art, and our employees, and volunteers, are all local. They help pass on cultural knowledge to the public. Our organization was formed in (give date) . In (put in the date) we were able to build the museum shop, which we received a grant for (grant specifics). This nice log building is on the scenic and historical Tanana River. From the picture windows can be seen the Native Gravesite up on Toghettele Hill, the historical railroad bridge, subsistence fish-wheels, barges hauling freight, and in short, is a very good location. Tour buses stop by and quite a few individual travelers...And so on and so forth

Grant writing, and looking for funding seems to be a big part of a small village's survival today. *I had never realized before, that small communities are subsidized by the cities!* But it is more complicated than that. When I think about it, *Nenana cannot pay for its post office on its own! Nor can our tax dollars support our educational system! Nor could we afford fire trucks, rescue tools, the airport or the roads. Without outside help, we would be a vastly different community!* So I ask if this is fair to everyone else to subsidize us? Would an answer be to live within our own means? Thinking that, as an individual, I would not ask for a bigger house than I can afford, better food, better clothes, etc., and ask someone else to pay for it! So how is a community so different? What can a community of 300 afford?

Yet all Americans, our entire culture, seems to have more than it can pay for. This is very odd. So then, who is paying for it all? *Very puzzling. Who is subsidizing us if it is not 'us?' Who would want to and why? What are 'they,' what are those subsidizing us, getting out of it?* I wonder.

Many people I talk to say,

"Big government! It's about paying our bills in trade for giving up control!" If so, where is government getting money? I thought government was 'us.' It is as if I got a gift from someone. The first thing I'd say is, "Wow! Cool! Who is this from, how kind!"

Maybe someone says, "Your big brother."

This brings a puzzled, "But, how come he has never been over to dinner? Do I know this brother?"

"Well, no, it's more like an uncle. Your Uncle Sam. He supports us, gives us all kinds of free stuff." If I do not know this Sam guy, my thoughts go from *'what a kind person'* to *'what is this Sam up to?'*

The subsistence life I believe in and wish to stand for has a lot to do with 'taking care of yourself.' I have a conversation with someone local that makes sense. "We in the remote villages are not being subsidized, Miles!" The price we pay is the loss of the natural resources around us, on our land. Timber, oil, gold, fish, furs. We do not get paid. These resources are taken from us who own the land. In fact our entire state gets the short end of the stick, as Federal government and big companies treat us like we are not here. We are kept pacified by getting some perks."

I'm not totally convinced, but this is a better answer then I had. In the news has been 'Enron' bank scandals, shell game schemes with loans, interest, the stock market. This involves trusted names like Ralph Nader. I do not fully understand this world of high finance and lending. Along with this has been the theft of many retirement plans. Social Security going broke. If I think about all this, I wonder if ultimately the 'trillion dollars' I'm told it amounts to, ends up in the government's hands, at least the hands of 'those in charge' who run things. This amount I'm told, is about $50,000 per man woman and child in the country. If this is so, at least a few things make sense. This answers, "Where is all the money coming from?" I concluded it can't possibly be our tax dollars at work. The average citizen is not paying in this kind of money.

Not much time to dwell on that, as I shift from grant work to checking my emails for the business. I have more free time due to the money I make at the fair and Tucson shows. That is why I can now give more to the community, and even pick and choose the art orders and deals I want to make.

An email arrives:

HEY MILES,

I HOPE YOU DON'T TAKE OFFENSE BUT MY OLD LADY WANTED ME TO DOUBLE CHECK WITH YOU ABOUT THE SKULLS. SHE WANTS ME TO MAKE SURE THAT THE ANIMAL WAS NOT KILLED JUST SO SOMEONE COULD HARVEST ITS SKULL. I TOLD HER YOU ARE ON THE UP AND UP. I SAID YOU GET THE CLAWS OFF OF SKINS, LIKE YOU TOLD ME WHEN I FIRST DID BUSINESS WITH YOU, BUT SHE WANTED ME TO CHECK ABOUT THE SKULLS. I KNOW SHE WILL WANT THE SEAL CLAW FOR SURE SINCE IT COMES FROM THE NATIVES. I WILL BE SENDING A US POSTAL MONEY ORDER SINCE I DON'T HAVE PAYPAL YET. I HAVE TO SET UP MY PAYPAL TO SELL SOME TARANTULAS AND GECKOS BUT IT WONT BE UNTIL AFTER THE HOLIDAY SEASON. I ALSO WANTED TO NOW IF YOU HAD ANY TURTLE CLAWS. I THINK IT IS STILL LEGAL TO GET TURTLE BECAUSE GUY IN QUARTZITE HAS THEM. IF

I AM, LET ME KNOW AND I WILL QUIT ASKING YOU IF YOU HAVE ANY OF
THEM. **LATER, BASEYMOUR**

I seem to have more people asking me for legal advice, and concerned about the
ethics of it all. But in truth, if someone in this business were 'unscrupulous,' would
they say to a customer, "Yup, I make sure everything suffers before it dies, and is
illegally taken, you bet!" The responsibility of doing the right thing doesn't end with
spending ten seconds to ask someone with a vested interest in the sale. If you really
care, it takes more time to check things out.

I offer references for example. In this case it would not make sense for anyone to
kill a wolf whose hide is worth $600 in order to toss out the hide and sell me a $25
skull. That would be pretty stupid, I'd think. But how much is the purchase of a
skull contributing to the overall profits and harvest of wolves? Who knows? What
kind of promises can I realistically make? I do know if I do not buy the carcass off
the trapper, he shrugs his shoulders and tosses it in the woods for the maggots to
feast on. $25 barely covers his interest in putting it in a sled and hauling it across the
village to my place. It will take at least an hour of his time.

It's difficult to explain, or prove, an entire lifestyle to a customer. In many cases
the local trapping villager does not have money problems, even though he is legally
called 'poor.' Natives get government money they do not work for. Given to them
because whites took their land (oil, timber, gold, gas…). In return, we keep them in
poverty with enough money to… whatever it is they choose to do. Drink? Trap? The
only 'fact' I know for sure is, local trappers will throw garbage away before they
bring it to anyone, unless at least $25 is involved. It would seem odd to call deliber-
ately dishing out pain, 'good business.' Trappers and hunters I know take pride in
clean quick kills that are not messy. Bloody bruised hides and parts are worth less.
Much less. Suffering brings less profit, and takes longer. Time is money. How many
farmers get into the business so they can torture chickens? What an odd question to
ask in the first place, *where is your head at to wonder?* It would never occur to me to
wonder if I should be buying eggs, because the farmer might be torturing chickens.

I'm unsure about the seal claw part of this customer's wish list. It used to be
legal and no issue, but the 1972 CITES agreement changed some views on marine
mammals, as more animals get added. *Remember we learned the government has no
obligation to make it known that a law changed, nor provide an easy way to find out.* The
laws in place are getting more enforced. Where at first it was just something on the
books to be used in extreme cases of abuse, overlooked in most situations where
someone is being reasonable and not trying to get greedy or slaughter animals in
large numbers.

I have accumulated over the years a lot of things in trades. I know some subsistence natives, some up north Eskimos who use such items as seal claws in crafts.

They ate the animal, and have a surplus of claws, saved up over a long period of time. But like Baron asking me, I can ask the Eskimo if this is a byproduct of a subsistence lifestyle. I'm going to hear a "Heck, yes!" every time. Again, it just does not make sense anyone would go out to hunt seals, then toss out the meat and hide in order to sell me a few dollars worth of claws.

No turtles up here in Alaska, but now I trade all over the world. One dealer in Tucson sells all kinds of animal parts. He has alligator teeth, armadillo hides, butterflies, etc., etc. It's all a matter of what to invest in. The bigger a business I run, and more diverse the materials I carry and far afield I go, the less control I have over how materials are acquired at the source.

There are items I do not deal in because the potential for harming the environment to get these products is great. I decided not to offer trophies or 'record' anything. Nor things like bear galls that are worth a thousand dollars, when bears are rarely harvested for food. Or salmon eggs, when there are so many people taking eggs and tossing out the fish, that I have witnessed. I do not deal in any elephant ivory and hardly any white walrus. I do not want my business to get so big I do not understand my sources. How many people deliberately limit their income I wonder? Out of a sense of responsibility.

I have trouble picturing this Baron customer saying to his boss, "Could you pay me less? I'm trying to cut back on my impact on the environment."

Likewise it would be rude for me to ask, "Hey, Baron, is that money you pay me with clean? It's not laundered mob money or anything is it?"

So why is it not rude to ask me if my product is guilt free? I'm not angry, just curious. The best answer is to try to educate people. My mind goes to the subject of mammoth ivory I find myself that is so popular. I did not follow up like I should have on the 'Mr. Egypt' offer. The guy in Germany who is interested in gathering the mammoth tusks big time by diving through the ice and getting them off the bottom of the river.

I explain to Will when he asks, "I agree with you, Will, it sounds exciting all right. Right out of James Bond or something, or Indiana Jones. Diving through the ice in winter and pulling up a hundred tusks off the bottom of the river."

"That'd be awesome, Miles! I have some snow track rigs perfect for the job of getting equipment in!" Will wants in on it, a job offering lots of money.

I tell Will again about the guy's house. "So, I'm talking to this guy next to a water fall in his house. Birds are chirping in the bushes as if we are in an outdoor garden. But we are in a heated house, sipping brandy, with his lady catering to us like is done with the rich people. A Playboy centerfold kind of woman." I think of something else. "If our plan hits the news media, the area will never be the same again. Mr. Egypt gets in and out, makes his fortune. In return there is a public uproar, an investigation, more laws, and suddenly I cannot go there again."

"Miles, do you think there are really hundreds of tusks at the bottom of the cliff in the river?" That does get the imagination going all right! But more, something to speculate on, and dream about, then to actually explore.

"Maybe, Will. I'm sure we do not see even one percent of what is there and it does fall in the river. Logic tells me it is heavy enough material to not be going anyplace, and will go right to the bottom. It should last for years there on the bottom. Possibly the current keeps the bottom scoured, so it may not get buried, and tusks simply pile up." I have a theory, though, against the notion of a pile of tusks. "The cliff is falling and moving. Probably at the same rate the land is being gained on the other side of the river, since it never changes width. So the river is moving at the rate of fifty feet a year, or whatever it might be."

So if say, ten tusks fell in one year. Next year the river has moved fifty feet, and another ten tusks fall in that new fifty feet. If this has been going on for thousands of years, the distribution of tusks on the bottom is about the same as the distribution of tusks in the cliff.

I have a theory the tusks may be much newer than thought. Possibly a few hundred years old, not thousands. There is, in fact, a small island off Alaska near Russia where it is believed mammoths lived up to 500 years ago. This supports the theory I had before this new information came to light. Carbon dating is less accurate as we get into modern times. It works best on carbon that is old. In fact, some of the bones still have meat on them, so probably have not been under water and moved before. If so, my guess is they are fresher than we think. But anyhow, who knows? There are various theories proposed. But no, I never followed up with Mr. Egypt. Will still does not understand why, and I am not really sure myself. I tried to explain, but it ends up sounding lame.

On another 'money' subject.

I find it amazing to be in a community of 300 people in a remote area, with the equivalent of a New York address on the internet. It's exciting!

😀 :)

I do not think much about what it means. Just discovering a new tool and running with it. I have no business, legal, or bookkeeping background. I have a high school education. I do not know how to do a spread sheet, so keep a word document with bookmarks archived every month. This is my customer data base and book keeping records. I make what I know work. As it grows and expands, it gets more complicated. I just deal with it; figure out solutions I can work with and get the job done. I file customers by their first name and only for a month. If I can't close a deal in a month, the deal is probably not going to happen. If there is not a problem with a deal in a month, the deal is probably fine. At worse, I have to ask what month that was, and go back to that document. Sometimes I give a bookmark reference to another month so I can go find something important.

"See Baron March 2001," for example.

If a customer looks like a regular, I create a separate file. I can record their preferences and some pictures of their order. I wish I understood how to do spread sheets for matching products with customers and sellers from suppliers and such. Now there is just far too much data to ever enter into a data base. I will never have time. Hundreds, thousands of transactions, customers, and inquiries. All listed by date and name, with no cross-reference. Oddly to me, once I see a file, the content of the file comes back to me without reading much. I go, "Oh yes." The trigger is the file. Without the file I know no one. The trigger is not a name or a face, but visual in the sense of a file document.

"Miles, have you met the new Nenana cop?" Josh stops me on the street, and I do recall seeing a new cop in town. Josh adds, "I feel sorry for him. The drug lord has put a contract out on him, and a couple of people want to collect. I don't think the cop knows."

"I wouldn't want to be in his shoes, Josh. It's doesn't seem right, fair of the community to hire a well meaning person and not inform him of what he's up against, and let him figure it out on his own or be dead." I'm not sure how Josh feels. Anyhow, it is only a rumor about the contract. Neither Josh nor I know it for a fact. Josh is in a hurry to get someplace, so I wave good-bye.

As luck would have it, there's the new cop around the corner coming my way. I hesitate but say, "Hi. Welcome to Nenana." He smiles and nods and thanks me and asks who I am and what not. Since he seems nice, I add, "You are new here. I heard talk the local drug lord does not want you here, and has a contract out on you. I think a heads up might help you cover yourself. I can point him out to you if you like."

"Yes, in any area there will be people who do not want to see a cop around, comes with the job. I appreciate your concern." Karl, the new cop, takes a liking to me. As weeks go by, Karl lets me know he is having problems getting information and evidence on the drug business, and possible crime ring.

I notice robberies seem organized. Someone knows who is home, and who is gone on vacation, what they have, is what it looks like. There is daily crime, sort of background noise against the hum drum sounds of life. Just annoying to the community and, of course, annoying to those getting targeted. The normal stuff is $10 to $20 thefts. Enough to buy a bottle. This newer organized theft is hundreds of dollars.

Something else is happening. Goods are not turning up in the normal places, like pawn shops, so I think stolen goods are getting shipped out, or taken to Anchorage instead of Fairbanks. Could be the same people involved in the drugs.

Naturally, Karl wants to get a handle on what is going on, and find out some details. I'm surprised he is not getting more help! In general, I get along with a lot of different groups. The criminal element has no serious problems with me. Some in that group even trust me. Why? Unsure, but some guesses. The biggest is, I am someone who thinks and lives 'outside the box'. There are a lot of conservative people in a small community. I think more so than in the city. Nenana is a place that has not seen a lot of change, and few want to see serious change. New ideas do not go over well. So I'm an outsider from the standpoint of wanting to introduce new ideas. I am also viewed as poor. I dress like I am poor. I tend to be dirty by most standards. Many think I am into drugs. The wilderness life as I live it, is not considered romantic or desired, but as lower class. 'Lower class' has a profile and generalization associated with it.

The outdoors is a big great topic for villagers. Most get out in well outfitted, good looking boats, or hot, new, big snow machines, with new high powered custom rifles. Like weekend warriors! I buy used items from local poor people who live subsistence as I do. I buy and trade for moose antlers and fish. This is associated with being poor, destitute, of low morals, probably doing drugs, and stealing.

Often I am approached to 'buy stuff,' usually legitimate. Someone needs cash and sells me a fishing pole, a few traps, or a boat propeller they don't need. But sometimes the items are stolen. That puts me in 'that group' of people. So I explain it to the cop, "Karl, I might be able to go under cover for you and get the evidence you need to stop the crime and drugs here." He for sure needs some local help. I care about my community, and do not like seeing what drugs are doing to the kids and our culture! Karl seems interested. I add "If someone wants to smoke weed, drink, do any drugs in the privacy of their own home or at parties with other consenting adults, I think people have the right to do that. But I think it is wrong to push it on kids, endanger the innocent by driving, or steal to support a habit. I'd want a say so in whom I help bust and why."

Karl agrees that is understandable. I want that part made clear because in my view, if the police want someone, anyone, for any reason, they can be had. No one is so squeaky clean as to pass a close inspection. Look what the government of the time did to Jesus, for example, as perfect as you can get. I do not want to be part of busting people to get rid of political rivals, or to make a cop look good with numbers of arrests resulting in more funding or a career move. I do not even know all the angles. But if I have a say so as to the situations to be part of, I can be more in control of my personal view of help.

Dear Miles,

Thank you for contacting PayPal.

I apologize for any inconvenience caused. Your web browser must be configured to accept "cookies" to access most secure web sites, including PayPal. Below are instructions on how to enable cookies for various browsers. If your browser is not listed below, we recommend consulting the Help section of **your browser.**

I reply—

Drop my security to give you free, unlimited access? I have no reason to trust a company just because it is big. In fact it gives me reason to be most watchful. I noticed my question wasn't answered. I didn't ask 'how' to let you in, I asked 'why.'[1]

Dear Miles,

Thank you for contacting PayPal. We apologize for the delay in responding to your service request. Cookies are simply bits of information… A cookie often functions as a small, digital ID badge. With them, websites can "remember" who you are and what your preferences are. Without such a record, a website must treat you like a brand new visitor every time you visit the site.

If you have any further questions, please feel free to contact us again.

Sincerely,

Mike

PayPal Customer Service

I have not yet decided if I want PayPal, or any company to put something in my computer they refuse to show me, that tracks and gathers information. What good is a security program, if I have to disable it to let in the very people I am most concerned about keeping out? PayPal is nothing but a bank. I do not trust banks. Yet not having PayPal is hurting my internet business. I'm between a rock and a hard place. The very act of complaining might well get me on the 'person of interest' list. Like I have something to hide. 'They' might say, "Let's watch and find out!"

I did a computer clean up, and it looked to me like I was reading a cookie that was a megabyte. About the size of my book. I take my cue from others I talk to. Few see any issues, few think I have reason for concern about security. I say, "Well this whole computer thing I can compare to buying anything else. I buy a car. I lock it in my garage."

I get a, "And so? What is your point?" look.

"Let's say I buy a car, and I assume I own it. Someone connected with the car company wants me to give them a key to the garage so they can come in and take a peek. Check the car out whenever they want. No, I cannot be there and watch." I come home one day and there is a mile more on the odometer than I drove. Others are asking me what is wrong? The car is OK. "That is how it starts. In truth, the dealer could come in and do about anything." Borrow my ladder, lawn mower. I may not like to go out one day and have mag wheels, no more chrome carb, but a fuel injector, and now it is blue. I bought a red car. I may not even recognize my car, it is no longer mine. Leather seats. I hate leather. The side mirrors are not adjusted as I left them, the seat is not forward, the radio station is not the one I set my radio at. On and on.

"What's the problem?"

I put it yet another way. PayPal is a type of bank. So turn this around. I say to the bank, "May I have the key to your bank? Do not worry, I will not rob you." I'm to trust PayPal? Why? PayPal is not my friend. Others are not worried. So I hold my breath and gulp.

I'm not understanding about this cookie thing. Why can't my computer ask, "Would you like this cookie to come in?" Followed by, "Would you like to see what it is, where it goes, and see a report on when the cookie is retrieved, what's left in the traveling cookie?" That is what seems fair and honest. So what's going on? It's complicated? It's not worth the bother?

Indulge me. Maybe once I take a look I might go, "Oh, that looks ok, fine, have at it."

Instead I hear, "No! Absolutely not! You cannot see what we put in, or know when we do it! No, we are not removing it!" If I go to the store with cash, no one knows my name, what I bought before, and what they might con me into buying again. Who I am, is none of their business. I do not find their knowing who I am, convenient to me, just to them. *It is not worth getting worked up over, nothing we can do to change this.*

Most friends say, "What is the big deal, Miles, are you trying to hide something?"

"Maybe not hide, but protect, like my money, my identity." I also think these people would not be asking why, if they were Jews, black, a minority under a powerful oppressor. I think of something else, "I let my security down to let certain people in. This is like leaving my home door unlocked. They do not lock it up again when they leave. I open, close, lock, unlock and what if I simply forget? I do not know when you came in and left last, or how long you need the door unlocked. It is now easy to get complacent, have it be such a bother to lock and unlock my computer." *So it would be easier to simply leave it locked, and manually let friends in.* I frown considering this thought. "So I have a locked door, and someone not a friend demands me to unlock it. There is no option to talk on the front steps, meet in a public place. No, I must allow you into my personal space." *Interesting.*

I get to my emails.

Hello Janet! I am ready to send the horn you ordered. Hey ain't the internet amazing? Poof—there you were—poof here I am. Address at Pay Pal? Well I only saw Pay Pal had a message, but I never went into the pay pal. Should I tell you why? Well... (um, er) I don't like cookies in my computer. I got this program that takes cookies away, and the program told me I had several megs of cookies—stuff other people put in my computer without my knowledge or knowing what it is. So, Pay Pal will not allow us to access unless we allow them to put something unknown in our computer. That bothers me.

Talk to ya later and will get this package off Monday, let me know when it arrives, my guess is three to five days. I suppose, to get my money, I will have to let Pay Pal in my computer with a cookie. I think I can immediately delete it! (smile). Hopefully when you say "You're pretty odd, Miles!" you smile. **Sunshine Miles**

"Miles, I have a situation and can use your help." Karl, the cop, has come to visit my home and remembers my offer. He seems to want to know if it was all talk, or if I can walk that walk. "I need some local help. I'm pretty sure Beaver is a major drug distributor here in the village. His drugs are getting to the kids. Hard drugs. Meth."

I reply, "This does look like the sort of situation I'd like to help out with. I want this off the street and away from our children for sure." I have not heard Beaver is involved. But he knows me as local, and is one of the Natives who traps and provides me with animal parts. I never thought of him as smart enough, or having it together enough, to run a major drug operation.

"He may be armed and dangerous, so you understand. But we appreciate your help."

"Everyone in the village is armed and dangerous!" We both chuckle. So it turns out there is a team or someone from the big city involved in this. I do not know that part of the details. I'm assuming this is one of those 'need to know' situations. I'm told only enough to do my part, and it's all about trust. Fine. I'll do my part. You do your part. I'm to be reporting to some lady cop I never saw before, Helen or Ellen or something. Whatever.

She says, "So can you set up a buy and get in? We'll be giving you marked money."

I reply, "I only know Beaver a little and in another situation. I think for this to work, I'll have to make an initial contact and set it up. I can tell him I have friends coming who want to get high. Tell him I'm only an occasional user, so do not know much. But since we know each other I thought I'd come to him as someone who can help me out."

I need to know how big a buy to make, what am I asking for, what would be normal? I'm guessing up to a $1,000 deal would not be suspicious.

"I'll tell him the friends will be bringing the money and be doing the buying and no, I will not bring them around, but they will be handing me the money, I just want to know if we can make it happen because we all want to take off on the river to have a good time at fish camp." This Ellen gal agrees this will work, and for me to make the initial contact. Of course if Beaver figures I am setting him up, he'll kill me. I have no doubts about that!

I have to wait for the right time and situation over the next week. The rest of 'the team' has their stuff to do. I'm at least a little familiar with this process. Years ago when Gene was killed, I worked with a cop. Well.. before Gene was killed, trying to prevent him or me from getting killed. *We talked about that a lot in the other book, remember?* The news headlines called it "Homesteader War!" In that case, someone got killed. In my opinion, no one had to die. It was preventable. The big plan fell through.

The cop I worked with in the Gene issue, told me he could not get a hidden tape recorder.

"There is no money in the budget for a new one, and all the owned ones are in use." In my opinion, for the lack of $100, a man died who did not have to die. I'm optimistic this present situation will go different!

September; in the news yesterday—the plane crashes—terrorist attack on the Trade Center—Pentagon.

"Miles, have you heard what happened? Did you see that film footage! How awful! Who do you think is responsible?" There is wild speculation as to who might be behind this. All we know at first is, it looks like a pilot flew a plane in a suicide bombing and a second plane is involved. Details begin to be made public slowly, as they are uncovered.

"My gut feeling? Our own country is involved somehow. Perhaps indirectly. Or at least knew about it, could have prevented it, and did not, much like the bombing of Pearl Harbor."

"Why would you think that, Miles? How cynical and unpatriotic! Our own government blowing up one of its own buildings and killing civilians? Why!?"

"You asked me my opinion, and I gave it. The 'why' is more complicated. I am not certain we have enough freedom of speech to freely discuss such matters." *The future will show what might have been gained by the government in all this. More funding for security, stronger regulations? Did the government get our attention in terms of 'we need more money to protect you!'? We need more powers, fewer restrictions!* This is what I think will come of all this. A stronger, more powerful government. At the expense of fewer rights for the citizens.

The King's horseman ride in with crossbows. Merchants and citizens scatter in fear as raids are made, taxes are collected. They go right on by the village idiot, the joker. The jester is overlooked and outlives many kings.

Memories from another time, I suppose a book I read.

I ATTEND A WELLNESS MEETING. WIN = 'Wellness In Nenana.' A new group meeting once a week for two hours.

"Will anyone volunteer to lead us in prayer?" We have no leader, no positions. As with the pledge, I do not see what God has to do with helping our community, although I can see how spirituality is important. In the beginning, we had various spiritual views, and each who spoke was careful not to turn this into a church gathering. More and more it is a, "Praise the Lord, thank you Jesus" recital. I sigh as we all bow our heads. Yes, once I was asked to say something spiritual. So I did.

"Lord, you gave Janis Joplin that Mercedes Benz, that cool color TV, and her night on the town. That was very kind of you, and has been a great inspiration..." I went on a little bit, not much. How she took God's gift and changed the world as we all know it and gave her life.

Yes. It's the truth. I think a lot about Janis when I think of God. Her expression on that album with the pimp mobile, with the peace symbol on it, that plume of pink ostrich feathers. A little piece of Heaven, here on Earth. I always smile when I think of it. God gave her a gift—to sing, and sing she did. I consider it an inspiration to take whatever talent we have and go for it. But no. I was not asked again to lead us in spiritual guidance. I was honest about my spiritual beliefs. I thought we were all open minded here. I meant no offense.

Others had spoken of Native beliefs. Someone had brought a feather and talked about a prayer feather. Others had talked about a medicine circle. There was talk about sun Gods and wind Gods. No one who believed in Jesus expressed any offense, but somehow, I screwed it up.

"Does anyone want to take minutes?" Once again, I used to volunteer and enjoy taking the minutes! *I'm a writer!* Everything became an elaborate story. With exclamation marks! There were side comments and references and humor. Some loved it! But no. The majority just want dry monotone, "Record the facts please."

I was told there is a huge difference between editorial writing and news. I suppose they mean like between the National Inquirer and a real newspaper? But no. I do not see a huge difference. Only slight, if any. I don't get asked any more. I honestly do not think I act as I do trying to get attention. It's all honestly me. I'd like very much to be accepted for who I am, but 'accepted' is not the same as craving attention. Sometimes I interrupt people who are talking. My own view is, I simply do not have a sense of when people are done, and the flow of how conversation communication goes. There was little conversation or communication in my childhood. I had few friends to interact with. In the military at sixteen, where most communication was orders barked. I made no friends in the military, always on the move and sticking to the joy of work that I truly liked. Then out in the wilds alone for all those years.

I think someone is done with their point and I jump in. They are in fact not done. "Oops! Sorry!" Other times I wait too long fearing interruption, and then the subject changes. I missed my chance. I get in the conversation and take it backwards, my timing is off. It's a social skill I never grasped well. But yes, it bothers some people. Others are more tolerant. I am changing, learning, getting better. It takes time. Going from a hermit to civilized.

"Are there any updates?" Usually we make the rounds one at a time around the table and give community news, when the ball games take place at the school, the next City Council meeting and what is on the agenda, and what took place at the last meeting. There are updates from subcommittees about the upcoming heath fair and the sober dance. Usually I give a Chamber of Commerce update. It's my turn. This same information I offer to WIN, had been given to the Chamber of Commerce with no interest beyond, " It's probably a scam."

"Something I got in the mail addressed to the Chamber of Commerce." I clear my throat and explain to the group. "Here is an ad that is something called 'Art Train' coming to Alaska. Some organization is thinking of stopping in our community with a train. Sounds like they expect financial contribution, so it could be a scam, or business deal we can't afford, but wanted to share it as interesting."

The concept sounds intriguing. I pass a copy of the communication I received around the table for a dozen people to see. I explain how a traveling museum is on this train, with artists and art. The theme for this trip is Indian art. The stated goal and intent is to bring culture to communities that do not have it, expose fine art to small communities.

The overall opinion of the group is, "Ya, well, sounds nice, but who has time to follow up? It sounds like a lot of work. Sounds like we need to contribute more than we could come up with. The last thing we need is more bills!" I save the flier. I think I will personally inquire and get more information. It would be fantastic I think, to show the Native kids who are gifted artistically, that it is an honorable trade that can make money and get respect. They could meet successful Indians and talk to them. Indians who make money, and are respected, educated, and maybe an inspiration to our youth.

"HEY BEAVER. How's everything going? Been out moose hunting yet?" I'm over at the drug dealer's place. A typical government HUD home, log cabin, small lot, stuff piled all over the yard. Beaver has the door only cracked open, looking up and down the street before replying. Only guessing now, he was looking out the window, and would not have even opened the door except he knows me.

"Come on in, Miles. Yeah, my brother got a moose opening day!" Now I see the moose rack in the corner on the porch as I enter his house, and the door closes behind me. Beaver is suspicious, since I have never come to his home before. He wants to know why. This is not time to stutter, be nervous, or break out in a sweat. His shotgun is in the corner, handgun on the table in front of him. Typical enough in any house in the village, but it does mean he is able to make good on any threat if it comes to that.

"I got some guys who want me to take them moose hunting coming up from Michigan. I said OK before I knew much about them. Friends of some other guys I took out, so figured they'd be OK. Well still OK, I guess. Only I just now find out they would like to get hold of some party drugs so they can have a good time. I'm not big on drugs and hunting at the same time. But it's their hunt. I want them to be happy. Sounds like a celebration getting away from the wives. They do not want beer. I figured you might be able to help me out. I do not even know the various choices or prices but they told me they had $1,000 budget."

I figured this line was the best approach because in truth, I do not know much about drugs. If I pretend I do, want some, and Beaver asks specific questions and I do not walk the walk I talk, I'm dead. Also, I do not want to be in the situation where he wants me to test the drug first, before I buy it. There is no way I'm testing any of that nasty stuff! So Beaver just stares at me with a mean look for a little while. Seems to make up his mind and breaks out in a smile.

"Sure, Miles. You got the money on you?"

"No, the guys are not here yet, two days. I just did not want to look stupid in front of them and make sure I had it all lined up. My guess is they do not know me or you that well, so it might work out for me to come by and get maybe half, like $500. That way they can test it out before we go out on the river and I can come back before we leave for the other half." I'm not sure how drug dealers and users usually work. Guessing it can come down in any number of ways, depending on the variety of situations. Guessing having all the money and all the drugs at one time for a first time is not common.

Knowing this group of guys in general I can assume it will be a cluster F=+@%k. So and so needs something for this other guy, and this third guy has half the money he got from his mother, while this fourth guy will come by after he sees his girlfriend, after they turn their food stamps into dollars. With a, "By the way do you need any steaks?" Tossed in as part trade-payment. Who has the drugs, who has the money, and who is on first, no one is quite sure of.

So yeah. I think this looks good, an easy mark. Couple of rich out of state hunters never been here before, do not know Beaver from Adam. Idiot, clueless Miles wants them to have a good time. Isn't that sweet. Yup, Beaver buys into my story. I follow it up with my village idiot grin.

"So $500 in two days, call me first!" So my part so far is going well. I relay the latest to my contact. This Ellen-Helen-whoever-red-hair-cop. I have not thought it all out. The bigger plan is up to the cops. Like, when the big bust comes down. I visualize I hand over the money and step aside, and the cops come storming in with guns and Beaver realizes I set him up. Well, no problem, he goes to jail. But he is going to be telling his buddies. And some day he is getting out. But I assume all this, is details cops deal with every day. They'll have a plan. Protect me. I do not know what that plan is yet.

Honestly, I am not impressed. I tell Josh, "I could stop all drugs in Nenana alone, by myself in a week if I chose to, wanted to."

"Yeah, right."

"We know who the drug dealers are, right?" He nods that he guesses.

No one wants to admit it. "So I break in their house." I break in, find the drugs, and substitute the drugs for crap. Dealers do not know they have been broken into and that the drugs are crap. Mr. Dealer begins selling. Mr. Customer is pissed. 'Hey Man, you ripped me off I want my money back you A%$# hole.' Followed by, 'Who you calling a ripper bro! You'all want a piece of this?' The conversation progresses. Use your imagination. Mr. Dealer goes to his supplier and says he got ripped off. Imagine.

"I'll give you three guesses what happens and the first two guesses do no count." *Can you spell problems?* Sit back and watch the fireworks. May be some mysteriously dead people. For sure Mr. customer is no longer trusting. No longer trusts the local dealers.

"Use your imagination how that goes." No one knows nothin about nuthin.

"You have a devious mind Mr. Mau-tin"

"Just call me, Wild Miles." I wink. However civilization both wants and needs drugs, including business people. It's a necessity, so I have no interest in stopping them. Just tone it down, keep it within acceptable limits. *I'm in it for the game, not out of any moral conviction.* "Well, I would not mind being on the 'in' with the local GESTAPO. You know, among the protected." In truth, getting along with the local Mafia is a good idea as well. *Same as the poh-lease do.* "Yeah, so I choose who to hit. Beaver is on the outs with the mafia." Yeah, in general, organized crime tells society's hired guns who to hit.

In the deep snow, this moose had trouble moving fast. I was able to snowshoe right up to take a picture!

CHAPTER TEN

MAKING MONEY, AN ART TRAIN ARRIVES, LEARN
TO DRIVE

The Wellness Group talks about alcoholism a lot. One driving force in the group is the Mental Health and Addictions Group. We talk about building halfway houses, sober houses. We do drives to get food to feed these people and have, 'free cycle,' where we give away free stuff like clothes. What I notice is, the people who have it together show up with free stuff to give away, and leave with someone else's free stuff. No goods seem to end up in the hands of the truly needy. My opinion of 'why,' is a class distinction. 'They' do not mingle with 'us.' There is a vast difference in how we each live. What does work? When one of the gals, 'Witty'- physically goes to the drunks hangout with boxes of food and clothes, then hands it to them. No lecture no questions.

She describes life among them—so all at WIN understand. Empty houses where the power and water have been cut off because no one paid the bill. They crap in buckets or plastic bags and stack that up frozen in the yard in winter. I have seen a few drunks going around with five gallon cans, begging for a little fuel oil to make it through the night. What does a community do with people like this? We are told this condition people get into is now considered a disease. Like any disease, does it help to cure someone by putting them in jail? *Well really any crime is a disease, because isn't any deviance an aberration, a disorder, break from 'how it ought to be'. Do 'well' people act in such non survival ways? But let me sort this out.*

I have known people like this in my life, in the days of living under a bridge and at the Salvation Army. Standing in food lines, work lines, talking, sleeping with, getting to know such people. *Wait! Was I by chance one of them?* I see a problem, but am unsure if 'feeling sorry for them' describes how I feel. There is a quote I think is true.

"If we gave everyone a million dollars, and left everyone alone to their own resources, in a year, the poor would be poor again, and the rich would remain rich." Giving away money or food or goods and tossing it at the problem is not a fix. Nor is education. I do not have a solution. I have not seen any solution. I wonder if there will always be a percent of any population that just can't cope, can't make it, is weak, and will always turn to cheap answers like drugs, stealing, and dysfunctional behavior. Some may just not be bright enough to survive. They need to be supported by society. Other times, I think it does not makes sense that 'addiction' is about just the weak and stupid. Some of the greatest minds in the world have been in the bodies of addicts. I confess, I do not get it.

I do believe, as a society, we create the drunk, because it is so profitable! Then we make money again treating the drunk! Well, someone is making money. Perhaps society at large loses more than it gains. Do we truly want alcohol and drugs to go away? I think a majority do not. *So in the big picture, where does that leave us? Where does it leave the do-gooders?*

Many of those 'problem people' I deal with, enjoy their lifestyle. It is always party time. Hardly any responsibility. There is always (so far) a meal and place to sleep. No need to get fussy about those details. Some are even happy, laugh a lot and... well... just do not wish to change. Welfare, food stamps, free stuff, and enough people feeling sorry for them to get some perks now and then.

"The problem, Miles? You get those kinds of people hanging around and they rob you. You get caught up in their game. You being more part of the problem than part of a solution."

Maybe. I mention the art train ad. How some of our youth could be affected in a positive way. Like, offer an alternative to drugs. "I meet a lot of the community artists, and have been the buyer for the Culture Center. There seems to be a feeling among the young Natives from the villages, that art is something Grandma does to keep busy; beadwork. But she is poor. Who can make a living as an artist among us? Schools seem to want to absorb the Native into the white culture, not educate them so they can go back to live in the village they come from." I say, how I think this is part of a community issue about our community being well. I know half our community is Native.

I'm told, "Talk is cheap; the one who brings something up should be the one willing to be in charge. Are you willing to do that?"

This concept is one I am seeing myself, and agree with. So often there is a complaint, or words about what we ought to be doing. It usually means 'you should do this' and the reply is, "What's this 'you' stuff?" An offshoot of, if we point out a problem, we need to offer a solution. Fair enough. I will be in charge, and get more information. Mostly find out if this Art Train is a scam.

I write an upfront letter to Art Train.

Dear Art Train:

Saw your ad for possible visit to my community addressed to our Chamber. Looks like it might be a scam, so I am here to find out.

There is a mention of a stop in Anchorage and other large places who can afford to pay you. Yet your mission statement says 'Small, poor communities we can introduce culture to.'

So is this about the money, or is this about your mission statement? In terms of your mission statement, Nenana is perfect. We are a Native village. This is Native art you are showing. We have a student living center which houses about eighty Native kids, from a dozen remote villages in a dormitory setting. Showing art from successful Native artists, with the chance to talk to the artist could be a wonderful education and inspiration.

Nenana has a train stop right on the tracks you will be traveling along if you come to the Interior to Fairbanks. We do not have any money to contribute, but could probably feed you and help out in other ways.

Miles Martin—Nenana Chamber of Commerce

I mail this off. We shall see if this is about a mission statement with meaning, or a scam about the money. The flier from Art Train reads, "The money comes from rich people who want to make a difference."

The city of Nenana got the same flier as the Chamber, as well as most communities along the railroad. Who is responding? I find out - 'none.'

The more involved in the community I get, the more I care. The more I care, the more involved I get. I want to 'do something' meaningful, I'm not just one of the talkers! *But Remember Canada!* Yes, my unconscious is always reminding me how things went then. 'But we were young then!' I reply to myself. I did not want to get involved again for a long time! Yet my natural personality is to care, and get involved. I simply… well… sometimes lack knowing what that looks like. *Define help!* Not everyone wants help on my terms! The Wellness group is not 100% behind involving the police or any government group. There is talk sometimes of 'taking care of ourselves'. *But how does that look?* We talk of building halfway houses for the big picture. *Take care of our own, fix people back up. OK. Well. Let us watch and learn then. Stop jumping in and volunteering for things I do not understand!*

"Hı Karl, what's up?"

Karl calls me over from his patrol car. He's thin and tall. I watch him unwind as he gets out. "I have a situation you might help with." I have been sort of infiltrating the drinking crowd and local theft ring. I have been buying stuff I need, while checking to verify if it is stolen. In the hopes of being able to set someone up who is doing big time ripping off, and help make a bust. I guess. Sort of. I mean on the one hand I get cool stuff cheap. Or, I started out with a good thought. *I am not going to just hand out money to the destitute and needy! What kind of 'help' is that? I did say I would help out by giving them a job, or working for the money, or "Sell me stuff you have that I need, that you have no use for." Like moose antlers from fish camp! In this way I am not an enabler, but offering a chance to have some pride and sense of having earned the money.*

But we got creative. "What else do we need?" Well! Let us together go down a list! Over the past year I have been offered guns. A stolen gun is a federal crime, something substantial. If the gun was used in a crime, all the more interesting. I have been feeding the serial numbers to another undercover local person I work with. Or he is an ex cop now, I think 'private detective.' I assume, working with the police and his former connections. I assume Karl's interest has to do with a hot gun off the list my buddy has been reporting. But no.[1]

"There is a new shipment of cocaine in Nenana. We think we know who it gets to, but we need proof and a buyer to step in."

"But Karl, I do not think I can get in with this drug group. It is pretty well known I am straight." This was not always true, so there have been some changes in how the community sees me. I'm thinking of how the previous fiasco went!

This Helen-Ellen-hot-shot-cop, had replied to me, "It's all off. We can't get the marked money for the project. Sorry!"

That's it. 'Sorry?' That's all she has to say is, sorry? I put my life on the line for sorry? *You did not hold up your end of the promise. Here we go again.* Now Beaver wants to know what happened with my needs, and the deal we had set up for drugs. I'm going to have a gun in my face trying to get out of that one, and the cops are 'Sorry?' So yes. I understand what the more 'civilization wise' community members mean when they say the heck with the cops. And let the lowlifes die, let the cops beat them up. But still. It would be nice to get along with the cops. That seems sort of necessary as part of survival. I do not blame our local Karl. He seemed put out with the outside help he was promised. He was as let down as I was.

Karl is 'one of us.' A local who cares. For all I know, the bigger drug dealers in town 'got to' the cops, paid them off, made a deal. Are as much a part of the problem as the solution. This Helen (Hell-and) cop treated me like a low life snitch. A criminal myself, getting involved for some crooked reason, like getting rid of my competition, or in trade for immunity of some kind on a pending charge. Like it is beyond her comprehension that a citizen in my position might actually care about the community. And be willing to take risks for no other reason than for the good of my community. One of 'us.' Instead I was treated like one of 'them.'

Karl understands how I feel, and why I am hedging and back peddling. He explains, "I am in a delicate situation. You know Phil, one of the Evans kids?" Karl goes on to explain he'd rather not bust this kid. But a big sting operation is in place, about to come down. This Phil is in on the fringes. Sort of an OK kid. "And has a girlfriend he is about to marry, who is pregnant." So Karl would like to give Phil a chance. Maybe save his marriage, and have a chance to be a father. Karl wants me to pass the word on, privately, to try to save this kid. Let him know he needs to clean up his act right now, as a big bust is coming down. Not give him time to pass the word to anyone else, but take care of himself. I agree, this is not a bad kid, and it would be a shame to lock him up. A warning might scare him into straightening out.

"Thanks, Karl, I'll pass the word to Phil. Wait till after six tonight? OK. Good luck on the bust." At ten after six, I go visit the Evans family. I work with Phil's mother on a community committee, and consider us friends. I do not agree with everything the family does, but prefer to be open minded. How do I put it? Small communities have different issues than larger cities. Issues that get handled by different methods. Rough riding over absolutely everyone is not how we do things. We can afford to be more patient, keep an eye out, protect ourselves, bring about change from within, through peer pressure and such. Anyhow, I let the mother know, since Phil is not home.

"I got word there is going to be a big bust. The cop would like to give your son a chance to get his life together, so a heads up a bust is coming down tonight."

I assumed I'd hear a grateful thanks. Instead she comes unglued. "Who is accusing my son of being involved in drugs? I want to know! That so and so cop! I am going to sue him!"

Oh great, that's all either the cop or the son needs. 'Try and help out, do a favor, and this is what we get?'

Mom says, "He has no right to accuse my son!"

"I think the cops are past the accusation stage. They have a search warrant, evidence, witnesses, and it's coming down. I'm only the messenger. I have no intention of saying anything to anyone. I care about your family and Phil. You are good people."

The father was tribal chief for a lot of years, invested a lot of money in good things in our community. She volunteers for many things, created the communities first web page voluntarily. Some of her children are good citizens. I do not know the situation that is behind a wayward son.

This incident is the end of our friendship, and all dealings, forever. There is no forgiveness for suggesting her son is involved in drugs. I'm sorry now I tried to help. *Years later Phil is involved in a stabbing in a parking lot where someone dies.* Maybe going to jail is what the son needs. Oh well. Life can be very complex sometimes. I am not great with various social situations. I suppose more street wise people would have known not to get involved. *Let the son of a bitch druggy son go to jail. To hell with his poor wife and unborn child.* I do wonder how many times help, forgiveness, intervention, of this sort actually woke someone up and good came of it?

A MONTH LATER, Karl stops me on the street. I am riding my three wheeler and I stop, smile, and chat. Karl tells me I need a license to ride this on the street. I'm shocked and puzzled. Every ten year old in town zooms up and down the roads on four wheelers, snow machines, etc. It is how I get my mail, and get around. None of the kids have licenses, and some drive recklessly! No one seems to care.

"Why am I singled out, when I drive safe?" In truth, the exact law says no license is needed within village limits, because these are not state maintained roads, and the village has no laws concerning the subject.

"Miles, someone complained and named you specifically, that's why."

"But I drive safely, there should be no reason to complain."

"Yes well, I know, but Phil was arrested for driving his four wheeler with a revoked license. He was also drunk. But the family claimed discrimination against Natives. Saying that others who were not legal were not touched. Saying we are picking on Phil. It's part of my job to not discriminate. I have been called on the carpet, so now it is a sticky situation, Miles, your name specifically came up." He goes on: "What is the reason you do not have a license, Miles? It's pretty strange for a civilized adult not to have one." So now it is illegal not to have one? I hem and haw and have no answer. It looks to me, like pay-back for getting involved, much like Canada. "Well get in, Miles, come with me, we'll go get your license."

"But, but, but…"

"Get in." So I have no choice. The cop tells me to get in and I do. "We'll go to Anderson, where the DMV is. I'm guessing you already know all the answers on the test, it's normal stuff everyone knows." So Karl drives me in the cop car all the way to Anderson forty miles down the road. We walk in, and there is the test. No time to think. I'm handed the test. I take it. I pass. He is right, it's 90% common sense stuff. OK, I pass.

"Now the driving test." Karl gets me in the cop car. We go to the airport runway, and then he turns the wheel over to me. I drive. He says, "A child is in the road!" I slam the brakes on. The right thing to do. He asks me to parallel park between barrels. It's easy. I have good eye-hand coordination. It's the first time I have ever done it, and it's easy.

"Now the highway." We get on the highway and I drive the speed limit. It is so much easier than my 1986 loose steering truck! The cop car is a breeze. We pull back into the DMV office, click a picture, turn, click again, smile. I'm handed a license. I never even had time to think about any of it, or make up excuses, or worry, or any of that. I blink, and poof, here is my license. First time in my life. It was easy. *How could it be so easy?* It was all in my head, I guess. I was raised to believe I couldn't do it.

"Well that's over with, Miles, and I will not have to pull you over again!" There is no talk of Phil or the bust and how it went. I assume things are on a 'need to know' basis. I consider it impolite to ask. I am not in a position to have insider information. Trying to help someone out turned out to be a big mistake. *At least in this case.*

"I'm still in hopes of being of help with stolen guns." I'm in a quandary on that subject though. I have acquired three to four legal guns. I can keep them or sell them. Hunting rifles and shotguns, not the sort criminals want. In most cases, a local drunk has something he does not use, and wants drinking money. Most of us locals own a dozen guns. Many drunks will sell a $300 to $500 item for $100 or less. Karl does tell me I can't be a pawn shop, or I get in trouble. Drunks want to get quick cash, then come back later and pick up their gun or whatever they got a 'loan' on. Reality is, they will never have it together to have that $100 (plus interest if it is a pawn shop they deal with). Or at least, so far, no one has come to me with any money wanting anything back.

They want to leave something and tell me at the time, "Can I come and get it when I get paid next Tuesday?"

I have to tell them what the cop said, "No. I can't be a pawn shop. I can buy something if you want to sell it." I make sure to say this, because any of these drunks could be wired, trying to bust me. Because if I am seen as a problem to organized crime people, this could be like being the only one who has to get a driver's license to drive on the city roads. I could be put in my place by getting busted for being a pawn shop without a permit.

Sure, it helps me out to get a $500 gun for $100! Or a box of movies for $5, or a boat propeller worth $300 for $50. I reason that if it is not me buying, it will be someone else. They will get their money and a drink someplace, somehow. *If they do not get it legitimately, they will steal it.* Yet several problems are developing over time.

If someone got robbed, something stolen, they call me and ask if I have it. Then ask if so and so brought me such and such to sell. Often a spouse or parent. Family members stealing from each other is a way of life. One family member might be sober and working, supporting a drunk or two or three, who steals from the family. I do not want to be part of that. Nor do I want to be getting calls asking if I have this or that. If I do, then what? What a mess. The entire family is dysfunctional and often violent. Something needs to change. 'These people' need help, *but in what way, and what will help?*

I explain to Josh how it all started. But think I already told him a hundred times! "In the beginning, someone came to me and wanted a free hand out! Needs cash for 'whatever'. I told them each time they could earn the money. I'm not just giving it away." Josh sighs. We have all run into that. "So I mention they have a fish camp. Spend a lot of time on the river and in the woods. So why not gather moose antler sheds for me. I will buy them!" This made sense to me. Teach this person to work. Maybe give them ideas for how to make a living and stay sober. Thinking, *They drink because they are depressed, do not think much of themselves, and 'working,' could give them their pride back!* "Problem is, Josh, they started stealing moose racks from relatives and out of neighbor's yards to sell to me. They told their friends I am a buyer and have cash. Out of the woodwork comes a line of drunks offering me who knows what. Used movies, broken wood stoves, anything they think is worth a bottle."

My conversation with Josh ends. He thinks we should just let them die in the street. Pretend they do not exist. Because that is how he was treated when he was a child. Drunk parents, him living with the sled dogs in a dog house to keep warm. "Nothing but trouble Miles, you'll find out the hard way!"

Except? "I feel this is as much a social problem as an individual problem. A problem we are all a part of and helped create. We are all partly responsible!" I have said this as well a hundred times! "First society creates alcoholics and dependency on drugs and pills. It's big money. We all like the profits. We advertise how much fun you can have. Or how the drugs help you, and go see your doctor to get addicted." Some users can handle it. Even most. But some cannot. "Oh good!" And explain how great that is. "All kinds of wonderful programs to help with your addiction!" Jobs for many! A whole government agency on mental health and addictions. Prison is a multimillion dollar industry with three fourths of those in prison there because of drugs. Anyhow, I see Josh is not listening, so on a different subject...

I get my winter moose. I am able to drag it home with the four wheeler and hang it up in my heated, well lit shop to skin it out and take care of it. Just at this time, one of the local drunks comes by. A Native whose family I know well, whose parents I respect a lot.

"Hey, Miles," long drunk pause as he thinks. "You got any money you can spare?" He has nothing to sell me. He used to sell me moose antlers he had at his fish camp in the woods, all kinds of antlers that had been lying around no good to anyone, rotting, getting chewed on by critters. Jonny is one of them who provided me with a lot of antlers over the years. But all his sources are dried up. As the alcohol ate him up, he was less able to get out to find antlers in the woods. He had tried to sell me his only boat and I had refused.

"Jonny, you need this boat for your hunting for food, getting fish. What will you do if you sell it?" If I was totally selfish I'd buy it. Heck yes, it's a good deal – he only wants $500 for it, it's worth $5,000. I had the $500 cash too, but I cared enough about him not to take away something he needs. But he sold it to someone else, and "Oh, well." Now he is down and out, a once proud hunter-trapper I respected, or more, his father, and feel for the family. He is a member of my community. I care. I want a healthy community.

"Jonny, I am not going to just hand out free money. But if you want to earn it, I have a moose here I shot. I'll pay you to skin it and take care of it for me. You must know how. You have got enough moose yourself in your life." I tell him it should be no more than a five hour job, and if he did good, I'd pay him $100. *My back is sore. I can afford to pay someone else to do the grunt work.* I'm trying to adjust my lifestyle to being out of my prime. Learn how to pay others to do the hard work. "I have more money now. I can afford to pay for help."

I'm confused. It is my understanding, that to hire anyone, I need to pay into workman's compensation, have insurance, file papers, keep records, and on and on. I suppose, consult with a lawyer. I'm puzzled. When I was growing up, I had jobs, learned responsibility. I mowed lawns, girlfriends did babysitting. The young helped out the elders and got paid a little bit. Not a lot, but it was like on the job training. This work taught the young ethics, work skills. Sure, I suppose it was slave labor. So what? That is all kids are worth as workers. It is often a financial loss to have children working for real wages. It would be like paying them to go to college. We pay them a little, and teach them how to mow a lawn, as they ruin our lawn mower. It's part of public service. That's how it was for me.

My first real job at fifteen, I took a greyhound bus out west to work the summer on a ranch. No social security number, no workman's compensation, no insurance. I earned $300 for three months of backbreaking dangerous work. I broke their truck and it needed a new transmission. I had to be taught everything. I was driving a combine, and truckloads of wheat to be sold. *So knew how to drive.* No one suggested I needed a license. No one suggested I was under age. In the big picture, the experience effected the rest of my life in a positive way. It was worth paying college costs, thousands of dollars. Yet getting paid was just so uplifting for a fifteen year old, and being treated as a real worker like an adult, and getting called 'Mr.' Well you cannot even buy this! So this has to do with a wish to pass this on.

"Sure, Miles no problem! Let me go home and get my own knife and stuff I need." So this is my plan. *No free stuff,* but maybe ways to earn some money. I'm not going to pay top dollar, I'm not rich, but to where Jonny is happy and I am happy. If this guy earns his money, maybe he can get some of his pride back? Who knows. I am not an expert on drunks or mental problems. But I'm trying to care, and find a solution to a community problem. My back is sore and I will be glad to have help with this moose.

An hour later, here comes Jonny with two of his buddies. Hmmm. Here comes beer. Hmmm. His two friends are belligerent, with 'white man' this 'white man' that in their speech. How my race owes the Indian. How the moose is really theirs, because I got it off land the white man stole from the Indian! All three drunks want to get $100 each. I should in fact give them the moose, that is what would be fair.

"Yeah, right!" I have to explain the job is worth $100. "This amount is plenty fair. The job should not take more than five hours for one person, that's $20 an hour. I am not paying $300. That would be ripping me off." But they think I have the $300. That is all that matters. Now they get threatening. As if maybe they will just take all my money, and not skin my moose at all. If I have the money, they should have the money. I'm curious where they learned that my money is their money?

I hold my ground and tell them "No." But now all are grumbling. I bring them in the warm shop, turn the lights on, and give them some plastic to set on the cement floor. Some bags are pointed out for trimmings, and a box for scraps for dogs.

"And I want the hide, so try not to cut holes in it. The hide can be in two pieces. I know that makes the hide removal work easier." I have other things to do. For $100, I am not going to also baby sit.

"You guys know what to do. I want to save the hide, put it over there." I feel I have to remind them. "And the quarters I want over here" and I point. "Do not get the rib cage dirty, I want it as well, and take the tongue out. The head can go in the cart to get hauled off later, unless you want it." And I leave them to the job.

About three hours later I come by to get a tool I need, and see how they are doing. They found one of my radios, and had spent half an hour trying to figure out how to get it to work, and find cords to hook it up. Beer cans are lying around, music is playing loud. My skinning knife I have had twenty years is bent, and has a huge hunk of steel missing. Someone was hacking and prying with it. Like someone did not know what they were doing. Like an amateur would do. People who know how to skin moose, know there is little prying needed if you understand the joints and where to take the moose apart. One of my doors is torn off the hinges. I am unsure why.

"No sweat Miles! You can fix it easy, you are skilled!" There are other broken things, moose blood all over, fur all over, and it is a mess that will take more time to clean up then it would take if I just skinned the moose myself. It appears to me, they are not capable of skinning a moose. *How can this be? They are Natives who should have been hunting all their lives. It is something they should know how to do, even drunk.* I look around. It is party time for them. They have zero respect for my property, my moose, me, or themselves.

I pay them $100 and ask them to leave. It is more work fixing their botched job than if I had just done it all myself. The mess they made will take days to clean up. What a disaster. *So much for saving my bad back by hiring someone to help me.* Obviously, the solution is not just to show respect and offer the needy work. All this talk of, *"All they need is to be given a chance!"* "Said by the church teary eyed group!" I point out to myself. *How many of these goody two shoes actually offered these people work themselves?* I'm not sure how to respond, or what to do. Oh yeah, one of my custom $300 knives is missing. I'm told it is in the hands of one of the guy's girlfriends, that he gave her as a present. No. I will never see it again.

The local cop Karl, only laughs and shakes his head. "No, Miles. They are the living dead. Zombies. I do not have time for them. There are domestic violence calls from them by the hour, rapes, stealing, and murders. I do not have time. If you choose to be with them, then I can't help you. If your place gets robbed, burned, I will not respond. There is just not enough man power. I, and all the communities resources would be sucked dry by the demands of the already dead. " *So basically his job is to take care of the tax payers.* Once again, I hear the concept, that these are the unprotected, who can expect nothing from society. Written off and dismissed. Dead, but not yet buried. *Yes, there really are zombies!*

"Miles, it would take ten police to keep up. Who is going to pay? Community tax payers? You can't even afford to hire me, one. I could go most anywhere else and make three times my wages. So what quality cop do you think you end up with for minimum wages, considering how dangerous a job this is." I have heard. Just last week Karl was about to get fired because he grabbed an Indian roughly. The Indian had pulled a knife on him. He is also being reprimanded for handing out speeding tickets. Too many of our fearless leaders like to speed, while drunk.

ONE OF THE other addicts I had tried to help a few times explained it to me. "We only take stuff worth $20. No big deal. No one cares or files a report for $20." Basically he knows who he can steal from, and get away with it, as part of his survival tools. This group steals from each other, from relatives, from others who are also unprotected. The cops only get involved when zombies cross the line, and mess with the protected.

"Oh. I did not know any of this." I'm stupid.

Wellness never explained this. "Wow." *I'm still brainwashed with the crap I was taught in school about everyone being equal.* So I do not want to be among the unprotected. How does one get on or off this list? Who decides? *Yes, I have been confronted all my life with this evidence I refuse to see. It can't be. Not my country.*

I'm puzzled. "So what role does mental health and addictions play?" *What is all this talk about helping the needy if going near them is to get on the unprotected list? To be among the protected, do you have to ignore zombies and pretend they do not exist?* No one can adequately explain this to me. But it must be something everyone understands, that I do not. But wait, if I think about it, this occurs to me... *We let the zombie come to us, in a protected professional setting like a clinic. Then, we sell them drugs, get them off other drugs, along with selling professional advice.* I wonder if something is wrong with me, that a part of my brain is missing, where social skills come from. *Can I survive among people, or will I be burned at the stake as a witch.* I am never 100% comfortable around people. I'm curious if this is the root of my high blood pressure. If I was still out in the wild, would I still have high blood pressure?

A REPLY COMES from Art Train. Apparently they are not getting a lot of replies or interest. *Sure! Because it sounds like a scam!* There is agreement from them, that if they intend to live up to the mission statement, Nenana would be an ideal place. They need a point person in Nenana. Someone to do all the work, put up posters, line up meals, places to stay, promote the stop so interested people will show up. If so, there will be no charge. The original notice mentioned paying for a stop. I already know there is no one else in Nenana who cares enough about this to make it happen, and do what is asked. If it is going to get done, I have to do it. So I agree. *Maybe this is how I can contribute to society!* Yet I'm scared to be in charge like this. So I try again to bring Art Train subject up to the Chamber of Commerce, the Wellness group, and the City Council. I need at least some secondary interested person or group, a committee, even if I am the point person.

It looks to me like a majority of the Chamber wants to have their name connected, but does not want to do the work. The Wellness group seems more willing to offer help and good advice. Big Mike, the cook at the school, tells me at the WIN meeting, "You can't ask, Miles. You have to take charge and tell people what they need to do to help, assign people, give specific tasks and deadlines. If you ask for volunteers and leave it at that, it will fall flat!"

I didn't know that. I have never worked with a group. I do not like to order anyone around, any more than I like others to order me around. I'm someone, if I say I'll do something and volunteer, it gets done, period. No follow up, no encouragement, no boss is needed. Motivation comes from within.

A lot of hours are spent going to the school to talk to teachers, working with the mayor. I need pictures of the rail yard. Art Train wants me to measure the length of the track after the turn off, and describe how the physical stop location is, so Art Train can prepare. They need permission to make the stop, and know the side line will be clear and the track opened. The mayor takes me to the railroad guys. I take pictures and measurements. There are other questions and needs.

Posters need to go up and down the road. I do not drive, so I need help with this. The gal who runs the newspaper is on the Chamber Board and tells me when she delivers the paper she can put the posters up. The school needs to work out a time frame, a visit by each class to the train. Times for the general public need to be worked out.

I tell the wellness group "Art Train used terms like 'poor depraved' and 'uncultured' to describe our community they will serve." I pause and go on, "I'd like to teach them something, as well as us receive something. Can we get our Native dancers to put on a show, and use the native George Hall and put on a potluck with salmon, and feed for maybe fifty people?" Salmon to us is almost free. One fisherman could feed 300 people easily. Salmon here, fresh out of the river is only worth $2 a fish, about twenty cents a pound. The same salmon New York pays $100 a meal for. Our community is used to putting on feeds, for free. Everyone chips in. I ask, "Can we do this for Art Train? Show them our culture, as they show us theirs?" It could mean some publicity for our dancers and community. Who knows, have an effect on tourism. The story could make national news.

I speak with Native Elders: "This is a good chance to show off the good side of Native culture. The Art Train is about Native art. Some very influential Native artists will arrive and meet with our young people. The news media will be here." I want the 'poor depraved backward' talk to change. I have seen how our community can be! Good caring people, able to take care of themselves. Art Train feels we lack culture. Let's show them we have culture. In the old days, wasn't it so, that the Natives were good at entertaining visiting tribes? "There were gifts, food, exchanges of friendship and new alliances made, isn't that so?"

No one wants to attend any meetings on the subject. "Just what we all need, more meetings!" Eyes rolled up. So, OK. To save everyone an hour of their time at a meeting getting updated and on the same page, I hand deliver updates to each and every interested party, then revisit each and every person to give the news of what everyone else had to say, until there is an agreement. I estimate I donate a total of hundreds of hours of my time over a six month period.

Fall 2002 Story knife

This Knife was designed to be a woman's decorative protection knife to be displayed on a nightstand or someplace in the home. The knife is made of 440 stainless steel with brass inlayed heart. The handle is Alaskan mammoth ivory found by the artist on the Yukon River. The sheath is from the same tusk and has a brass, silver and copper hand cut, soldered and pinned unicorn. The stand base is the same ivory with local caribou antler. The stand has silver, copper, brass and Mexican opal flower centers.

Story—On one side is the tranquil unicorn in a beautiful setting. Symbol of love, peace, magic and non-violence. Yet we know the unicorn is a mythical animal! Is the scene also mythical?? Is there ever love, peace, perfect and forever beauty? Turn the sheath over. The back shows the unicorn rearing in anger. You never really know—or can predict the future of every situation.

Perhaps it is wise to have the ability to defend yourself close at hand—just in case. Thus, the functional dagger as part of a beautiful art piece, something that does not have to be hidden away where you can't get at it if you ever need it. The heart in the blade? A symbol of love. This is not for attack or for crazy people. This is for someone who loves life, peace, honesty, and simply understands they need to be defended sometimes. If you have anything—be it beauty or material goods—there is always someone out there who wants to take it from you. **Life should not be lived in fear.**

"So Will, I am exploring different markets. I think there are not so many hunters these days. It is illegal in most places to wear a hunting knife. If you can't use it or wear it, I'd think that would cut down on the interest. I am trying some kitchen chef knives. But also this idea of knives for women. It's a brave new world now, Will, with women screaming about equality."

"Yeah, I know Miles. I get cussed out sometimes for opening doors for women. Geez."

"So, along that line, Will, maybe women hope to defend themselves as well?"

A lot more single women these days, and women paired up with other women, and just the concept they are able! I support that. There is no reason a woman can't defend herself! These days, many women are just as strong as men. Men do not do as much physical work in this day and age. "What do women need us for, Will? Men are obsolete." I actually feel I am not interested in a relationship based on need. We should be equals who want to be together. "Anyhow, we'll see. Trying to find a niche market."

Will does not have the imagination I do, and tends to want to stick to old ways. This is fine. We do not have to agree on everything to be friends. He tries to think of something nice to say, but I know he thinks it is a stupid idea,

"Miles, for sure we need to figure out how to keep making money. It is tough on our own. I try working for myself, and just can't make it, so at least you can do it. I'm not sure how you do it, but you must be doing something right." It has been good seeing Will. We do not see each other as much as we used to, but he is passing through the area and stopped in to see me. "Well got to get going. I want to use a bulldozer to make a loading ramp to get equipment into and out of the back of the truck." He described a ramp earlier he can back his truck up to and drive a snow machine right into the back of the truck. Maybe he has imagination and ideas after all, just in a different direction.

"OK, hope it works out, watch your top knot and stay below the horizon." He nods as he waves good-by from one of his beat up trucks from the '70s. He does not like all the electric gadgets in the new machines. I watch him hand crank his window up. He's been my friend now for over thirty years.

I write a letter to the 'Made in Alaska" and 'Silver Hand' people. I am more involved in art than ever before, and concerned about artists in general, maybe the Native artists, because I understand them, since I live their lifestyle.

Hello Saunders!

I have an interest in the Silver Hand program and have talked to Kieth Gianni some, and Guy (from the Fairbanks Chamber of Commerce) and we have gone over some ideas. I will be working- well time has already gone—was working, during the symposium and wish I could have made it. I'm an artist myself, hand-crafter-white-but with many Native friends. I'm also the buyer for the Nenana Cultural Center.

I've recognized the problem with authentication and verification for a long time, but it really struck home when about five years ago I brought some Native art to sell for friends down at the big Tucson gem show. I read a flier handed out there, saying that 70% of all Native crafts are 'fake.' This did not encourage anyone to buy. I heard "prove it" a lot.

I pause in the letter, re-read it and breeze through it again, catching the points I want to make.

One major flaw is, the Silver Hand sticker is not very hard to get. I have been offered the tags from Native friends. I have a pile I acquired but never used. Tags that says my work is authentic native handcraft. Oh, yes, a local shop in Nenana noted for lack of ethics, paid employees to take off Korea stickers, and put 'Native hand crafted in Alaska,' stickers on gift items. The fine for doing this when confronted was very minor, compared to the profits she made, and it didn't slow her down.

An artist known all over the Interior, made and sold grass basket scenes. Zola sold these as, 'Native Alaska hand crafted,' and she got approval from the Silver Hand. It turned out she is Asian, only looked Native, and had her relatives in Viet Nam sending these grass items to Alaska, that she sold as local Native handcraft for 100 times their real value.

My mind wanders to the concept of some method of verification, like the BIA number all Natives have assigned, or number, some identification in a data base that can be easily verified. Like a registered trademark. I've gone back to this topic many times, and do not know what can be done. It would not help me a lot, but would help out the Native artists. Related to the 'Sharing our Culture through art,' a grant proposal I am working on as part of my job as buyer for the Cultural Center. No. I do not get paid for that job. Many locals assume I took the job in order to favor my art in the gift shop.

There is quite a bit of my art on display now. But I have product, and not many of the other artists have inventory. I have at any given time 5,000 items, a good $100,000 worth of art in inventory. No. I do not know why others do not. I set the rule as buyer, to spend $200, give me anything. But to make more money, your art has to be selling. My work sells, I can prove it through gift shop records. I buy from artists whose work sells. I show up, and work on my own displays at my expense.

"You can do the same."

"That's the shops job!"

Yes it is, but do you want to sell or not? I mean what matters more—whose job it is, or that you make money?" I learned a long time ago to supply my own displays anyplace my work is shown. More than that, all my displays are handmade, to match my work.

I have never watched another artist at work, been to another artist's shop, nor had any artist in my shop beyond a few minutes. I do not consider it a great feat, or hard, or time consuming. I feel I could in fact, double my production if I had the sales to justify it. I feel I am slow because the motivation is simply not there, when the art is not moving any faster. I have hope, but in truth, my raw material, not the finished art, sells faster, and makes me more money. I try not to let it bum me out. There is much more potential profit in add-on value of doing art, over dealing in raw material.

I smile. Much of what I learned I got from Crafty. I hear comments from the other artists when I buy, that Crafty taught me to deal with.

"I have not been inspired,"

"I do not have enough material right now,"

"Saving money for materials." Those comments are the most numerous. Inspiration? Well I suppose I have this work I just do that is my bread and butter to make a living, that requires no inspiration. If I am not inspired, I do prep work, slice and dice raw materials I need for later. Grunt mindless work that needs to be done. I then have lots of raw to choose from when I am inspired. I do not comprehend other artists who do not have enough material. I have more than I can use in a lifetime and am considered poor. *Meaning if I can do it, anyone can.* I see other artists buying cigarettes, taking time off, buying nice cars. So my guess is 'art' is not their priority. Instead of cigarettes, a nice car and time off, I put all that into my passion, I guess is how I'd put it. In truth, I do not average in a year but about two hours a day doing art. I tell another artist,

"Maybe the secret is that two hours done consistently over a year ends up being a lot of art." The average $50 pendant takes me about half an hour total time to create. Now I do casting, so I have that time down to as little as fifteen minutes.

"Yes, right Miles! So how come you are not rich then!"

I have no answer. I do not know. Beyond, "But I am rich." But no, not with a fancy car, chic home, good clothes and such.

"But Miles—like the casting you tell me about. You use wax patterns, right?" I am talking to a friend – fellow jeweler at a gift shop in Fairbanks. I like to show him my latest ideas, and get some feedback. He does cast work as well, so understands the business. "You can buy a wax pattern for forty cents in volume, even if it's sixty cents by the dozen. So how does it pay for you to reinvent the wheel, and make your own wax injections from your own molds?"

We just do not think the same way is all. I do less production than he does. I can create a short run of my own designs that sell higher because they are one of a kind, not bought from someone who has thousands. I can cater to a more local market. I answer my friends question.

"Well if so, what do you have to show for it, Miles?"

"Four homesteads, a home that is paid for, a shop, truck, boat, snow machine, four wheeler, a dozen nice guns, $100,000 in inventory, lots of tools…" This is just off the top of my head. No, I just do not look or act the part. *Oh well, never mind. I make a joke of it.* "Ignorance is bliss!" He chuckles at that response. So I get my reply honed down based on this. I want people to be happy.

"You got that right, Miles." So I pretend I am too stupid to understand how vastly more rich he is than I am. One of the prices of being outside the box. The standards change. What is valued changes. But yes, sometimes I get a hint he envies some of what I have, the different freedoms, the sense of adventure and fun I have, that he can't buy. He has his own airplane, but no time to fly it. So what good is it?

"Miles, maybe we could work together and I could meet you with my plane at the boneyard and get some tusks?" *And I need his help because? I do not need his help. He needs mine. He does not know how to find the fossils.* "I just got floats for the plane!" I know from working with Seymour surveying in his plane, the floats can costs as much as the plane! Now he can get into places to go fishing—if he ever has any time off that is.

"Well, there might be a legal aspect to the plane that holds you up. You could get your plane confiscated by Fish and Wildlife." *Possibly true. But in fact, I have never heard of any arrest, citation, or confiscation of gear, just confiscation of fossils with no receipt or ticket. I consider it is in fact not illegal as we are told. It is simply 'undesired.'*

After all, where would we all be if everyone with a boat or plane went out to find fossils? What a mess! So there are hints it is not legal. No one gets the truth, there is no where to look it up, and most people stay away.

A handful of people 'fool around', dabble in and out of the area. No proof, no real interest in getting proof, as long as it is somewhat low key. There has never been a court case, a precedence, to show as example. I think no one especially wants a court case. In the same way, few civilized people want to define subsistence, and go to court with subsistence cases. It's a can of worms, just like fossil hunting is. But my friend, I think, only understands black and white. Half truths and vague policy is the same thing as 'illegal' to him.

Yup! You got it, you stay away. Cuts down on the competition. It is also to my advantage to be vague and imply this, imply that, and keep my legal activity in the dark. For even finding fossils on legal mine claims or Indian lands has issues, and no one wants a huge market in fossils. The miners might get shut down as archeological sites if word got out how many fossils they are finding. I'd lose my permission to be there if I had pilots flying in to help me! Legal activity can become illegal if attention is brought to it. Others get jealous. Some preservation group will add it to their cause for publicity and fund raising.

I have this Indiana Jones image I enjoy, and part of that is 'mystery'. Friends in high and low places, dealing with the criminal element off and on. People with patches over their eyes, pirates. People in the wilds without permits or papers or social security numbers. Off the grid so far, they do not exist. Savages, knowing secrets about the land. Secrets only special people like Yours-Truly-here, are privy to. Sworn to secrecy in return for a relationship of trust! *I can't really blow that story over a guy who has a plane and owns a big shop!* I got the hint that, hey, didn't he just imply I'm stupid? Imply I'm poor, while he is rich?

Now I can wink with a, "Catch you later", hinting *Maybe I will show you my latest finds. Share an adventure story.* Who is rich and who is poor now? Who envies who? Put your nose to the grindstone, good buddy. The whip cracks; there are bills to pay! While I will get paid more than you make to go have fun.

My attitude could be different! I consider the issue has to do with trust. If I bring in anyone else on my exclusive, profitable agreements with remote people, we need to, at the very least, be equals. It makes a good cover to hint I, like others, sneak into the boneyard in an illegal preserve.

But oh, yes! There are those who would like to clean my clock, wipe that smile off my face. The world is filled with dark enemies. Gas has been set aside for the long trip. The boat engine has been tuned up. Not even I know when I will go. I will simply, suddenly, be gone. I might be out fishing and back in two days. Who knows? I plan on keeping it that way. Trust no one. I return. Who knows when or from where? Absolutely no one knows. Not a best friend, not a relative. Suddenly 'home' after being gone a week or two, tired, muddy with many hours on the boat engine. A tarp over the boat. Covering who knows what? Singing, "Bringing in a couple of keys, please don't bother me, Mr…" With a sweet four stroke quiet engine I slip into my private river parking spot at a very off hour. Quiet trips back and forth in the dark with four wheeler and cart, covered with tarps, going between the boat and the huge shop with no windows.

After an appropriate amount of time. Hints, vague references, to past trips with no exact details, and possibly something ready for the market. *All legal!* But in truth, who really knows? I agree with the government! We need to protect (to some extent) the things that come off and out of the land! Imagine if it was all 100% 'Let's go get fossils!' I'd be out of business. There'd be fences and bulldozers and big companies involved. The land would be ruined. Like civilization does, harvesting wood by clear cutting and strip mining. Greed.

I'm sure my jewelry friend would tell me I have made up my own story, my own reality, to suit my own needs and justify… Bla, bla. Smile. *No use upsetting the man!* Different people get told different sets of facts. Is that what makes me known as a bullshitter? Hmmm. I wonder. I thought bullshit was… well… something said with no substance. *Does that pile of fossils in my shop have no substance?* Anyhow. Sigh. Being a good bullshitter makes a good cover. *I am Oz! I do not want too many people to listen or believe. While I buy boat engines with cash, others use credit, and struggle.*

My jewelry friend changes the subject, "Miles, whatever happened to that experiment with casting more than one metal at once? Those pieces you showed me were sure interesting!"

No one else has seen anything like it. Something I stumbled on. Being so far out of the box, doing things so wrong as to be on another planet, and suddenly an unexpected anomaly. Pieces of casting coming out like a marble cake of copper and white bronze or brass. Done with one sling of the molten metal. How? How can two metals not mix and go in at the same time? He had been intrigued, and thought if I could duplicate it, come up with a special crucible, I might make a million dollars on it.

"That is on a back burner now. Held up by obstacles I cannot overcome without a lot of money or time." I explain how I hoped it might be easy. A crucible with two sides. Melt two metals, spin them at once into the mold. "I have to understand more about centrifugal force, vortex science and weight, volume, density science." I explain how it is not as simple as I hoped. "The heaviest metal spins in first. I need to restrict the metal that wants to go in first in some way. Let it go in the slipstream of the other metal, by how I design the divider." I explain how I tried to divide one on top of the other, instead of side by side. But it was too hard to melt the bottom metal. I explain how it is hard to create unique crucibles. It might take a dozen tries to figure out what direction to go with this. "It's just not that important to me.

Another idea I had, one of many," I explain "So much is an experiment with me. I may have as high as a one third failure rate."

"Geez, Miles, if I had a failure rate like that I'd be laughed out of the business!" Once again, the respect that was beginning to show, is lost in disgust. I only smile. *Why remind him Edison had 9,999 failures before his first light bulb lit up. Failures? Why is this word used? Is that what Edison called them? I'm sure he got up each day inspired, with a big smile, because now he knows 9,999 ways it will not work, zeroing in on the one way it will!* My view is that, even one exciting result, can financially pay for thirty items I have to re-melt and try again. I'm the only one who has it. Suddenly I can name my price. *When we fish, do we focus on all the fish in the river we are not getting? All the ones that missed our net? All the ones that started to get caught and got loose? Why?* Be happy with the ones that ended up on the dinner plate! My friend is waiting for a comment as I think.

"I'll keep at it. See if I get any better at it. You asked, so I was just letting you know where I'm at. Hey, are you going to make it to the fair this year?" *Change the subject.*

AT THE TANANA STATE FAIR, the equivalent of, "Step right his way and be amazed! The magical mystery tour…"

A lot of, "Yeah, right!" snorts, and keep on walking.

"Step right…"

"Hi, Miles, what you got this year?" Look to the right, look to the left. Reach under the counter and pull out a saber tooth tiger fang.

"Holy *&%!!! Where did you get such a thing?" A vague reply,

"I'm the man!" I do the wavy jive hand wobble, like a sidewinder rattler movement that says, "Here, there, someplace, no place. Maybe I found it? Maybe I got it off an Indian? Maybe it's stolen? Maybe off a museum. Maybe I time travel. Who knows?" *If you need a story I'll make one up, or maybe it's the truth that sounds like a story. Who knows?* "For you, a special deal."

The man who supplied Obi Wan with a star ship, that kind of transaction. It's all part of the fun. Passing myself off as a vagrant. The village idiot. Behold, and be amazed. If a Fish and Wildlife badge comes out, "Oh yeah, I got it in Tucson, here's the receipt." *Off a reputable dealer of course.*

Some customers fancy themselves connected with the occult. I say,

"A raven in a dream showed me…" Some customers are wanna be paleontologists. I say, "From the layer of shells at the 40,000 year old plasticine level…" Some are proud Indians and I say, "From a Shaman…" Some customers are artists who want it to make jewelry, some want to display it in a museum with an accurate story.

All stories are true. I just leave out some facts. Maybe the entire truth is not going to set anyone free, or be very marketable. The truth is the reality of a real saber tooth. Behold, and use your imagination. The truth is, it is not fake. That's not bullshit. 90% do not have an issue. Some percent do not think much of me.

"I just want to hear your bullshit, Miles, it has such imagination."

"Almost everything is bullshit if that is what we focus on. The fact the earth is round is bullshit."

"So how is that bullshit, Miles, enlighten me?"

"The Earth is not in fact 'round.' To be honest and precise, it is, slightly pear shape. It's simply easier, and more convenient, to call it round, and we all nod in agreement, because it is what we want to hear. A techno geek might beg to differ and argue. But why? As long as it's the Earth we all love, and it's sort of roundish."

My customer walks away shaking his head, "I give up!"

While I have a happy smile. *Next! Step right this way and be amazed!* I move a lot of stuff. A whole lot of stuff. *I may need a second booth next year.* How am I going to run two booths? I'm tired. I'm glad the fair is only ten days.

Honestly, how do I explain my life?

"Wow what nice art, what cool ideas, how do you do that?" Where would I even begin? I used to try, and got blank looks, and simply lost people.

"I cut the stone with diamond wheel, then eighty grit grinding wheel. Four other wheels. Finally in a tumbler with cones I designed myself. I had to use a vibratory, not a rotary, and adapted it. Then I dip the top in wax.. well sort of, first in water soluble wax to account for the shrinking of the cast metal. Cool idea, huh?"

Blank stare, walk away, no sale. Try another tactic.

"Magic!" *Defined as anything exciting that we do not fully understand, and when understood by a few, is difficult to explain.*

"Cool, I'll take it!" *People!* I smile. So what will my answer be, behind door #1 or door #3? *The door that has the prize of course!*

"Will that be paper or plastic?" He knows I mean how are you paying, not how I expect to wrap it, so we laugh. "I'm not really set up for plastic. I send the plastic people to the ATM machine."

"Have a nice day."

My neighbor with the booth next to me is a lady I have known a long time as I know many others here. The lady who handed me money collected after the homestead fire, who I dance with here at the fair. She and her husband work together. He does woodwork items and she does interesting bead work using nicely cleaned bones and teeth somewhat as I do, but with her own more feminine style. She is tall and willowy, from Germany with an accent. We have spent a lot of time talking over the years, when business was slow. Often sharing ideas about how to sell, how to display, how to attract the kind of customers we want.

"Miles, I want all my good stuff up front where the customers with money can see it!" I give my own selling concept,

"I put out one or two attraction pieces, but keep low end near the front to occupy the kids and keep them out of the interior of the booth." That works for me, but she says she does not want children around at all, and has nothing for them. She wants high end people around, like a gallery. I think that is going to be hard to acquire in a fair setting. Also, I have had problems with theft if too many high end items are right in front by the door. But we talk about things like this, compare notes, and things we learned over the past year since we met each other. She overhears the conversation where I find out I lost my homestead cabin last year. I explain, once again, about all the things I lost. I imagine what life would be like if this was my only home as a few years ago! "What then?" *I am lucky I have two homes, one in town to fall back on. I have a place to live at least.* "Life can be strange."

I was smug thinking I had it made. That when civilization fails, I have my get away safe place that will save my bacon. Others do not have this, so I am better off than others. I feel sorry for those without such an escape. Now, Mother Nature takes my wilderness home and supplies. "It is civilization that saves my bacon." We cannot predict the future, or know what direction survival will come from. Quite a life lesson.

We are being prepared for an unknown-to-us-future, headed for our destiny. Lessons, getting trained, prepared. This thought keeps me going, open minded, accepting whatever life hands me.

I sigh and keep on selling, and enjoying seeing regular customers, enjoying the fair food. Some is good food, like the cooked corn on the cob. There are turkey drumsticks. Big Daddy's sells pork in a sandwich.

Mostly I eat with Dan at the Patty Wagon, since we are friends and he gives me a line of credit giving me the #1 in the vendor book! It is fun to order and say,

"Yes put it on my tab, it's number one in the book!" Loud enough for everyone to hear. Burger, fries, and a soda is a rough diet every meal though. Now and then I see the Asians, who remember me, and give me a good portion of rice and stir fry for a nice price. I do not tell anyone about the fire and losing my home. That is not a good fair subject, a topic expected to make me any profits. I learned a while back, to keep the subjects moving in the direction of leading to a sale. That's why I am here. That took me a long time to learn.

I tell Kristine, my German fair neighbor, "Coming here used to be more a social event for me. I wanted to talk to people. I considered it rude to turn the subject to their buying something. I saw however, that I'd fill up my selling space standing and talking, so customers had trouble getting in to look and buy."

Kristine understands the problem, but sees it more with her husband Gary, who does the wood work. He enjoys talking, while she counts the money. At least there are two of them to work the booth. Gary sits out in front of the booth in one of his rustic handmade birch chairs. Tall and thin, with his hillbilly hat on, crooked knife in hand whittling on something.

Heidi still brings her children by and leaves them with me. Now they are older, and able to be of help. Forest and Skyler now straighten out twisted tangle chains for me, in return for ride tickets or trinkets I have. I notice they help out of politeness and are not as interested in the rides. Teenagers now.

"Oh Miles, what a beautiful watercolor! So soft and subtle, so dreamy and sweet!" Here it comes, a customer with the puzzled look, the frown, the reprimand. I keep smiling and nodding. "But Miles, the back is dirty! The sides were not cut to match, it is out of square, and one edge here is not trimmed. See?"

I lean closer as if to inspect something I was unaware of, with my, "I'll be darn, how did that happen?" look. Big grin still on my face.

"Miles, I don't get it, so beautiful and you ruin it with mistakes so easy to fix, why?"

I keep smiling my stupid grin like, *Amazing isn't it?* A grin that says: "So beautiful, yet at the same time so ugly." *Such a wonderful work of art, ruined by minor details, ruined by reality. What a shame!* My look of, "The world is such a puzzling place, don't you think?" *All is not as it appears or as we expect!* In my mind,

Will you notice? Such bold, strong, sure lines, done with swift, fast strokes of confidence, clean, neat, pure, to the beat of music – as a dance. Such a contrast to how I dress, the paper it is painted on. Do you notice? I trust the gift God gave me. I am honoring nature, not myself. A mere mortal God has given a gift to. The part that is me, filled with sin, as we all are. But the brushstroke will not falter. I refuse to let it. I will hang on to the one thing I understand, and know, as one sure thing I trust. If my art sells, I do not necessarily want it to sell for its perfection. That would be a lie. I get distracted when my neighbor in the next booth comes by.

"Kristine, have you seen the labor people from the government come by?" Each season now, more government regulators check more often and punish more severely for infractions. The weight and measure people come by and want to certify that our scales weigh the correct weight in order to protect the customers from people who deliberately alter their scales. For a fee we get a certificate of approval.

"Now for a mere $5 everyone knows your scale works!" Big thank you smile. Kristine answers me.

"I'm from Germany. I get it."

I reply, "Next year it will be our calculator."

"No Miles, no government agents by today yet, you did not miss anything." I am here at the fair and supposed to be having a good time, that's what fairs are for.

"Step right this way for the magical mystery tour!" It's show time! Be amazed. I am Oz, the great and powerful. *Who can't get a pee break without a contract with the government, how powerful is that?* I step aside for the inspector, who makes sure I have a fire extinguisher up to code, my table covers are fire approved retardant, electrical cords are up to code. All about safety! Costs are passed on to customers, who complain about high prices! *Be glad someone cares and makes sure you are safe! Don't worry, $5 of your entry ticket goes to insurance and safety officer's salaries.* "Obviously you are too incompetent to look after yourself. But have no fear, the government is here!" I go back to thoughts of my customer, who is still looking,

Ah yes, out of such ugliness, beauty is made. Behold and be amazed. What else lurks within? Be puzzled, ponder, rise and have questions. View the world in a different way. All is not as it seems. Beauty has a beast in it, the beast has a beautiful streak. Ying and Yang meet. What goes up is coming down. Are you glad? Do you accept the ways of the world? Or will you be upset all is not as you want? Will you open your eyes and see what is before you? Or will you see what you wish to see? Behind eyes of the court jester; I watch, nod and smile dumbly. The lady buys the piece, saying,

"Yes, it is profound. I have never seen anything like it. I'm drawn to it. I do not know why. It's so raw and real!" She will pay someone else twice as much money to make it square, clean it, and put it in a perfect frame. That's fine. I have done my part. I could 'do all that,' and put another zero on my prices. I would not be happy. *I hate clean and perfect.*

THE ART AUTHENTICITY issue is on my mind once again. I notice at the fair, that I run into situations where customers want proof of it comes from the designation of the area I am set up in as 'craft section.' Vendors should have made the items they sell themselves. But did they really? These customer worries lead to a conversation with Crafty at the fair. We have had many talks, this is an on-going topic.

"Crafty, it seems to me we talk about what is legal. Many of us are not clear on what is OK to do, and what not. In general, we are asking each other what the various laws mean."

"Well, Miles, the law books spell it out clearly, if we can find the laws. I just do what the wildlife people say when I ask." Crafty forgets that each officer you ask has a different interpretation. Wildlife parts is only a small segment of his inventory, so the subject does not concern him as much as it concerns and affect me.

"Maybe I could get an informed wildlife officer to come speak at a group?" I'm thinking of maybe a Highways Companion meeting of the tourist industry. "The gift shop owners and employees could be informed what they can buy from the artists, and know better what can be sold and to whom." The Nenana Chamber has been paying for me to attend a meeting of tourist related industries up and down the highway. The group seeks topics of interest to focus on, or have guest speakers inform us about.

"Yeah, Miles, it is confusing. Eskimos can do things no one else can. Yet discrimination by race is not legal. Can we buy ivory from a Native, then sand his work off, and put our own work on like we did in the '70s, or has that law changed?"

"I know we used to be able to, but heard that law got changed. I do not know for sure, and have no way to find out."

"I'm also pretty sure there are different levels of 'Native' now. There are different laws for Eskimo, different from Alaska Native, and different again from lower 48 Indians."

All we can do is speculate. Fish and Wildlife will not put answers in writing when asked, and are not obligated to give the right answer. I was told, "Because they are not lawyers."

Lawyers I ask are not sure. I get told, "It depends on court cases. Without knowing the cases I can't look it up." So who can? It'd be nice to get someone in charge to give us a basic rundown on where to get answers, and give helpful advice. That thought is put on the back burner for now. The whole question of just what laws are, what is their purpose, how do they get made, and changed, comes out of this conversation.

Crafty, and many other vendors I know are concerned with being law abiding. Is that the priority? They say, yes. My priority is integrity, honesty, morality, and intent. 'Legal' is about #6 priority. I think because I do not trust our lawmakers to be looking out for my our society's best interest. I argue that laws are supposed to be a reflection of the morality of the culture. It often lags behind a bit, but this is the purpose and intent. For many, answers are spelled out in Fish and Wildlife hand outs, with simple answers for basic commonly asked questions. Written in the game book we all get at the beginning of each hunting season. *Who wrote the book? These are not in fact, laws.* This is what Fish and Wildlife would like to see. So the simple answer is to follow that! This simple book does not address 'crafts' much.

"There is fine print at the end of the book we get handed."

This says, "These are not the laws, please look up the exact laws that apply." With no source to find these laws given.

Not so simple. What is expected has changed since I got into this business. I'm committed now, with a lifetime investment of money, knowledge, a built up reputation, and clientele that took over thirty years to build. Will this all now be called 'illegal?" Do I smile, say ok, quit, find a new occupation? Some people decide this is what they will do, quit. I can study the law, and work out at the edge, understand the intent, stay out of trouble and at the same time keep my occupation.

I hear a lot of complaints against Crafty. Many will not go in his store. Crafty will follow the letter of the law, including the fine print at the bottom. He also knows various legal loopholes. Crafty has no qualms about importing thousands of items from overseas, to be turned into authentic local hand craft. I say many times in his defense, "It is legal to alter a product by 10% and call it yours." Crafty has street people do the work for trade. Trading for maybe food and a place to stay, like our buddy Wess—the 0mess. He does not have to pay Workman's Compensation, or have any withholdings. Legal slave labor. The item he paid a dollar for, and invested another dollar in slave labor to have altered, now has a 'hand crafted in Alaska' sticker on it, that sets on his store shelf for $100 has a $10 investment on his part. Very slick, till he lectures me about the letter of the law, concerning my own activities.

I agree with Crafty, that what he does is legal. I think it is immoral, and does not uphold the intentions of why the laws he follows were made. Which is to protect the public from fraud. The proof of what I say is in the fact that so many people complain and feel ripped off by him. Where I get very few complaints. Crafty does not agree saying,

"It will be you who ends up in jail, Miles, not me. I follow the law, and you follow some sense of ethics in your head that you made up! While going over the legal line sometimes!" Two different viewpoints. I smile, and wonder if we each justify our actions to suit what we do, so we can feel ok about ourselves and what we do! He is not interested in how I do things. Many customers agree with Crafty. Crafty makes a lot of money, as in, a million a year. And I never will. That is the bottom line. "There will always be dissatisfied customers, Miles!" True. However, I have almost zero dissatisfied customers or complaints. My complaints are before any deal takes place, so the customer is not out anything.

I do some of the things Crafty does, to make a profit. But I prefer to tell the customer what is going on. My hope would be, that customers get educated and plugged into reality. I often get in trouble for exposing the truth. Customers often get indignant when I tell it like it is.

"Yes, dear customer, that is a nice price for turquoise. Because it is low grade turquoise ground into dust, mixed with glue and dyed, squeezed in a mold and not cut." *Dear customer is angry at me.* I shrug my shoulders, and feel sorry for their ignorance. "If you do not want to know, that is your choice. You asked, and I do not want to be a liar. It's a fine product for the price. That is why I offer it. If you want fine, authentic natural turquoise, I have that over here." I repeat this interaction with customers, when discussing what approach we venders should take.

Dear customer often says: "But this is $100! That's an outrage!"

"No, it is not an outrage. Quality cost."

"I can buy that for $25 down the street!"

I doubt that very much. I paid $25 wholesale for the raw stone and had to buy $500

worth to get that price. I had to hand cut the stone and create the setting by hand. Is the customer always right? In this case, Yes. I calmly reply:

"Perhaps this particular piece is overpriced." I get out my tray of, 'Anything in this tray, $35.' I pick out a big honker turquoise item, and hand it to the Dear Customer. "I can go $25 on this one." He happily buys a piece of blue plastic, thanking me for giving him a deal on this lovely turquoise.

Dear Customer number two shows up later and looks at the same $100 genuine turquoise necklace saying,

"Wow, a great price, Miles. I saw one similar across town for $200!" This set of events is common. A variety of customers with different expectations, budgets, understanding of what they expect, and what is acceptable.

I can see the merit in Crafty's view of, "Just follow the law and pay attention to the fine print to cover your butt." I used to feel my views were better. Now I think 'just different.' In school, I thought about knowledge and education.

I got told, "Do not worry about your question, it is not on the test," as if passing the test is everything, as Crafty would argue.

"That's why there is a test, that's why there are laws! Do what those in charge tell you to."

I would say, "I do not care so much if I pass the test or not, I want to know something." I feel the same about laws I suppose. Laws should properly reflect being honest, kind, and doing what's right. In other words, if I care about morality, I should not go very far astray of the law. I recall a Fish and Wildlife officer asking me to sell him large amounts of illegal fish eggs and bear parts. Telling me, "If you work with me you will not be arrested. If you do not, you may go to jail." The idea was to kill bears to get him the gall. Those I knew were killing the bears, taking the gall out, and wasting the rest of the bear. I refused. He was right. Neither he nor those under his protection got arrested or in trouble. It was me who got in trouble. Sometimes laws have to do with politics, power, and money. Laws may not be biologically sound, or kind, moral, fair.

Laws appear to me to focus on some people having rights others do not, favoring the rich, holding back the poor. The subsistence lifestyle I live has a lot to do with the idea that we take care of ourselves, and know how to think, and make our own decisions. When I was young, our country told all of us the United States fought for, and believes, in, personal freedom. Doing whatever you like and believe in, as long as you do not bother anyone else. That sounded good to me, and was how I was raised. If that is not workable, I do not know what to say. Am I being told the basic premise our country was founded on is false? If so, then what does our country now stand for? I sigh, and at home get my thoughts together.

I had missed a couple of city meetings. I have been working a while on the Art Train visit, several months! It is time I give an update at a WIN meeting.

"Art Train seems on track." Everyone laughs at my pun. "Crowley gave permission for the stop in their rail yard. I sent pictures of the area. Art Train responded that this looks do-able. Mayor said we will have to hook up an electrical box to supply power when the train shuts down. But another option is to supply fuel for the train generator. Crowley might donate fuel. I have not heard for sure on that. I have eighty salmon in the Senior freezer. Big Mike will oversee the cooking on the school grill. All the posters are up around town, and up and down the road."

"What about the dancers?"

"I have not talked to Jackie yet. Does anyone know her well, who might get an answer? I know there was something about needing some money. If it's dance outfits, maybe they can be made locally."

A hand comes up and Karen adds, "The Native Council has some grant money connected with the school I am in charge of. I will cover the cost of the dancers with this grant." Out of the blue, money is found, and comes forward. Grant money so many others had been fighting for.

"I think you will make this happen, Miles! I was not sure in the beginning, but you are working hard! The dancers deserve the chance to perform at such an event. The Native council is grateful for what you are doing to bring renowned Native art to Nenana."

Thus, many of my quirks and odd ways get overlooked by some, in the light of the big picture. I refuse to feel guilty for my quirks. It is like war wounds of life. I am lucky to be alive, but it comes with a price. I came out of my younger years tweaked. Fine. Lesser people under the same conditions did not even survive. Some live in hell, like my sister. Will we laugh at someone in a wheelchair? The wounds of the mind are as devastating as the wounds of the body. Anyhow, maybe I can make up for my faults by focusing on my strengths! *Anyhow, my quirks are harmless, aren't they? Should they be such a big deal?* Maybe others will try to do the same, like Karen.

"That's great, Karen, I'm sure that was the only holdup with the dancers. I will have Jackie go talk to you then? I'll have a timeframe, schedule, as the date gets closer." I explain the plan now is to open first for the school kids, and move the classes through in order by grades. "In two groups, with the younger going first. The school bus will bring the children from outlying areas. We are trying to coordinate with Anderson down the road. About 3:00 pm., it will open for the public. Ending about 6:00 pm., to allow those who work to get in after five. There will be two days. Art Train wants some local help with guiding people through the train, snacks, and other duties. Looking at a need of about twenty-five people in shifts over two days. The Chamber of Commerce is going to take care of that. Mostly us Board members it looks like! Anyone interested in helping can see Christine. She is in charge of that."

There are some other details, but my update is over in ten minutes. We are done with the meeting in our usual two hours. There is no sub- committee. It has worked best for me to just go around and update everyone, individually deal with everyone, passing messages back and forth. Sometimes it occupies the entire day. But for some reason, no one is excited about having meetings. I hear yet again,

"That's all we need, one more meeting!" It simply increases my workload by ten times.

"That's how it is, Miles, for those movers and shakers who are the ramrod behind an event." I guess so. I mean, I see and understand it now. I just never realized or gave it any thought. All those events I just showed up at for the free food. Now I understand what it took to put them on. I have new knowledge, and do not want to suck the event dry showing up for free stuff. I will make up for the past by trying to give more in my later years. *Or so are my thoughts and grand plans.*

I did not mention that outlying communities are getting to be a problem.

Without giving names, at least one is angry that the train is not stopping in their community, so refuses to cooperate, and demands the train stop at their village. In their protest they may get left out completely and not even have the opportunity to come to Nenana.

The argument goes, "Why did Nenana get picked? Who decided that? What's wrong with stopping here also?" Art Train informs me of the complaints, politics, and issues going on. There is a possibility Art Train will simply bypass us after all, as too many problems, too much bickering, not enough focus on the purpose of the stop. Art train does send out a communication,

"We sent out a notice all up and down the train route to every community. Besides Anchorage and Fairbanks, Nenana was the only community to reply." I just cannot believe outlying communities would be so petty as to refuse to come to Nenana. Nenana is covering all the planning and extra costs, all they need to do is show up, give us a time so it can be scheduled in. The ones who suffer from this pettiness is the public, especially the schoolchildren.

Art Train also explained, "We are putting the train car on a barge in Washington and sending it up, having it lifted and put on the tracks. This takes a long time and cost a lot of money. We have never done this before. Up till now, we kept the train in the lower states. This is exciting for us to make such a long trip to outlying areas who can most benefit, and need to be exposed to culture." If this whole event inspires even one child to go into an art career, it will be a success, and worth all the work I have done. This would be my greatest reward.

I have been exposed to culture as described. I saw the original King Tut exhibit when it traveled the U.S. I was exposed off and on to great museums and music. Art Train is getting closer. The event is getting more real. The train needs a water hook up. I need to ask the mayor what kind of hoses and fittings we have in that area. If we do not have the right things we have to figure out where to get them! The community is already asking what all this will cost the tax payers. So many want it all for free, will contribute nothing, but show up, and consider it an honor to have their presence. I show up for my appointment with the mayor.

"I am getting asked why you are in charge, Miles. Now that most of the work is done, others want to get the credit. It's a big event, and who are you?"

"Well, not the end of the world, Mr. Mayor. It is not the credit I care about. If Art Train wants or needs to put our great leader's names in their thank you and credits, that looks good. The main thing with me is the event itself, the good it can do. I heard the Chamber is claiming it is all their idea, and as a group, wants the credit. When in fact, if anything, they held the project back and have been more of a stumbling block than a help. If any group deserves credit, it would be the Nenana Wellness Group."

Mayor and I both know, the one who runs the newspaper is on the Chamber Board and printing stories praising the Chamber and its foresight. Likewise, is ready to do news coverage, possibly getting national attention for the local paper. One of the issues being covered is publicity. This whole news coverage issue is exactly my point about the news and reality. Art Train wants good glowing coverage to get back to the ones who contribute the money. Pictures of poor deprived Indians being shown the light, looking grateful. Humanitarian pictures. Stories the rest of the world will get Moon- eyed over.

I understand what is required. After all, I am in the business of selling romance and dreams. There are other interests. I have promised to take the Art Train leaders in my boat on a fishing trip while they are here. Lifelong dreams of several of the Art Train people. Their personal perk. If this is the grease that makes the gears turn, OK. I donate my time, boat, gas and expertise as a local fisherman. No one else is interested in offering a free trip,

"To some 'Ya-hoo' outside clowns," as it was put when I asked around, and, "They can take their high class culture and stuff it," and, "What are you getting out of it anyhow, getting paid under the table or something?"

It is Jack Corncob, who has befriended me for some reason, who explains, "Those who get things done learn to ignore the hecklers." He has given advice over the years. Like, "It is better to beg forgiveness than ask permission." In some cases, at any rate, it does seem better to just do it. By the time you get a consensus and permission, opportunity is gone.

Jack adds "Good for you, keep it up," and with a friendly nod, heads for his Laundromat. So far from the heavy politics on a high level he once knew. *The man who helped write the Alaska constitution!*

Art Train stops in Nenana.

THE END OF BOOK 4

A PERSONAL NOTE—

Reviews help! If you enjoyed this book, please leave a review where you purchased it—it would be greatly appreciated!

Sign up for my newsletter, "Keeping Up With Miles," @ www.milesofalaska.com Deals, new books, comments, links to YouTube. Stay updated!

The Alaska Off Grid Survival Series Summary

Book 1 - Going Wild

In 1973, I am 22 years old, and a city kid. I enlisted in the Navy and got out after the Vietnam War.

I travel to interior Alaska, a 'Cheechako' (Greenhorn) by Alaskan standards. But I have been raised on Walt Disney and feel qualified to be a mountain man!

I arranged with a pilot to drop me off in the wilds of Alaska. I do not have everything I need and have things I do not need. I learn about guns, trapping, and the loneliness of living in the vast wilderness with no other humans around.

I do not see anyone for many months, then walk out of the wilds to civilization in the spring. After working odd jobs to make supply money, I return to the wilds in the fall and have a hard time my second winter. I almost die, and need to be rescued.

I decide to build a houseboat so I can travel around without having to build another cabin. I have to accept summer work in Fairbanks to pay for the boat materials and work under a builder. The boat takes much longer to build than expected.

I live as a street person much of the time to keep expenses down.

Book 2 - Gone Wild

I have many adventures on the houseboat and acquire a dog team. There are issues with the police, a bear on my boat, and a trip to see my family who live a civilized life.

My houseboat sinks. I get lost and learn other hard lessons. I start doing artwork and end up on TV. I win a land lottery and start my first homestead.

There are mail order women, and I live with a woman and her kids. Ten people are murdered in a village we visit, and myself and the family are almost among them. Family life is more difficult than I imagined.

Fish and Game becomes a concern.

I head back into the wilderness, which leads into book 3.

Book 3 - Still Wild

I acquire a couple more homesteads and cut more trapline.

I give up sled dogs and enter the world of snow machine adventures.

I winter in Galena and visit many native villages. There are bear encounters, and many survival situations to learn about.

I become a serious mammoth hunter and find fossils as part of my living. I work with a land surveyor specializing in homesteads and wilderness surveys, getting paid to use my boat.

My art sells well, so I do some big shows. I become more social and understand civilization better. I see the wisdom of being accepted by others. I learn. I grow. I try to change, as the world does.

The economy changes. It is less acceptable to be a trapper. I never become totally civilized as a city person defines it, but maybe I do, relative to the life I had in book one.

Book 4 - Beyond Wild (This Book)

I am getting past just survival and doing well, even prospering. I own more than the houseboat can easily haul. Gas gets expensive. I need a new houseboat engine.

There is a homestead and trapline that keeps me in one place now. There are more bear stories and adventures into the wilds, including a 300-mile boat trip looking for mammoth tusks, which has disastrous consequences.

I find where I want to live on the Kantishna River. A river 300 miles long with about five people on it. I hang out in the native village of Nenana, spending a lot of time here.

I get my first computer and learn to build a website. People are looking at the pictures and buying my raw materials and art. This is a chance to make a difference.

Life is beautiful. Life is precious. I Dare to live it.

Book 5 - Back To Wild

I acquire a home in Nenana and start a web store. I am forced out of my subsistence lifestyle, partly because of changes in the laws. I do some serious mammoth hunting.

Unstable power causes a lot of computer data loss. I learn by punching keys to see what happens. It takes a long time to get good enough to create a book.

I continue the Mammoth hunts. The Tucson fossil gem show and State fair do well for me.

This period of 'being civilized' that I am trying out, has advantages, but also a price to pay—a big change from the wilderness life and being alone!

I am a suspect in a murder investigation. Another trapper tries to move in on my territory. There are neighbors and infringements on my property.

I fear I cannot change who I am. There is difficulty blending the two lives and ways of thinking. There are mail-order women coming and going, as well as the usual adventures and situations I manage to get myself into.

Book 6 - Surviving Wild

Iris is my partner. Business grows, with money coming in, but causes 'complications.' I understand why I left for the wilds in the first place.

I get better at fossil hunting and have some exciting trips getting mammoth tusks and other ancient treasures. I am viewed as an expert on a few subjects and Discovery TV and reality shows contact me several times.

The new life in town causes legal issues that have been nipping at my heels off and on throughout my time in Alaska. Fish and Wildlife ask, "Why are you alone out here where we cannot keep an eye on you? We know you are up to something. What is it you have to hide? We will find out!" This mentality is that different is bad and of concern. I end up being investigated. A SWAT team shows up at my property with a dozen cars and 20 cops.

My arrest makes headlines. I'm sentenced to Federal Prison for six months as a felon. This is a stark contrast to 'Book 1-Going Wild,' where I have as much freedom as it is possible to have.

How did I get from there to here?

Book 7 - Secretly Wild

I am a convicted felon, describing life in prison from the viewpoint of someone used to freedom and the wilderness life. The same feather in the hat I wore on the cover of Ruralite magazine in 1979, is now worth five years in prison.

What do I need to do to survive here? There are classes to take, books to read, farm work to do, and people to help. There are interesting felon stories.

I observe more crime within the prison system by the system than I am accused of committing. "The prison could not survive if we operated legally," I am told by officials. I do my time. Now what? Am I a better person? I see the error of my ways. I am saved. Society is safer now.

Book 8 - Retiring Wild

I talk about news relevant to living off the grid as an individual in the wilderness that few citizens are aware of. I adapt my business, and still have adventures, depending as much as I can on the subsistence life I love and understand that is now becoming illegal as a white man.

I ponder whether the end of my life is in agreement with the views I held dear from the beginning. I have hope that even in times of control and suppression, I can still focus on the plus side, and continue to find ways to enjoy personal freedoms and individuality.

I continue to explore choices, how to have better control of my destiny, happiness, and success. I refer to this as 'Survival.' I have few regrets, and hope my life's path as written can provide entertainment and insight.

As someone who is interested in being different, not one of the sheep, I look realistically at the rewards that choice offers, but also the price that has to be paid.

Please visit www.alaskadp.com for links to the books.

Visit www.milesofalaska.com to find a bio of Miles, additional photos, stories, how-to videos, handmade artwork, and raw materials for sale.

Magazine and News Stories

Alaska Magazine

Alaska Magazine July 77—Survive by Miles Martin two pages, Photos. By Miles about my rescue, walk out on the Yukon River, five days at 50 below zero.

Nomadic House Boater Have Cabin Will Travel January 81—by Miles. Three pages, four color photos, a map. About life living on a houseboat, trapping and selling art (photo of my art), and all the adventures I have had on the river.

Would You Make A Good Bush Homesteader? June 86—by Miles four pages, six color pictures (One shows my custom knives.) A story I wrote about what it takes to be a homesteader.

Surviving The Big Lonesome— March 98—by Jim Rearden five pages, two color photos, one double page photo of Miles. Photos by world-famous photographer Jean Erick Pasquier. Describes life in the wilderness.

GEO Magazine

GEO in Germany is like "National Geographic" in the US.

Life in The Wilderness Alaska Special—87 by Miles Martin ten pages, sixteen color photos, a map

Photos by Jean Erick, one of the best photographers in the world, I Wrote it myself, winter life in the wilderness.

Alaska Special - 95 Einer gegen den Rest der Welt

Eight pages, seven color photos, three are double page. A follow up story to the first, written by New York Times reporter Ted Morgan, with Brigitte Helbing, photos by New York Times photographer Rex Rystedt. My fight for a lifestyle.

The New York Times

New York Times Magazine an insert to the paper, April 17, 1994, section six, The Vexing Adventures of the Last Alaskan Bushrat.

Six pages, four color photos, one is a double page Written by New York Times writer and bestselling author Ted Morgan. Photos by Rex Rystedt (World-renowned photographer). Facing twenty years in jail and a $10,000 fine for putting artwork on a bear claw and selling it.

Book-- A Shovel Full of Stars 95—Published by Simon and Schuster — New York

By Ted Morgan about ten pages with Miles. About one of the last homesteaders, and the lifestyle I live, of a Subsistence person.

Ruralite Magazine

Put out by Golden Valley 180,000 circulation

Wild Miles August 79, two pages, four black and white photos, Full cover page photo of Miles doing artwork. Story and photos by Margaret Van Cleve — Mostly about my artwork, some about my lifestyle on a houseboat

Newspaper, Daily Newsminer, Fairbanks Alaska

Associated Press, date unreadable, think a Thursday, and think spring of circa 74 **'Trapper rescued by Chopper**; Vows to Return to the Bush' headline, one column, National news, about my rescue after five days walking at 50 below.

Alaska Trapper Magazine

Put out by Alaska Trappers Association, a cover photo of me with Wolf. Five-page story by Miles comparing snowmachine and snowshoe trapping Nov. 99—four pages. Over the years, another six-seven articles on various trapping and related issues. Contact organization for exact issues.

Me in 1975.

OTHER TITLES AVAILABLE FROM ALASKA DREAMS PUBLISHING

Visit www.alaskadp.com to see these titles.

Books by Miles Martin:

- Going Wild
- Gone Wild
- Still Wild
- Beyond Wild
- Back To Wild
- Surviving Wild
- Secretly Wild
- Retiring Wild

Titles by other ADP authors:

- Rookie
- Alaska Freedom Brigade
- Apache Snow
- In Search of Honor
- A Coming Storm
- Arizona Rangers Series – Blake's War
- Legend of Silene
- Inspiring Special Needs Stories
- My Life In The Wilderness
- All Over The Road
- Ghost Cave Mountain
- Inside the Circle
- The Silver Horn of Robin Hood
- Alaskan Troll Eggs
- Through My Eyes
- The Professional Ghost Investigator
- The Adventures of Jason and Bo
- Seeds Of The Pirate Rebels

NOTES

PROLOGUE

1. **Past flash** = a term I make up based on the music industry. "Knock out nifties of the past, golden oldies." Songs, that when we hear them, spin us back to another time. Take us, as if we were really there, stuck in time for a moment. So a past flash is spinning back to a memory important to me. usually triggered by key words, sounds, a cue, like a hypnotic suggestion.

CHAPTER 1

1. And no one told me till years later, a chiropractor is not a real doctor, so cannot prescribe real pain pills as a doctor can. The Chiropractor gave me pineapple pulp extract, and tells me I'll be fine. Incidents like this are important in the formation of an opinion of doctors, ethics, human nature, respect, and authority.
2. Refer to the map on first page. Much about the homesteads etc. was covered in the first 3 books.
3. Covered in book one 'Going Wild.' Though it is not absolutely necessary to have been reading the past books in the series, it does help as many subjects I talk about, I briefly review, that have been discussed at great length in my previous books. Helping to explain what makes me tic.

CHAPTER 2

1. 'Mail order women' would be a topic worthy of a book by itself I suppose. I did indeed meet many, with letters from hundreds over the years. I did not want hundreds or dozens. I only wanted one, 'the one.' It is difficult to tell it as an exciting wonderful experience. It's a story of failure. I do eventually end up with a good woman, as a senior. That is 'ahead' yet—stay tuned to the next, or the next book after that.
2. I have an agreement with local miners to not reveal where their mine is, or where I find mammoth tusks. There is a certain amount of vagueness concerning exact locations identifying the area.

CHAPTER 3

1. I still have no driver's license. I'm only driving a few blocks once a month when it is necessary to deal with the boat, which I usually keep parked on the river. This subject becomes an issue off and on with friends, my relatives, and the law. It doesn't make sense to me to have all the horrendous costs of driving when I put three miles a year in on the truck. I'm careful, sober, and not a hazard. In a small village we tend to do things our own way. I think I have legal tags and plates. I forget how I accomplished that. Creatively I assume.

CHAPTER 4

1. In 2014 I read a best seller book 'Blink' that gets into the scientific studies of the unconscious. How quick but accurate unexplained decisions can be made by the unconscious mind. I cover in previous books the issues I had, how long it took to learn to run the river, years and years! My abilities were a joke for a very long time. I used to ask myself in frustration, "If I were water, where would I be, what

would I do?" All I can say about this is, primitive people's around the world do not wonder what I mean. Being close to the land and nature, is not just a quaint phrase.

2. Said before 911. There have been a lot of changes since this conversation. These thoughts would be more common now, but profound and not as accepted when said. I have never trusted banks. I learned about interest and compound interest. I learned what banks pay compared to what they ask. Later, Seymour loses almost all his money in the bank. Where I never lost all my cash in the coffee can.

3. This is the earlier days of computers. Computers are still unstable, and not as user friendly as now. Trying to create a book using a pirated version of word, could mean not all the features work correctly. An unstable program may create unstable or corrupt. Code. My community has unstable power. Picture edit programs were more crude and harder to understand and work with. Everything I learned, I learned by punching keys to see what happened.

CHAPTER 5

1. In years ahead I hear common stories of people following their car GPS into rivers, across airport runways, believing the machine more than what they see out the window. Begging the question, "What is reality?"

2. This subject of how mountain men, remote people were treated throughout history is discussed in all my books, so not repeating it here.

3. 2012 news, vast amounts of millions given to Japan for a hurricane clean up did not go to the people in need. Investigation shows, much got passed around among the rich, for exchanged favors – not in the name of equality. So whom and what exactly did we help?

4. My father I now feel is- was-(he is dead now) a quite complicated person. In his ending years he has IRS problems and is put out of business, dies broke. Way more than that though. I review various aspects throughout my books.

CHAPTER 6

1. In 2014, fifteen years after finishing book one, I do a 're work' and new edition of book one. I noticed over the years of writing with the computer, I learned more. In 2020 yet another serious rework! A few years after this visit with Dad, he dies at seventy-two years old.

CHAPTER 7

1. Discussed in the same words on a different level way back in Book One in the early 70's when the drug freaks stole the leather jackets. The owner would not file charges because he had smuggled the whole shipload through Customs. No one pressed charges on the big guy, but the small fry, the cops wanted to beat up out back.

CHAPTER 8

1. In years ahead Nenana floods. My biggest worry is my boat! I say "I can always live in my boat, I cannot go boating in my house!" I believe Dad once felt that way. For a year or so he lived on his sailboat in England where he bought it, and sounded happy reworking and fixing up the old boat. No one alive knows this but me.

CHAPTER 9

1. In the beginning of the wonderful world of computers, cookies seemed such an invasion of privacy! In time the shock to the public disappears. There is more and more acceptance, till this becomes normal. Before computers, phones were the fast method of communication, considered 'public' yet the laws were very strict concerning listening in on other people's conversations over public telephone lines. This is a major turning point in the concept of privacy.

CHAPTER 10

1. Helping the police has been a touchy subject fraught with conflict. Often as not, doing more harm than help, but I seem to never give up. For where are we as a society, if we can't work with the police, or where am I as an individual. Survival would be getting along with those that have the big stick. Only second choice would be, avoid them.

www.ingramcontent.com/pod-product-compliance
Lightning Source LLC
Chambersburg PA
CBHW072134090426
42739CB00013B/3185